THE AMERICAN
CIVILIZING PROCESS

THE AMERICAN
CIVILIZING PROCESS

Stephen Mennell

Polity

First published in 2007 by Polity Press

Polity Press
65 Bridge Street
Cambridge CB2 1UR, UK

Polity Press
350 Main Street
Malden, MA 02148, USA

ISBN-13: 978-07456-3208-7
ISBN-13: 978-07456-3209-4 (pb)

A catalogue record for this book is available from the British Library.

Typeset in 10 on 12 pt Sabon
by Servis Filmsetting Ltd, Manchester
Printed and bound by Replika Press Pvt Ltd, Kundli, India

The publisher has used its best endeavours to ensure that the URLs for external websites referred to in this book are correct and active at the time of going to press. However, the publisher has no responsibility for the websites and can make no guarantee that a site will remain live or that the content is or will remain appropriate.

Every effort has been made to trace all copyright holders, but if any have been inadvertently overlooked the publishers will be pleased to include any necessary credits in any subsequent reprint or edition.

For further information on Polity, visit our website: www.polity.co.uk

Contents

Preface   viii

Prologue: Civilizing Processes   1
  The theory of civilizing processes   4
  Established–outsiders relations   18
  Conclusion: The plan and major themes of the book   20

1 **'American Civilization'**   23
  The Founding Fathers as *philosophes*   25
  'Progress'   26
  Fugitive government   28
  'Human nature'   33
  Conclusion   38

2 **'Fellow Americans' and Outsiders**   40
  Others: the Native Americans   41
  Others: the blacks   43
  Others: the Europeans   44
  Anti-Americanism: how the outsiders view the established   48
  Conclusion   50

3 **American Manners Under Scrutiny**   51
  American manners books   53
  Americans observed   56
  Technology, hygiene and deference   67
  Victorianism   73
  Informalization   75
  Conclusion   80

4 American Aristocracies   81
   The colonial gentry   82
   The South: American *Junkers*?   85
   The North: *working* upper classes   94
   From cumulative to dispersed inequalities?   100
   A significant absence: an aristocracy of office   103
   Conclusion   104

5 The Market Society   106
   The constraints of the market   107
   The constraints of organization   115
   Conclusion   120

6 Violence and Aggressiveness   122
   Long-term trends in violence   123
   Is America peculiarly violent?   133
   The Western myth as a form of romanticism   137
   No duty to retreat   138
   Capital punishment   149
   Conclusion   154

7 And Wilderness is Paradise Enow: 158
   From Settlements to Independence
   Autarky, but not *terra nullius*   160
   Population   163
   Early phases of the American state-formation process   165
   Conclusion   179

8 But Westward, Look, the Land is Bright: 180
   From Frontier to Empire
   Manifest destiny and latent dynamics: 181
     a necessary theoretical digression
   The balance between the planned and   183
     the unplanned in US territorial expansion
   'Sovereignty' as a function of power ratios   190
   The frontier   193
   Beyond manifest destiny: the beginnings of an American   209
     empire
   Conclusion   212

9 Integration Struggles   214
   Urbanization and resentment of the city   215
   Immigration   218

Growth of the means of ruling   223
The breakdown: the Civil War and its aftermath   233
A central ambivalence: the armed forces   240
Conclusion   247

10   **The Curse of the American Dream**   249
Equality and inequality in America   250
The American welfare state   254
Social mobility in America   262
Conclusion: Upwards identification,   263
    not mutual identification?

11   **Involvement, Detachment and American Religiosity**   266
Fantasy and the growth of knowledge   268
American religion in long-term perspective   273
Some explanations   282
Odd one out – Europe or the USA?   289
Conclusion   291

12   **America and Humanity as a Whole**   294
'American social character': diminishing   298
    contrasts, increasing varieties
The problem of the American *homo clausus*:   301
    the we–I balance
Market fundamentalism and diminishing foresight   305
Functional de-democratization   311
The American empire   314
Conclusion: path-dependency in America and the world   320

Notes   323
References   346
Index   373

Preface

A book's intellectual antecedents can often be traced back in an author's mind far beyond the time spent in actually writing it. My own fascination with American history, society and politics dates from when, as a first-year undergraduate (in economics) at Cambridge in 1963–4, I attended the lectures of Sir Denis Brogan and Lord Annan, and tutorials with Maurice Cowling.

After graduating, I spent a year in the old Department of Social Relations at Harvard University, in which the cohabitation of sociologists, anthropologists and clinical and social psychologists offered an unrivalled interdisciplinary stimulus to young social scientists. I had been drawn there by the reputation of Talcott Parsons, then the world's most famous sociological theorist. Parsons was in his late 'evolutionary' phase and I read his book *The System of Modern Societies* (1971) in draft, finding its depiction of America as the 'lead society' irritating but not demonstrably wrong. Other members of that star-studded department lit long-delayed time fuses which have made more positive contributions to this book. I was inspired by Seymour Martin Lipset, and took a seminar with Robert Bellah when he had just completed his celebrated first essay, 'Civil Religion in America'. I read *The Lonely Crowd* and went to talk to David Riesman – who did not care much for teaching graduate students, but was friendly, helpful and encouraging if one specially sought him out. These early influences are shown in the fact that my very first published journal article was on Prohibition in the USA; and a little later (with John Stone, my friend from Cambridge days) I edited the volume on Alexis de Tocqueville for the University of Chicago Press's Heritage of Sociology series.

Something else which I took back with me from Harvard when I returned to Europe in 1967 to begin my career as a university teacher was a preoccupation with the set of intellectual problems that sociologists refer to as 'macro/micro relations', the 'action/structure' or 'agency/structure' dilemma, and the 'individual and society' issue. Under whichever label, these concern the question of how to reconcile two equally obvious propositions: on the one hand, that people's behaviour and feelings and social character – what sociologists now fashionably call 'habitus' – are shaped within the structure and culture of the societies in which they live; and, on the other, that the structure and culture of societies are the product of, and continuously re-enacted through, the activities of individual people. I remember timidly discussing the question with George Homans, who was critical of many then-prevalent ideas in sociology. He shrugged his shoulders and barked that it was a non-problem. Quite right. But there has long been a tendency among sociological theorists and philosophers to believe that the *apparent* contradiction between these two truisms could be resolved conceptually. If the macro/micro problem really *is* a problem, though, it is essentially one to be resolved through the theoretical–*empirical* investigation of social processes of change or of relative persistence in particular times and places. C. Wright Mills put it best in his still inspiring book *The Sociological Imagination* (1959), when he described the task of sociologists as being 'to grasp history and biography and the relations between the two in society'.

In retrospect, I can now see how serendipitous was my encounter with Norbert Elias, whom I met for the first time in 1972. At that time, already 75 years old, Elias had just begun to achieve belated academic celebrity in Germany and The Netherlands, but was still almost entirely unknown in the English-speaking world. His two early masterpieces, *Über den Prozess der Zivilisation* and *Die höfische Gesellschaft*, written in the 1930s, were still unavailable in English, and Elias was yet to write or complete another dozen or so books in the remaining 18 years of his life. I only slowly came to know *The Civilizing Process* – as it subsequently came to be called – but in the end it certainly made a great impression on me. For here was a theoretical *and empirical* study which suggested how very long-term trends in European society – the division of labour, urbanization, and the growth of trade, the formation of states and the monopolization of the means of violence – were connected with changes in people's habitus, seen in rising social pressures towards more habitual self-constraints and foresight, and the advance of thresholds of shame and embarrassment. In 1998, in a straw poll of members of the International Sociological Association, *The Civilizing Process* was even voted seventh in a list of the ten most influential sociology books of the century (there was no pretence, however, of the poll being properly representative of all the world's sociologists). Vigorous, if minority, groups of researchers were busily using Elias's ideas in their own research, testing and extending them to new topics and in new areas – not just in Europe, but in the other continents: South America, Asia, Australia.

Yet a puzzle remained: why (to adapt the famous question posed by Werner Sombart about the absence of strong socialist movements) was there no 'Eliasianism' in the United States? Or, if not literally none, then very little.

One reason why Elias's work may not have achieved the resonance in the USA that it has elsewhere is the long tradition of 'American exceptionalism'. From John Winthrop's vision of the New World as a 'city upon a hill', a beacon for Old Europe, there has been a proud sense that America is different: it is not Europe. And Elias often seems to be preoccupied with just those features of European societies – notably aristocrats and courtiers and well-defined class boundaries – that Founding Fathers like Thomas Jefferson were very determined they had left behind. But debates about American exceptionalism often resemble the proverbial dispute about whether a glass of water is half full or half empty. It depends on the observer's angle of vision. If one looks at human beings from a sufficiently high level of abstraction, they and their societies can all look alike. If one chooses a very low level of abstraction, the differences between human groups are so numerous that any pattern is lost in a mass of detail.

The chapters of this book can be read as a series of essays centring on why America is as it is, and especially on how it resembles and how it differs from Europe. But why I have chosen to write on these topics, and how they are connected with each other, can only be understood through their relation to Elias's theory of civilizing processes and its various extensions. For that reason, in the Prologue I have provided a brief sketch of his main ideas.

It is now common for sociologists to concoct a theoretical pot-pourri of concepts drawn from a number of recent 'theorists' and invoke them at will at various points in what one is writing. Elias, in contrast, even when he was little known, wrote – in Richard Kilminster's phrase (1987: 215) – as if his own theory had 'the right of way'. I have done so too, using it as a 'central theory' (Quilley and Loyal, 2005) even though it is by no means familiar to all social scientists, especially in the United States. Although I refer to many other sociologists, historians and political scientists, this book is laid out along the lines of Elias's *The Civilizing Process*, the structure of the two books loosely corresponding to each other. After reading Elias's masterpiece many times, I am still overawed by it, still finding new insights. Yet Elias saw it as just one step along the way towards understanding the problems of human coexistence with which it was concerned; if his book was only exploratory, my own must emphatically also be regarded as little more than an exploratory stimulus to further research and discussion.

I am very much aware that an undertaking such as this carries risks for an author who is not himself American. Introducing a book about America by the great Dutch historian Johan Huizinga, Herbert Rowen shrewdly wrote:

> When a foreign historian undertakes the study of the history of another country, he characteristically seeks to combine the native's familiarity with the outsider's freshness of approach. It is seldom that he can achieve the insider's full sureness of touch, but he can come close to it by dint of sustained study. His new thoughts may on occasion betray not novelty but naïveté, yet at his best he sees clearly and sharply things that the native in his very familiarity with the material takes for granted. (In Huizinga, 1972a: viii)

Responsibility for any remaining outsider's naivety is my own, but many friends and colleagues have helped to divert my steps from many more pitfalls. For their encouragement, advice and assistance, I should like to thank Rod Aya, Godfried van Benthem van den Bergh, Reinhard Blomert, Peter Burke, Randall Collins, Mark Cooney, Manuel Eisner, Alice Feldman, David Garland, Tom Garvin, Ademir Gebara, Daniel Gordon, Johan Heilbron, Andreas Hess, John Hudson, Tom Inglis, Richard Kilminster, Hermann Korte, Helmut Kuzmics, Steve Loyal, Arthur McCullough, Herminio Martins, Kevin Matthews, Bruce Mazlish, Barbara Mennell, Aogán Mulcahy, Ian O'Donnell, Margaret O'Keeffe, Steve Quilley, Chris Rojek, Richard Sennett, Richard Sinnott, Pieter Spierenburg, Ruud Stokvis, John Stone, Bram de Swaan, Arpád Szakolczai, Ariadne van der Ven, Nico Wilterdink, Alessandro Guardamagna and other members of my Master's classes at UCD in 2004–6, and Stephen Hannon who drew the maps. Eric Dunning, Johan Goudsblom and Cas Wouters read each chapter as it was written, as well as the complete draft; my intellectual debt to them and to other members of the 'figurational family' over many years is immense. I should also mention that this already large book would probably have contained even longer discussions of informalization and relations between the sexes, and of sport and the rise of spectatorship, had it not been for the existence of comprehensive publications, especially by Cas and Eric, which I saw no reason to duplicate.

I should also like to acknowledge the indispensable gift of time to conduct this research arising from the award by University College Dublin of a President's Research Award; it enabled me to spend the year 1999–2000 at St Antony's College, Oxford, once again as the guest of Theodore Zeldin. Later, Tom Inglis, as a good friend and colleague, kindly agreed to deputize for me as Head of the Department of Sociology at UCD so that I could spend the first half of 2004 working on the book. Last revisions were made at the start of a sabbatical year in 2006–7 back in

Cambridge through the hospitality of my old college, St Catharine's, and with the support of a Government of Ireland Senior Research Fellowship awarded by the Irish Research Council for the Humanities and Social Sciences. Finally, my thanks to the Toledo Museum of Art, Toledo, Ohio, for permission to reproduce the painting by Broughton on page 165.

Writing about American history today often raises questions of nomenclature in light of powerful standards of political correctness, which nevertheless change so quickly that there is a danger of the rapid onset of anachronism. Over the last few decades, there has been a whole sequence of terms considered to be the polite way of referring to the descendants of African slaves: 'Negroes', 'coloured people', 'blacks', 'African-Americans', 'people of colour'. Similarly, 'Native American' has superseded the older 'Indian'. I have attempted to avoid both offence and anachronism by using an older term whenever a newer term might read incongruously.

Prologue: Civilizing Processes

Viewed from Europe, America is a land of familiar paradoxes. An agreeable civility habitually prevails in most everyday relations among people in America – yet the United States is almost the last bastion among advanced democratic nations of capital punishment.[1] In most parts of America, the laws and social customs strongly restrain people from doing harm to themselves and others by smoking – yet the laws and social customs only weakly restrain people from doing harm to themselves and others by the use of guns, and the murder rate is about four times as high per capita as in Western Europe. Ever since independence, Americans have fostered a spirit of New World egalitarianism proudly contrasted with the stuffy and hierarchical Old World – yet that spirit has coexisted with social inequalities greater in many respects than those found in Western Europe. The USA is the world's remaining superpower – yet internally the American state is in some ways strikingly weak. America leads the world in science, technology and higher education – yet religious belief and observance has risen there while it has fallen in Europe.

Can history and the social sciences help to explain these seeming paradoxes and show how they are related to each other? This book is intended to make a contribution by using Norbert Elias's theory of civilizing processes to shed some light on the course of American social development since the beginnings of European settlement. Elias developed his theory through the study mainly of European history. He linked changes in people's everyday behaviour, in the codes of manners they followed and in their typical feelings and emotions, to the formation of states with relatively effective monopolies of violence and to changes in the balances of power between social groups within states. The aim of this book is to look both at whether underlying processes similar to those traced by Elias through European history can also be seen at work in the development of the USA, and at those aspects in which the American experience is evidently different.

The sense of being different from Europe has played a leading part in American thought since the beginning of European colonization. So too, however, has been the sense of America's being an offspring of Europe, and of Europe's sternly critical parental watchfulness over all things American. Both elements were already present in the famous remarks of John Winthrop, first Governor of the Massachusetts Bay Colony, supposedly delivered on board the *Arabella* just before landing at the site of Boston in 1630:

> wee must be knitt together in this worke as one man, wee must entertaine each other in brotherly Affeccion, wee must be willing to abridge our selves of our superfluities, for the supply of others necessities, wee must uphold a familiar Commerce together in all meekenes, gentlenes, patience and liberallity . . . allwayes haveing before our eyes . . . our Community as members of the same body, soe shall wee keepe the unitie of the spirit in the bond of peace . . . : for we must Consider that we shall be as a Citty upon a Hill, the eies of all people are uppon us; soe that if wee shall deale falsely with our god in this worke wee have undertaken and soe cause him to withdrawe his present help from us, wee shall be made a story and a by-word through the world. (1994 [1630]: 111–12)

The relevance of Europe to subsequent American social and political development has been debated among American intellectuals for many decades. In the late nineteenth century, at the high tide of social evolutionism, Herbert Baxter Adams of Johns Hopkins University was the leading advocate of what came to be known as the 'germ theory' of American institutions. Against the view that America represented a new beginning, he argued:

> Wherever organic life occurs there must have been some seed for that life. . . . It is just as improbable that free local institutions should spring up without a germ along American shores as that English wheat should have grown here without planting. Town institutions were propagated on New England by old English and German ideas, brought over by Pilgrims and Puritans, and as ready to take root in the free soil of America as would Egyptian grain which had been drying in a mummy-case for thousands of years. (1882: 8)

A little later, Edward Eggleston set out to make an inventory of the 'mental outfit' of the early colonists, because:

> In taking account of the mental furniture of which the early English emigrants carried aboard ship with them, we shall gain a knowledge of what

may be called the original investment from which has been developed
Anglo-Saxon culture in America. The mother country of the United States
was England in the first half of the seventeenth century, or, at most, England
before the Revolution of 1688. (1901: 1)

The early colonists' minds were thus furnished not just with various
kinds of Christian religious belief but also, among other things, with
beliefs in astrology and horoscopes, spontaneous generation, an invisible world and witchcraft, a taste for brutal pastimes such as bull-
baiting, and codes of behaviour deeply permeated by the consciousness
of hierarchy.

How far, though, did the European 'germs' multiplying in American
soil develop into strains distinct from those which grew in eighteenth-,
nineteenth- and twentieth-century Europe, and why? The most celebrated
counterblast to the germ theory was Frederick Jackson Turner's 1893
paper, 'The Significance of the Frontier in American History'. In essence,
Turner contended that from the earliest decades of European settlement
in America, the availability of free land on the westward-moving frontier
had set American society on a profoundly different track of development
from that followed by European societies. Life on the frontier had meant
a recurring return to 'primitive conditions', from which American social
development had been 'continually beginning again'. At first, the wilderness mastered the colonist, and then 'little by little he transforms the
wilderness, but the outcome is not the old Europe' (Turner, 1947: 3). Later
in this book I will argue that, for all its imprecision and overstatement,
the 'Turner thesis' contains insights still valuable in understanding important facets of American society. In the middle decades of the twentieth
century, however, it fell greatly out of favour and was picked to pieces by
historians drawing on a wealth of later research. In fact, the political theorist Louis Hartz swung to the opposite pole. The Turner thesis, commented Hartz, 'by seizing on the "native" factor of the frontier, reflected
the loss of memory of Europe in American history as a whole' (1964: 69).
Hartz himself revived something resembling the old Johns Hopkins germ
theory. He viewed the USA as one of several 'fragment societies' which
broke off from Europe in the early modern period – other examples being
Latin America, South Africa, Canada and Australia. He suggested that
such societies continue to exhibit the characteristics of Europe at the time
they broke away, and that 'when a part of a European nation is detached
from the whole of it, and hurled outward on to new soil, it loses the stimulus towards change that the whole provides. It lapses into a kind of
immobility' (ibid.: 3). This is surely an overstatement in relation to the
United States, and could seem even barely plausible only to someone
whose preoccupation was principally with the history of political ideas

rather than with the development of social structures, institutions and people's social character.[2]

The fundamental fault in debates of this kind is that they have tended to be cast in dichotomous and static terms. It is not an either/or question. America's institutional and intellectual debt to Europe cannot be assessed for all time as a fixed percentage. Nor can the relative autonomy of the development of American society from that of Europe. The debt plainly diminished and the autonomy equally plainly increased over time, as America grew and as the balance of interdependence between it and the countries of Europe swung in America's favour. Yet even if the autonomy of American development increased over time, it has never been total.[3] What is needed, in understanding the connections between superficially disparate aspects of America, is a thoroughly processual and relational model which takes into account how the connections change over time.

In this context, Norbert Elias's theory of civilizing processes is useful in several ways. As a model of the interconnectedness of many strands of European social development, it shows something of what Eggleston called the 'original investment' that European settlers brought with them to America. At the same time, it helps in avoiding the shopping-basket image in which American borrowings from Europe (and vice versa) are recorded as lists of discrete items: the inheritance was of highly interconnected processes, not just of shreds and patches.[4] The rest of this prologue will be devoted to sketching Elias's theory in outline, in preparation for a prolonged investigation of how far it can help to account for the character and development of American society.[5]

The theory of civilizing processes

All the main elements of Elias's theory are to be found in *The Civilizing Process*, although many of them were further developed and refined in later books and articles. His *magnum opus* was first published in German in 1939, but little known until reissued 30 years later, and not available in English until 1978–82.[6] Elias saw his work as exploratory, never as the definitive and exhaustive study, and later he often spoke of 'civilizing processes' in the plural, because there are many interwoven component parts. Moreover, although he was studying Europe, he did not intend to imply that what had unfolded in Europe was *the* single and unique civilizing process. Nevertheless, the book has become known as *The Civilizing Process*. It is organized into four parts, to which corresponds the structure of the present book.

Civilization and culture

One of the ways in which people in the modern West most like to see themselves is as 'civilized'. The connotations of collective self-approbation which have become attached to the word 'civilization' certainly complicate the use of the concept of 'civilizing process' as a tool of relatively detached analysis. Elias confronts this problem in Part I of *The Civilizing Process*, where he discusses the origins of the concepts of *civilisation* in France and *Kultur* in Germany. He makes it clear from the beginning that his is not a theory of 'progress', let alone of inevitable progress. Nor is it an instance of the Western triumphalism that Edward Said (1978) would later discuss under the rubric of 'orientalism'. Elias was not putting his own moral evaluations of good and bad on the ideas of 'civilization' and 'civilized behaviour', but showing the social historical context in which all sorts of positive evaluations had accreted around particular facets of behaviour and of cultural expression (and negative evaluations around others). As a 'commonsense' rather than a scientific concept, the term 'civilization' had come to serve a specific social function:

> [T]he concept expresses the self-consciousness of the West. . . . It sums up everything in which Western society of the last two or three centuries believes itself superior to earlier societies or 'more primitive' contemporary ones. By this term Western society seeks to describe what constitutes its special character and what it is proud of: the level of *its* technology, the nature of *its* manners, the development of *its* scientific knowledge or view of the world, and much more. (Elias, 2000: 5)

The new word *civilisation* came into use in France with these collectively self-approving connotations from the latter half of the eighteenth century.[7] Enlightenment intellectuals were the first to use it in connection with ideas of progress and social reform, deriving it from *civilité*, the word which courtly aristocrats had used since the sixteenth century to describe their own polished manners and courtly modes of behaviour. By the nineteenth century, the ways in which people in the West used the *word* civilization showed that they had forgotten the long *process* of civilization through which their ancestors' behaviour and feelings had changed and been socially moulded from generation to generation. They had come to think of the traits they considered in 'civilization' as innate in themselves and their fellow Westerners, and indeed as inherent in what they unabashedly then termed the 'white race'.

Elias, however, regarded these evaluative connotations simply as sociological data, as changes at the level of ideas corresponding in complex ways to changes in people's actual behaviour and feelings. To be more exact, his central concern was with changes in what he called *Habitus*.[8]

Elias defined habitus as 'second nature' – it refers to that level of habits of thinking, feeling and behaving which are in fact learned from early childhood onwards, but which become so deeply ingrained that they feel 'innate', as if we had never had to learn them. These are especially the characteristics which individuals share with fellow members of the groups in which they have learned them, and they become unconscious of the process of learning. So the next section of *The Civilizing Process* is a study of the changes in the course of which certain forms of behaviour came to be regarded among the secular upper classes in Western Europe as superior and others as inferior.

Civilization as changing habitus

Central to Elias's conception of a civilizing process is the *increasing social constraint towards self-constraint*. The long-term growth of complexity, of the spreading web of social interdependence, is associated with a tilting of the *balance* between external constraints (*Fremdzwänge* – literally constraints by strangers, or more generally by other people) and self-restraints (*Selbstzwänge*), towards the latter's greater weight in the steering of individual people's conduct. Steady and consistent social pressure towards self-constraint is most effective in tilting the balance in favour of more demanding social standards of habitual self-control.

For evidence, Elias looks to changes in manners in Europe since the Middle Ages. His principal sources are the numerous 'manners books' of Germany, France, England and Italy which, from the thirteenth to the nineteenth century, set out the standards of behaviour that were socially acceptable among the secular upper classes. The earlier ones dealt with very basic questions of 'outward bodily propriety' which it would later become embarrassing even to mention. They told their readers how to handle food and conduct themselves at table; how, when and when not to fart, burp or spit; how to blow their noses; how to behave when urinating or defecating or encountering someone else in the act of doing so; how to behave when sharing a bed with other people at an inn, and so on. In earlier centuries, such matters were spoken of openly and frankly, without shame. Then gradually, from the Renaissance said Elias, thresholds of shame and embarrassment advanced: a long-term trend became evident towards more elaborate codes of behaviour, towards more demanding standards of habitual self-control and towards silence in later centuries on some of the topics that earlier books had discussed at length.

Eating, drinking, urinating, defecating, spitting, blowing one's nose, sleeping, having sex are things that human beings cannot biologically avoid doing, no matter what society, culture or age they live in. All societies have always had some conventions about how they should be handled – there is no zero-point, no 'state of nature' in which there are no social constraints whatsoever on how people handle these things. On the other hand, there *is* a zero-point in the individual lifetime: human infants are born without such habitual constraints and have to learn whatever are the standards prevailing in their time, place, social stratum, national or ethnic group. Since the *lifetime* point of departure is always the same, if changes take place from generation to generation in the social conventions that children have to learn, changes are especially clear in relation to these universal matters of outward bodily propriety. But changes can also be tracked in conventions governing other matters which will be more central to this study of the USA, such as in the use of violence and in ways of expressing superiority and inferiority.

Priests had for centuries drawn up Latin compendia of precepts of Christian behaviour, but the manners books studied by Elias were addressed to the *secular* upper classes, and mainly in the vernacular languages of Europe. Early authors in the genre include some famous names: Tannhäuser in the thirteenth century, Caxton in the fifteenth, Castiglione and Erasmus in the sixteenth. The books' audience was in the beginning specifically a *courtly* one. All the early terms for good behaviour – courtesy, *courtoisie, cortezia, Hofzucht* – refer to courts, to a specific powerful and prestigious location in society. Standards appear to have been set first in courtly circles around great lords. Later, the audience for the books widened to include provincial knights and nobility – and even the higher bourgeoisie who might aspire to join the court and to emulate the courtiers' standards of seemly behaviour. By the eighteenth century, separate books for the bourgeoisie appeared, setting out standards which resembled those of courtly circles perhaps a generation earlier. As we shall see in chapter 3, there was a ready market in America for European manners books or imitations of them.

Table manners illustrate the general pattern of development. Compared with later periods, the medieval books place relatively few prohibitions on behaviour at table. One was told not to slurp soup from one's spoon or smack one's lips noisily. Everyone took food from a common dish, placed it on a plate or a trencher of bread and ate with the fingers, but it was bad manners to put something one had chewed back in the pot. One should not blow one's nose on the tablecloth. For cutting up food, one used one's own general-purpose knife or dagger. By Caxton's time (about 1477–8), there were some prohibitions on the use of knives – they were not to be passed blade first to other people, nor pointed at one's own face. The fork made its appearance in elite circles in the sixteenth century, but took centuries to trickle down the social scale. By 1560 it was more common for each guest to have his or her own spoon. By the late seventeenth century, one no longer ate soup directly from the common bowl. Courtin reported in 1672 that there were now some *gens si délicats* that they would not wish to serve themselves from the soup tureen when someone else had helped himself to a second helping with a spoon that had already been in his mouth. So one must at least wipe one's spoon on one's napkin or, better still, ask for a clean spoon for the purpose. Such was the stage reached by table manners in the best circles in Europe a few decades after the beginning of European settlement in North America, and there is no reason to suppose that most of the early settlers were among the *avant garde* in these matters. In later manners books, many of these things no longer needed to be said (except to small children), and even to mention them would be embarrassing and/or amusing. A similar sequence is found in what the successive manners books have to say about nose-blowing, spitting, the 'natural functions', dressing and undressing, and sexual relations.

What common pattern of development underlies these changes in social standards in relation to the various aspects of behaviour?

In general, says Elias, the medieval standards, in comparison with later times, could be described as simple, naive and undifferentiated. The impulses and inclinations were less restrained, the commands direct: don't slurp; don't put gnawed bones back in the common pot; don't blow your nose on the tablecloth; don't urinate on the staircase. Over and over again, down the centuries, the same good and bad manners were mentioned, and yet 'the social code hardened into lasting habits only to a limited extent in people themselves' (Elias, 2000: 70). Then, at the time of the Renaissance, change becomes perceptible: the social compulsion to check one's behaviour increased. To Caxton, in the late fifteenth century, it was already evident that social standards had been set in motion: 'Things once allowed are now reproved', he remarked in his *Book of Curtesye* (c. 1477). Erasmus, writing half a century later, was himself a pivotal figure in an age of transition – in his minor work on manners as much as in his important contributions to the larger intellectual world. He showed all the old medieval unconcern in referring directly to matters later too disgusting to mention, and yet at the same time his recommendations were enriched and nuanced by considerations of what people *might* think. He tells boys to sit still and not constantly shift about because that gives the *impression* of always farting or trying to fart. This tendency became more pronounced over the generations. In 1672 Courtin told his readers not to use fingers when eating greasy foods, since that led to the need to lick one's fingers, which was 'distasteful to behold'. The rule about not eating with one's hands was not at first as absolute and consistent as later, and only very gradually did the prohibition become an internalized habit, an aspect of 'self-control'.[9]

As many things were no longer spoken about, so were they increasingly moved *behind the scenes of social life*. This is seen most obviously in the case of urination and defecation, in the greater privacy of the bedroom and in feelings about nakedness. It is also seen in the requirements for greater care and discretion in spitting or blowing one's nose in the presence of others. It is also possible to speak figuratively of things being moved behind the scenes of mental life. Since newly forming standards were at first generally not absolute and unambiguous but conditional upon circumstance – especially the company one was in – conformity with the latest in refinement might require conscious effort even among adults. But in due course children were trained by adults not only to conform in their behaviour, but also to feel shame, embarrassment and disgust – automatically, and in circumstances which a generation or two earlier would not have been felt at all, even among adults. Why, for instance, did people come to feel disgust at eating with sticky fingers? Because social superiors made subordinates feel inferior when eating like that, and because adults told children that such habits were disgusting:

> [T]he displeasure towards such conduct which is thus aroused by the adult finally arises through habit, without being induced by [the present action of] another person. . . . The social standard to which the individual was first made to conform from outside by external restraint is finally reproduced more or less smoothly within him or her, through a self-restraint which operates to a certain degree even against his or her conscious wishes. (Elias, 2000: 109)

The advance of the threshold of shame and embarrassment (or repugnance) thus involves a tilting of the balance between external constraints and self-restraints in the steering of conduct that is central to Elias's conception of a civilizing process.

What were the social and psychological processes that led to these changes? They were not driven wholly by rational consideration of, for example, hygiene – changes in standards of behaviour tended to predate advances in relevant medical knowledge. A clue lies in the reasons given in the manners books for the merits of the newer over the older standards. The earlier and less restrained behaviour was said to show a lack of respect for one's social superiors. Only after a long period of transition did shame in such matters come in the nineteenth century also to be felt by the superior in the presence of inferiors, and as the standard came to apply more equally to all ranks, so the controls became more and more automatic, 'unconscious' and 'natural' for all adults. In the seventeenth and eighteenth centuries, however, this process had not run its full course in Europe, so the very great concern of early settlers in America with questions of social rank is not so surprising as it sometimes appears to modern readers who have been brought up to think of the settlers as egalitarian.

Correct behaviour and its relation to social rank appear to have become more of a problem in Europe at the time of the Renaissance. In the feudal society of the Middle Ages, 'the behavioural differences between different estates in the same region were often greater than those between regionally separate representatives of the same social stratum', and models of behaviour developed in one stratum permeated only slowly and imperfectly to other ranks of society (Elias, 2000: 100). Towards the end of the Middle Ages, however, the old ruling class of warriors was in decline – thinned out through warfare, economically undermined by the growth of the market economy and the emergence of rich and powerful entrepreneurs, and increasingly subordinate to a small number of powerful kings. There was no sudden emergence of an egalitarian, non-hierarchical society, but old social ties were loosened, individuals of different social origins were increasingly thrown together and the social circulation of ascending and descending groups and individuals speeded up (ibid.: 68). Then, slowly, in the course of the sixteenth century, a more rigid social hierarchy began to be established once more, as a new aristocratic upper class began to form *from elements of diverse social origins*. This started earlier in some parts of Europe than others – England was among the earliest – and there were reversals well into the seventeenth century. But everywhere in Western Europe there was emerging a new upper class of courtiers. The old warrior nobility was being tamed; over the generations some families sank into provincial obscurity, but others adhered to the growing royal courts. Also attracted to the courts were other people whose origins lay in the professional and commercial bourgeoisie. Forced in the courts to live with one another in a new way, these people were more acutely confronted with the problem of what constituted a uniform standard of good behaviour. As Elias shows in more detail in *The Court Society* (2006), very gradually, in accordance with the newly emergent power ratios, courtiers had by the reign of Louis XIV (1643–1715) developed a high level of sensitivity to status on the basis of fine nuances of bearing, speech, manners and appearance.

Nuances of behaviour, indeed, became a principal mark of distinction among the courtly elite; for it was what Elias (following Georg Simmel) termed a 'two-front stratum'. With the growth of absolutist monarchies in France and Spain, and later in Prussia, Austria and other states of the Holy Roman Empire and Italy, courtiers became highly dependent on kings 'above' them for lucrative offices and positions of prestige – all the more dependent because their social identity became more and more tied up with a style of life that many could ill afford to maintain. At the same time, they were exposed to 'pressure from below' by the rising commercial and official bourgeoisie. The customs, behaviour and fashions of the courtly elite were continually being imitated by the strata immediately beneath them. Indeed, by asserting their power as definers of *savoir-vivre*, courtly circles actively promoted the adoption of their ways by inferiors: in effect they 'colonized' the bourgeoisie, as Elias puts it. Yet, as elite manners were imitated, they inevitably lost something of their value as a means of distinguishing the upper class. This compelled those above towards still further refinements of their standards, as a means of 'repulsion' of those below.

Courtly characteristics were never dominant in the North American colonies – though stronger in some colonies than others. That should not blind one to the possibility that some of the processes at work in courtly circles in Europe could be observed at work in rather different times and contexts in America; one need only mention Thorstein Veblen's account in *The Theory of the Leisure Class* (1899) of 'conspicuous consumption' among American plutocrats in the 'Gilded Age' at the end of the nineteenth century.

Violence and state-formation

Aggressiveness, violence and cruelty are another area of habitus in which a similar long-term curve of the civilizing process can be discerned among Western European people. Theologians, philosophers and social theorists have speculated for centuries about whether aggression and violence are innate and universal in human beings. Certainly they have never been absent from any human society, and the shocking wars and genocides of the twentieth century make it tempting to believe that they are constant and universal. Yet the social moulding even of aggressiveness is well documented: not its elimination altogether, but its modelling or moulding.

In the early Middle Ages, the majority of the secular ruling class in Western Europe were leaders of armed bands. For them, war was a normal state of society, and they had little social function other than to wage it.[10] It is difficult, says Elias, for many people today to grasp the joy and exultation they felt in the clash of arms, but still less easy to come to terms with the sheer pleasure warriors then derived from cruelty, from the torment and destruction of other human beings. Long into the Middle Ages, the mutilation of prisoners was practised with evident relish. So were rape and pillage in victory. Very gradually over the centuries, these military pleasures were subjected to increasingly strong control anchored in the state organization.[11] Indeed, tighter discipline and control over the impulses came more and more to be conditions of success in the changing circumstances of military conflict: the wild venting of aggressive impulses in hand-to-hand combat became a steadily less sufficient condition for victory. The pleasure taken in cruelty, torment and killing was by no means confined to a military context. For centuries, people at large

also experienced well-documented pleasurable excitement in the spectacle of burning heretics, public torture and executions.

Elias did not suggest that medieval people were constantly aggressive,
violent and cruel. More characteristic of their temperament – and here
Elias drew on the insights of Johan Huizinga (1972b [1924]), confirmed
by much subsequent historical research – was their volatility, their propensity to switch suddenly from mood to mood, from merriment via sudden
offence at a joke taken too far, for example, to violent brawling. Elias
argued that aggressiveness and impulses towards cruelty and ready resort
to violence – not unlike eating behaviour or the 'natural functions' –
underwent a long-term process of moulding, curbing and taming.[12] They
too came to find expression in more 'refined' and indirect forms. But something resembling the earlier volatile habitus may survive, or be recreated,
in parts of modern societies where levels of danger and incalculability
remain high and where 'civilizing' pressures are weak and inconsistent (see
chapter 6). Today, some criminologists describe delinquents in much the
same way as Elias's account of the medieval character-type, and offer much
the same explanation in terms of uneven social controls and poorly developed self-controls (see, for instance, the concept of 'control balance'
advanced by Tittle, 1995).

The taming of aggressiveness is thus linked, according to Elias, to a
broad change in the structure of society. Medieval society had lacked any
central power over large territories to compel people to restrain their
impulses towards violence, but he contended that, 'if in this or that region
the power of central authority grows, if over a larger or smaller area the
people are forced to live in peace with each other, the moulding of the
affects and the standards of emotion-management are very gradually
changed as well' (2000: 169; translation modified). This proposition
leads Elias into an extended investigation of the formation of states in
Western Europe, which occupies the major part of the original second
volume of *The Civilizing Process*. Readers are still sometimes surprised
and puzzled by this jump from the apparently 'micro-level' study of
behaviour to the apparently 'macro-level' study of states. Elias was later
to explain it as follows:

> One could imagine a condition of human coexistence where people do not
> need external restraint in order to refrain from the use of violence in their
> relationships with others. One could imagine a society whose members are
> able to rely entirely on self-restraint – without any extraneous restraint –
> in observing the common rules that they have worked out over the course
> of generations, as regulators of their lives together. In that case, individ-
> ual self-restraint would be strong and reliable enough to make any exter-
> nal restraining force unnecessary. . . . That would be a very advanced form
> of human civilization. It would require . . . a measure and a pattern of

individual self-constraint all round which, at the present stage of social development, and within it, of the civilizing process, are not yet attainable. Nor is it certain that they will ever be attainable, though it is worth trying. As long as this condition has not been reached, the individual self-restraint of men and women requires reinforcement through external restraints, by means of agencies which are specially licensed to threaten or to use physical violence if that is necessary, in order to ensure a peaceful coexistence of people within their society. (2007a: 140–1)

Elias's account of state-formation takes its departure from Max Weber's (1978 [1922]: I, 54) definition of the state as an organization which successfully upholds a claim to binding rule-making over a territory, by virtue of commanding a monopoly of the legitimate use of violence. (Throughout my book, the term 'state' is used in this sense, unless the context makes clear that I am referring to the states of the Union. The normal meaning of the word 'state' in America denotes an entity that under other systems of government might be called 'provinces' or *Länder*.) To the idea of a monopoly of violence, however, Elias added 'and taxation'. In the earliest stages of the formation of effective states, it is futile to try to draw a clear line between the 'economic' and the 'political'. The threat of or the actual use of violence are the necessary means by which warrior lords – leaders of armed bands – extract tribute in kind (or, less probably, in cash) from peasants and tradesmen. Such tributes, equally, are the necessary means by which an armed band can be maintained, its monopoly established and its territory extended. To call them taxation at this early stage would be to beg the question; the line between taxation and what in a different context we would now call a 'protection racket' is a fine one. The word taxation becomes justified only when an effective and stable monopoly apparatus has been established, and (generally even later) when the subjects at large within the territory have come to recognize that only that apparatus has a legitimate right to make such exactions. By that stage, the violent aspect of the monopoly may – like so many other repugnant aspects of life – to some extent be *hidden behind the scenes* of social life. Force is, literally and figuratively, confined to barracks.

To say that a monopoly of the legitimate use of violence and taxation has been established does not mean, of course, that other people – outside the apparatus – never resort to violence in their dealings with each other. What it means is that, however legitimate and justified people may consider their own resort to violence in their private dealings with each other, the agents of the monopoly do not consider it so, and take action to assert their monopoly. Less abstractly, if one commits an act of violence against one's neighbour within the territory of an effective state, one must reckon with a high probability of being punished for it. Indeed, like 'taxation', the word 'punishment' becomes justified only when an effective and stable monopoly apparatus has been established: without established state authority, there are only feuds and revenge killing. 'Punishment' requires a monopoly of the power to punish.

Elias sought to show in much more detail than did Weber the long-term *processes* through which increasingly effective monopolies of violence and taxation have taken shape. The first section of the original second volume of *The Civilizing Process* (2000: 195–256) discusses the period of the early Middle Ages, after the fall of the Roman Empire in the West, when the centrifugal forces dominant in the process of feudalization resulted in the extreme fragmentation of Western Europe into countless tiny territories each controlled by a local warlord. The process proceeded faster in the area approximating to what we now call France than in that centred on what we now call Germany (although political fragmentation was to persist in Germany, and in Italy, for a long time after a large state had emerged in roughly the hexagon of modern France). The principal reason why centrifugal forces dominated over centripetal tendencies – in an era of reduced population, decaying roads, declining long-distance trade and repeated invasions by marauding bands – was that the only means kings then had of paying subordinates to administer distant territories was to give them the land from which they could support themselves. The means of supporting themselves were identical with the means of making them rulers of the territory independent of the king to whom they nominally owed allegiance. Political autarky went hand in hand with economic autarky: they were mutually reinforcing.

Early in the second millennium AD, at least in the region that was to become France, the balance tilted once more in favour of centripetal, centralizing forces. A very long section of Elias's work is devoted to the twists and turns of how the early modern French state emerged (2000: 257–362). It was not inevitable that there would be a single country corresponding to France in its present boundaries: it was not preordained nor in any sense planned that the kings whose principal seat was Paris would extend their territories until they reached the boundaries of the hexagon, and then stop. For much of the Middle Ages the Paris kings were locked in combat with other French-speaking kings whose principal city was London, but who often controlled more of what is now France than did the Paris kings. Even towards the end of the medieval period, there was a resurgence of centrifugal forces when members of the royal family, assigned regions as apanages to govern on behalf of the king, used them to reassert their autonomy.

Even if state-formation in Europe did not unfold in linear fashion, and its outcome was in considerable measure affected by chance and accident, Elias was able to point to a number of part-processes running fairly consistently through it in the long term. State-formation was a violent competitive process through which there emerged successively larger territorial units with more effective monopoly apparatuses. Initially, around the year 1000, there were relatively small disparities in strength between the rulers of the many small territories, who fought out an 'elimination contest' with each other, the victor in each round absorbing his defeated rival's land, so that a smaller number of steadily larger territories arose. In explaining this, Elias alluded to the westward expansion of America, quoting what was once said of an American pioneer: 'He didn't want all the land; he just wanted the land next to his' (2000: 312). The more or less continuous warfare between neighbouring magnates in the European Middle Ages is not to be explained primarily by the aggressive psychological characteristics of warlords. In an age when power was so directly correlated with the amount of land one controlled, it was impossible for a ruler of unusually pacific temperament to sit idly by as his neighbours slugged it out with each other, for the victorious neighbour would then control a larger territory and be able next to defeat the would-be passive observer. True, there is much evidence that most medieval warriors thoroughly enjoyed warfare, but they had to: they would not have survived in a social situation so structured had they not. Aggressiveness, remarked Elias, may more nearly be explained as the outcome of conflict than conflict as the outcome of aggressiveness – though, to be more accurate, it is a two-way relationship through time.

The state-formation process was Janus-faced. On the one hand, larger territories underwent *internal pacification*. On the other hand, the scale of *warfare steadily increased* through European history. In what became France, for instance, the local skirmishes in the early stages of the elimination contest gave way to a struggle between the Paris kings and the London kings, which was prolonged over several centuries. When the Valois were finally victorious, they immediately entered a lengthy contest with the Habsburgs and the Hohenzollerns, the process culminating in the Franco-Prussian War of 1870 and the two 'World Wars' of the twentieth century. Long before that, of course, several of the European states had begun to control territories beyond Europe, to acquire empires in other continents – including in North America – where they fought wars both with each other and with previous inhabitants.

Although the precise outcome differed from case to case,[13] within each of the developing states of Western Europe certain common processes can be discerned. One of them Elias calls the *monopoly mechanism*.[14] In the course of the elimination contest between many territorial magnates, a smaller number of central rulers emerged with more extensive lands and, by extension, with more of other power resources by which they were able gradually to make their monopoly of the means of violence and taxation within their territories more complete and effective. Alongside this operated the *royal mechanism*, the accretion of power to the social position of kings and princes through their ability to play off rival social interests against each other – typically, by the late Middle Ages, the relatively evenly balanced forces of the old warrior nobility and the rising commercial bourgeoisie. Kings often threw their weight on the side of the second most powerful group as a counterbalance to the most powerful. A necessary third component was the *transformation of private into public monopolies*. Administrative functions became too large and varied to be handled by a king and his immediate staff, so bureaucracies of an increasingly 'public' character developed.

Each stage in these processes was fought over. The old warrior nobility did not give up its regional autonomy without many struggles. In France, the last big aristocratic rising was the Fronde, early in the reign of Louis XIV, after which *le roi soleil* completed the 'courtization'[15] of the remaining warrior caste and its thorough subordination to the royal power, which played so important a part in the development of courtly civility. In England, in a period that coincided with the first decades of European settlement in America, events took a different turn. Although the Tudors and early Stuarts appeared to have established a more secure royal monopoly than their French contemporaries, and to be well on the way to creating a court society and royal absolutist regime, the consequence of their efforts was the civil wars of the mid-seventeenth century, the beginning of a cycle of violence which diminished but did not finally die away until the early eighteenth century. Although the monarchy was restored in 1660, the balance of power between the king and the landowning class was never afterwards so unequal as it became in France. Moreover, as much by chance as otherwise, the outcome of the cycle of violence in England was a relatively equal balance of power in Parliament between two factions of the landowning class, a circumstance conducive to their evolving into the Whig and Tory parties, which peacefully alternated with each other in office.[16] This was the social context in which John Locke wrote, and such were the nascent institutions which were to influence the early development of America.

If Elias pays most attention to state-formation, he sees it as only one important thread interweaving with others in a long-term overall process of social development which enmeshed individuals in increasingly complex webs of interdependence. It interweaves with the division of labour, the growth of towns and trade, the use of money, and increasing population, in a spiral process. Internal pacification of territory facilitates trade, which facilitates the growth of towns and division of labour and generates taxes which support larger administrative and military organizations, which in turn facilitate the internal pacification of larger territories, and so on – a cumulative process experienced as an increasingly compelling, inescapable force by people caught up in it. Furthermore, according to Elias, the gradually higher standards of self-restraint engendered in people contribute in turn to the upward spiral – being necessary, for example, to the formation of gradually more effective and calculable administration.

Pressures towards increasing foresight

Elias thus linked questions of violence and state-formation through the level of security and calculability in everyday life to the formation of habitus. He argued that as chains of interdependence become longer and webs denser, a gradual shift takes place in the balance between external constraints and self-constraints in the habitual steering of people's behaviour. The social web formed by increasing numbers of people tends to be experienced as exerting a compelling impersonal pressure and, in order to fulfil their needs and achieve their goals with such a web, individual people have habitually to exercise greater foresight. The necessity of coordinating more and more complicated sequences of activities means that each person, at his or her node in the web, has to peer further down chains of interdependence. Spreading webs of interdependence, Elias hypothesized, tend to be associated with *relatively* more equal power ratios and *functional democratization*, meaning more and more reciprocal controls between more and more social groups. Less abstractly, 'More people are forced more often to pay more and more attention to more other people' (Goudsblom, 1989: 722). The pressure towards greater consideration of the consequences of one's own actions for other people on whom one is to a greater or lesser extent dependent tends to produce a widening of the circle of *mutual identification*. This tendency had already been noted by Alexis de Tocqueville who, in *Democracy in America*, observed 'that manners are softened as social conditions become more equal' (1961 [1835–40]: II, 195–200).[17] Whether longer chains of interdependence *always* have these consequences will be questioned at several points in later chapters. A major thesis of this book is that the long-term historical experience of the USA is the opposite of functional democratization: it has seen increasing inequality, in some respects internally, but more certainly in its power position vis-à-vis its neighbours. For reasons I shall attempt to explain later, the result is that it has become more, not less, difficult for Americans to understand people who are not like themselves; and, perhaps more important, it has become more difficult for Americans (collectively) to see themselves as others see them (collectively).

Pressures towards greater foresight are also involved in the process of *rationalization*. Elias was careful to stress that there is no point in history prior to which human beings were entirely 'irrational'. Nor is 'rationality' a fixed property of individual minds in isolation from each other: 'There is no such thing as "reason"', contends Elias, 'only at most rationalization' (2000: 403). What actually changes is the way people are bonded with each other in society, and in consequence the moulding of personality structure or habitus. Elias's argument is that the forms of behaviour we call 'rationality' are produced within a social figuration in which an extensive transformation of external compulsions into internal compulsions is taking place:

> The complementary concepts of 'rationality' and 'irrationality' refer to the relative parts played by short-term affects and long-term conceptual models of observable reality in individual behaviour. The greater the importance of the latter in the delicate balance between affective and reality-orientated commands, the more 'rational' is behaviour. (2006a: 101)

Thus, underlying the emergence of what Max Weber (1978: I, 24–6) called purposive or instrumental rationality (*Zweckrationalität*) are changes in emotional habitus, the habitual curbing of immediate impulses or drives in the interests of attaining longer-term objectives. The modern businessman rationally calculates how best to dispose of his current revenues in order to maximize his future profits. 'Economic' or 'bourgeois' rationality is not, however, the only possible form this *Zweckrationalität* may take. Elias showed how French court society imbued its members with a 'court rationality', in which expenditure was geared strictly to what was expected of one's social rank, not to one's income (which, for many French aristocrats, was inadequate to support their lifestyle, and some were ruined). In America, as we shall see, bourgeois–industrial rationality has played by far the larger role, but something like court rationality has been at work in American history at certain times and places.

Arising out of his ideas about the connection between 'rationality' and the management of the emotions, Elias developed an important extension of the theory of civilizing processes in his writings on the growth of knowledge and the sciences through the course of human history.[18] This is relevant to understanding the persistence of religiosity in American society, the subject of chapter 11.

Established–outsiders relations

In later writings, Elias extended the theory of civilizing processes in many directions. One of these extensions, which will play a significant part in the present book, was his model of 'established–outsider' relations. In the late 1950s and early 1960s, Elias carried out a study of a small community near the city of Leicester in the English Midlands (Elias and Scotson, 1994 [1965]), and he linked what was observed there to ideas already present in essence in *The Civilizing Process* to develop a model of wider applicability. The community contained two areas of working-class housing, one dating from the late nineteenth century and one from the 1930s. The residents of the two areas differed little from each other according to conventional 'objective' sociological measures. The main difference between them was the length of time the families had been living in the locality. The older group, the 'Villagers', looked down upon the more recent arrivals who lived in the 'Estate'. One of the most remarkable aspects of Elias and Scotson's fieldwork was what they found concerning the role of gossip. The longer-established Villagers were linked in a dense social network; over the years, these families had intermarried and were closely connected. Moreover, the Villagers had monopolized the strategic sites in the local networks – the church, the clubs, even the pub. Along these networks they passed a tide of both 'praise-gossip' about themselves, and 'blame-gossip' chiefly about the benighted residents of the Estate. The praise-gossip was based on a no doubt unrepresentative 'minority of the best' among their own members; in it, themes of good behaviour, considerateness, respectability and self-restraint – themes associated with the notion of 'civilization' – played a key part in establishing the claim to social superiority. The blame-gossip was based on a 'minority of the worst' among the denizens of the Estate, who were collectively depicted as lazy, dirty, drunken, violent, sexually immoral and prone to commit crimes. There was indeed a very small minority of 'problem families' on the Estate, who drank and fought, whose children constituted the local delinquents, and so on. The vast majority of the Estate people were not like that. But, lacking the dense established networks, they were unable to retaliate against the Village with a wave of blame-gossip of their own or through praise-gossip about themselves. And, Elias and Scotson found, the people of the Estate to some extent accepted the picture painted of their own inferiority by the Villagers. It is a general principle that one group's *'we-image'* is defined in large measure in relation to its *'they-image'* of another group or groups.

In his introduction to the second edition of *The Established and the Outsiders* (1994: xv–lii), Elias drew more general conclusions. Established–outsider relations are the normal concomitant of a process in which formerly more or less independent groups become more interdependent, and such processes have occurred throughout human history. Where the power ratio between established and outsider groups is extremely unequal, it is very common for people to believe that the differentials in power are inherent in the 'nature' of humankind. Where the oppressed and exploited cannot escape from their position, it is likely that they will take into their 'we-image' what the established say about their inferiority. Nevertheless, pressures towards equalization frequently arise when groups are forced together in growing interdependence – functional democratization – in which established groups become relatively more dependent than formerly on the outsiders. The tensions thus created often result in a shift – either slow and oscillating or sudden and dramatic – towards a more even power ratio. The imposed sense of inferiority is then weakened. Inequalities once taken for granted are challenged. The twentieth century saw an astonishing sequence of emancipation struggles: of workers, of colonial peoples, of ethnic groups, of women, of homosexuals. These dynamic aspects of established–outsider relations have played an enormous part in the history of the USA (see Dunning, 1999: 179–218), and arise in several parts of this book.

Conclusion: The plan and major themes of the book

Although Elias's *The Civilizing Process* is the single most important reference point for this book, I also draw upon many of his other writings that at present few American scholars know well. Elias advanced not just a single theory, but a whole way of doing sociology, or, better indeed, of looking at human society. His approach was labelled (initially by opponents) 'figurational sociology'; he himself preferred 'process sociology'. It is better not to label it as something separate, for there is much in it that all social scientists and historians can agree with. But it does have some distinctive emphases.

Above all, Elias always gave primacy to the study of *process*, rather than to the identification of structural constants supposedly underlying the surface flux of social life. It has been said that he tried to practise 'concept avoidance' (Gleichmann, 1979: 176; cf. Blumer, 1930). Of course, that is not literally possible; what it means is that Elias tried to avoid the use of substantives, which have so often given rise in the social sciences to chicken-and-egg debates about 'individual and society', 'agency and structure' and many others. Here, a contrast with the theories of Pierre Bourdieu may be illuminating. Elias and Bourdieu enjoyed warm personal relations and were interested in many of the same intellectual problems. But Elias always avoided such devices as Bourdieu's repertoire of forms of 'capital' – social, cultural, symbolic and so on – all of them conceived as static entities which then have to be made to move and change. They, and many similar concepts in traditional sociology, tend to give rise to 'static polarities' or dualisms, which Elias always strove to avoid. He was, so to speak, Heraclitean: everything changes all the time.

By extension, in this book I try to follow Elias in thinking in terms of *balances*. The changing balances between self-constraint and external constraint in the steering of behaviour, and between involvement and detachment, play prominent parts. But a concern with *balances of power* or 'power ratios' is all-pervasive in what I have written. Human beings are ineluctably interdependent with each other in a variety of ways. They may be allies or opponents. Sometimes their interdependence is relatively equal, but more often it is unequal; and it thus always involves balances of power between the people and groups concerned, balances that change over time. Central to history and the social sciences, therefore, is the study of the asymmetrical power balances that fluctuate and shift in the course of social conflicts.

Elias's great talent was for *synthesis*, for making connections between aspects of sociology and history that may hitherto have seemed unconnected. In this book, I only occasionally point out the provenance of an idea of which he makes use – Simmel's 'two-front stratum' for instance – but I do not spell out in every case where he has drawn upon a major figure such as Max Weber. Academic readers of the book will be able to see that for themselves.

The architecture of *The American Civilizing Process* loosely resembles that of Elias's *The Civilizing Process*. Chapters 1 and 2 discuss the popular usage of the concept of 'civilization' – which returned very much to prominence in political rhetoric after the attacks of 11 September 2001 – and the part this and related ideas have played in the formation of American 'we-images'. Chapters 3–6 deal with various aspects of the development of manners and of attitudes towards violence in America. Then, like Elias's original work, the book turns in chapters 7–9 to processes of state-formation: both territorial expansion and the internal integration of the American state, with a particular focus on the extent of the monopolization of the means of violence. Because a strong tradition of opinion in America not only favours a weak state, but sees the country as essentially held together by shared 'values', the emphasis on violence and on the unequal distribution of power-chances may jar. But although the constraints of the market and of life in modern large-scale organizations have been prominent components of American civilizing processes, it cannot be emphasized too strongly – as Adam Smith recognized perhaps more clearly than many contemporary writers who pay homage to *The Wealth of Nations* in their celebration of the merits of free markets and open competition – markets can only function within a stable framework of 'law and order' provided by an effective state apparatus. Chapter 10 deals with problems of equality and inequality that arise in a market society, and chapter 11 – as already mentioned – is concerned with the problem of religiosity in American life.

Although I hope that what I have learned from Elias's thinking may cast some aspects of American history in moderately new light, some more familiar themes and problems also run though the book. First, there is the question of 'American social character', much discussed from Crèvecœur through Tocqueville and David Riesman to Christopher Lasch. The whole issue was never simple, but has become more complicated with the ever-increasing diversity of American society and shifts of power within it. One argument running through this book is that there never was a single 'good society' or model-setting elite in the USA to the extent that there was in many Western European societies, but rather a number of competing centres. Nevertheless, the tendency of many earlier writers – perhaps especially European observers – to give great prominence to the New England legacy was not so misleading in the past as it has become today: as a British journalist commented, 'There is an America beyond Massachusetts, and it is firmly in control' (Clark, 2005). The rich internal political and cultural differences and dissension to be found in the contemporary USA makes it difficult to write in a way that is neither over- nor under-generalized. There are no doubt instances where I have failed to strike the right balance; in such cases, readers should understand me to be thinking of traits found among circles of particularly powerful people, or to be pointing to traits that appear to be more common in America than in Europe.

Comparison between the USA and Western Europe is another thread running through the book, and with it the old question of 'American exceptionalism', which is too often framed in terms of ideology rather than of a balance of similarities and differences. I hope it will become evident that research on civilizing and decivilizing processes in America can clarify the specific characteristics of European development, as well as vice versa.

Finally, questions concerning the USA's place in the world today cannot but arise even from an essentially historically orientated study.

These various themes are interwoven in a complex and often implicit way through the book, but I return to address them more explicitly in the final chapter.

1
'American Civilization'

> Since we are condemned as a nation to be a superpower, let a growing sense
> of history temper and civilize our use of that power.
>
> Arthur M. Schlesinger Jr (2006)

In their response to the terrorist hijackings and attacks on the World
Trade Center and Pentagon on 11 September 2001, political leaders and
commentators in the United States and the rest of the world repeatedly
referred to 'civilization' and 'the civilized world'.

President George W. Bush, in a proclamation, declared that 'Civilized
people around the world denounce the evildoers who devised and executed
the terrible attacks'.[1] Secretary of State Colin Powell spoke of a 'war
against civilization' (BBC World Service, 12 September 2001, 14.20 GMT).
Echoing him, former US Ambassador to Britain Philip Lader said the terrorist attacks had been 'an attack on all civilization' (*Newsnight*, BBC2, 12
September 2001). Speaking on behalf of the British government at a special
sitting of the House of Commons, Prime Minister Tony Blair described the
perpetrators of these hideous atrocities as enemies of the civilized world:
'These were attacks on the basic democratic values in which we all believe
so passionately, and on the civilized world.' In response, the leader of the
Conservative Party, Iain Duncan Smith, said that democracy must always
triumph over evil: 'It is the responsibility of civilized countries everywhere
to do whatever is necessary to prevent such atrocities ever happening again'
(<www.bbc.co.uk>, 14 September 2001). At the United Nations, the British
Ambassador, Sir Jeremy Greenstock, said that the events were 'a global
issue, an attack on modern civilization and an attack on the human spirit'.
From Germany, Kurt Voigt of the Social Democratic Party promised his
country's 'help in this common struggle against the evil in the world': this
was 'a war against civilization, and we are with you' (both in *New York*

Times, 12 September 2001). Josef Joffe went further in a leader article in the German weekly newspaper *Die Zeit* (13 September 2001): the terrorists, he wrote, were attacking America and Israel 'as the spearhead of modernism and of Western civilization. They hate the free market, the liberal order, the individual pursuit of self-interest, the freedom of self-determination, the separation of Church and State.' Here, 'civilization' is being used as a term of broad self-approbation for 'us Western people'. The *New York Times*, in its leader on 12 September, admitted, however: 'The distaste of Western civilization and culture that fuels terrorism is difficult to overcome.'

In the face of the repugnant events of 11 September 2001, it is easy to understand how people were drawn to use the concept of 'civilization' in this Manichaean way, as the antonym of 'barbarism', 'savagery' and plain 'evil'. Yet even in the immediate aftermath, a few commentators were uneasy at its use. The Irish historian Joe Lee expressed it well:

> The self-indulgent rhetoric of good versus evil, of 'the civilized world' versus the rest, is the mirror image of the jihad thinking of Muslim fundamentalism. The rhetoric of 'the civilized world' was commonplace a century ago to mean the white world. Blacks are now too visible in America for that to be said out loud. But there is still unfortunate potential for dehumanizing Muslims lurking beneath the surface of the Bush rhetoric, however little he may himself intend it. (*Sunday Tribune*, Dublin, 16 September 2001)

These misgivings were not without cause. In the days and weeks after the attacks, there were sporadic incidents of verbal abuse and violence against Muslims in America and other Western countries. Especially after President Bush's gaffe in speaking of a 'crusade' against terrorism – an unwitting allusion to episodes in the history of the Middle Ages when, judged by modern standards, it is hard to say whether Islam or the Christian Europeans were more nearly 'civilized' – he and other Western leaders had later to go to some lengths to stress the peaceful character of most branches of Islam and the vast majority of Muslims.[2] The effect of their assurances was negated when, a little more than a year later, the United States invaded Iraq.

It was Susan Sontag who wrote what became the most celebrated rejection of the prevailing rhetoric about 'civilization':

> The disconnect between last Tuesday's monstrous dose of reality and the self-righteous drivel and outright deceptions being peddled by public figures and TV commentators is startling, depressing. The voices licensed to follow the event seem to have joined together in a campaign to infantilize the public. Where is the acknowledgment that this was not a 'cowardly' attack on 'civilization' or 'liberty' or 'humanity' or 'the free world' but an attack on the world's self-proclaimed superpower, undertaken as a consequence of specific American alliances and actions? How many citizens are aware of the ongoing American bombing of Iraq? And if the word 'cowardly' is to

be used, it might be more aptly applied to those who kill from beyond the range of retaliation, high in the sky, than to those willing to die themselves in order to kill others. (*New Yorker*, 24 September 2001)

These passages are enough to show not only that the concept of 'civilization' and related ideas are still quite near the surface of modern political thinking, but also that connections remain between the 'everyday', relatively unreflected and the more technical, social scientific senses of the word. How the words 'civilization' and 'civilized' were used in the heat of the moment was very different from the technical meanings of those concepts that Elias developed in his theory of civilizing processes. One link between the everyday and technical, or what anthropologists (Headland et al., 1990) would call the 'emic' and 'etic' meanings of civilization, is that both are connected to means by which one group of human beings expresses its superiority over other groups. The scale of America's historic achievements is such that Americans would not be human if they did not feel and express their collective pride. This pride has always involved a firm faith in *progress*, in things of all kinds having improved and become better, and in their continuing to improve and become better in the future. Irrepressible optimism is commonly recognized as a key American trait. It can be traced back at least to the beginnings of the American state in the era of the Enlightenment, the very period when the word 'civilization' came into use and started to acquire its range of meanings.

The Founding Fathers as *philosophes*

The Enlightenment, that great movement of eighteenth-century European thought marked by a growing faith in reason, science and humanity, comprised many local Enlightenments.[3] Of these, the Enlightenment of the British colonies in North America was only one. It came relatively late, and – at least in the estimate of Peter Gay (1997 [1968]: 35) – was intellectually fairly minor when compared with the French, German or Scottish Enlightenments. In its long-term consequences for world history, however, the American Enlightenment was arguably the most important of all because several of the leading American intellects – Benjamin Franklin, Thomas Jefferson, John Adams, Alexander Hamilton, John Jay, James Madison – had an exceptional opportunity to implement their ideas. They played decisive parts in the American Revolution and in the formation of the American Republic. The most distinguished literary products of the American Enlightenment, moreover, were in the field of political and social thought.

Whatever else of their European heritage they believed they were casting off, the intellectual leaders of the American Revolution certainly did not abandon the concern with problems of 'civilization' characteristic of the Enlightenment. In the Declaration of Independence, when denouncing George III for 'transporting large Armies of foreign Mercenaries to compleat the works of death, desolation and tyranny',[4] they described him acting with 'cruelty and perfidy scarcely paralleled in the most barbarous ages, and totally unworthy of the Head of a civilized nation'. Charles and Mary Beard (1942) traced how, from Thomas Jefferson in the early Republic to Robert MacIver in twentieth-century American sociology, Americans followed European discussions of 'civilization' and later of 'culture', contributed to them, and considered how these issues related to the United States.[5] From an early date, a conception of 'American civilization' became bound up with a sense of American superiority over Europe – as well as of European Americans' superiority over the Indians and blacks – just as in Europe 'civilization' gradually became a badge of superiority, first of upper-class people over the lower classes of European societies themselves and then of all Europeans over the natives of lands subjected to European colonialism. Moreover, while in America there was always a strong sense of human progress, this was combined with at least as strong a sense that the virtues of 'civilization' were, if not innate in every individual American, then at least inherent in the founding conditions of American society. In other words, Americans, like their European contemporaries, came to forget the *process* of civilization through which they had, over the generations, arrived at where they were, and to take the *state* of civilization very much for granted.

In all this, Thomas Jefferson (principal author of the Declaration of Independence and third President of the United States) is highly significant, not so much because he was entirely typical of the founding generation – on the contrary, he was a rather extreme figure – but because the ideas with which he is associated have strongly endured in American political thinking.

'Progress'

In Jefferson's collected writings, the word 'civility' occurs half a dozen times, always in the sense of politeness or consideration for others. He uses 'culture' frequently, but only with the original agricultural meaning: the notion of culture and cultivation in the human and social sense was only just beginning to emerge in his lifetime (Williams, 1958; Goudsblom,

1980). 'Civilization', however, was almost a favourite word, which Jefferson employed about 50 times in publications and correspondence.[6] While representing his newly independent country as Minister to France (1784–9), Jefferson had travelled extensively in Europe (Shackelford, 1995), meeting many leading intellectual figures, and he always read extensively. One of his acquaintances was the Marquis de Condorcet, whose *Sketch for a Historical Picture of the Progress of the Human Mind* (1955 [1795]) traced nine stages of social development, starting from the lowest form of 'savagery' in which humans were barely better than other animals, and drew from this theory a vision of the infinite perfectibility of humankind. Not surprisingly, then, Jefferson uses 'civilization' in most of the senses current at the time in Europe – although not in the derogatory anti-French sense that would become prominent in Germany. Generally he uses the word to signify a peaceful, settled and technically advanced agricultural and commercial society such as the USA then was. Often the word occurs in conjunction with allusions to other symptoms of progress: 'agriculture, manufactures and civilization' (1907: III, 491); 'improvements in arts and civilization' (ibid.: IV, 185); 'the progress of philanthropy and civilization' (ibid.: IV, 17).

Perhaps Jefferson's most vivid statement of his belief in progress is found in his vision of an imaginary journey from the far west of the USA to the more settled East:

> Let a philosophic observer commence a journey from the savages of the Rocky Mountains, eastwardly towards our seacoast. These he would observe in the earliest stage of association living under no law but that of nature, subsisting and covering themselves with the flesh and skins of wild beasts. He would next find those on our frontiers in the pastoral state, raising domestic animals to supply the defects of hunting. Then succeed our own semi-barbarous citizens, the pioneers of the advance of civilization, and so in his progress he would meet the gradual shades of improving man until he would reach his, as yet, most improved state in our seaport towns. This, in fact, is equivalent to a survey, in time, of the progress of man from the infancy of creation to the present day. I am eighty-one years of age; born where I now live, in the first range of mountains in the interior of our country. And I have observed this march of civilization advancing from the seacoast, passing over us like a cloud of light, increasing our knowledge and improving our condition, insomuch as that we are at this time more advanced in civilization here than the seaports were when I was a boy. And where this progress will stop no one can say. Barbarism has, in the meantime, been receding before the steady step of amelioration; and will in time, I trust, disappear from the earth. (Ibid.: XVI, 75)

The famous correspondence[7] between Jefferson and John Adams towards the end of their lives, after their reconciliation following political differences that had emerged at the end of the eighteenth century, is highly revealing about currents of thought in the early Republic concerning matters of 'civilization' and 'barbarism', 'progress' and 'human nature' in Europe and America, and how these were connected to social and political arrangements. In the aftermath of the French Revolution and while the Napoleonic Wars dragged on, Adams expressed some doubt about the inevitability of human progress:

> Let me ask you, very seriously my Friend, Where are now in 1813, the Perfection and perfectibility of human Nature? Where is now the progress of the human Mind? (Adams to Jefferson, 15 July 1813)

And, in a later letter:

> I can only say at present, that it should seem that human Reason and human Conscience, though I believe there are such things, are not a Match, for human Passions, human Imaginations and human Enthusiasm. (Adams to Jefferson, 2 February 1816)[8]

Yet the second and third presidents showed that they still shared an admiration for the achievements of the age of the Enlightenment. Jefferson concurred with Adams's 'eulogies on the eighteenth century':

> It certainly witnessed the sciences and arts, manners and morals, advanced to a higher degree than the world had ever seen. And might we not go back to the era of the Borgias, by which time the barbarous ages had reduced national morality to its lowest point of depravity, and observe that the arts and sciences, rising from that point, advanced gradually thro' all the sixteenth, seventeenth and eighteenth centuries, softening and correcting the manners and morals of man? (Jefferson to Adams, 11 January 1816)

These remarks show Jefferson's characteristic philosophical idealism – he saw ideas and the growth of knowledge as the very cause of the softening of manners.

Fugitive government

The most important legacy of the Enlightenment faith in 'human nature' and in progress – especially American progress – that Jefferson retained, even when the bloody excesses of the French Revolution had shaken it in many others, was a preference for minimal government. With the benefit of hindsight, it must indeed be seen as a gross underestimate of the powers of government necessary in a large and complex society. In a letter to

Judge Johnson, written in 1823, nearing the end of his life, Jefferson recalled that it was the belief of himself and his political allies

> that man was a *rational* animal endowed by nature with rights, and with an *innate* sense of justice; and that he could be restrained from wrong and protected in right, *by moderate powers* confided to persons of his own choice and held to their duties by dependence on his own will. We believed that men, enjoying in ease and security the full fruits of their own industry, enlisted by all their interests on the side of law and order, *habituated* to think for themselves, and to follow *reason* as their guide, would be more easily and safely governed, than minds nourished in error and vitiated and debased, as in Europe, by ignorance, indigence and oppression. (1907: xv, 441; my emphases)

The long-term influence of this view of a universal 'human nature' may perhaps be seen in such spectacular mistakes as the American viceroy's disbandment of the army and much of the administrative structure of Iraq after the occupation of that country in 2003.

With the advantage of hindsight and two subsequent centuries of research and debate among social scientists, Jefferson's eloquent statement can easily be seen to contain a central contradiction. On the one hand, he rightly speaks of habituation, recognizing that people's social habitus is shaped by their experience – including the accumulated experience of generations. This line of thought came to be associated with conservative political theorists, notably Jefferson's older contemporary Edmund Burke (1729–97). On the other hand, the overall impression given by Jefferson's writings is that a peaceful, 'civilized' society is more the outcome of consciously enlightened political institutions than of a long-term, unintended and 'blind' process of development. He appears to take for granted an American habitus in which a strong and stable habitual self-constraint stands almost alone in the steering of conduct, requiring little support from the forces of external constraint by other people. Jefferson asserts that all people can be governed, and govern themselves, by reason, and sees rationality as well as rights and the sense of justice as innate or endowed once and for all by 'nature'. Much later, Elias would contend that rationality or reason was not some fixed and timeless quality of human beings (2006a: 120–3). Rather, the long-term process of rational*ization* is a process of emotional as well as cognitive change – more exactly, a change in prevailing social standards of emotion management – in which, given appropriate social circumstances, external constraints can be converted gradually into habitually greater self-constraints and foresight. Perhaps the founding conditions of American society did constitute appropriate circumstances for this purpose. But an immediate consequence of this belief seems to have been that, from the start, dominant white groups took internal pacification in America too much for granted.

Historically, the most famous and influential statement of Jefferson's point of view was the human rights section of the Declaration of Independence, which he drafted in 1776 on behalf of the Continental Congress with the help of Adams and Franklin:

> We hold these truths to be self-evident, that all men are created equal, that they are endowed by their Creator with certain inalienable Rights, that among these are Life, Liberty and the pursuit of Happiness. That to secure these rights, Governments are instituted among Men, deriving their just powers from the consent of the governed, That whenever any Form of Government becomes destructive of these ends it is the Right of the People to alter or abolish it, and to institute a new Government, laying its foundation on such principles and organizing its powers in such form, as to them shall seem most likely to effect their Safety and Happiness.

Subsequent commentators have frequently dwelt upon the assertion that 'all men are created equal', pointing out that 'all men' plainly failed to include the Indians, slaves and women. Undeniable though that is, it is arguably not the most fundamental criticism that can be made. For even among the 'men' who are included, there never subsists a factual equality in the real social world; there are always to varying degrees inequalities in power between people, whether those inequalities rest on wealth, prestige, political office, knowledge, age, sex or physical strength. More or less unequal power ratios are inevitably part of all relations of interdependence between human beings; and, furthermore, human beings are ineluctably interdependent from birth with numerous others. Whenever the capacity of one person or group of people to withhold something that a second person or group wants or needs is greater than the second's capacity to withhold what the first wants or needs, then there is an unequal power ratio between them, in the first's favour.[9] This principle too ought to be a self-evident truth, but it is a truth which the Declaration of Independence denies (if we take its rhetoric literally).

This rhetorical diminution of the factuality of human interdependence is even more explicit in the Virginia Declaration of Rights, drafted by member of the state legislature George Mason as a preamble to the state's new constitution and adopted on 12 June 1776. Jefferson drew upon it in drafting the more famous Declaration of Independence, adopted three weeks later. Mason wrote:

> All men are *by nature equally free and independent* and have certain inherent rights, of which, when they enter into a state of society, they cannot, by any compact, deprive or divest their posterity; namely, the enjoyment of life

and liberty, with the means of acquiring and possessing property, and pursuing and obtaining happiness and safety. (<www.nara.gov/exhall/charters/billrights/virginia> (Section 1); my emphasis)

Mason's text makes evident even more than Jefferson's their indebtedness to John Locke's political theory of the social contract.[10] Of course, the subsequent accumulation of biological, anthropological and sociological understanding has made us aware that this old philosophical myth is entirely invalid. There never were any separate and isolated human beings who decided, each independently, to enter into interdependence with each other in a 'state of society'; we are *born* into a state of society, and *become* functioning human beings only through our social interdependence with others.[11]

To say that human beings are inherently interdependent with each other is, however, very far from saying that they are inherently capable of living together in harmony. The classic political philosophers were certainly right in fretting about 'the problem of order' – the question posed by Thomas Hobbes: why do people cooperate with each other in society? Why is there not a continual 'war of everyone against everyone', as individuals pursue their own self-interest by whatever means, including force, that are at hand? Why is life not, in consequence, 'solitary, poor, nasty, brutish and short' (Hobbes, 1904 [1651])? Thomas Jefferson's stance on this problem is revealing.

The vision that pervades Jefferson's political thinking is, as Joseph Ellis (1997: 69) cogently argues, of 'a world in which all behaviour was voluntary and therefore all coercion unnecessary, where independence and equality never collided, where the sources of all authority were invisible because they had already been internalized'. Read literally, the human rights section of the Declaration of Independence makes two monumental claims, claims that Jefferson continued to uphold even in such late formulations as that found in the letter to Judge Johnson quoted above:

> The explicit claim is that the individual is the sovereign unit in society; his natural state is freedom from and equality with all other individuals; this is the natural order of things. The implicit claim is that all restrictions on this natural order are immoral transgressions, violations of what God intended; individuals liberated from such restrictions will interact with their fellows in a harmonious scheme requiring no external discipline and producing maximum human happiness. (Ellis, 1997: 11)

In other words, freely interacting individuals would 'create a natural harmony of interests that was guided, like Adam Smith's marketplace, by invisible or veiled forms of discipline' (ibid.: 360). At the time he was drafting the Declaration, Jefferson could hardly have read Smith's *The*

Wealth of Nations, which was published in the same year, 1776; even so, the similarity between his political vision and Smith's famous 'hidden hand' is striking. Yet Smith recognized that free markets could only function in this ideal way if government power was at least adequate to hold the ring, to uphold the peace and to enforce contracts. Smith came a little closer than Jefferson to recognizing that when the 'freedom' of the individual is stressed, 'it is usually forgotten that there are always simultaneously many mutually dependent individuals, whose interdependence to a greater or lesser extent limits each one's scope for action' (Elias, 1978: 167).

Ellis contends that Jefferson's utopian vision came from deep within him, that it was first of all the vision of a young man projecting his personal cravings onto the world. Certainly it fits with his curious and persisting distaste for the cut and thrust of political conflict, and his use notably of Madison and James Monroe to dirty their hands on his behalf in the conflicts which inevitably accompanied his later political career. Yet were this vision no more than the product of the youthful hopes and illusions of a particular young man in the 1770s, it would be of little significance. In fact it was engraved in the founding document of the American Republic: 'The American dream . . . is . . . the Jeffersonian dream writ large' (Ellis, 1997: 69). Nor should it be supposed that the vision would have been accepted by the members of the Continental Congress if they had found it hopelessly juvenile. We must infer that it resonated more widely in the America of the time. These ideas were in the air of late eighteenth-century America. They were, for example, articulated by Hector St John de Crèvecœur in his *Letters from an American Farmer*, first published in 1782 and widely read on both sides of the Atlantic. Crèvecœur paints a picture of the settler's idyllic and almost absolute independence:

> [W]here is that station which can confer a more substantial system of felicity than that of an American farmer possessing freedom of action, freedom of thoughts, ruled by a mode of government which requires but little of us? I owe nothing but a peppercorn to my country, a small tribute to my king, with loyalty and due respect; I know no other landlord than the lord of all land, to whom I owe my most sincere gratitude. (1981: 22)[12]

Crèvecœur was well aware that life among the 'back settlers' on the westernmost frontier, especially in Virginia and the Carolinas where it could be dangerous even to travel, was substantially less idyllic. He spoke of them as 'barbarous' and 'lawless'. But time and increasing population would reform these regions, and make them 'polished and subordinate'. The government neither could nor should seek to crack down hard: 'better it should wink at these irregularities than that it should use means inconsistent with its *usual mildness*' (ibid.: 79; my emphasis).

These ideas were not merely inscribed in classic texts. They were also the underlying attitudes of the political party that won the first great political struggle after the adoption of the new Constitution in 1787, between the 'High Federalists' around Alexander Hamilton, who favoured the development of a much stronger federal government, and the 'Democratic Republicans' around Jefferson. The Federalists, dominant under the first two presidencies – George Washington and John Adams – never recovered from Jefferson's decisive defeat of Adams in the presidential election of 1800. Though undergoing vicissitudes such as its mutation into the rougher-hewn form of Jacksonian democracy in the late 1820s and 1830s, the Jeffersonian current remained dominant in American social and political thinking for most of the nineteenth century.

Even so, an eighteenth-century utopia would not still be of such moment – worthy even now of the attention of anyone who wishes to understand the USA at the beginning of the twenty-first century – if it did not continue to resonate in the social and political life of Americans to this day. Radical changes in American social structure that first gained momentum between roughly 1890 and 1920 – the growth of cities and of industrial production, mass immigration and the supposed 'closing of the frontier' – made the urban worker and professional a more typical American than the independent farmer, and the twentieth century an age of big and growing government; yet powerful elements in America have remained reluctant to accept the political implications of a 'post-Jeffersonian' society. Jefferson himself is often seen, perhaps anachronistically, as a man of the left. But in the late eighteenth century, the 'left' – those such as Condorcet who sympathized with the Enlightenment and the Revolution – were the severest critics of the state. The 'right', those who opposed the Revolution, were the defenders of the state (Rothschild, 2000: 29). During the nineteenth century these positions reversed, and Jefferson's legacy passed to the radical right.

'Human nature'

Political theorists have debated whether the Jeffersonian ideal society was fundamentally individualistic or fundamentally communal; but the matter can scarcely be resolved, because within this utopia such choices do not need to be made: they reconcile themselves naturally (Ellis, 1997: 69). Sociologists will recognize this vision as substantially similar to that which critics in the 1960s contended was embedded in the theories of Talcott Parsons (1903–79), then dominant in American social theory (and more widely), which were seen as representing a 'consensus' view of society, in which the 'problem of order' was solved largely through the assumption that people internalize 'common values' through the process of socialization.[13] Parsons was accused of having adopted an 'oversocialized conception of man', which minimized the chances of conflict both between competing interests within society and between competing impulses within the individual (Wrong, 1961).

It is better not to think about the 'problem of order' in dichotomous and polarizing terms – 'consensus' versus 'conflict', 'shared values' versus 'power', or 'freedom of action' versus 'social control'. In the steering of individual behaviour, *both* external constraint *and* self-constraint *always* play a part. The relevant question, posed with notable clarity by Norbert Elias, is how much of each of these ingredients enters into the steering of conduct in any particular social situation, and whether the balance between external and self-constraints tilts in the course of social change or differs between groups and contexts at a given point in time.

By the late 1780s, others were decidedly less sanguine than Jefferson about what would later be called the problem of social control. Benjamin Franklin observed that 'we have been guarding against an evil that old states are most liable to, excess of power in the rulers, but our present danger seems to be defects of obedience in the subjects' (1905–7: x, 7). Under the Articles of Confederation, the Continental Congress had few powers, and the central government had no executive arm. Since independence, the states had meanwhile generally adopted constitutions that provided government of no more than Crèvecœur's 'usual mildness'. Debtors in particular welcomed weak government. Shay's Rebellion in western Massachusetts in the winter of 1786–7, a local movement of civil disobedience on the part mainly of farmers aiming to prevent county courts sitting to enforce the payment of debts, was fresh in the minds of members of the Constitutional Convention which met that summer in Philadelphia. The need for a government more effective than that established under the Articles was widely recognized among the more prosperous strata in all states.[14] Common to the thinking of Hamilton, Madison and Jay – and also of John Adams – around the time of the new Constitution was a lack of confidence in people's capacity, individually and collectively, to exercise a steady and principled self-constraint. The authors of *The Federalist Papers*, argues Isaac Kramnick, shared

> a profound pessimism, scepticism or realism that continually surfaces in the contributions of all three authors. Men are constantly depicted as vindictive, ambitious and rapacious seekers after power. Visionaries and philosophers who seek perfect worlds are repeatedly objects of ridicule. Government, itself but a reflection of human nature, is necessary only because men are less than angels. (1987: 79)

Madison, Hamilton and Adams, though later to be political opponents, all saw the need for more 'vigorous' government. In *The Federalist* No. 26, Hamilton spoke of 'a zeal for liberty more ardent than enlightened' and asserted 'that greater energy of government is essential to the welfare and prosperity of the community'. Madison, in No. 37, equally recalled the difficulty of 'combining the requisite stability and energy in government with the inviolable attention due to liberty and to the republican form'. To achieve this difficult balance, Madison, as principal architect of the new Constitution, crafted the elaborate system of checks and balances that are its hallmark. He also contrived to succeed in the almost equally difficult task of retaining the support for the Constitution of his patron, Jefferson; Jefferson's absence abroad as American Minister to France helped in this. But Jefferson, then and later, showed little appreciation of the need for Madison's constitutional craftsmanship. As Ellis remarks, Jefferson's ideal remained one of a world 'in which individual citizens had internalized their social responsibilities so thoroughly that the political architecture Madison was designing was superfluous' (1997: 120).

The Federalists, proponents of the new Constitution, won the hard-fought campaign for its adoption. Their opponents, known as the Anti-Federalists and including great names such as Samuel Adams, Patrick Henry and Elbridge Gerry, have been characterized by Isaac Kramnick (1987: 54) as 'nostalgic communitarians, seeking desperately to hold on to a virtuous moral order threatened by commerce and market society'. (It is hard not to think that Jefferson could easily have found his way into their ranks had he not been away in Europe at the time.) In contrast, the Federalists were agreed upon the necessity of the Constitution to provide for the development of commerce through the creation of a national market, a uniform currency, public credit and the protection of contracts and property rights. They were also agreed on the need for government by 'worthy, enlightened and deliberative' men, who would not pose the threat to property rights that the state legislatures had done. Kramnick sees this as one of the eternal polarities of social and political thought, as the contrast between Rousseau and Locke, between Tönnies's *Gemeinschaft* and *Gesellschaft* or (he might have added) between Durkheim's mechanical and organic solidarity. That the difference was both more subtle and less static is evident from the way in which within a decade Madison had seemingly become a 'nostalgic communitarian' in opposition to the High Federalists led by Hamilton. The battle that developed between them has left an enduring mark on American political debate.[15]

A certain disdain for the people who had dominated the early state legislatures, and even a distrust of the common people in general, were widespread among those who supported the new Constitution. Hamilton was especially outspoken. In a famous speech to the Constitutional Convention on 18 June 1787, he went so far as to express his strong admiration for the British Constitution and to advocate that senators serve for life, that the federal government have a right of veto over all state legislation and that governors be appointed by the central government. On none of these matters did he have his way. But as the first Secretary of the Treasury – effectively Washington's Prime Minister – and later as Inspector-General of the Army, Hamilton championed the expansion of the federal government as a good in itself. He understood that for republican government to succeed, the people had to be knitted together by common ties of interest and affection (Walling, 2000: 14–15). Unlike Jefferson, though, he did not believe that the sense of a wider common interest would arise simply from a nation of self-reliant farmers; it would come rather from the ties of complex commercial interdependence, not from agrarian virtue but from successful trade. Commerce would weave the bonds that would restrain the local prejudices and hot passions that had marred the state legislatures. However correct he may have been about that, the growth of commerce was also associated in the early Republic with the emergence of a commercial elite. Both Jefferson and John Adams viewed such an elite as self-serving and standing in need of being kept under control, although the two men differed in subtle ways about how that should be achieved.

After their reconciliation in 1812, the second and third presidents pursued their discussion of the principles of good government and, by extension, of 'human nature', through a somewhat esoteric distinction drawn by Jefferson between a 'natural' aristocracy and an 'artificial' or 'pseudo-' aristocracy based on wealth. Virtue and talents were the marks of the 'natural *aristoi*', those people whom he valued most highly for 'the instruction, trusts and government of society'. There was also 'an artificial aristocracy founded on wealth and birth, without either virtue or talents; for with these it would belong to the first class'. The best system of government was that which most effectively placed the natural aristocracy or best people in government offices. Jefferson wrote:

> *You* think it best to put the Pseudo-aristoi into a separate chamber of legislation where they may be hindered from doing mischief by their co-ordinate branches, and where also they may be a protection to wealth against the Agrarian and plundering enterprises of the Majority of the people. I think that to give them power in order to prevent them from doing mischief is arming them for it, and increasing instead of remedying the evil. For if the co-ordinate branches can arrest their action, so may they that of the co-ordinates. Mischief may be done negatively as well as positively. (Jefferson to Adams, 18 October 1813)

Adams, on the other hand, expressed scepticism about the distinction between the 'natural' and 'artificial' aristocracy, and stated that

The fundamental Article of my political Creed is, that Despotism, or unlim-
ited Sovereignty, or absolute Power is the same in a Majority of a popular
Assembly, an Aristocratical Counsel, an Oligarchical Junto and a single
Emperor. Equally arbitrary cruel bloody and in every respect diabolical.
(Adams to Jefferson, 15 November 1813)

Differ as they might about how the 'best' people should be placed in government, Adams and Jefferson had a common conception of what constituted these best people: the criteria bear a close resemblance to what
European as well as American intellectuals increasingly understood as
'civilized'. The intellectuals of the American Enlightenment placed a high
value on 'self-government', in both a political and a psychological sense
– and the two senses went together. Daniel Howe (1997: 9) has summarized the dominant view as being that 'Only people who could govern
themselves psychologically – that is, who could rationally control their
own impulses – would be capable of governing themselves politically'.
While conscience and reason were certainly acknowledged to exist, they
were typically considered a weaker force in the steering of conduct than
the 'passions'. Prudence – that is, self-interest – could however be enlisted
on the side of conscience in the balanced character, and in the cause of
socially responsible behaviour. This line of thought is seen, for instance,
in Franklin's dictum of Poor Richard that 'Honesty is the best policy'; and
'What the wise and virtuous citizen, dedicated to the common weal, might
do out of principle, a prudent one might do out of self-interest' (Howe,
1997: 13).

In fostering and sustaining a capacity for self-government, Jefferson
believed that gentle constraints were most effective in this task. In that
respect, he may be seen as having anticipated Elias's insight that, in the
more recent stages through which he traces the European civilizing
process, external constraints on people's conduct became increasingly
indirect, and older forms of constraint, notably overt force, became
hidden behind the scenes or 'confined to barracks'. But, for Elias, this
stage is attained only through a very long process of sociogenesis and psychogenesis. Jefferson's trust in a natural aristocracy among men, on the
other hand, was of a piece with his faith in education and in human
progress. Jefferson was very conscious of the long processes of development through which human society had passed, but was perhaps too
ready to assume that all the advances were securely fixed and irreversible
in the founding conditions of the American Republic. It was secure, he
thought, at any rate in an America made up principally of free farmers,
and provided that literacy and education were as widespread as they were
in the states of New England. He was gravely disappointed that Virginia
had not accepted his scheme for universal education in the state, which

would have raised the mass of the people to the high ground of moral respectability necessary to their own safety, and to orderly government; and would have completed the great object of qualifying them to select the veritable aristoi, for the trusts of government, to the exclusion of the Pseudalists [the pseudo-aristocracy of wealth]. (Jefferson to Adams, 18 October 1813)

With such small reservations, Jefferson and those who thought like him may be said to have anticipated the attitude that came to prevail among upper-class people in Europe during the nineteenth century: as noted above (pp. 5, 26), the ways in which people in the West used the *word* civilization showed that they had become unconscious of the long *process* of civilization through which their ancestors' behaviour and feelings had changed and been socially moulded from generation to generation; and they had come to think of the traits they considered 'civilized' as qualities that they themselves possessed innately and self-evidently.

Conclusion

In the debates among the Founding Fathers, doubt was rarely expressed about the peculiarly favourable situation of the white Americans, its legitimacy and moral rightness. Jefferson averred that a government adapted to the character of men as they had been formed in Europe would be very different from one adapted 'for the Man of these states':

Here every one may have land to labor for himself if he chuses; or, preferring the exercise of any other industry, may exact for it such compensation as not only to afford a comfortable subsistence, but wherewith to provide for a cessation of labor in old age. *Every one, by his property, or by his satisfactory situation, is interested in the support of law and order.* And such men may safely and advantageously reserve to themselves a wholsome controul over their public affairs, and a degree of freedom, *which in the hands of the Canaille of the cities of Europe, would be instantly perverted to the demolition and destruction of every thing public and private.* (Jefferson to Adams, 18 October 1813; my emphases)

Jefferson is again making the case for a mildness of government, and in doing so he provides one of the clearest early statements of what came to be known as 'American exceptionalism', of how American 'Man' differed from his European counterparts. (There is a certain tension between this and the more universal conception of human nature implied in Jefferson's letter to Judge Johnson, p. 29 above.)

It can be argued – indeed it was argued at the time – that this current of thought in the early Republic fostered an underestimate of the continuing need for an effective state monopolization of the means of violence, possibly with long-term consequences such as the weakness of American gun-control legislation to this day. In a similar way, Jefferson's idealism (in all senses of the word) led him to see the dominance of kings, nobles and clergy in *ancien régime* Europe as something to be condemned as unenlightened, rather than to ask himself why agrarian societies have to a late stage been dominated everywhere by priests and warriors (Goudsblom, 1996a, 1996b). To pose that question leads to the recognition that the taming of warriors is a necessary element in any process of state-formation. That the pacification of warriors – including the transformation of elements of the old warrior nobility into courtiers – had proceeded relatively far in the European states which founded the American colonies was one reason why early Americans were able to take it so much for granted. It perhaps led them and the generations that succeeded them to underestimate the renewed task of taming their own warriors. In other words, it was an easy assumption that spilled over into a persisting illusion that pacification more generally – the internal pacification of American territory – was a completed process.

2

'Fellow Americans' and Outsiders

The intellectual and emotional construction of a group's 'we-image' and 'we-feelings' always takes place in tandem with the construction of a 'they-image' about some other group or groups of people, and with the development of feelings about them. The other groups may be stronger or weaker, and will simultaneously be forming their own we- and they-images in relation to the first group (see above, pp. 19–20). All this is true of the construction of the idea of 'American civilization', a term of collective self-approbation that by the middle of the twentieth century was used quite unselfconsciously – as for example in the titles of books by Charles and Mary Beard (1940), Curti (1953), Lerner (1957), Kammen (1972), Boorstin and Goetzmann (1972), and even by Mauk and Oakland as late as 1995. The process can be traced back to the earliest phases of European settlement in North America. In colonial times and in the early Republic, for most people their we-images as Bostonians or Virginians may have remained stronger than their we-image as 'Americans'; indeed, until not long before Independence, most seem to have felt themselves to be British, with a regional loyalty akin to that found in British counties (Greenfeld, 1992: 407). This we-image as British-in-America was surprisingly strong, despite the considerable proportion of the white population of the colonies that came not from Britain but from other parts of Europe; though it was later to embarrass him, in 1749 Benjamin Franklin expressed alarm at Americans' Britishness being diluted by the influx of German-speaking settlers (Morgan, 2002: 72, 77). More decisively, the we-image of 'Americans' was from the beginning quite strong enough to demarcate the colonists of European stock from the Indians, as they were then called. It also demarcated them from the African slaves they imported; and, a little less emphatically, from French traders and settlers. The key 'others' in the development of an American identity are the

Indians and the blacks on the one hand and the Europeans-in-Europe on the other.

Others: the Native Americans

In so far as they had occupied the land for many centuries before the arrival of European settlers, the 'Indians' were initially the 'established', and the power ratio at the centre of the established–outsider figuration of the European settlers and the Indians was at first much more nearly equal than that between the white settlers and their African slaves. Before 1492 most of the New World's inhabitants were agriculturalists who lived a settled existence in towns and villages. The earliest European settlers had some resources that gave them certain power advantages over the Indians: horses, guns and, not least, the diseases they brought with them. Nevertheless, the celebrated story of how Plymouth Plantation would have perished during its first year had the local Indians not explained the use and cultivation of such crops as corn and squash represents a memory that the balance of interdependence was initially in the Indians' favour. But, by the time of the War of Independence, the writing was already on the wall for the Indians. Although it must be recognized that ideology and discourse were not the driving forces in the treatment of the Indians – they provided useful rationalization of a process that was mainly driven by white settlers' lust for land – Roy Harvey Pearce (1988) has shown the significant part that the discourse of 'savagery' and 'civilization' played in their downfall. It can be seen very explicitly at the end of the nineteenth century in, for instance, Theodore Roosevelt's *The Winning of the West* (1995 [1889–99]).

Once again, the enigmatic Jefferson is a point of reference. Both he and John Adams from their childhoods had first-hand knowledge of Indians, who were then still living locally in Massachusetts and Virginia. Adams unambiguously pitied their fate. Jefferson was as slippery on the Indians as he was on the question of slavery. He pioneered the study of Indian languages, made one of the first archaeological excavations of their burial mounds and took an interest in the languages and social organization – overall, in what would later be called the anthropology – of the Native Americans. In the thought of the time concerning ways of life, intellectual development and systems of government, the American Indians are often a third corner in a triangular comparison with Europe and the United States. The Indian way of life in small, self-governing communities, in which a fairly stable and violence-free society was maintained apparently without any police or other state agents of coercion, had some obvious appeal to Jefferson and others who thought like him.

In Jefferson's writings, the notion of 'civilization' arises as often as not in connection with the Indians. While President, Jefferson explicitly referred to their 'progression from barbarism to civilization', speaking with special optimism about the Cherokees, 'the upper settlements of whom have made me a formal application to be received into the Union as citizens of the United States, and to be governed by our laws' (1907: XII, 75). But whatever sentimental attachment Jefferson may have entertained for Indian society, he had a stronger attachment to his vision of the westward expansion of white American society into the 'free' lands to the west. It was during his presidency that the foundations were laid for the destruction of the Indians in such later episodes as the expulsion of the 'five civilized tribes' (including the Cherokees of whom he had spoken with apparent sympathy). Throughout his life Jefferson supported a policy of 'civilizing the Indians', a policy fully articulated by his colleague in George Washington's cabinet, Secretary of War Henry Knox, who wrote:

> [I]t has been conceived to be impracticable to civilize the Indians of North America. This opinion is probably more convenient than just. That the civilization of the Indians would be an operation of complicated difficulty; that it would require the highest knowledge of the human character, and a steady perseverance in a wise system for a series of years, cannot be doubted. But to deny that, under a course of favourable circumstances, it could not be accomplished, is to suppose the human character under the influence of such stubborn habits as to be incapable of melioration or change – a supposition entirely contradicted by the progress of society, from the barbarous ages to its present degree of perfection. (Cited in Wallace, 1999: 168)

If the Indians could not be civilized, wrote Jefferson, 'we shall be obliged to drive them, with the beasts of the forests, into the Stony [Rocky] Mountains' (cited in Remini, 2001: 115). That was beginning to happen as a matter of policy by 1817, when General Andrew Jackson was negotiating with the Cherokee, who were being offered a choice of moving to Alabama or becoming citizens of the United States. They could no longer survive as hunters, and as long as they roamed in search of game, wrote Jackson to President Monroe, 'they will retain their savage manners, and customs'. He advised that it was necessary by law 'to circumscribe their bounds – put into their hands the utensils of husbandry – yield them protection, and enforce obedience to those just laws provided for their benefit. . . . In short, they must be civilized.' Monroe replied, a little more cautiously, that perhaps 'a compulsory process seems to be necessary, to break their habits, & to civilize them' (ibid.: 119).[1]

Interestingly, the Cherokee themselves adopted this discourse of civilization and savagery. In their negotiations with Jackson, their leaders said that the truth was that 'we are not yet civilized enough to become citizens'. But, if forced to move,

> we would, in the course of a few years, return to the same savage state of life that we were in before the United States, our white brothers, extended their fostering care towards us, and brought us out of a savage state into a state similar to theirs. . . . Our choice is to remain on our lands, and follow the pursuits of agriculture and civilization. (Ibid.: 125)

This appears to be a paradigmatic instance of a weaker, outsider, group taking into its we-image elements of the stronger, established, group's they-image depiction of them (see above, pp. 19–20).

A similar rhetoric of 'civilization' and 'savagery' was employed more than a century later in the United States' rule in the Philippines, although opposition to the 'civilizing' process there 'had the support of distinguished men and women . . . who held that the new policy departed ominously from the letter and spirit of American civilization' (Beard and Beard, 1942: 580; cf. Go, 2003: 13).

Others: the blacks

From the earliest days of the Republic, many Americans were only too conscious of how the rhetoric of liberty ignored the slaves of African origin. John Adams, for one, was always opposed to slavery, as were his distinguished descendants. So too was the slave-owning Thomas Jefferson in a decidedly ambivalent and uncomfortable way. The problem could be swept under the carpet to a limited extent; it was predicted that the slave population would in time decline and disappear. The vast expansion of cotton production and of black slavery in the Deep South in the early decades of the nineteenth century following Eli Whitney's invention of the cotton gin refuted that prediction. The protean concept of 'civilization' was pressed into service by both sides in the great conflict which culminated in the Civil War. Abolitionists drew upon its universalizing connotations to denounce slavery as incompatible with a 'civilized' society. On the other hand, the conception of human progress from 'savagery' to 'civilization' was employed to stigmatize the blacks as inherently inferior and 'savage'.

Slaves lived in varying degrees of powerlessness, the most extreme case being that of field hands on the cotton plantations of the New South. Legally, slaves were no more than chattels whose owner could do with them as he pleased. First-generation slaves were disorientated by the sufferings of capture and transport and by the severing of all their bonds to their own families, communities and cultures. Very often, slaves on a particular plantation would not even speak the same language as each other. Even in subsequent generations, the conditions of life made it difficult for slaves to communicate and form any kind of social cohesion wider than the single plantation. This made the stigmatization of 'the Negro' as an inherent inferior to 'white' people relatively easy. 'The Negro' was represented as lazy, feckless, lacking any foresight and having a happy-go-lucky, child-like and essentially helpless nature. Indeed, Stanley Elkins (1959; cf. Abrams, 1982: 241–50) argued that their situation did have 'infantilizing' effects on them, most especially those who were merely 'field hands' on the plantations. Yet the owners *needed* the slaves. They were a means of production, a form of property and wealth, and did have a function for their owners. This tended to place some limits, by and large, on their maltreatment. In contrast, where an outsider group has no such function for the established group, where they are – as, for instance, in the case of the Amerindians both in North America and parts of Latin America – simply in the way, they may be exterminated or driven out and left to die (Elias, 1994: xxxi).

Others: the Europeans

From the earliest beginnings of settlement in North America, Europeans served as 'others' in the construction of an American we-image and we-feelings.[2] The idea is present in Winthrop's metaphor of the 'city upon a hill'; but that is two-edged. It implies an intention to create a community better than that found in the country they were leaving; but more strongly, it conveys an awareness that the settlers were a tiny outsider group, the very visibility of whose experiment imposed on them a pressure towards collective self-constraint. Any failings would be observed, albeit from a great distance, and decried by the more powerful established group represented by the watching parent society. The colonists had to strive for respectability – in part, respectability in the eyes of Europeans. Yet such relationships are always marked to a greater or lesser extent by ambivalence, by the sense both of inferiority and superiority to 'the others'.

Summarizing their discussion of the notion of 'civilization' in the early USA, the Beards discern certain propositions underlying its use (1942: 162–4). There was the belief in human progress, noted above, and in the special scope for human progress found in the USA. And there was the belief 'that America, though an offshoot of Europe, was no mere duplication of European ideas, institutions and practices', with the consequence that civilization in the USA, being different from that in Europe, 'must continue to differ, for history is irreversible'.

American individualism

While the *philosophes* of the American Enlightenment shared much of their thinking with their European counterparts, there was – as we have seen notably in Jefferson – an undercurrent of individualism which subsequently became more emphatic and more clearly linked to a rising nationalism. The word 'individualism' itself seems to have been first used in 1820, in a pejorative sense, by the French conservative thinker Joseph de Maistre (Curry and Goodheart, 1991: 10–11), but was applied to America by Tocqueville, who used it to describe what had been growing for some time:

> Individualism is a mature and calm feeling, which disposes each member of the community to sever himself from the mass of his fellow-creatures, and to draw apart with his family and friends; so that, after he has formed a little circle of his own, he willingly leaves society at large to itself. (1961 [1835–40]: II, 118)

After the Civil War, the doctrine of individualism became more widely current, and the Beards depicted it as 'a new doctrine of the perfect good' which came to be *opposed* to the older idea of civilization (1942: 332, 334). Tocqueville had contrasted individualism with selfishness: 'Our fathers knew only selfishness', which he defined as 'a passionate and exaggerated love of self that brings man to relate everything to himself alone and to prefer himself to everything'.[3] For the Beards, the distinction was less clear:

> The spirit of this arbitrary act of . . . declaring one's complete independence from all social relations, entered into the idea of individualism as it was developed, especially in relation to economic activities and vested rights. When it reached full formulation the idea embraced several very concrete affirmations, such as the following: Society is merely an aggregation of individuals struggling for existence competitively. The qualities or talents of the individual which prepare him for that struggle are to be attributed solely to personal merits and efforts; the individual is 'self-made'. In unrestrained competition, victory goes to the strong, the ambitious, the ingenious, the industrious, the 'fittest to survive', and their rewards as victors are proportioned to the contributions of their labours to the total product, as justice requires; they get what they deserve, in short. . . . Poverty is due to the indolence, lack of initiative, improvidence, dearth of ambition, the inebriety, or the restlessness of the poor themselves. (1942: 333–4)

The ideology of this high form of individualism embodies a pessimism far removed from the Enlightenment faith in the 'Perfection and perfectibility of human Nature'; it rather represents a view of human nature that is essentially unchanging. Just as the *process* of 'civilization' was forgotten, so too was the process of individual*ization* – individualism as a social characteristic was taken to be something self-evident and innate, which it is not. The stress on the individual soul in the Calvinist theology of the early New England settlers can be seen as a stage in the development of individualism, but those settlers in their tight communities were very different from the individualists of the late nineteenth century. High nineteenth-century individualism was linked to the dominance in the late Victorian period of laissez-faire economics and of Darwinism. The Beards, speaking from the standpoint of the American left in the first half of the twentieth century, saw the idea of individualism as 'hostile to the social principle in the idea of civilization' and as 'a disintegrating force in many directions'. The most prominent American champion of individualism and of Social Darwinism, the Yale sociologist William Graham Sumner, well expressed this sense of hostility to 'civilization' as follows:

> This civilization has cost mankind many inconveniences and it has, in many respects, involved experiences which we do not like. It has subjected us to drill and discipline; the civilized man is disciplined in his feelings, modes of action, the use of his time, his personal relations, and in all his rights and duties. As civilization goes on the necessity grows constantly more imperative that any man who proposes to pass his life in the midst of a civilized society must find a place in its organization and conform to its conditions. At the same time the civilized man, instead of living instinctively, as his ancestors did only a few centuries ago, has become a *rationalizing* animal. (Quoted in Beard and Beard, 1942: 344)

There was no longer any liberty 'in the sense of unrestrained self-will' (ibid.). This sentiment is reminiscent of Nietzsche's almost contemporaneous exaltation in Germany of the warrior code (Elias, 1996: 113–19).

The special significance of individualism, however, is that it came to be seen as 'the chief and distinguishing characteristic of American civilization' (Beard and Beard, 1942: 338). In the USA, there was never effectively a rival concept to 'civilization' such as *Kultur* posed to *Zivilisation* in Germany, where *Zivilisation* came to be tarred with connotations of foreignness. Individualism was part of American 'civilization', but as its most distinctive feature it nevertheless served to heighten the contrast with Europe. In that sense, the development of the individualistic ideology in late nineteenth-century America paralleled 'the recession of the social element and the advance of the national element in the antithesis between *Kultur* and *Zivilisation*' described by Norbert Elias (2000: 26–30). That is all the more true because individualism was championed by politically and economically powerful figures of the time, including two Presidents – Woodrow Wilson in his *History of the American People* (1918), and Theodore Roosevelt in such writings as *The Strenuous Life* (1923–6: XIII, 319–31) where, in an echo of Jefferson, he identifies urban life with the danger of creating 'overcivilized man'. Rotundo (1993: 251–2) and Bederman (1995: 23–5) both noted how the fear of becoming 'overcivilized' applied especially to males, and how, in consequence, the term 'civilization' acquired connotations of femininity and softness. There is a distant echo here of how in Germany '*Zivilisation*' came to be identified with aristocratic affectation and superficiality, and masculinity with a 'hard' behavioural style.

Within any society, especially one as vast and diverse as the developing United States became, there are always many contradictory currents of thought. Some American voices were always raised against the ideology of individualism. In the extreme form in which individualism was articulated in the late nineteenth and early twentieth centuries, it is now confined to the far right of American politics. Yet it is also fair to say that this far right is more strongly represented in America at the beginning of the twenty-first century than are its counterparts in most Western European countries. And, in milder form, individualism also flavours the outlook of a much broader spectrum of American opinion. One reason is that, given its power position in the world, the USA has undergone fewer changes than have occurred elsewhere. In the twentieth century, almost all European countries experienced defeat (or near-defeat) in war at least once; as the Native Americans could testify, nothing is more upsetting to a way of life than defeat. In consequence, America has to a certain extent been able to continue to live in the 1890s, and to European eyes has come to appear in some respects curiously old-fashioned or even backward.[4] Perhaps a strong individualism (a kind of *collective individualism*, if that is not an oxymoron) sometimes flavours American foreign policy too, in a sense that is captured in the following comment – less than five months after the events of 11 September 2001 – by a European journalist who steadfastly maintained that he was not anti-American:

> The era of guilt (Vietnam) and the era of dithering (Clinton) have been replaced by a fresh discovered triumph of American will, that more and more permits Washington to take decisions which have to pass only an exclusive test of national self-interest. [This] carries costs, which a pro-American should be the first to lament. . . . [I]t negates the notion of a world community of self-respecting nations, many of which have much to contribute to making this a safer place. In George Bush's America, there's evidently little room for a sense of *noblesse oblige*. This America is an alliance-builder only for her national purposes. . . . But world power surely carries the responsibility to look wider, towards a benign shaping

of decisions that are collective, not unilateral. (Hugo Young, *Guardian*, 31 January 2002)

What Senator Fulbright (1966) called 'the arrogance of power' has many roots besides the cultural and ideological – sheer power and the opportunity to exercise it come first – but the USA is sometimes seen in Europe as acting collectively in the world on principles akin to those of individualism.[5] Given the position of the USA today as the world's pre-eminent 'established' group and its powerful cultural influence throughout the world, it is not surprising that hostility to this individualistic strain is one of the key elements in anti-Americanism in Europe and elsewhere. On the other hand, the USA is also widely seen in Europe as having saved democracy in that continent from Nazism and communism. Now that Europe is the weaker, 'outsider' party to the old relationship – politically, militarily, economically and culturally – European intellectuals often display the ambivalence towards the USA that many Americans at one time felt towards Europe.

Anti-Americanism: how the outsiders view the established

As already noted, we-images and we-feelings are always constructed in relation to they-images and they-feelings about other groups of people. But at the same time, the other groups of people will be forming their own they-images and they-feelings in return. Anti-Americanism, especially in Europe, is long established, far antedating the world dominance of the USA, even if it has competed from the beginning with strongly pro-American currents. It must not be overlooked that in Britain, even during the War of Independence, there was a considerable body of radical opinion that supported the American cause. William Blake's poem 'America' (1958 [1793]: 110–26), celebrating the military leaders of the American Revolution, is just one symptom of that. On the other hand, disparagement of America started very early too. The notion of 'civilization' proved a useful tool in these rivalries, used by all sides to assert their superiority in the hierarchy of nations. A British traveller in the United States in the 1840s asserted that 'England has her fixed position in the family of nations, and at the head of civilization – a position she has long occupied, and from which it will be some time ere she is driven', and sneered that 'the true citizen of the United States exalts his head to the skies in the contemplation of what the grandeur of his country is *going* to be'. And Victor Hugo wrote condescendingly that 'French civilization is so above and apart from that of all other peoples, that my countrymen need not shrink from encouraging people like those of the United States in their ambition to imitate the glories of France' (Beard and Beard, 1942: 485).

Much similar talk was, as we shall see in chapter 3, directed by upper-class European travellers at the manners of nineteenth-century Americans. This kind of superficial social condescension has not disappeared. It is more difficult to sustain, however, against the people of what is now the richest and most powerful country in the world rather than against some seemingly pretentious upstart in the nineteenth century, especially in the face of the popularity of the products of American culture among large swathes of the world's population. What has taken the place of simple condescension has been a sustained discourse among European intellectuals that has made 'America' a negative symbol which, James Ceaser (1997) has argued, has little connection with the real society that is America. This tradition of thought has been shaped by writers both from the 'right' and the 'left'. Ceaser has traced it from De Maistre through Baudelaire to Baudrillard in France, and from Hegel to Ernst Jünger and Heidegger in Germany. Many of the remarks Ceaser unearthed would be funny were they not full of hatred. Baudelaire described America in 1857 as 'a great hunk of barbarism illuminated by gas'; and a former secretary to Jean-Paul Sartre described Disneyland, on its opening in Paris in 1992, as 'a cultural Chernobyl . . . a construction of hardened chewing gum and idiotic folklore written for obese Americans' (Ceaser, 1997: 11, 8). But in the following passage, Ronald Wright (2001) gives a more serious denunciation of 'America'. He distils just those shameful elements, the exclusion of which underpins the pride in the American we-image – elements of which some Europeans take a certain pleasure in reminding their transatlantic friends. He speaks of America's

exceptional capacity for self-delusion. Perhaps no other modern nation is such a prisoner of its mythology, or so needs to be. The United States views itself as a beacon of freedom planted on virgin soil, where great wealth has been built up by the honest sweat of pioneer brows. Certainly many Americans have toiled hard, but the ultimate source of their prosperity – their 'start-up capital' – was the theft of the continent and the destruction of the millions who lived there. [America is] a nation that regards itself as quintessentially modern, yet is strangely archaic. One in two Americans believes the earth was created by divine will within the past few thousand years. Almost as many cannot recognize the outline of their country on a map. The American conservative is a social Darwinist who does not believe Darwin. . . . Other nations have horrors under the concrete too, but reckoning with their pasts does not threaten their national being in the same way, because they do not believe themselves to be the End of History. Unabashed historical amnesia . . . is essential to America's utopianism. White America can live with itself only if it forgets the past.

Conclusion

Chapters 1 and 2 have been concerned with some of the ways in which Americans, especially American intellectuals from the early days of the Republic, came to think about themselves and the world. The notions of 'civilization' and 'American civilization' played a significant part, directly and indirectly, in this. As in Europe, the idea of civilization as something of which to be proud also involved things to be forgotten, including much of how the happy stage attained at any time had in fact been reached. As Elias wrote of the *European* civilizing process:

> [N]ations came to consider the *process* of civilization as completed within their own societies; they came to see themselves as bearers of an existing or finished civilization to others, as standard-bearers of expanding civilization. Of the whole preceding process of civilization nothing remained in their consciousness except a vague residue. Its outcome was taken simply as an expression of their own higher gifts; the fact that, and the question of how, in the course of many centuries, civilized behaviour has been attained was of no interest. (2000: 43)

So far we have been concerned mainly with the formation in intellectual and ultimately popular discourse of an American collective pride similar to that of which Elias spoke in Europe. Hitherto, we have taken what anthropologists call an 'emic' view of how many Americans see *themselves*. In place of this 'insider' perspective, we shall now turn to examine the factual processes through which were created various components of what Americans feel proud of. For this task we shall attempt to adopt an 'etic' approach, the perspective of the outsider – not literally, except incidentally, of non-Americans, but the perspective rather of relatively detached historians and social scientists seeking to understand the sociogenesis and psychogenesis of the we-images and we-feelings that have become attached to 'the American way of life'.

3

American Manners Under Scrutiny

> In America, where the privileges of birth never existed and where riches
> confer no peculiar rights on their possessors, men unacquainted with each
> other are very ready to frequent the same places, and find neither peril nor
> advantage in the free interchange of their thoughts . . . their manner is there-
> fore natural, frank and open.
>
> Tocqueville, *Democracy in America* (1961 [1835–40]: I, 202–3)

Alexis de Tocqueville, the most famous of all foreign commentators upon
the United States, attributed the distinctive features of American manners
to the relative equality of social conditions which prevailed there when he
visited the country in the 1830s.[1] *Democracy in America* is not just about
America; even if Tocqueville does not loudly proclaim it, the book is in
effect a three-way comparative study of the USA, France and Britain,
and his sense of the exceptional character of American manners arose
from that transatlantic comparison (Stone and Mennell, 1980: 9–10).[2]
'Manners' – *mœurs* in French – he understood, moreover, in a very broad
sense. He applied the word 'not only to manners in the proper sense . . .
but also to the various notions and opinions current among men, and to
the mass of ideas which form their habits of mind' (1961: I, 354).
Manners in this sense, he argued, were more important than laws and
geographical circumstances in maintaining democratic institutions in the
USA. Yet the manners were themselves the product of 'democracy' in the
sense of relative social equality. Tocqueville constantly compared 'democratic society' – America – with 'aristocratic society', by which he meant
France, and he implicitly placed Britain on the continuum between the
two, but closer to the aristocratic pole. For him, there was little doubt that
America represented the future direction in which aristocratic societies
would evolve, and he inferred that as society became more equal many

consequences followed: attitudes to the suffering of fellow men became less harsh; social interaction became less stiff and formal (although striving for invidious status distinctions increased); and relations between masters and servants, between the sexes and even between officers and men in armies became less hierarchical. The relative equality of social conditions, furthermore, had cultural consequences. In a new and rapidly expanding society, the ideas of earlier generations have little authority; where social mobility is high, people do not adopt ideas dominant among their social class, for class consciousness scarcely exists; and where social conditions are so nearly equal, there are few people whose social standing lends authority to their ideas. Tocqueville went on to suggest how 'democracy' would affect the arts, literature and language, and foster an interest in applied rather than pure science.

It would be hard to disagree that American *mœurs* have distinctive characteristics. Every nation's history leaves its mark upon a people's habitus. As Norbert Elias remarked: 'In the conduct of workers in England, for example, one can still see traces of the manners of the landed gentry, and of merchants within a large trade network, in France the airs of courtiers and a bourgeoisie brought to power by Revolution' (2000: 386). Or, writing much later about the Dutch: 'having an upper class composed of urban merchants has left deep marks on the habitus of the Dutch. Fostering equality is of prime importance' (1996: 12). What would be the ingredients from which an equivalent American habitus was composed? The Puritan preacher, the slave-owning planter (or, for that matter, the slave), the frontiersman, the *nouveau riche* businessman? Perhaps the American cocktail is less thoroughly stirred, for it is much less clear than in England, France or the Netherlands that there was ever any single model-setting central social group. Rather than any single 'good society', there was more open social competition between a multiplicity of groups. Tocqueville was aware of the diversity of American society, but equality of social condition was for him the overriding characteristic. Yet, for all that so many of his insights have stood the test of time, he may have been misled simply by the date of his visit: he arrived in America just after Andrew Jackson had swept into the White House, and the Jacksonian era is generally seen as the high water mark of American egalitarianism. Snapshots taken at one moment often prove insecure evidence from which to infer processes over time. In comparing civilizing processes in America and Europe over the longer term, certainly some contrasts endure; there are leads and lags in the constituent part-processes, with the USA sometimes outstripping some or all European countries, and sometimes vice versa; but there are also great similarities in the underlying processes. This can be seen, in the first instance, in the history of American manners books.

American manners books

American exceptionalism was again the first note struck by Arthur
Schlesinger Sr in his pioneering study of American etiquette books,
although the final impression he leaves with the reader is of the broad similarity to Europe. He began by listing five conditions which flavoured the
American behavioural canon from the outset (1947: viii–ix):

1 The colonies were settled in the main by people who would not have
   been familiar with the usages of good society in the Old World.
2 No native hereditary aristocracy of the kind which in Europe set standards of taste and behaviour ever existed in America. (Schlesinger
   should more exactly have written 'hereditary nobility'; there were
   never hereditary titles and legally enshrined privileges but, as we shall
   see, approximate functional equivalents to aristocracy in the broader
   sense did emerge in particular regions and periods.)
3 The 'necessity of taming a wilderness before cultivating the graces of
   living' was constantly renewed as the frontier was pushed westwards.
   (Here Schlesinger invoked Frederick Jackson Turner's 'frontier thesis',
   which will be discussed more fully in chapter 8.)
4 There was a constant influx of immigrants, 'who faced all the difficulties of the native-born as well as the additional one of having to master
   the unfamiliar customs of their English-speaking neighbours'.
5 Finally, as in many other new countries (such as Australia), for a very
   long time men outnumbered women, whose role as a source of civilizing pressures on men has been recognized by sociologists at least since
   Sombart's essay on luxury (1969 [1913]).

While Schlesinger was probably right that all these circumstances contributed something to the overall flavour of modern American manners,
it is hard to assess how distinctive was the process through which they
developed without first looking at what early European settlers took to
America from their home continent. In particular, what point in the
European sequence of development traced by Norbert Elias through
European manners books had been attained in the seventeenth and eighteenth centuries?

The European point of departure

Translated into many languages, manners books from the previous century,
such as Della Casa's *Galateo* (originally 1558), Erasmus's *De civilitate
morum puerilium* (1530), Castiglione's *Il Cortigiano* ([*The Courtier*] 1528)

and many imitations and derivatives, continued to circulate in seventeenth-century Europe. If they no longer represented standards at the highest ranks of society, they could have been read only in the wider but still relatively restricted ranks of the literate, from which it may be inferred that – there at least – their instructions about good behaviour were not yet risibly irrelevant. The more demanding standards reached at the court of Louis XIV were set out in Courtin's *Nouveau traité de civilité* in 1672; it was Courtin, for instance – as we saw in the Prologue – who noted that some 'delicate' people would be so disgusted if a fellow diner were to use a spoon that had already been in his mouth to help himself to soup from the tureen that they would refuse to take soup from it themselves (Elias, 2000: 91). In the foreword to his book Courtin strongly implies that people at court do not need to be told how to behave – they learn simply by seeing how others behave – and claims to be writing simply for the 'information' of provincial noblemen who are rarely able to visit the court (ibid.: 85–6). By the early eighteenth century, books were appearing – in France at least – that were more explicitly addressed to wider bourgeois strata (ibid.: 80ff.). It is evident from them that the use of the fork was still filtering down the social scale, and some eating with the fingers persisted. A book such as La Salle's *Règles de la bienséance et de la civilité chrétienne* still spelled out good and bad table manners in great detail. So also did it the use of the handkerchief as opposed to the fingers when blowing one's nose and in spitting, and it discussed at length conventions surrounding the 'bodily functions' – urination, defecation, breaking wind – and undressing for sleep. But by 1774, when a heavily revised edition of La Salle's work was published, the latter topics were mentioned only briefly, mainly in terms of the need to preserve 'modesty'. When standards of 'refinement' in colonial America appear 'low', it is as well to remember that it is highly questionable whether – class for class, stratum for stratum – they differed dramatically from those that prevailed at the same period in Europe.

Manners books come to America

If there was an audience for instruction on good behaviour among the provincial gentry and the bourgeoisie in Europe, the same certainly applied to their counterparts in America. John Winthrop the Younger (1606–76), Governor of Connecticut, owned a copy of Castiglione's *Cortigiano* (Schlesinger, 1947: 6). The famous *Rules of Civility* that the young George Washington copied out for his own use (eventually published in 1890) were taken from a seventeenth-century English translation of a French book derived from Della Casa's sixteenth-century *Galateo* (Bushman, 1993: 32). One of the first manuals of manners for children written in America, Eleazer Moody's frequently reprinted *The School of*

Good Manners (1715), was similarly adapted from a 1595 English version of a French original dating from 1564 (ibid.). Seventeenth-century English books such as Richard Brathwayt's *The English Gentleman* (1630), Henry Peacham's *The Compleat Gentleman* (1622) and Richard Allestree's *The Whole Duty of Man* (1658) could be circulated and reprinted in America without need for adaptation. Jefferson is known to have owned a copy of *The Whole Duty of Man*, and Benjamin Franklin to have recommended it to his daughter (Schlesinger, 1947: 9). Wright (1940) found that copies of these books were commonly to be found on the shelves of Virginia gentlemen. The manners these books described and prescribed were on the whole less decorative than those to be found in a book from the French court like Courtin's – in part because they were based on social standards at a somewhat earlier period, and perhaps also in part because virtuoso display became less central to the English upper-class way of life than to the French[3] – but their pedigree was essentially from the common European courtly tradition. Although the courtly ideal was altered and adapted in England, comments Bushman (1993: 36), 'gentility never lost the marks of its origin in the royal courts'. The demand for manners books of European courtly provenance continued into republican America. Lord Chesterfield's *Letters to his Son* – a not untypical courtly mixture of highly polished manners with somewhat cynical attitudes to personal relations – was published in London in 1774, and 18 editions and adaptations were published in America before the turn of the century (ibid.). Eventually, in 1827, a naturalized version was published under the title *The American Chesterfield* (Schlesinger, 1947: 14).

The dominance of European influence in the manners books read in America should come as no surprise. It has to be remembered that, until well into the nineteenth century, a majority of books of all kinds published in America were by English authors. It has been estimated that as late as 1820 only 30 per cent of titles were by American writers and roughly 70 per cent by British. These figures were, however, rapidly reversed in the space of the next three decades.[4] Kasson (1990: 47) notes that although reprints and adaptations of English etiquette books continued to be published throughout the century, the proportion they represented steadily declined.[5] Moreover, at the beginning of the nineteenth century, there began to appear a distinct series of manners books addressing an audience of 'middling people', as Hemphill (1996, 1999) terms them.

Nevertheless, as Schlesinger drily commented: 'The continued repute of British courtesy books through the tumultuous years of Revolutionary agitation and armed strife and during the early decades of the Republic suggests how little political separation affected subservience to the parent country in matters of decorum' (1947: 13). Such 'repute' is one symptom of an established–outsiders relationship between Britain and America –

with Americans as the outsiders – that arguably persisted until into the twentieth century, when the USA finally manifestly overtook Britain in economic, political and military power in general; a gradual reversal of the deference relationship then ensued, in the wake of changes in the distribution of those other more tangible power resources. It is certainly a mistake to project backwards a stereotype of American society as always militantly egalitarian, where people were always indifferent to the striving for 'gentility'.

Deference and American gentility

In his study of the 'mental outfit' that the early European settlers brought to the North American colonies, Edward Eggleston pointed out a century ago that 'the prevalent notions of life and obligation were everywhere monarchical and aristocratic. Primary duties were to those above you – to God, to the king, to the magistrate, to the social superior', and he quoted Peacham's prescription that 'Noble or Gentlemen ought to be preferred in Fees, Honours, Offices, and the other dignities of command and government, before the common people' (Eggleston, 1901: 141). There is no reason to suppose that this Old World habit of mind vanished instantly in the New. Even though Schlesinger was very broadly correct that the colonies were settled in the main by people who would not have been familiar with the usages of good society in Europe, modern research has repeatedly confirmed that that did not prevent many of them from wishing to *become* familiar. In addition to Wright's (1940) demonstration of how commonly copies of European manners books such as Peacham's were to be found on the shelves of the colonial Virginia gentry, subsequent studies, such as Persons (1973), R. D. Brown (1989), Bushman (1993) and Hemphill (1999), have shown that, while there was a particularly buoyant market for such books in the southern states, status-striving and deference to English models were widespread in the middle Atlantic and New England states as well. Counting all kinds of 'conduct' literature – not just manners books in the narrow sense, but also books of sermons, child-rearing guides and advice books – according to Hemphill (1999: 5) more than 200 works prescribing proper face-to-face behaviour were published in or imported into America before 1861.

Americans observed

It is true that the motives for buying and reading manners books are mixed, and it is dangerous to assume that purchasers read them in order immediately to enact their prescriptions in their own everyday behaviour. As in the parallel case of cookery books (or of the modern celebrity magazines) there is often an almost pornographic interest in seeing how socially superior (or just richer) people live, eat and behave, without a corresponding intention or opportunity to live, eat or behave in exactly the same way. Little can be inferred from the ownership of certain books about people's actual behaviour at specific points in time. On the other hand, if (as Elias found) there is a discernible pattern of change in the social standards set out by the authors of manners books, and if we further make the not unreasonable assumption that the gap between those standards and actual behaviour did not widen or narrow at random, then we can still cautiously use the manners books as evidence of change over time. Moreover, such evidence can be compared with other, less prescriptive, sources such as diaries and travellers' accounts of manners as they were actually observed, sources which in recent centuries have become far more abundant than in the medieval and early modern period studied by Elias.[6] So, combining the two, what patterns of change in Americans' behaviour and habitus can be discerned, and how, if at all, did they differ from their counterparts in Europe?

Authors and their audiences

Comparing the European and American manners books over four centuries is not altogether a straightforward task. From an early stage, American ones were probably addressed on average to a slightly lower modal social stratum of readers than were the European ones. Two related reasons are worth mentioning. First, in early colonial days, relatively few members of the real English social elite were to be found in the colonies. Those who formed the elite of the colonies were at best university-educated professionals such as lawyers and clerics, who would have occupied the lower ranks of the class of gentlemen in England. But equally, there were relatively few members of the unskilled and deeply impoverished underclass that was to be found in England (Hemphill, 1999: 15–16). Secondly (and following on from this), literacy was higher in America than in England or in most other European countries, so readership extended further down the scale. These considerations may help to explain why, in such matters as table manners, at a given date the American books appear somewhat more 'basic' than their European equivalents: some of the advice they give on behaviour at the table, or spitting, seems almost more reminiscent of the famous medieval examples quoted by Elias. On the other hand, they help to explain why in other respects the American books appear to be ahead of their European contemporaries. Most notably, they take an early lead in playing down outward displays of deference towards social superiors, and in discouraging both lack of consideration towards inferiors (such as servants) and 'self-aggrandizement' (more prosaically, showing-off and boasting) among social equals.

Travellers' descriptions of *actual* behaviour in America also have to be interpreted with some care, for parallel reasons. As Nevins (1948: 79) pointed out, until around 1825 British visitors to the USA were mainly working- and middle-class people, especially businessmen, who tended to speak with respect of the manners of the social equals they met. After 1825, however, more upper-class and professional visitors arrived from Britain, and there is in general a more marked note of condescension in their reports about what they saw and the people they met. Subsequently, this trick of perspective was further complicated by the changing balance of power between Britain and America. By the inter-war years of the twentieth century:

> For the first time, the great majority of British visitors showed themselves distinctly respectful of the rich, powerful, and exceedingly complex nation beyond the seas. During the period we have described as one of Tory condescension [1825–45], the travellers have tended to look down on the Americans; during the later period we have described as one of analysis [1870–1922], they tended to look at the United States with level gaze; but now they frequently tended to look up at America! (Nevins, 1948: 403)

Alternatively, using Elias's concepts, we may say that over the century 1825–1925 British visitors gradually changed from being an established group looking down upon outsiders to being outsiders looking up to a new established group.

With all these caveats, a few observations about the course of American manners can still usefully be made.

Table manners

Around 1800, according to Jack Larkin's authoritative study of everyday life in America over the first half-century of the federal period (1988: 132, 180), homes on the frontier were commonly short of both furniture and cutlery, and he tells of a diminishing minority of households where the family still ate out of a common bowl, all dipping their spoons into the same dish in the medieval fashion. Where forks were to be found, they were generally of the old type with two sharp prongs, designed for skewering food while it was cut up on the plate, rather than for conveying food to the mouth, which was often achieved with the round-ended knife. During the period 1800–40, however, change was rapid, and the knives, forks – which had sprouted first a third and then a fourth, less sharply pointed, tine – and spoons, as well as tables and chairs, that were already taken for granted in the cities were spreading to rural areas too. The impression remains, nonetheless, of strongly persisting regional and social differences, symptomatic of the absence of any single, strongly influential model-setting class whose writ ran throughout the country. The British naval officer Captain Basil Hall, visiting the USA in 1827–8, remarked upon 'the luxury of silver forks and spoons in New York' (Nevins, 1948: 105). Yet Charles Dickens, travelling on a Pennsylvania canal barge in 1842, observed how his fellow travellers 'thrust their broad-bladed knives and the two-pronged forks further down their throats than I ever saw the same weapons go before' (1957 [1842]: 147), while as late as the presidential election of 1884 Grover Cleveland was accused of eating with his knife and regarded it as a serious slander (Kasson, 1987: 125). Among the socially superior, seeing others eat in an inelegant and unrefined way gave rise to feelings of disgust, while, for the inexperienced, negotiating the unfamiliar rituals of formal dining carried the fear of shame. For the latter, books and magazines continued to dispense advice such as not slurping one's soup noisily that had appeared in the precursors since medieval times (ibid.: 130ff.).

The discrepancy in ways of eating between urban and rural or rich and poor households was not unique to America, although its extent may perhaps have been greater for some time than in Europe. While at first glance 1800 may seem very late for anyone still to be eating from a common bowl, or not yet using the fork, it must always be remembered that Elias's study is entirely of changing standards among upper-class Europeans. We know that at about the same time the broad-ended knife, used to convey food to the mouth, was common enough in rural homes in England (not necessarily the poorest). As for the fork, the use of which Elias shows to have been gathering pace among the European upper classes in the sixteenth and seventeenth centuries, according to Eugen Weber (1977) it was only in the latter half of the nineteenth century that it was reaching the peasantry in the remoter parts of rural France.

One respect in which the USA did come to differ from Europe, however, was in the social standard for the handling of the knife and fork; and, although seemingly a minor detail, it is of great interest in the light of Elias's discussion of the use of the knife at table (2000: 103–7). Most (right-handed) Americans today use their knife in their right hand and fork in their left to cut up the food on their plate, and then put down the knife and transfer the fork into the right hand, using it alone to transfer the food to the mouth. Europeans generally do not do that, keeping the knife always in their right hand and fork in their left. Among those who take notice of these things, the American method tends to be looked down upon, even viewed with mild disgust, possibly (here I speculate) because it reminds them of how children – including themselves – first eat, when they have not yet mastered the coordination of utensils in both hands. Indeed, many upper-class Americans are brought up to eat according to the European model.

Yet the more general American convention about the use of the knife and fork can be interpreted as representing a stage beyond the European standard of today in the direction of development charted by Elias. He notes that from medieval times, use of the knife at table was surrounded by taboos. One of the earliest was the rule that, in passing a knife to another diner, one should always offer it handle-first. Rationally, that can be explained by the fact that knives are dangerous, and people then used their own personal daggers to cut up food; offering it with the blade towards oneself showed there was no intention of a surprise stabbing. Other rules developed about never pointing the knife at one's face, never putting it in one's mouth, and later about various items of food that were to be cut not with the knife but with a fork or a spoon. Rational explanations can go only so far, though, and Elias argued that the 'knife became a symbol of the most diverse feelings, which are connected to its function and shape but are not deduced "logically" from its purpose' (2000: 104). There was 'a tendency that has slowly permeated civilized society, with pressure from the top to the bottom, to restrict the use of the knife . . . and wherever possible not to use the instrument at all'. In 1714, a manners book published in Liège instructed its readers: 'Do not keep your knife always in your hand, as village people do, but take it only when you need it' (ibid.). By 1859 an English manners book recommended that 'everything that can be cut without a knife, should be cut with fork alone' (ibid.: 106), but that does not apply today. In this sense, the prevalent American way of eating is 'more civilized' than the European. But then the Chinese, who use chopsticks and have long since banished the knife from the dining table, tend to regard either of the Western ways of eating as 'uncivilized'.

That points once again to the trickiness of the concept of 'civilization': it is possible in principle to trace a civilizing *process* through the development of more numerous and elaborate rules, the observance of which requires more stringent habitual self-constraints and associated emotions, yet the actual *content* of the developing rules may be to a large extent arbitrary. In his remarks about the use of the knife at table, Elias seems to be pointing to a trend that is less arbitrary than most because of cutlery's connection with weaponry.

Spitting and nose-blowing

Many of the manners books that circulated before and shortly after American independence, being derived from European texts of far earlier origin, continued to repeat advice about blowing one's nose and spitting that was already redundant among the European upper class. Medieval and early modern people had blown their noses with their fingers. Erasmus instructed that any mucus which fell to the ground must be trodden on immediately. To wipe one's nose on one's clothing was already 'rustic', but still common enough. By the late seventeenth century, upper-class people had ample stocks of handkerchiefs and it was obligatory to use them. Eighteenth-century books laid down polite ways of using them, and for a person to gaze at the product or to poke his or her nose was described as disgusting. Again, by the nineteenth century, it was no longer necessary or acceptable for the books to discuss the topic. It is hard to be sure whether the habitual use of the handkerchief had spread as far down the social scale in America as in Europe. Kasson (1990:14) cites a French traveller in Virginia in 1788, who noted that even the 'best-bred' gentlemen blew their noses with their fingers, or sometimes employed a piece of cloth that fulfilled the triple functions of napkin, handkerchief and cravat. While, again, social and regional differences may have persisted strongly in the USA, there is no doubt that the underlying social trend was the same as in Europe. By the peak of immigration in the late nineteenth century, newcomers quickly learned that Americans were embarrassed and disgusted by habits that did not conform to their own – relatively lately acquired – standards, and they came to feel corresponding shame themselves. Thus Hoy (1995: 125) mentions Jewish girls who had used rags to blow their noses on, but who immediately stopped doing so when their teacher told them it was disgusting.

Spitting underwent a similar pattern of change. In medieval Europe, people spat freely on the floor (though preferably not on the table or in the common washbasin). In the sixteenth century, it was required that spittle be trodden on. Gradually the use of a handkerchief became necessary, at first if one were spitting in a great house, then in churches and other places kept clean, then finally everywhere. For centuries, spitting was regarded as a bodily function as necessary as urinating, but by the nineteenth century it was described as 'at all times a disgusting habit'. Spitting appears to have been the case where a gap between European and American habits and feelings persisted longest, mainly because of the prevalence in America of chewing tobacco – a practice that never seems to have been very common in Europe. Chewing stimulated saliva, which necessitated frequent spitting; tobacco was cheap, and the addictive effect of nicotine probably made the habit persist more strongly at equivalent social levels in the USA than in Europe. Floors not just of saloons but also of homes and public buildings were stained by gobbets of brown spit (Larkin, 1988: 6). Complaints about the habit were a constant refrain in nineteenth-century visitors' accounts of America. Spitting was only one in a whole list of habits found unsatisfactory by Fanny Trollope, whose consistently hostile *Domestic Manners of the Americans* caused something of a sensation on its publication in 1832. On a steamboat on the Mississippi in 1828, travelling with gentlemen who were 'nearly all addressed by the titles of general, colonel, and major', she observed:

> The total want of all the usual courtesies of the table, the voracious rapidity with which the viands were seized and devoured, the strange uncouth phrases and pronunciation; the loathsome spitting, from the contamination of which it was absolutely impossible to protect our dresses; the frightful manner of feeding with their knives, till the whole blade seemed to enter into the mouth; and the still more frightful manner of cleaning the teeth afterwards with a pocket knife, soon forced us to feel that we were not surrounded by the generals, colonels and majors of the old world. (1997 [1832]: 20)

A generation (literally) later, Fanny's novelist son Anthony was a much more sympathetic observer of America at the start of the Civil War, but he too described how in the West men 'sit in silence, with the tobacco between their teeth. . . . They drink often, and to great excess, but they carry it off without noise, sitting down and ruminating over it with the everlasting cud between their jaws' (1968 [1862]: 199).

Dickens, again on his canal boat in 1842, wrote equally vividly but with more amusement than outrage of

> men, in foul linen, with yellow streams from half-chewed tobacco trickling down their chins. . . . You never can conceive what the hawking and spitting is, the whole night through. . . . *Upon my honour and word* I was obliged, this morning, to lay my fur coat on the deck, and wipe the half-dried flakes of spittle from it with my handkerchief; and the only surprise seemed to be that I should consider it necessary to do so. (Letter quoted in Forster, n.d. [1872]: 169)

The journalist Alexander Mackay, in his *Western World* (1849; see Nevins, 1948: 244, 251–2), like Dickens before him and Anthony Trollope after, wrote in an amused tone about the spitting habit, admiring the precision with which the jets of spittle were aimed. But again, it is clear that while spitting persisted in some social circles, it was becoming invested with feelings of repugnance, especially among the 'respectable' strata of the eastern cities, and that their influence was gradually spreading.

Undressing and behaviour in the bedroom

Feelings of repugnance and embarrassment are also centrally involved in changes in social standards concerning nakedness and, especially, sleeping in the company of other people.[7] 'The bedroom', observes Elias (2000: 138), 'has become one of the most "private" and "intimate" areas of human life'. In medieval society, this 'privatization' had not yet come about. People were received in bedrooms, even from the bed. It was common for many people to spend the night in one room – in all but the upper class, these might not unusually include both men and women (cf. Flandrin, 1979: 98–102; Shorter, 1976: 39–44). People generally slept naked. The sight of the naked human body must not have been uncommon – and not only in the bedroom. In some parts of medieval Europe, at least, people of both sexes unconcernedly shared the communal bathhouse,[8] and in some towns it was customary for the family to undress at home and go to the baths naked or very scantily clad (Elias 2000: 138–9).

The early manners books often concern themselves with how one should behave when sharing a bed with another person (of the same sex), for example in an inn. One is told to lie still and lie straight, and to keep to one's side of the bed. Special nightclothes slowly came into use during the Renaissance, like the fork and the handkerchief, and Erasmus instructs his readers: 'When you undress, when you get up, be mindful of modesty.' Something was happening to people's feelings akin to how the Bible describes events in the Garden of Eden: 'and they saw that they were naked and were ashamed'. By the eighteenth century, to have to share a bed was quite exceptional (for the upper classes). Details of how to behave if the necessity arose were left unspoken, and La Salle advised 'You ought neither to undress nor go to bed in the presence of any other person'.

In America and in Europe, poorer people often continued to share bedrooms until into the twentieth century. As Larkin points out:

> Sleeping and sleeping space only slowly became individualized and private. Families in one- and two-room houses necessarily slept within sight and hearing of each other, even for parents' sexual intercourse. In most larger dwellings, parents were still the only family members to gain private sleeping quarters. In 1800, only a few wealthy households provided individual rooms for anyone other than the heads of the household, or occasionally a widowed grandparent. In the great majority of American families, the concept of one's own room, and even one's own bed, would have been a strange one. Children and other adults living in the household slept together in hall, garret or bedchambers, although they usually separated the sexes if there was enough room. (1988: 123)

The trend towards greater privacy in sleeping arrangements was international (Gleichmann, 1980), but, like other changes in social standards of comportment, slow. Larkin (1988: 125) notes how, in America in the early decades of the nineteenth century, 'some men and women of higher status adopted the mores of the English travellers whose "one person, one bed" requests so surprised country tavern keepers'.[9] New England lawyers travelling together on circuit generally slept two to a bed until the 1820s, when they came to insist on sleeping alone. Further west, changes came later. Abraham Lincoln, seeking lodging on his arrival in Springfield, Illinois, in 1837 thought nothing of it when Joshua Speed offered to share his bed, and he and his partner William Herndon generally shared when out on circuit in the 1850s, after Lincoln had already served a term as a Congressman in Washington (Herndon and Weik, 1983: 148, 248).[10]

The 'natural functions' and standards of cleanliness

By the nineteenth century, neither in Europe nor America did manners books any longer need – as they had in the sixteenth or seventeenth century – to tell members of the best circles of society that they should go to the appropriate place to defecate and urinate, and to do so in private. Medieval people had been able to perform and speak about their bodily functions in the presence of others. Erasmus in 1530 still discussed these functions quite openly, although he advised that it was bad manners to engage in conversation with someone encountered in the act of urination or defecation. Gradually, however, they were invested with feelings of shame and repugnance, hidden behind the scenes of social life and not even spoken about without acute embarrassment. It would be wrong to draw from that the conclusion that the standards that came to prevail by the twenty-first century had already been attained in the first half of the nineteenth. People usually used earth closets, often built in their gardens, or less commonly in a suitably remote part of the house, but the evidence is that in rural areas, many just used any corner of a field or a wood. In the towns, men not infrequently relieved themselves in the street or against a wall. Well-appointed houses would have a chamber pot under each bed for use in the night, which housewives or servants had to slop out in the morning, into the privy or – very often – out of the window into the street or otherwise just outside the house. The streets were not uncommonly full of ordure. In the better-organized areas, the night-soil men made their rounds, emptying privies and taking the contents away for disposal, sometimes for use as manure (Larkin, 1988: 159–69). In short, people lived in closer contact with bodily waste and its smells than it is easy for an inhabitant of the USA or Western Europe to imagine today. It should not be thought, however, that they always 'really' felt this to be repugnant, but lacked the means to avoid it. Most of the accounts of the dirt and smell of nineteenth-century America are written by people – whether better-class Americans or Europeans – whose threshold of repugnance had already advanced further, but their descriptions make clear that those who lived thus batted not an eyelid. Nevertheless, the new social standard of repugnance was plainly spreading more widely and continuing to advance, along with technology, in the second half of the century. In 1840, only a tiny minority of the wealthy city-dwellers had running water and flushing water closets in their homes, but both had spread much more widely by around 1890 (Ogle, 1996). It is hard to say whether America lagged behind or led comparable countries such as Britain, France or Germany. A French historian has suggested that the French tended to remain olfactorily more tolerant than the British (Corbin, 1986), but similar trends were clearly under way in industrial societies generally.

Changes in plumbing formed part of a broader picture of changing social standards of personal cleanliness. In a long note that is easily overlooked, Elias pointed out that in Europe social standards governing washing and bathing followed much the same trajectory as those relating to eating, nose-blowing, spitting and so on:

> At first it was taken for granted that people cleaned themselves regularly only out of respect for others, especially social superiors, i.e. . . . under the pressure of more or less perceptible external constraints. Regular washing was omitted, or limited to the minimum demanded by immediate personal well being, when such external constraints were absent, when the social position did not demand it. Today, washing and bodily cleanliness are instilled in the individual at an early age as a kind of automatic habit, so that it more or less disappears from his consciousness that he washes and disciplines himself to constant cleanliness out of regard for others and, at least originally, at the instigation of others, i.e., for reasons of external constraint. He washes by self-constraint even if no one else is present who might censure or punish him for not doing so. If he omits to do so, it is today – as it was not earlier – an expression of a not altogether successful conditioning to the existing social standard. (2000: 530n; translation modified)

Americans appear to have travelled along this particular civilizing curve at high speed during the nineteenth century. According to a remark attributed to the West Indian intellectual C. L. R. James, 'American civilization can be summed up in one word: plumbing'. By the mid-nineteenth century, Europeans often remarked upon what they saw as a general American obsession with cleanliness. Yet it was not always so. There is little doubt that in its earlier decades many of them were very dirty by later standards. For every Alexander Mackay who thought they were the cleanest people he had met (Nevins, 1948: 209), there were dozens of other visitors who said the opposite. This is by no means conclusive evidence that they were any dirtier than their European counterparts. Well-to-do British travellers, especially, probably travelled to wilder parts than anything they had ever before encountered, stayed there in hotels of a kind they would not have countenanced at home and mixed with classes of people from whom they would have been to a greater extent segregated. Even Harriet Martineau, who in general wrote very favourably of American manners, commented on the 'odours more pungent than agreeable' at President Andrew Jackson's White House levées, when the prominent people with clean clothes and washed hands mixed democratically with 'men begrimed with all the sweat and filth accumulated in their day's – perhaps their week's labour' (quoted by Larkin, 1988: 162–3). But, comments Larkin, 'many even of the best-turned-out visitors at Jackson's levées would not have passed unnoticed at a social gathering today' (ibid.: 163), and it was virtually impossible for them to have been 'clean and decent' by today's standards. From contemporary accounts and from the architecture and furnishings of houses, it is clear that those who washed daily did so at the kitchen sink, or at the pump in the yard. Lack of privacy meant that water regularly reached no further than the hands and the face, and soap was mainly used for laundering clothes. Feelings of shame about nakedness appear for a time to have outstripped any concerning lack of cleanliness. Gradually, nevertheless, the better off equipped their bedrooms with washstands and ewers, enabling family members to close the door, remove all their clothes and sponge themselves down all over. By the 1830s, the bathtub and daily bath were beginning to spread beyond the very rich. But the poor stayed dirty: 'in cleanliness, as in much else, Americans' material lives were becoming increasingly unequal' (ibid.: 166).

By the later decades of the nineteenth century, however, cleanliness was becoming next to Americanness. As Hoy (1995: 88) remarks: 'Although hardly dirtier than poor whites fresh from the countryside, most immigrants soon caught on that prosperous Americans cared about cleanliness.' In thinking about the lower orders as 'the great unwashed', prosperous Americans were no different from their European counterparts, although the vast scale of immigration from Eastern and Southern Europe in the late nineteenth century (see chapter 9) brought the conflict between the new – only recently adopted – and the older standards to the fore in the USA. The bulk of immigrants settled first in the cities where the prosperous classes had already adopted the newer standards. Social workers, educators and employers set out to teach immigrants – adults and children – how, where and how often to bathe with soap and warm water, how to clean their teeth and how to keep livestock out of their hair and clothes. New arrivals soon learned that 'there was an American way to brush teeth, an American way to clean fingernails, and an American way to air out bedding' (McClymer, 1982: 109, quoted by Hoy, 1995: 89). These campaigns, usually benevolent in intention but often tinged with American nativism, have the hallmarks of 'civilizing offensives' (or 'civilizing campaigns') – highly characteristic of established–outsider figurations, where small details of behaviour and conduct form important components in the group charisma of the established group, and of the group shame of the outsiders.[11]

Technology, hygiene and deference

A reminder is in order at this point: Elias focused particularly on the most basic, 'natural' or 'animalic' of human functions – eating, drinking, defecating, sleeping, nose-blowing, even walking and sitting – because these matters of outward bodily propriety are things that humans cannot biologically avoid doing, no matter what society, culture or age they live in. For that reason, it is relatively easy to identify any differences between societies and strata in the social standards of behaviour and feeling by which these matters are handled. Moreover, although there has never been such a thing as an 'uncivilized' society in the technical sense of being devoid of socially induced self-constraints, there *is* a zero-point in the individual lifetime: infants are born in the same emotional condition everywhere and in every generation, devoid of self-restraints. Therefore, if change occurs from generation to generation in the way these functions are handled, it can be seen rather clearly in the social standards that young people are taught.

The general picture that emerges from studies of American manners is that they followed broadly similar trends to those seen in Europe, but that there was probably a greater measure of social and regional diversity, and that in some respects American conventions may at times have lagged behind, yet in other ways run ahead of Europe. How are both the similarity of overall trends and the differences to be accounted for?

From the vantage point of the knowledge available to us early in the twenty-first century, it can appear all too obvious that most of the changes in customs, manners and behaviour just described can be explained by 'material' reasons (the forward march of wealth and technology) or by reasons of health and hygiene. Thus, for instance, Larkin, in his wonderful study of the changes that took place in everyday life in America between 1800 and 1840, quite casually remarked:

> In a long, slow process of change that had begun in early Renaissance Europe, American families since the time of first settlement had on average, over the generations, improved the material conditions of their domestic life. The gradual growth of commercial networks in early America, the slowly decreasing cost and greater availability of household goods, made possible an awakening interest in domestic consumption and comfort. (1988: 133–4)

Larkin goes on to comment (ibid.: 188) that cheaper cotton fabrics meant that people could change and wash their clothes more frequently – no doubt true, but a change in the technology of textile manufacture does not entirely explain the growth of the desire to put on clean clothes daily, and of the feelings of embarrassment if one did not.

To the modern mind, it seems yet more obvious that considerations of health and hygiene must have played a part still more significant than material advances in bringing about higher standards. Surely the fear of the spread of infection must have been decisive, particularly in regard to changing attitudes towards the natural functions, nose-blowing and spitting, but also in aspects of table manners such as putting a licked spoon back into the common bowl.

Over the period of European history that he studied, however, Elias was able to show that in each case standards of restraint rose first, and only later were reasons of hygiene advanced as *a posteriori* justifications of the new standards. For instance, when spitting was accepted and frequent, it was said to be unhealthy to retain sputum; only *after* spitting became socially unacceptable was it declared unhygienic. In Erasmus, medical arguments are not found very often. When they are deployed, it is almost always on the side of not restraining the natural urges: it is unhealthy to try to hold back a fart (so do it as discreetly as possible, disguising the sound with a cough). Later, especially in the nineteenth century (but even before the discovery of microbes), reasons relating to health nearly always served to justify the restraint of natural urges. That extended sometimes even to standards the breach of which in fact carried little risk of infection or damage to health. The supposed hazards of masturbation are possibly the most famous example. Reasons of health and of morality at this stage often overlapped and served a similar purpose:

> Much of what we call 'morality' or 'moral' reasons has the same function as 'hygiene' or 'hygienic' reasons: to condition children to a certain social standard. Moulding by such means aims at making socially desirable behaviour automatic, a matter of self-control, causing it to appear in the consciousness of the individual as the result of his own free will, and in the interests of his own health or human dignity. (Elias, 2000: 127)

There is nothing in the historical evidence to suggest that manners changed, or thresholds of sensitivity and embarrassment advanced, for reasons that we can describe as 'clearly rational' and based on a demonstrable understanding of particular causal connections such as how infections are spread. At most, writes Elias, the advance of the threshold of repugnance

> may be connected at some points with . . . indefinite fears and therefore rationally undefined fears and anxieties which point vaguely in the direction

subsequently confirmed by clear understanding. *But 'rational understanding' is not the motor of the 'civilizing' of eating or of other behaviour.* (Ibid.: 98–9; my italics)[12]

Thus, for instance, middle-class feelings of repugnance towards their inferiors' smelling and lack of cleanliness in the nineteenth century seems to have motivated a concern with sanitation even before it was clearly understood how diseases such as cholera were spread. In America, as in Europe, it is clear that there was some awareness of a link between dirt and epidemics in the overcrowded cities, even before the microbial nature of the link had been discovered. And the work of the US Sanitary Commission in reducing the incidence of disease in the Union armies, which in the early stages of the Civil War had killed or disabled more men than did combat, was extremely influential. But the changes among upper-class people in feelings about cleanliness appear to antedate any clear understanding of any reasons of health and hygiene justifying the new standards.

The reason most often initially given in European manners books from the sixteenth to the eighteenth century to justify new standards was that the old, relatively less restrained, behaviour showed a lack of respect for one's fellows, but *particularly towards social superiors*. People were told to turn away from a person of higher rank if they needed to blow their nose. They were told to spit only into a handkerchief, or not at all, when people of higher ranking than themselves were present: to do otherwise evoked disdain and showed disrespect. An especially vivid illustration of the principle concerns states of undress: it was said to be disrespectful for a man to appear unclothed before another of superior rank, yet for the superior to do so in front of an inferior could be a sign of his benevolence and affability. This pattern – in which forms of behaviour were considered distasteful or disrespectful in social inferiors which superiors were not ashamed of in themselves, and in which reasons of respect served as the main justification for new standards – was transitional. Later, by the nineteenth century especially, shame in such matters was felt also by the superior in the presence of inferiors, and as the standard came to apply more equally to all ranks, so the controls became more automatic, 'unconscious' and 'natural' for adults. It was, again, at this stage that reasons of hygiene and morality came to the fore, retrospectively, in training children to the seemingly 'natural' standard.

'Reasons of respect',[13] requiring conformity to certain standards of behaviour as a mark of deference to social superiors, may seem distinctly un-American. In Elias's account of the civilizing of manners in Europe, the courtly nobility play a key part. Especially with the consolidation of royal absolutism in France under Louis XIV, courtiers became a 'two-front stratum'. They became squeezed between the king above them and the rising merchant class below. Their dependence on royal favour increased as their economic resources were eroded – partly as a result of the 'system of expenses' through which a certain level of spending was dictated by their rank, irrespective of their income – and as any independent political and military power they had once had became thoroughly subordinated to the royal power.[14] Virtuoso consumption, *savoir-faire* and habitual impulse-control came to be central to their means of distinguishing themselves from those below them. A concertina-like process set in, which Elias describes as a mechanism of 'colonization' and 'repulsion'. The more courtly circles proclaimed their modes of conduct as socially superior to those below them, the more they were copied, and in consequence they had to elaborate their distinctive codes all the more vigorously. But in America there were no royal courts and no courtiers and, by the time discussions begin about the character of American manners in the early nineteenth century, all observers are agreed that the country was marked by a spirit of egalitarianism or, as Tocqueville termed it, 'democracy'.

One sign of this egalitarianism is the apparent low level of self-constraint in social interaction described by travellers in America. The great geologist Sir Charles Lyell noted in an amused tone the unabashed curiosity of fellow passengers on a steamer travelling from Vicksburg to Cincinnati in the mid-1840s:

> [O]ne passenger after another eyed my short-sight glass [monocle], suspended by a ribbon round my neck, with much curiosity. Some of them asked me to read for them the name inscribed on the stern of a steamer. . . . Others, abruptly seizing the glass, without leave or apology, brought their heads into close contact with mine, and looking through it, exclaimed, in a disappointed and half reproachful tone, that they could see nothing. . . . Meanwhile the wives and daughters of passengers of the same class were sitting in the ladies' cabin, occasionally taking my wife's embroidery out of her hand, without asking leave, and examining it, with many comments, usually, however, in a complimentary strain. (Quoted by Nevins, 1948: 213)

No doubt British travellers found themselves mixing more closely with people of classes that they may not have been forced into contact with at home, but as Wouters (1998c; 2007) has demonstrated, at home social segregation was taken more for granted by both sides, and the lower orders would have known to keep their distance to a greater extent.

Foreign observers in the period often commented unfavourably on American boastfulness. Fanny Trollope is a predictable example (see Nevins, 1948: 137–8). Among the French aristocracy under the *ancien régime*, competition for status was intense, but carried through by means far more subtle than verbal self-aggrandizement. In the nineteenth century, the same self-restraint was the norm among upper-class British people too, and it was almost certainly conditioned by the relatively strict segregation of social strata. Within the ranks of gentlemen and their ladies, norms prevailed against boastfulness and self-aggrandizement, but this apparent egalitarianism was possible only because of the clear social boundaries that in Britain separated gentlefolk from outsiders.

The egalitarianism of American society was already more all-encompassing. It can be seen in small details as well in the considered reflections of travellers. Larkin makes a significant point about the way men dressed:

> Men's shorter coats and longer pants [trousers] were in reality an embellished version of the working costume of sailors and labourers. As a whole society donned working dress, the new men's fashions defined a transition into commercial and industrial ways. . . . [M]en never returned to anything remotely like the old ways of dress. (1988: 183)

The adoption of the short jacket in place of the frock coat or tailcoat, and trousers in place of breeches, are good examples of the 'trickle-up' of lower-class and more informal traits, characteristic of periods when power ratios between upper and lower strata are becoming relatively less unequal. Twentieth-century examples of 'trickle-up' include the almost universal adoption of blue jeans – originally workmen's wear – for leisure time, and still more recently the popularity of body piercings and tattoos, formerly the prerogative of sailors, prostitutes and rougher social elements. Most dances – the Charleston, the tango, jiving – also seem to have been socially frowned upon as 'indecent' before being enthusiastically adopted (Wouters, 2004: 19–23).

America often seems to have led the way in both 'trickle-up' and 'trickle-down', to the confusion of visiting Europeans confronted with the unfamiliar mixing of social ranks on relatively equal terms. The novelist Captain Marryat, visiting in 1837, noted how Americans of all ranks habitually shook hands – then a sign of relative intimacy in Britain – and, as Larkin comments,

> Americans were not blind to inequalities of economic and social power, but they less and less gave them overt physical expression. Bred in a society where such distinctions were far more clearly spelled out, Marryat was somewhat disorientated in the United States; 'it is impossible to know who is who', he claimed, 'in this land of equality'. (1988: 156)

Thirty years later, Anthony Trollope complained that 'when one is bidden to follow "that young lady", meaning the chambermaid, or desired with a toss of the head to wait for the "gentleman who is coming", meaning the boots, the heart is sickened' (1968 [1862]: 64). Thirty years later still, Dr James Muirhead was still expressing dismay at being told that 'the other *gentleman*' – meaning a porter – would take care of his luggage (Nevins, 1948: 282). And Max Weber observed – though without any note of outrage – that when he visited the USA in 1904, 'an American farmer would not have led his guest past a ploughing farmhand . . . without making his guest "shake hands" with the worker after formally introducing them' (1946: 310).

Many commentators have applauded the results of this social egalitarianism. Lord Bryce considered that the gain in manners consequent upon social equality was far in excess of the loss, writing that 'I do not think that the upper class loses in grace. I am sure that the humbler class gains in independence' (1891: II, 625). Anthony Trollope before him (in spite of the snobbish remark just quoted) had taken the same view. After eating in Lexington, Kentucky, with 75 'very dirty' teamsters of the Union army, he noted how orderly and well behaved they were, with better manners than their British equivalents, and reflected that

> It is always the same story. With us there is no level of society. Men stand on a long staircase, but the crowd congregates near the bottom, and the lower steps are very broad. In America men stand upon a common platform, but the platform is raised above the ground, and though it does not approach in height the top of our staircase, the average height is greater. (A. Trollope, 1968 [1862]: 188–9)

The essential point, perhaps, is that 'social rank can rarely assert an open claim to deference in this country, and it usually makes at least a pretence of conformity to equalitarian ways' (Potter, 1954: 95).

Yet for all that America's egalitarianism was so striking to European visitors, it is not the whole story. With leads and lags and many variations, America proceeded along much the same track of changes in manners that Elias had attributed in Europe to the status-striving competition among its different strata. Could the same results arise from a more equal society? Tocqueville apparently thought so, advancing the thesis that under conditions of 'democracy' social interaction became less stiff and formal, *but also* that striving for invidious status distinctions increased. Here is a paradox. It can be seen in the coexistence of the discouragement of deference towards superiors and inconsiderateness towards inferiors on the one hand with, on the other, the early and continuing reputation of Americans for boastfulness. How is the paradox to be resolved? Probably the answer is that in a class-segregated society, such as Britain and France, with a unifying 'good society', a greater certainty of status made self-aggrandizement less necessary and more counterproductive. In contrast, uncertainty of rank had both levelling and unlevelling functions:

a constraint to avoid giving offence in encounters with people whose rank was uncertain, but also a need to signal one's merits to others who were uncertain of one's own status.

The paradox must also be connected with the fact that egalitarianism is an ideology, and is not synonymous with factual social equality. The American Dream has always been that through hard work and self-help, individuals could ascend the ladder of opportunity. But the ladder was always a long one: the factual inequalities have always been great, and there has always been scope for economic and status insecurity in the broad middle rungs. So it is no surprise that self-control, punctuality, cleanliness and devotion to duty became marks of superiority for middle-class Victorian Americans. Social competition as a driving force for changing habitus cannot be easily dismissed.

Victorianism

Later generations have come to use the adjective 'Victorian' as a close synonym for 'puritanical' (in its loosest sense). Not just in Britain but also in the USA and other countries, Queen Victoria (who reigned 1837–1901) has given her name to what is seen as a period of intense repression and self-denial. Of course, no precise starting or ending dates can be pin-pointed for the prevalence of such attitudes, but in the mid- to late nineteenth century they did find particularly vocal expression. The Marxist historian E. P. Thompson spoke of 'an all-embracing "Thou Shalt Not!"' (1963: 411) that in England permeated *all* religious persuasions in varying degree. Sexual pleasures were especially disapproved, but disapproval spread to gambling, drinking, dancing and other sensual pleasures and forms of impulsive behaviour.[15]

Of course, few lived up to the proclaimed ideals of 'Victorianism' completely, and many did not live up to it at all; it has long been known, for instance, that brothels prospered in the period. Nevertheless, in America at least:

> What is surprising . . . is not that so many Victorians failed to meet the Victorian ideal, but the extent to which they did meet it. Premarital pregnancy rates dropped sharply; alcohol intake was down two-thirds from the dizzying heights of the previous era; church attendance rose dramatically; homes, farms, and streets became cleaner; casual violence was curbed. (Collier, 1991: 18)

Collier, following many other scholars (although he does not cite Elias), defines the central tenets of Victorianism as 'self-control' and 'discipline', and contends that this went along with an extended circle of mutual identification:

> It brought with it a rededication to Christian religion, to honour in human relations, to a general decency in manners and expression. Underlying everything was the idea that human beings could not live solely to gratify themselves, but must in every sphere of life – in politics, in philosophy, in social commerce – take into account the needs of the family, the community, the country, or even the whole of humankind. When choices were being made, not merely must others be thought of, they must be given first consideration. (Ibid.: 10)

Collier moralistically conceptualized this as a decline in 'selfishness',[16] but it can equally well be described in the more neutral terms of an extending circle of mutual identification or, better still, as a change in the 'we–I balance' (Elias, 1991: 155–237). The use of high standards of self-constraint as a mark of social respectability certainly also played its part.

The period between the end of the Civil War and the outbreak of the First World War seems, with benefit of hindsight, an aberration in the history of American manners, at odds with trends dominant before and afterwards towards more egalitarian social manners. This was the so-called Gilded Age, an age when parvenus managed to crash into quasi-aristocratic circles in the cities of the eastern seaboard hitherto comprised of old families tracing their origins to colonial times or the very early Republic. The cascade of new etiquette books in this period, unlike their ante-bellum precursors, sought to instil a more aristocratic style of behaviour. 'For the most part', Schlesinger commented, 'these manners were borrowed consciously, if sometimes to bizarre effect, from Europe, where an hereditary leisure class held the position which America's newly rich anguished to attain in their own country' (1947: 29). If this period seems aberrant in American history, in comparative perspective it fits perfectly into a common pattern of periods when the pressure from below upon established elites is at its greatest, and when rising bourgeois groups are forcing open the gates of exclusive society circles in the face of strong resistance. It is then that we can expect the strongest reaction of repulsion on the part of established groups, leading to rapid innovation in standards of behaviour, which become ever more demanding of emotion management and self-constraint, even becoming ritualized as a means of demarcating members of established groups from outsiders. At the same time, the outsiders are pushed, both by the attempted exclusion of them and by their own 'anticipatory socialization', into adopting the new standards. This was true of the last century of the *ancien régime* studied by Elias in *The Court Society* (2006a). It was also true of London society between the end of the Napoleonic Wars and the 1890s, when the number of participating families more than quadrupled (Davidoff, 1973). And, for similar reasons, it was true of late nineteenth-century America. There were transatlantic differences, however. It may seem curious that Henry Adams (1999 [1919]: 156) considered that English 'good society' was much more easy and tolerant than American. But what Adams did not recognize was that the boundaries of London 'Society' were much more clearly demarcated than those in America (even though both were expanding). As Wouters (2007) has documented, within English 'Society' everyone was to be treated equally, so manners within the circle could be relatively relaxed, but relations with lower classes outside the circle were much more distant and formal. In America, the boundaries were more strongly disputed, the pressure from below more insistent and therefore – if Adams was right – the standards, for a time, more rigorous.

Informalization

In retrospect, the relative stiffening of manners among the upper strata in late nineteenth-century America – even though it was less marked than in Britain – appears to have been a deviation from the main trend before and after. All commentators are agreed that in the twentieth century the trend in manners in American society very broadly was towards a more relaxed, easy and egalitarian style. In long-term perspective, this can be seen as a resumption of the trend that Tocqueville observed in Jackson's America. Its outcome is something that runs deeper than surface manners, an emotional habitus which Stearns (1994) calls 'American cool'. Many writers have suggested reasons for this. They include the exodus to the suburbs breaking up city elites as bastions of ceremonious intercourse; Schlesinger commented that, 'Oddly enough, the result was to flavour urban sophistication with a naturalness that smacked of bucolic folkways' (1947: 58). Then there was undoubtedly popular antagonism to great fortunes and conspicuous consumption, fanned by the campaigning journalists known as Muckrakers. The greater economic and social independence of women, hitherto the main custodians of the codes of good behaviour, also played a part, and was certainly reflected in changes in those aspects of behaviour and feeling that relate to relations between the sexes. Films, radio and television, and car ownership are also frequently mentioned. The effects of the media are notoriously difficult to ascertain precisely, but Beth Bailey, in *From Front Porch to Back Seat* (1988) was quite precise about the impact of car ownership in emancipating young people from the surveillance of their parents. All these suggested reasons contributing to an overall process of what has been called 'informalization' relate in one way or another to an underlying tendency towards functional democratization, towards somewhat more even power ratios between social classes, between age groups, between men and women and between many other social groups. And although in much of the twentieth century the USA may have led the way in many aspects of functional democratization, the underlying trends can be observed in Europe and many other countries too. As will be seen in chapter 10, there have also been contrary trends.

Apart from the changes in matters relating to sexuality that are especially evoked by the popular (but sociologically inadequate) expression 'the permissive society', the apparent relaxation of controls and pervasive process of informalization can be seen in many symptoms that came to the fore especially in the 1960s and 1970s. They include, for instance, the much more immediate and widespread use of forenames, which was once confined to the circle of family members and very old and close friends. In many European languages, although not in English, this trend was also linked to the increasing use of the familiar second person pronoun – *tu* in French, *du* in German, and so on.[17] This aspect of informality extended in the workplace not just to how colleagues on the same level addressed each other, but how they addressed their bosses, who would in the past have been strictly 'Mr' this or 'Miss' that. A decline in the use of ceremonious titles – Lord, Lady, Sir, Madam, Professor, Doctor – was also evident. (Curiously enough, the deferential use of 'sir' is now more prevalent in the USA than in Britain.) Similar processes of informalization can be seen very markedly in conventions concerning clothing, music and dancing, and in the less formal regulation of the written and spoken languages. Even mourning customs and attitudes towards death became less formally defined than before (Wouters, 2002). It may at times have appeared that there was emerging what Miss Manners humorously called 'an etiquette-free society' (Martin, 1996). On the other hand, there were those who called the 'etiquette-free' attitude the 'new etiquette'; to call the new standard 'etiquette-free' is much the same as calling one mode of pronunciation 'accentless'.

Inevitably, and rightly, these informalizing trends have led to debates about whether they invalidate Elias's whole theory of civilizing processes. After all, over the period of European history that Elias documented, from the late Middle Ages to the mid-nineteenth century, the main trend was towards formalization, the proliferation of rules and more demanding social standards of habitual self-constraint. Do informalization and the 'loosening of morals', as many saw it, mean that the civilizing process has gone into reverse? Or is there a cyclical pattern? The wave of informalization that took place in the 1960s and 1970s was not the first, either in Europe or America. People perceived the *fin de siècle* and then again the 'Roaring Twenties' in much the same way. Generally speaking, there was then in most of the Western world a subsequent period of consolidation, or even a retreat from informality and 'permissiveness', until the rather dramatic wave of the 1960s. In the 1980s, another period of reformalization appears to have set in (Wouters, 2004; 2007).[18]

Elias was well aware of this ebb and flow when he was writing *The Civilizing Process* in the 1930s. He discussed the apparent 'relaxation of morals' which had taken place since the First World War (2000: 157–8, 439–40).[19] Reversing Caxton's dictum that 'Things once allowed are now reproved' (see p. 8 above), he observed that 'Many things forbidden earlier are now permitted.' On the one hand, he remarked that the informalization of the inter-war years was probably just another such fluctuation. On the other hand, he also pointed out that some of the symptoms of an apparent relaxation of the constraints imposed on the individual by social life actually took place within the framework of very high social standards of self-constraint. He gave the example of bathing costumes and the relatively greater exposure of the body, especially the female body, in many modern sports. In the nineteenth century it would have meant social ostracism for a woman to wear in public a bathing costume as relatively scanty as those worn between the wars. The bikinis and the topless bathing of the decades after the Second World War were, of course, still over the horizon. This development, Elias had already argued in 1939, could take place only 'in a society in which a high degree of restraint is taken for granted, and in which women are, like men, absolutely sure that each individual is curbed by self-control and a strict code of etiquette' (2000: 157). Later research has yielded a good deal of evidence in favour of the wider applicability of this last insight.

For instance, the modern informal office, in which colleagues of every rank are on forename and bantering terms, calls for a far more subtle capacity for emotion management and sensitivity to invisible boundaries than was the case when there were rigid and formal rules and conventions. Peter Stearns detected signs of such a change in emotion management in the workplace in response to the changing American economic structure as early as the 1920s:

> Families in managerial and service work pioneered new concerns, regarding the need for new emotional styles on the job. Creation of smooth personalities, able to sell goods and relate comfortably in bureaucratic interactions, dictated a new list of banned emotions and new means of keeping these emotions under control. What the workplace increasingly called for . . . was a superficially democratic style . . . 'friendly but impersonal'. (Stearns, 1989: 187)

Similarly in relation to sexual relationships, the 'commandments of the new freedom' (Brinkgreve, 1982) are more rather than less demanding. For couples to live together without the formal framework for marriage pro-vided in the past by church and state, and without the external constraint of strong social disapproval, requires more internalized self-constraint, not less. The 'new divorce', in which former partners are expected to remain friends and continue to move with equanimity in the same social circles, is also quite demanding.

Moreover, some convergence appears to have occurred in ideals of the feminine and masculine selves. Cancian (1987: 7–8) found evidence in national surveys in America from the 1970s onwards of a trend to more 'androgynous' gender roles, in which feminine intimacy and emotional expression was combined with masculine independence and competence. Wouters, drawing on etiquette books, agony columns and handbooks on 'self-development', in Britain, Germany and the Netherlands as well as the USA, found much the same trend, which he described more precisely as a change in the 'lust balance between love and sex' (Wouters, 1998a; 1998b; 2004: 124–39). The twentieth century witnessed a 'sexualization of love' and an 'eroticization of sex', undermining the traditional lust-dominated sexuality for men and a complementary romantic love-dominated sexuality for women. The ideal of marriage came to be expressed less in terms of an ideal of 'harmonious inequality' between the sexes, and more in terms of competing interests, in which negotiations played a more decisive part than fixed roles. Blanket rules were no longer given for what was right and what was wrong. It was less a matter of judging and censuring, and more one of considering a situation from all angles. 'Increasing varieties' were permissi-ble: couples living together 'out of wedlock', extra-marital affairs, volun-tary childlessness and homosexuality had once all been frowned upon, but were now far more widely accepted. By the 1970s, however, desires had to be kept in check not because they were considered evil in themselves, but more because giving in to them could lead to so many problems.

These trends alarmed some academic commentators, such as Bellah et al. (1985) and Lasch (1979), who believed that 'a good society required strong communities and a strong moral code', and were concerned at 'the increasing tolerance and declining respect for authority that has accom-panied the trend to self-development' (Cancian, 1987: 9). Wouters's thesis is reassuring on that score. While a lessening of power inequalities is con-ducive to greater informality, '[c]ontrary to the superficial impression, greater informality in the relationships of interdependent people induces and requires more deeply built-in self-restraints than relationships of a more formal nature, characteristic of greater and more overt status and power inequalities and more authoritarian behaviour by social superiors' (Wouters, 1977: 447).

The level of 'mutually expected self-restraint' (Goudsblom's phrase used by Wouters, 1987) has risen. Like most important insights, this is not altogether new: in his historical study of American manners books, Schlesinger quoted one observer as early as the inter-war period who made the perceptive comment that the greater 'liberty of behaviour' required 'more real breeding' than ever; people had to have 'an innate sense of the fitness of things, and sure feeling for the correct time and place' (1947: 58). 'Innate' is not strictly the right word, but otherwise this remark anticipates the main thrust of Wouters's interpretation of informalization processes. Informalization involves a *highly controlled* decontrolling of emotional controls.

Most of these trends are international in the West, with America leading the way in some respects and lagging behind in others, yet showing an overall similarity. The trend of informalization is not linear in any country. It proceeds in spurts or waves. A spurt of informalization is typically succeeded by one of 'reformalization', which is not, however, simply a return to the *status quo ante*. Rather, although codes of behaviour and of emotion management become more codified and formalized than in the period of rapid change, when it may have appeared that 'anything goes', the new standards incorporate patterns that emerged in the informalizing phase. A good example is the emergence in America between the wars – much more explicitly than in Northern Europe – of a formalization of more informal behaviour in a widely recognized code of dating behaviour. It was an aspect of an emerging 'youth culture', involving the loosening of the former formal codes in the context of an emancipation of the younger generation from parental authority. In America, the expectation was that petting went further than would have been respectable before the informalizing spurt following the First World War but, at least in college circles, the sequence, timing and limits of the permissible came to be quite clearly defined and widely recognized (Wouters, 2004: 49–50).[20] And again, after the informalization of the 1960s and 1970s, in most countries the 1980s represented such a reformalizing phase, but there was no widespread reversion to the formal and deferential manners or the attitudes to courtship and sexuality typical of the 1950s.

In all countries, informalizing trends – especially those related to sexuality – have provoked social, political and religious controversy. Those who dislike the new ways often see them as representing a decivilizing process, while those who favour them see them as liberating and indeed often as 'more civilized' standards. What is unusual about the USA is that, rather than rumbling along in the background of political life as most people gradually adjust to and adopt the new standards, these controversies have attained an extremely prominent place in the foreground of American politics. They have formed the basis of the 'culture wars'. Rather than dying down, as they did in Europe after their heyday in the 1960s when 'permissiveness' became subtly linked to more conventionally political issues like opposition to the Vietnam War, in the USA 'moral' issues – attitudes to abortion, contraception, homosexuality, formal marriage and 'family values' – have become more divisive. One trend has certainly been towards greater flexibility and tolerance, but in America there has also been a contrapuntal trend towards adherence to traditional, rigid structures, institutions and lifestyles (Doob, 1988). Rather than being moderated by cross-cutting memberships and allegiances, the two models have become aligned with other divisions: Democrat/Republican, liberal/conservative, secular/religious, urban/rural and North/South.

Conclusion

This long and complex chapter can be summed up in a few sentences. The broad trend of development of manners in America is very similar to that found in Europe, and is compatible with the explanations offered by Elias and subsequently by Wouters. In some respects, notably in the avoidance of *overt* expressions of social superiority, America has been ahead of the curve, and in some minor respects it has lagged. The main differences in manners between the two continents appear to be related to differences in social stratification, and in particular the absence from American history of any single dominant model-setting elite of the kind that was to be seen in many Western European countries. This will be explored further in chapter 4.

4

American Aristocracies

America never had an hereditary nobility. But its history certainly records various groups who fulfilled, or aspired to fulfil, a function equivalent to that seen in the European 'good societies', the upper-class circles which laid down the standards and set the models for the aspirant lower strata. The difference is that no single group in America succeeded in monopolizing the model-setting function to the same degree.

In his correspondence with Adams (see p. 36 above), Jefferson used the term 'pseudo-aristocracy' – or 'pseudalists' for short – to refer disdainfully to the *nouveaux riches* commercial interests, whose representatives had wealth but lacked refinement, intellect and the finer feelings of (in effect) *noblesse oblige*. The very disdain, however, draws attention to the fact that the correspondents were themselves members of two of what may better be called the quasi-aristocracies or 'good societies' of the post-Independence era: the third President was a slave-owning southern planter, while the second belonged to the New England intellectual–professional elite. Indeed, Adams was the progenitor of a dynasty that played a distinguished part in American national life throughout the nineteenth century. Before their two quasi-aristocracies, there had earlier been a distinct native colonial gentry not unlike its British counterpart. Later, in the last decades of the century, fulfilling Tocqueville's insight that 'aristocracy may be engendered by industry' (1961: II, 190–4), there emerged a plutocracy, part of which became prominent for its 'conspicuous consumption' reminiscent in some ways of the display of rank associated with *ancien régime* courtiers. The extremely wealthy have continued to occupy a prominent position in the American scene, and to that extent their style of life has served as a model to which others may distantly aspire. Whether, like the model-setting 'good societies' of Europe described by Elias, they can be said to have exercised self-constraint as a badge of their superiority is an altogether different question.

In examining upper-class strata in America, it will be useful to pose questions about them in the light of several interrelated characteristics of the 'good societies' of France, Germany and Britain discussed by Elias. Such 'good societies' were to varying extents:

- in a structural situation in which a strong curbing of affects and an elaborate code of self-discipline could function for them as a mark of rank;
- being 'defunctionalized' by social changes that deprived them of the social position they formerly enjoyed;
- 'two-front strata', ground between the upper and nether millstones of a powerful class above them and a rising class below them;
- in situations where social groups of diverse backgrounds were being thrust together willy-nilly, thus activating the patterns of development associated with established–outsider mechanisms.

On the whole, the trend of American history appears to be towards the differentiation of more numerous elite groups, among which some, but not all, compete directly with each other. Not all of them, either, have conspicuously sought or unwittingly come to exercise a model-setting role. At the same time, as a counterpoint to this differentiation, processes of integration appear also to have eventuated in a fairly distinct central power elite.

The colonial gentry

In Britain, the groups of relatively 'old' families who constitute the hereditary titled nobility, together with the slightly wider class of 'gentry', have until surprisingly recently played a dominant part in setting social standards for manners, behaviour and feeling that were copied by an aspirant middle class and even by a 'respectable' working class. The same is true to varying degrees of several other European countries, including some that have been republics for many decades. The British aristocracy and gentry were never so closed a social formation as those of some other countries. Rich merchants could always aspire to an estate for themselves and a title eventually for their descendants, and during the nineteenth century the number of families taking part in the London 'season', and thus constituting 'Society', grew fourfold (Davidoff, 1973). But upward mobility essentially involved what Robert Merton (1968: 319–22) called 'anticipatory socialization', adopting the manners of the stratum to membership of which one aspired.

The early leaders of the colonies were not, with a few exceptions, drawn from the upper reaches of English society. They consisted mainly of university-educated professionals – clergy and lawyers – together with a growing proportion of merchants. Of these two categories, the first would have been socially acknowledged by the landowning gentry class in England and the second rather less certainly.[1] The demand for deference often asserted by the early colonial elites appears to have been stoked by a sense of status insecurity. From an early stage, a striving can be observed for the security of social standing that the gentry enjoyed on the other side of the Atlantic. As Stow Persons argued:

> By the time of American colonial settlement, the gentleman had achieved a well-defined status among the privileged classes of Britain and the continental European countries. Everywhere, he combined a measure of authority and prestige with a prescribed code of manners and style of living that distinguished him from less favoured social types. In the rapidly growing colonial societies of British North America, a gentry class modelled explicitly on the British gentry formed the apex of the social structure. Composed of merchants, planters, professional men, and civil servants, the colonial gentry well nigh monopolized both the tangible powers of the community and its formal intellectual and cultural life. (1973: v–vi)

The basis of their power was wealth, and in North America it mattered much less than in Europe whether that was derived from ownership of land or from mercantile enterprise. The colonial gentry experienced continual 'pressure from below'. Although the tendency of the gentry within each colony to intermarry 'resulted in a growing sense of the value of heredity and family ties', everyone knew that 'new men were constantly pushing up into the class and marrying their children into established gentry families'. The pressure from below was no doubt one reason why the 'colonial American gentry modelled themselves on the English gentry, carefully imitating their manners and their style of living, and frequently seeking further reassurance by establishing family derivation, however dubious, from British landed families' (ibid.: 31; cf. R. D. Brown, 1989: 42–64). But, while the British gentry was less closed than was the minor nobility of other European countries, the colonial American gentry was still less of a closed stratum than its British counterpart, and educated people were accepted on terms of equality. Nor were they a 'two-front stratum' of the kind that Elias saw in the French courtly nobility, increasingly ground between the upper and nether millstones of the monarchy and the rising bourgeoisie. In no real sense were the colonial gentry in any significant numbers economically dependent on the patronage of colonial governors, or indeed of the London rulers. Eventually, it is true, through conflicts over taxation and over access to lands to the west, the colonial authorities came to be seen as an obstacle to the prosperity of the merchants and gentry, but they were not dependent on royal policy for their social status.

The colonial gentry did, nevertheless, make a claim to superior social status on the basis of their manners and way of life. John Adams, himself coming from only the middling ranks of the colonial gentry, is an interesting case study. Returning after years of diplomatic service in Europe to take office as George Washington's Vice-President, Adams wore a sword on official occasions and clearly expected a good measure of deference; for these and other apparently courtly affectations, he was mocked as the 'Duke of Braintree'. Significantly, it has been noted (Hemphill, 1999: 65) that his letters and diaries show him to have been greatly concerned with self-command and with observing other people's facial expressions. This is certainly reminiscent of what Elias (2006a: 113–16) called the courtly 'art of observing people'. People who frequented courts – as Adams had done – developed an extraordinary sensitivity to the status and importance that should be attributed to a person on the basis of fine nuances of bearing, speech, manners and appearance:

> [R]ank at court can change very quickly; [each courtier] has rivals; he has open and concealed enemies. And the tactics of his struggles, as of his alliances, demand careful consideration. The degree of aloofness or familiarity with everyone must be carefully measured; each greeting, each conversation has a significance over and above what is actually said or done. (Elias, 2000: 398)

Observing, dealing with, relating to or avoiding people – and the self-observation that was inextricably bound up in that – became an art in itself. It always involved observing an individual person not in isolation but always in social context as a person in relation to others. It can thus be seen as a tendency at odds with the individualism later celebrated as central to the American habitus.

Not many of the colonial gentry had the direct experience of European courts to which Adams, Jefferson, Jay or Franklin had been exposed. In some of the colonies at least, though, a few more would have had contact with the mini-courts that arose around the governors appointed by the crown, where, for a relatively short period, some families could aspire to membership of a quasi-courtly circle and to perform as quasi-courtiers. As Arthur Schlesinger Sr wrote,

> the aristocratic idea was firmly enthroned in the life of the people in colonial times. At the apex of the social pyramid stood the colonial governor

with the official class that surrounded him, constituting a class that looked to England not only for its governmental authority but also for its models and standards of social conduct. Life at the governor's court was gay and extravagant, and frequently brilliant; to become members of the charmed circle was the aspiration, and sometimes the despair of the colonial aristocracy which ranked next in the social scale. (1922: 73)

Even those who had no direct contact with either European or gubernatorial courts, however, took as their models a European gentry class who were themselves influenced by models set in courtly society. The pervasive concern with social status is well illustrated by the fact that Harvard freshmen were listed not in the alphabetical order of their names, but by their social rank (Bushman, 1993: 40), and throughout New England and the middle Atlantic colonies, precedence was given to the 'well born'. Class distinctions and the emulation of English fashions and conventions were even more rigidly maintained in the southern colonies (Schlesinger, 1922: 74).

Yet as a single elite – if indeed the elites of the 13 colonies ever were a single elite – the colonial gentry barely survived Independence. As Persons contends: '[T]he colonial gentry had scarcely attained maturity as a class before the political and social changes initiated by the Revolution and culminating in Jacksonian democracy destroyed its class character and substituted a number of functional elites' (1973: vi). These included, to begin with, the professional and intellectual elites typical of New England, and the southern planters. Both, in their very different ways, used codes of strict self-discipline as marks of their rank.

The South: American *Junkers*?

Literally, 'aristocracy' means 'rule by the best', who by implication are only a few. In that sense the great planters of the Old South were an aristocracy, for they always represented a small proportion even of the white population of the southern states. According to Clement Eaton (1968: 26), those who owned 100 or more slaves numbered not many more than 2,000 even in 1860, after the great expansion of cotton planting. Even among the white population (and setting aside the 'poor white trash'), they were far outnumbered by the professional middle class and the yeoman farmers. The latter group tended to be involved in mixed farming and, even if they owned a few slaves, they lived fairly roughly, for example in log cabins; they also tended to be far less well educated than their counterparts in the North.[2]

What the great planters lacked in numbers, they compensated for in political and cultural power. V. O. Key Jr. (1949) regarded it as their great political triumph that they enlisted so many others in their cause in the Civil War. Culturally, they acquired a distinct flavour that still leaves a strong taste in the social character of the region.

In a number of respects the planters shared social traits with the *ancien régime* nobility. For a start, plantations and slavery were linked to disdain for manual labour. Darcy Ribeiro made this point in explaining the differences between the social and political development of North and South America, contrasting the predominance of the wage-earner class in the colonies of North America with the hacienda system, slavery and serfdom predominant in Latin America: 'These two forms of labour recruitment left deep marks on the societies resulting from them. On the one side, they occasioned a dignification of manual labour, contrasted with a conception of work as denigrating, proper to the servant class only' (1971: 350). The contrast is not a dichotomy, however, but a continuum, along which the South was placed nearer than the North to the Latin American pole.

Another respect in which some at least of the quasi-aristocrats of the South were closer than most northerners to the courtly attitudes of the *ancien régime* was in how they viewed expenditure. Many of them pursued a costly lifestyle that to northern eyes appeared extravagant, even reckless, to the point of 'irrationality'. This is reminiscent of French courtiers, who spent according to the demands of their rank rather than to their income, often financially ruining themselves in the process. Elias pointed out that expenditure on consumption of many kinds was a necessary expression of the seigneurial ethos of rank. He argued that the conspicuous consumption of court society represented a specific form of rationality under a specific form of social compulsion, a 'court-rationality' very different from bourgeois or 'economic' rationality. Both require rational foresight and calculation. Both therefore require restraint of short-term affects for the sake of certain vital interests. But what is being calculated and made calculable is very different: 'Bourgeois-industrial rationality is generated by the compulsion of the economic mesh; by it power opportunities founded on private or public capital are made calculable. Court rationality is generated by the compulsion of the elite social mesh; *by it people and prestige are made calculable as instruments of power*' (Elias, 2006a: 121; my italics). Traces of a similar court-rationality can be seen for instance in Thomas Jefferson's mounting debt, resulting in the forced sale of Monticello upon his death. Or in the following extract from the diary of Mary Chesnut, dated 11 March 1861 in Charleston, just immediately before guns firing on Fort Sumter in the harbour signalled the beginning of the Civil War:

Mr Ledyard thought the twenty thousand (and little enough it is) was given to the President of these United States to enable him to maintain an establishment of such dignity as befits the head of a great nation. It is an infamy to economize with the public money and to put it into one's private purse. Mrs Browne was walking with me when we were airing our indignation against Mrs Lincoln and her shabby economy. (1961 [1905]: 18)

While this trait is reminiscent of the French courtiers described by Elias, in other respects the southern planters were quite different from them too. *The Court Society* focuses on France at a stage when the 'taming of warriors' was far advanced, when the old *noblesse d'épée* had been thoroughly subordinated to the power of the state – that is, royal power – and deprived of the capacity to use independent military force that their forefathers had (literally) enjoyed. Rather than with the French courtiers, or indeed the English gentry, the ante-bellum planters of the South may be more fruitfully compared – as Shearer Davis Bowman (1980; 1993) has argued – with the *Junker* class that became a dominant force in Germany.

The aristocratic – noble and non-noble – landowners of eastern Prussia did not own slaves, but until 1807 their lands were worked by serfs 'subject to the personal, nearly despotic, authority of the owner' (Bowman, 1980: 782). Agriculture in parts of Eastern Europe had become refeudalized from the late fifteenth century onwards, just as the remnants of feudalism were disappearing from Western Europe. That process was set in train by the development of the international grain trade, which made it advantageous for landowners to develop capitalist agriculture by enforcing hereditary bondage on their labourers (Wallerstein, 1974: 90). There is an obvious parallel with the growth of the transatlantic cotton trade that led to the expansion of cotton planting in the South. Some irony, then, that both *Junkers* and American planters disdained the free-market society. Conservative thinkers in Germany provided ideological justification for serfdom, even after its legal abolition (Mannheim, 1953: 141ff.), just as their counterparts did in the ante-bellum South (Bowman, 1980: 797ff.). George Fitzhugh, in his book *Sociology for the South* (1854), drew on the then-recent thinking of Auguste Comte (who had invented the word sociology) and his socialist disciple Fourier. He depicted slavery in warm, paternalistic tones, contrasting it with 'the failure of free society'. The free market in wage labour was leading, he argued, to the emiseration of the working class, reducing it to a condition inferior to that of the slaves. (Besides conditions in northern factories, he referred to how free-market doctrine had contributed to the disaster of the Irish potato famine.) Slavery, he went so far as to argue in his highly intelligent if wholly misguided book, was a form of socialism – slaves were provided with food, housing and nurseries – and, following Fourier, he foresaw socialism superseding free-market capitalism.

In both cases, Prussia east of the Elbe and the Old South, the dominance of the landowning class depended ultimately on their capacity to use violence in its defence. As Bowman (1993) points out, both the slave-owners and the *Junkers* enjoyed the benefits of the 'private law state' – their right to adjudicate and enforce their judgments in their own domains – which, although it implied some limitation of the national state's monopoly of the legitimate use of the means of violence, in the end rested on the confident expectation that the forces of the state would uphold landowners' rights.[3] In both cases, the landowning class was also the military class. The *Junkers* provided the Prussian officer corps and also, though less exclusively, the backbone of its administrative corps. In a similar way, before the Civil War, most of America's Presidents and a disproportionate number of Justices of the Supreme Court came from the South; planters and their sons typically served in the state militias, and provided a large part of the (admittedly small) federal army. Visiting the US Military Academy in 1861, Anthony Trollope (1968: 105) was told that before the Civil War 'no officer or board of officers then at West Point was able to dismiss a lad whose father was a Southerner, and who had friends among the Government'.

What Elias called a 'warrior ethic' was still a strong element in the habitus of the planter aristocracy. Again, Mrs Chesnut's diary is illuminating. Writing on 5 December 1864, as the Civil War neared its end, she first remembered Stonewall Jackson, the Confederate general who had died the previous year of injuries received at the battle of Chancellorsville:

> He classed all who were weak and weary, who fainted by the wayside, as men wanting in patriotism. . . . He was the true type of all great soldiers. Like the successful warriors of the world, he did not value human life where he had an object to accomplish. He could order men to their death as a matter of course. His soldiers obeyed him to the death. (1961 [1905]: 262–3)

She then recounts a conversation with her own husband, formerly a US Senator, then an aide to Confederate President Jefferson Davis and a brigadier-general in the rebel army:

> My husband, as I told him today, could see me and everything he loved hanged, drawn and quartered without moving a muscle, if a crowd were looking on; he could have the same gentle operation performed on himself and make no sign. To all of which violent insinuation he answered in unmoved tones: 'So would any civilized man. Savages, however – Indians, at least – are more dignified in that particular than we are. Noisy, fidgety

grief never moves me at all; it annoys me. Self-control is what we all need. You are a miracle of sensibility; self-control is what you need.' 'So you are civilized!', I said. 'Some day I mean to be.' (Ibid.)

This emotional style is very close to that which Elias (1996) describes as dominant in Germany under the *Kaiserreich* (the period from 1870 to 1918 when Germany had achieved national reunification through force of arms rather than through the aspirations of a liberal nationalist middle class).

In *The Germans*, Elias attempted to explain how, in the specific circumstances of Germany in the nineteenth century, a form of the 'warrior code' of behaviour and feeling not only persisted among the *Junkers* and higher aristocracy, but also took hold among the higher-middle-class civil servants, lawyers and other professionals, and even permeated relations between employers and workers. A stable hierarchy of dominance and subordination anchored an autocratic form of rule in the very habitus of individual people. It was expressed in a hard, highly self-constrained, rigidly unemotional style:

[I]n order in life to be man, one had to be tough. As soon as one showed any weakness, one was lost. Therefore it was a good thing to display one's strength. Anyone who showed weakness deserved to be expelled; anyone who was vulnerable deserved to have salt rubbed into his wounds. (1996: 112)

The similarity to the qualities Mary Chesnut observed in her husband and other southern gentlemen is striking. The style was an essential badge of membership of a dominant stratum.

In Germany, another essential badge of membership consisted in being deemed worthy to give satisfaction in a duel, a qualification that – by the nineteenth century – upper-middle-class men principally gained at university, along with a degree, through membership of one of the fighting fraternities:

[T]he duel was characteristic of a socially strategic type of behaviour which was widespread in the less pacified societies of earlier times, and now, hemmed around with formalized ritual, still remained alive in later, more strongly pacified societies, even though it breached the central ruler's and the state's monopoly of violence. It raised above the masses those who belonged to certain social strata; in the first place the nobles and officer corps, and then the fighting fraternities of middle-class students and their Old Boys – in short, the stratum of those entitled to demand satisfaction. Through it, they submitted to the constraint of a special norm which made the formalized use of violence, possibly with lethal consequences, a duty for individual people under certain circumstances. In this form was preserved the typical social strategy of warrior castes: a scale of values in which physical strength, skill and readiness personally to do battle were ranked particularly high, if not highest of all. Alternative, more peaceful forms of competition and social strategy, especially the art of verbal debate through argument and persuasion, were accordingly regarded as of lesser value or virtually contemptible. (Ibid.: 65)

Although the social hierarchy of the Old South was a great deal more open and fluid than that of Prussia, the persistence of duelling there was something that marked it out for visitors as quite different from the North. Harriet Martineau (1837: III, 56) noted that in 1834 more duels were fought in New Orleans than there are days in the year, almost all of them for what – from her point of view – were frivolous reasons. Sir Charles Lyell, visiting the city in 1846, recorded that: 'Over the grave of one recently killed in a duel was a tablet, with the inscription – "Mort, victime de l'honneur!" Should any one propose to set up a similar tribute to the memory of a duellist at Mount Auburn, near Boston, a sensation would be created, which would manifest how widely different is the state of public opinion in New England from that in the "First Municipality"' (in Nevins, 1948: 239). Duelling, for Martineau (1837: III, 55), betokened a 'recklessness of life which is not confined to the semi-barbarous parts of the country'. But although it was not unknown in the North, it was never so prevalent, and it more or less died out after Alexander Hamilton's death at the hands of Aaron Burr (Lane, 1997: 84). The Ohioan Ulysses S. Grant expressed what was probably the attitude even of fighting men from the North:

> If any man should wrong me to the extent of my being willing to kill him, I would not be willing to give him the choice of weapons with which it should be done, and of the time, place and distance separating us, when I executed him. If I should do another such a wrong as to justify him in killing me, I would make any reasonable atonement within my power, if convinced of the wrong done. I place my opposition to duelling on higher grounds than any here stated. No doubt the majority of duels fought have been for want of moral courage on the part of those engaged to decline. (1994 [1885]: 40)

The motives of individuals for duelling in the ante-bellum South – as in nineteenth-century Germany, and as it had been in many countries at an earlier stage of development – could, however, only be understood as part of a complex social code of 'honour'.[4] In his classic book *Southern Honour: Ethics and Behaviour in the Old South*, Bertram Wyatt-Brown shows how 'honour' is both internal and external to individual men:

> [H]onour is reputation. Honour resides in the individual as his understanding of who he is and where he belongs in the ordered ranks of society. . . . The internal and external aspects of honour are inalienably connected

because honour serves as ethical mediator between the individual and the community by which he is assessed and in which he must also locate himself in relation to others. (1982: 14)

Roger Lane contrasts the code of honour dominant in the South with that of 'dignity' prevalent in the North. The leaders of New England from the beginning, and certainly by the nineteenth century,

> had consistently challenged the traditional, external code of honour in the name of the newer, internal concept of dignity. The difference between the two . . . is that between two different conceptions of the relation between individual and society. 'Honour' is a matter of reputation, as judged by the community; a person's worth is what it appears to be, to outside observers. 'Dignity' is a matter of the soul; a person's worth cannot be judged from the outside, but only by the individual conscience . . . or by God himself. . . . An insult, then, to a 'man of honour' must be answered publicly; a 'man of dignity' may ignore the same insult, as not touching his inner worth. (1997: 85–6)

Lane's conceptualization is too dichotomous;[5] Wyatt-Brown expresses the idea better in his recognition that a code of honour includes both an external and an internal component. A better way still of expressing the distinction with which both authors are concerned is Elias's idea of differences, and changes over time, in the balance between external constraints (*Fremdzwänge*) and self-constraints (*Selbstzwänge*) in the steering of individual people's conduct. Since he defines a civilizing process as involving a tilting in this balance in favour of a greater weight being carried by self-constraints, the dominant code of honour in the South was in a technical sense less civilized, representing an earlier point on the curve of a long-term civilizing process, than the code that Lane labelled one of 'dignity'.

Lane notes that the New England 'man of dignity' would very likely take a quarrel to court rather than fight a duel; but the propensity to litigation through the legal apparatus of the state is a function not only – not mainly, indeed – of culturally conditioned individual dispositions, but also of the degree of internal pacification and the effectiveness of the state monopoly of the legitimate use of violence in a given territory. In the antebellum South, Steward (2002) has contended, upper-class duelling over issues of 'honour' stood at the apex of a pyramid of violence, and served to legitimate less refined forms; widespread violence against blacks, for instance, was another symptom of the weakness of the state monopoly.[6] In the North, on the other hand, Lane is right to argue that:

> Dignity, with its emphasis on self-control, discipline, and delayed gratification, was well suited to the conduct of life in an increasingly commercial

and capitalist North, and to a polyglot society in which people of other religions and ethnic groups could not be expected to share the same standards
of conduct and propriety. Honour, in contrast, continued to flourish in the
more ethnically homogeneous white South, where all of a man's peers –
blacks and other social inferiors did not count – were assumed to hold the
same values. (1997: 86)

As far as the blacks were concerned, the difference was of course only
one of degree; they suffered many forms of social exclusion in the 'commercial, capitalist . . . polyglot' North too, until the Civil War era and
afterwards. But the general point is correct: the white southern code of
honour, involving a type of 'hard' self-discipline as a mark of rank,
applied only within the restricted circle of its members' mutual identification. In that, too, they somewhat resembled members of court society
in *ancien régime* France who, for all their watchfulness, self-command
and honour among themselves, felt no necessity to treat people outside
their rank in the same way – as Voltaire found when a courtier whom
he had rashly challenged to a duel instead sent his servants to thrash
him.

By way of summary, how far did the quasi-aristocracy of the Old South
share in the four interrelated characteristics that are associated with
European 'good societies' in Elias's writings?

Certainly to some extent, its members were in a structural situation
where the curbing of affects was used as a mark of membership of an
upper class; this can be seen especially in the prestige of a 'hard' warrior
exterior and in the code of 'honour' linked, as in Germany, to the cult
of duelling. Yet it was a rather circumscribed form of self-constraint,
exercised mainly among members of the same class. As Eaton (1968: 31)
commented, 'With all his virtues and charms, the "high-toned"
Southern gentleman had pronounced defects and limitations', which
largely stemmed from the institution of slavery. Ruling over their plantations like little kings, they 'were not accustomed to having their wills
crossed or opinions contradicted', and were not to the same extent as in
the growing capitalist North subject to the pressures towards self-constraint and foresight that arise from long chains of interdependence
between people who are relative equals. An illustration can be found in
the memoirs of Frederick Douglass, the freed slave and a leader of the
abolitionist cause. Speaking of a relatively good master, Douglass nevertheless recalled that 'Mr Freeland had many of the faults peculiar to
slaveholders, such as being very passionate and fretful' (1995 [1845]:
46). This offers a striking comparison with Tocqueville's remarks on the
easy and considerate relations between masters and (paid) servants in the
North (1961: II, 211–20). Moreover, slave-owning was not conducive to

effective emulation of some of the virtues associated with the English gentry:

> They did not keep up their property as the English squires and there was in many plantation homes an air of shiftlessness and untidiness owing to lazy and careless servants. Their young sons were often tempted into ways of immorality with the Negro servants and both boys and girls were rendered lazy by having slave valets and maids assigned to them. . . . While both master and mistress were often industrious, their children had nothing to do but amuse themselves by hunting, shooting, fishing, riding horses, visiting, and drinking. (Eaton, 1968: 31)

The extremely unequal power ratios that marked the situation of the old slave-owning elite were not conducive to a strong conversion of external constraints into habitual self-constraints that is a hallmark of a civilizing process. Indeed, until the latter half of the twentieth century, the pressure on southern whites for rules of behaviour to apply 'all-round' – equally to all, irrespective of social rank, a tendency Elias saw developing in Western Europe by the nineteenth century – was relatively weak.

The Old South quasi-aristocracy, unlike Elias's *ancien régime* courtiers, was not undergoing a 'defunctionalization' – military, political and economic – that left it with little more than exclusive manners and virtuoso consumption as a means of displaying its rank. On the contrary, in the decades after the introduction of the cotton gin, the numbers and wealth of slave-owners were increasing. Nor were they a two-front stratum, since they faced little threat from below or subordination to central rulers above; if threat there were before the Civil War, it was from a growing economic dependence on northern manufactures and from the emancipation movement burgeoning in the North. Only during and after the Civil War did their defunctionalization begin in earnest, and then indeed they did become a two-front stratum; then indeed, in Reconstruction and for many decades afterwards, did the characteristic features of established–outsider figurations come into play: ruthless exclusion of the blacks, bitter resentment of central authority, a romanticization of a better past and of a 'minority of the best', the stigmatization of the outsiders in terms of a 'minority of the worst'.

How far did the southern aristocracy, with its code of honour and its *Junker*-like warrior ethic, survive the Civil War? The Scot David Macrae, visiting the South five years after the war's end, reported that he 'found the old aristocracy still in the dust, with less and less hope of ever recovering its old position' (in Nevins, 1948: 347); it had, so to speak, gone with the wind, and Macrae described former Confederate generals and other officers labouring in humble occupations. Yet, however attenuated, a cultural legacy from the ante-bellum South is still visible nearly a century and a half later; indeed, the legacy may be said to have increased in visibility in the last quarter of the twentieth century, as the southern states became increasingly dominant in national politics. And it can be heard in the hard, unemotional, speak-your-weight-machine mode of speech affected by US military spokesmen in American wars today.[7]

The North: *working* upper classes

In the North, the successors to the colonial gentry included several groups, the boundaries between which were relatively blurred and shifting over time. But, in contrast with the wealthiest of the southern plantocracy, they were essentially *working* upper classes, a professional and commercial bourgeoisie of the kind that emerged in Britain, but also – just below and in tension with the courtly nobility – in France and Germany.[8] They arose in the nineteenth century through the processes of functional democratization. It has been said that 'it more and more came to be thought that a gentleman was what a gentleman did', and that 'he could be anybody, no matter how lowborn, if he thought and acted in the right ways' (Collier, 1991: 10). On the other hand, after the high point of equality – social and political – in the Jacksonian era of the 1820s and 1830s, the division between what are commonly called the middle and (manual) working classes became more clearly marked, and differentiation was also taking place within the upper and middle classes. Persons (1973) distinguished between what he called the 'gentry elite' and the 'social elite'. The 'social elite' gradually became the more prominent and numerous; among them, matters of 'lifestyle' and social display were more prominent, and public activism less so.

An American Bildungsbürgertum

Learned cosmopolitanism had long been part of the we-image of the educated colonial gentry, along with the dream of English gentility. English connections and aspirations became less significant after Independence, but the ideal of the cultivated gentleman survived; in the Virginia Tidewater it was transformed, according to R. D. Brown, into a kind of classical ideology: 'Now clad in the classical robes of Republican Rome, whence the ideal originally derived, Virginia became the new centre of civilization' (1989: 63). The tradition persisted most strongly, however, in the Northeast; indeed Henry Adams remembered Boston society before the Civil War as still deferring to London: 'The tone of Boston society was colonial. The true Bostonian always knelt before the majesty of English standards; far from concealing it as a weakness, he was proud of it as a strength. The eighteenth century ruled society long after 1850' (1999 [1919]: 22). Yet when he went to London as secretary to his father Charles Francis Adams, who served as Lincoln's ambassador during and after the Civil War, Henry was rather disdainful of English society (ibid.: 156, 171, 172). English men and women treated each other with 'atrocious insolence and brutality', and 'the manners [and the dress and the cuisine] of English society were notorious, and the taste was worse'. But it was above all the level of education and intellectual cultivation that Adams deplored in London. Significantly, 30 years earlier, Harriet Martineau had admired the respect for intellect that she encountered in elite circles in America:

> In the capitals of States, men rank according to their supposed intellect. Many mistakes are made in the estimate; and (far worse) many pernicious allowances are made for bad morals, for the sake of superior intellect: but still the taste is a higher one than is to be found elsewhere: and where such a taste and a gradation subsist, the essentials of good manners can never be wanting. (1837: III, 102)

Thus, even if the educated elite in America imagined that it still to some extent looked to its Anglophone counterparts across the Atlantic, a closer similarity in fact probably subsists between it and the *Bildungsbürgertum* (intellectual bourgeoisie) in Germany. The great German universities – far ahead of Oxford and Cambridge in the leadership of scholarship until the ancient English seats of learning began to revive in the latter half of the century – were the key institutions of the *Bildungsbürgertum*, just as Harvard, Yale, Princeton and the College of William and Mary were for the American intelligentsia. It is not surprising that so many nineteenth-century American scholars, such as George Bancroft, went to study in German universities. It was the university-educated German middle class who, as Elias showed, elevated *Kultur* above *Zivilisation*, intellect and true feeling above the superficiality of polished courtly manners. For the American educated upper class, as for the *Bildungsbürgertum*:

> A code of polite conduct was part of an elaborate set of inducements and sanctions – which also included religion, education, enlightened self-interest, and of course the law itself – upon which virtue was believed to depend. . . . [T]he idea of politeness included not only outward behaviour but also inward qualities of mental cultivation and good taste. Thus it was an aspect of self-development considerably more important than learning table etiquette. (Howe, 1997: 16)

In the 1830s, Harriet Martineau (1837: III, 10) commented upon the great cautiousness that was entrenched early and deeply in northern people; she described as 'fear of opinion' something very similar to what Elias termed the habitual 'checking of behaviour' in anticipation of what others would think. Kasson (1990: 114–15) speaks of a 'new kind of embarrassment' that 'became a normal, even an essential, part of American urban life' in the nineteenth century. This appears to be at odds with Tocqueville's assertion that Americans 'find neither peril nor advantage in the free inter-change of their thoughts', resulting in manners that were 'natural, frank and open'.[9] On the other hand, Tocqueville also pointed out that in 'democracy' – a society characterized by relatively even power ratios – the 'readiness to believe the multitude increases'. Martineau's social 'cau-tiousness' is an aspect of Tocqueville's 'softening of manners as social con-ditions become more equal' (Tocqueville, 1961: 195–200). The social situation of the northern educated professional and commercial elite was not such as to be conducive to their showing open disdain towards their fellow citizens, even if they were inwardly confident of their superior edu-cation, understanding and feeling.

These emerging aspects of the habitus of northern elites stood in con-trast – for a considerable period – with the persistence of the sense of honour and in the more hierarchical local communities in the South. Discussing the disappearance of duelling in the North and its persistence in the South, Martineau, perceptive as always, commented:

> It will not do for the duellists of the south to drop in conversation, as they do, that good manners can exist only where vengeance is the penalty of bad. The fear of imputation and the dread of vengeance are at least as con-temptible as bad manners; and unquestionably lower than the fear of opinion prevalent in the north. (1837: III, 13)

What this contrast involves is again the balance between external con-straints and self-constraints in the steering of behaviour. The increasing sensitivity to embarrassment among the northern upper and upper-middle classes 'reflected the unstable, altered context of honour, shame and rep-utation in the market economy and democratic ethos of the nineteenth-century city' (Kasson, 1990: 114), in contrast with the persistence of older notions of honour in the well-defined and local social hierarchies of the Old South.

While there are striking parallels between the educated upper-middle class of the North and the German *Bildungsbürgertum*, one important difference is that in the USA there is little in the way of an equivalent to the transition from 'humanist to nationalist middle-class elites' that Elias (1996: 134–54) describes in Germany from the middle of the nineteenth century, nor especially to the infiltration of the militaristic ethos into the middle class via the universities. The liberal middle classes had not achieved the reunification of Germany in the failed revolution of 1848, but the warrior class had brought it about shortly afterwards on the battlefield, and gained great prestige by so doing. Nothing quite similar happened in the USA after the Civil War.[10] To oversimplify somewhat, the *Junker* class of the South had eventually been defeated on the battlefield by a Union army led in the main by generals, like Ulysses S. Grant, of humble origin,[11] and by the northern industrial power behind it. The Federal army fairly soon reverted to its tiny pre-war size (see chapter 9 below). If anything, it was the common man and the common businessman who gained prestige from the outcome of the war.

Henry Adams ironically pictured the changed society to which he and his father and their friend the historian John Lothrop Motley returned in 1868 after a decade representing their country in Europe. They were:

> survivors from the forties – . . . ornaments that had been more or less suited to the colonial architecture, but which had never had much value in Desbrosses Street or Fifth Avenue. They could scarcely have earned five dollars a day in any modern industry. The men who commanded high pay were as a rule not ornamental. Even Commodore Vanderbilt and Jay Gould lacked social charm. Doubtless the country needed ornament – needed it very badly indeed – but it needed energy still more, and capital most of all. (1999: 202)

The 'ornaments' were encountering a new kind of 'business tough guy' – tough, albeit not in quite the same way as the warrior-planter elite of the South – whose emergence as a characteristic American figure Wilkinson (1984: 37) dated from the Jacksonian 1830s and 1840s, 'when business took on more of the tone of a competitive scramble'.

The rise of the plutocracy

The growth of a new elite of *nouveaux riches* and a plutocracy was the key feature of the half-century after the Civil War. Besides the names of Gould and Vanderbilt, Henry Adams could have mentioned Rockefeller, Carnegie, Armour, Huntington, Frick and countless others among the fabulously wealthy who emerged during and after the Civil War – through war-profiteering, then manufacturing, mining, banking and railroads. These parvenus managed to crash into the older aristocratic circles, and 'the owners of these regal fortunes – or, more accurately, their wives – helped to set the social pace of the times' (Schlesinger, 1947: 28). At the end of the century they were parodied by Thorstein Veblen (1899) as a 'leisure class' preoccupied with 'conspicuous consumption'.

Yet 'leisure class' is a misnomer: both elements, the old educated upper class and the *nouveaux riches*, were *working* upper strata whose income derived from commerce, industry and the professions. No social derogation attached to employment in commerce and the professions (Mead, 1942: 58), as had been the case – at least in theory – among continental European aristocrats. Edith Wharton's novels depict young men of traditional upper-class background, such as Newland Archer in *The Age of Innocence* (1982 [1920]), who, like Henry Adams, went out to work as lawyers and in similar 'respectable' professions. But they also depict the uneasy coexistence of the old and new upper classes. The intermingling of old families with *nouveaux riches* in post-bellum America produced anxieties about status and manners and called forth what Schlesinger called an 'avalanche' of new etiquette books, the overall tendency of which was 'to instil a more aristocratic style of behaviour' (1947: 34). Even among the old families of 'Proper Philadelphia', according to E. Digby Baltzell, 'a rigid code of drawing-room manners gradually replaced the more ancient moral values' (1958: 13). As so often in times of high social mobility – for instance in Europe at the end of the Middle Ages, when, as Elias showed, the formation of a new court aristocracy out of elements of diverse origins was associated with an early spurt of printed manners books – a process of formalization followed upon a period of fluid and uncertain social standards. Schlesinger quoted *Appleton's Journal*, which asked 'Are not over-refinements better than under-refinements? . . . Training is necessary to repress, and art to express'. The earlier trend not to defer to European models appears to have been temporarily reversed. From his visit to the USA in 1904, Max Weber observed:

> At the present time affiliation with a distinguished club is essential above all else. In addition, the kind of home is important (in 'the street' which in middle-sized cities is almost never lacking) and the kind of dress and sport. . . . All these phenomena . . . belong in the broad field of the Europeanization of American 'society'. (1946: 309)

Such baroque features of the English upper-class world as chaperoning and the complexities of the visiting card social mobility game (see Davidoff, 1973) did not take root for any great length of time. Even so, Wharton caught a certain similarity between the New York upper class in the Gilded Age and seventeenth and eighteenth-century French court society described by Elias: the same need for observing oneself and others, the exaggerated consequences (especially for women) of making a social mistake. In *The House of Mirth*, Lily Bart has (quite innocently) had tea with bachelor Lawrence Selden in his rooms, and has been seen leaving by a distant acquaintance. She thinks:

> Why must a girl pay so dearly for her least escape from routine? Why could one never do a natural thing without having to screen it behind a structure

of artifice? She had yielded to a passing impulse in going to Lawrence Selden's rooms, and it was seldom she could allow herself the luxury of an impulse! This one, at any rate, was going to cost her rather more than she could afford. She was vexed to see that, in spite of so many years of vigilance, she had blundered twice within five minutes. That stupid story of her dressmaker was bad enough – it would have been so simple to tell Rosedale that she had been taking tea with Selden! The mere statement of the fact would have rendered it innocuous. But, after having let herself be surprised in a falsehood, it was doubly stupid to snub the witness of her discomfiture. If she had had the presence of mind to let Rosedale drive her to the station, the concession might have purchased his silence. . . . He knew, of course, that there would be a large house-party at Bellomont and the possibility of being taken for one of Mrs Trenor's guests was doubtless included in his calculations. Mr Rosedale was still at a stage in his social ascent when it was of importance to produce such impressions. . . . Lily was sure that within twenty-four hours the story of her visiting . . . would be in active circulation. (Wharton, 1990 [1905]: 20–1)

Wharton, incidentally, makes Rosedale a Jew; this serves as a reminder that the pressure from below experienced by older-established families was associated not just with the *nouveaux riches* in general, but also with ascendant ethnic communities. It has been noted that in the late nineteenth century 'gentlefolk were supposed to know the maiden names of their four great-grandmothers', it being assumed that 'only people whose families had been in America for several generations could perform this feat' (Collier, 1991: 40).[12]

Overall, how far did the upper classes of the late nineteenth-century North share in the four interrelated characteristics that are associated with European 'good societies' in Elias's writings?

The long-preserved ideal of the cultivated gentleman was clearly associated with a much more rigorous standard of habitual self-constraint than that typical of the southern planters. It involved more 'dignity' than 'honour', embodied in a certain cautiousness, an habitual 'checking of behaviour' and 'fear of opinion', even (according to Martineau, 1837: I, 145) a more deferential way of walking. Far less than the ante-bellum southern elite (or post-bellum southern whites in general) could they show open disdain for their social inferiors. These northerners were living in a far more functionally democratized society, and it was from this – more than from an intra-elite contest for status – that the external constraint towards self-restraint stemmed. These social conditions rested in turn upon state-formation and internal pacification having proceeded further in the North than in the South, which had the further effect in private disputes of discouraging resort to violence and encouraging the seeking of redress through the courts.

Not in any real sense was this professional and commercial bourgeoisie being 'defunctionalized' in society as a whole, although Henry Adams's dry irony about them becoming 'ornaments' among the new men after the Civil War hints at a measure of displacement. They were not excluded from positions of command in the state as were the nobility under Louis XIV, but they had to compete for them with more and more other groups (thus resembling their British counterparts more than the French or German). They were not a two-front stratum, if that conjures up the image of a simple sandwich, with a royal or equivalent state apparatus clearly 'above' and a rising merchant class 'below'.[13] Nevertheless, they were competing with at least two other strata: the *nouveaux riches*, who may be thought eventually to have overtaken them, and a variety of middle-class rivals rising from more recently plebeian origins.

What is certainly true is that people of diverse social origins were being thrust together in circles at the 'top' of American society, and this enforced social mixing goes a long way to explaining the spurt of reformalization observed in the last decades of the nineteenth century and the early years of the twentieth. As for the 'conspicuous consumption' of the so-called 'leisure class', it was not quite the same as that seen under the *ancien régime* – where there were quite clear rules about the expenditure appropriate to each social rank (Elias, 2006a: 58–9, 65–6). The conspicuous consumption of the Gilded Age was rather a symptom of newer groups crashing into older elites in the absence of such clear rules, and the result was a cruder form of social display.

From cumulative to dispersed inequalities?

The social and political development of New Haven, Connecticut, appears to represent in microcosm the trends that are evident in the macrocosm of the USA. In an historical prolegomenon to his classic study of the distribution of power in the city in the 1950s, Robert Dahl traced a trend that he summarized as 'from cumulative to dispersed inequalities' (1961: 85–6). He traced four broad stages in the city's political history. From colonial times until around 1840, it had been dominated by a tiny 'patrician' elite, members of old families who simultaneously held most of the available forms of power resource: besides their wealth and high social standing, they provided the elders of the Congregational Church, were the most highly educated and filled the political offices. The 'elect' were also the elected. Then, from about 1840 until towards the end of the nineteenth century, the arrival of industry and wealthy businessmen drove a wedge between social standing and education on the one hand – which remained with the patricians – and business and public life on the other. These were the decades of 'the entrepreneurs', when the leaders of local industry overtook the patricians in wealth and held the major elected offices in local government. Next, the early decades of the twentieth century witnessed the rise of what Dahl calls 'the ex-plebes': upwardly mobile representatives of groups formerly at the foot of the social scale, especially the children and grandchildren of people who had arrived in New Haven as immigrants – the Irish and Italians among many others. They were not wealthy, and their route to public prominence depended principally on their electoral popularity. Their arrival further fragmented the distribution of local political resources, a fragmentation that proceeded so far that Dahl contended that after the Second World War a long-term transition 'from oligarchy to pluralism' culminated in the dominance of the 'new men' – the fourth stage – principally professional politicians whose power derived essentially from their political skills in formulating policies behind which they could assemble sufficiently broad alliances from among the many competing interest groups in the city.

There was much debate among sociologists and political scientists about whether Dahl had proved his case (Lukes, 1974). In particular, had he taken sufficient account of the possibility of 'covert power'? Was it not possible that the politicians were in practice tailoring their policies in advance to make them acceptable to members of an economic elite who did not themselves hold public office but could, from behind the scenes, block policies inimical to their interests? Although there is no need to explore this question in detail here, it is indirectly germane to a broader issue. Did Dahl's study refute that of C. Wright Mills (1956), who had sought to demonstrate that, above the local and middle levels of open, pluralist competition in public life, there was a military–industrial power elite at the apex of American national life? Mills and Dahl, however, agreed upon one thing: the old kind of 'good society' was no longer central to the exercise of power in America.

The New Haven study casts especially interesting light on the fate of the 'patricians', the descendants of the old-established families who formed an early quasi-aristocracy in the Northeast. At the time of Dahl's study half a century ago, the patricians no longer played any discernible part in local politics. They still formed a clearly defined and highly connected local network, and attended such exclusive events as annual 'high society' coming-out balls for the daughters of the best families. In spite of what has been said earlier about the *nouveaux riches* crashing into the old social elite in the Gilded Age, in New Haven the social elite overlapped little if at all with the wealthy corporate elite. Nor does there seem to have been much sign of members of other social groups desperately anxious to be accepted into the old social elite, and striving to emulate their ways in order to do so.

New Haven may have been an extreme case. Besides the proliferating etiquette books in the late nineteenth century, another sign of the fluidity of the upper class was the *Social Register* which, in separate editions for several major cities, listed the membership of the social elite in each (Baltzell, 1953). This formalization would have been unnecessary earlier, when the view would no doubt have been that if one had to ask, one was definitely not a member. On the other hand, this was also a sign that the old social elites were essentially local rather than national, and in a society that was then, as it is now, marked by high geographical mobility, such works of reference were at least useful to newcomers.

One major difference between the USA and nearly all European countries is that it created a new capital city that has not become its pre-eminent commercial, financial or cultural centre. Even at the end of the nineteenth century, 100 years after John and Abigail Adams first occupied the White House, Washington society could not compete in social prestige with the old families of Philadelphia, Boston or New York. Only in 1900 was a *Social Register* published for the nation's political capital. It listed 2,100 families, 40 per cent of whom were either people already listed in one of the other *Social Registers* or members of Congress, senior government officials, army and navy officers, or foreign diplomats who were not necessarily long-term residents of the District of Columbia. When members of old families such as Henry Adams, Henry Cabot Lodge and Theodore Roosevelt came to live permanently in the capital, they 'raised Washington's social standing simply by moving there' (Zimmerman, 2002: 179). Other cities continued to be effective rivals to Washington as model-setting centres in matters social, cultural and economic. Richard Wade pinpointed the widespread effect this has continued to have:

> Unlike the Old World, where capitals dominated the nation because of their mixture of public and private functions, the American pattern has been dispersal rather than concentration. New York, to be sure, has had an unchallenged supremacy in many fields, but it lacked the political dimension which could have given it the national domination of a Paris, London, Rome or Berlin. The pattern meant, too, that while other places suffer from a 'second city' psychology, they have escaped the 'provincial city' relationship. In every part of the country the regional capital, like Chicago, Atlanta, Houston, San Francisco, or Detroit, is self-contained enough to exercise an independent influence over a large hinterland. (Wade, 1968: 191)

Again, the USA and Germany offer an interesting comparison. Until the nineteenth century, Germany remained a land of numerous little statelets (with a few larger states emerging around the periphery of the German-speaking region); if they differed greatly in their political and military power, the many regional cities and courts served effectively as regional social and cultural model-setting centres. Even after the Franco-Prussian War and the designation of the King of Prussia as German Emperor, subsidiary kings and their courts endured until 1918. Elias (1996) stresses the problems faced by people who held a clear rank in their own local good society but who were unknown in other cities, notably in Berlin when it became the national capital. He argues that *Satisfaktionsfähigkeit* – being judged socially qualified to challenge and be challenged to fight a duel, mainly through having been a member at university of one of the fighting fraternities – provided a kind of common social currency transferable from one city to another. In America, something similar happened in the twentieth century, though to a lesser extent. Baltzell (1958: 13) contended that there had gradually emerged an 'inter-city aristocracy', based on acquaintanceships formed at fashionable boarding schools, universities and clubs more than on family connections. Eventually, from 1977 onwards, *The Social Register* was no longer published in separate city editions, appearing only as a single national edition. Its continued existence testifies that family connection, if diminished in importance, remains of some significance, at least for those who belong to it (Broad, 1996). What is more doubtful, again as in the local case of New Haven, is whether there are any longer large numbers of outsiders trying to emulate the manners and mores of the social elite of old families and crash into these circles. One *Social Register* does not signify the formation of a single model-setting social elite in the USA much resembling those that existed in the past in European countries.

A significant absence: an aristocracy of office

One form of elite that has never strongly developed in the USA is an aristocracy of office. In many parts of the world and in many periods of history, people who hold offices under the state have formed some of the most powerful groupings in their societies. They range from the mandarins over much of Chinese history to the *noblesse de robe* in *ancien régime* France (surviving in attenuated form even in republican France today in the form of what Pierre Bourdieu [1996] called the *noblesse d'état*), and from the *Junker* bureaucracy in Prussia or the officialdom of Habsburg Austria to the *nomenklatura* of the Soviet Union. Their power derived essentially from their relationship to and position within the apparatus of the state, although in the longer term that form of power resource typically also leads to the accumulation of wealth and status honour too.[14] In America, what in German is called *Amtscharisma* – the charisma of office that helps people to feel that they should obey, emulate or defer to the office *per se* rather than to its holder *pro tempore* – has been only weakly evident. It is not entirely absent. Americans still appear commonly to have feelings of deference towards the President as head of government because he is also head of state, and the same may be true to some extent of other very senior offices such as the Justices of the Supreme Court and Senators. Mark Twain's Tom Sawyer was disappointed, when a Senator visited his town, to find that holders of this vaunted office were not 12 feet tall but of the same stature as other human beings. Perhaps since the Second World War some charisma has begun to attach itself to the American military officer corps. But, on the whole and despite such prominent dynasties as the Adamses, the Roosevelts, the Kennedys and the Bushes, the respect accorded to public office has not been a major source of intergenerational elite formation. *Amtscharisma* has not been a significant ingredient in the formation of American habitus, which is far less oriented to the state than to the market.

Conclusion

A number of quasi-aristocracies have existed in America. Southern planters, northern educated elites and the super-rich have all left their mark here and there on American social character to this day. Other groups have left their mark too, if only as implicit reference groups rather than as acknowledged social superiors – including the Hollywood and media celebrities of the twentieth century and (to be discussed in chapter 8) the frontiersmen of the nineteenth century. These are not to be thought of as separate ingredients or 'factors' in some actually non-existent homogeneous American habitus; rather, they have served as a source of conflict between groups and also to some extent conflicts *within* modern American individuals.

None of the dissimilar quasi-aristocracies established a clear central monopoly position. None of them acquired on a national scale the four interrelated characteristics of European 'good societies' seen in the writings of Elias. Rather, they competed with each other. The Civil War was the most dramatic instance of conflict between (among many other things) different elite ways of life. Nor is this competition merely a thing of the past: since about 1970, in accordance with political realignment and a shifting balance of economic power between North and South, there has been a reassertion of the prominence of the southern tradition in the overall flavour of the USA.

Emulation of social 'superiors' – more powerful groups – whether by restrained respectability or by the imitation of consumption-oriented lifestyle, has played a part in the USA as it does everywhere, yet it is not the whole key to understanding the formation of American character. Questions of manners and lifestyle appear to have been relegated to the highly competitive middle levels of power in American society. Above that pluralist middle may tower the power elite of the military–industrial complex, but it is a general rule of thumb that those who wield real economic and political power are less concerned with manners, the display of conspicuous self-constraint and 'setting an example' than are groups whose power position is under threat or ambiguous.

In short, although there is plentiful evidence of the social constraint towards self-constraint in the development of American society, it appears to have stemmed somewhat less than in Europe from intense status competition, and much more emphatically from the pressures exerted by people's interweaving into long chains of interdependence – most especially from the constraints imposed by markets. The forces of the market have left an imprint in all modern industrial societies, but the 'American Dream' makes their impact especially severe in the USA. For it amounts to a belief that, in a market-based society, everyone has an equal chance to succeed – to gain wealth and social status – through his or her own individual efforts. That in itself imposes a severe incentive for self-discipline. This idea is explored further in the next chapter.

5
The Market Society

Aristocracy may be engendered by manufactures. . . . if ever permanent inequality of conditions and aristocracy again penetrate into the world, it may be predicted that this is the channel by which they will enter.

Every man allows himself to be put in leading-strings, because he sees that it is not a person or a class of persons, but the people at large that holds the end of his chain.

Tocqueville, *Democracy in America*
(1961 [1835–40]: II, 190, 194, 382)

The consequences for American social character and culture of there never having been a court society, nor any single social formation that performed a similar role as a central standard-setting elite, have been considerable. Tocqueville was among the earliest to comment upon the tendency towards conformism in such a 'democratic' society. In matters of everyday social behaviour, as well as cultural taste and style, this was the equivalent of the 'tyranny of the majority' in the realm of politics. He was well aware of the paradox that such a society promoted both individualism and a regression to the social mean. A century later, David Riesman spoke of an 'other-directed' type of character becoming dominant in America. The common feature of other-directed people, he wrote, was 'that their contemporaries are the source of direction for the individual – either those known to him or those with whom he is indirectly acquainted, through friends or through the mass media' (Riesman et al., 1961 [1950]: 21). Their behaviour was not guided solely by what Elias termed 'external constraints', however. Rather, the dependence on guidance by others was internalized early in life through socialization. 'Paying close attention to the signals from others' became deeply habituated, and permitted 'a close behavioural conformity ... through an exceptional sensitivity to the actions and wishes of others' (ibid.: 21–2).

From this, if Riesman was right, a striking conclusion may be drawn: a society lacking any social formation resembling a court society may make *everyone a courtier*. For, as Elias (2006a) showed, *within* the absolutist court in early modern Europe the art of observing oneself and others became highly developed, and a sensitivity to subtleties of speech and conduct was essential to keeping or improving one's own position in the courtly hierarchy. The members of the court, moreover, became entrapped in its routines so that it was a risky strategy to attempt to break out of them.

The parallel is not exact. Courtiers were not striving especially to be liked, which was one of the central features of Riesman's other-directed people:

> [This] need for approval and direction from others – and contemporary others rather than ancestors – goes beyond the reasons that lead most people in any era to care very much what others think of them. While all people want and need to be liked by some of the people some of the time, it is only the modern other-directed types who make this their chief source of direction and chief area of sensitivity. (Riesman: 1961: 22)

Nor is this a matter simply of personality structure and everyday social interaction. It extends to matters of cultural taste – as again Tocqueville observed in the second volume of *Democracy in America*, and as Elias noted in his 1935 essay on kitsch where he spoke of the 'tension between the highly-formed taste of the specialists and the undeveloped, unsure taste of mass society' (2006b: 92). Social standards of taste and behaviour form in such a society through something akin to the impersonal (as they seem to any single one of the persons who enact them) mechanisms of the marketplace.[1] What emerge are a standard practice, a going rate, a common style, a typical taste, a conventional wisdom, a market price. In this chapter, this principle will be explored in relation to the social effects of actual markets and large-scale organizations.

The constraints of the market

The effects of spreading markets on social character in early capitalist societies have been widely discussed, from Karl Marx and Max Weber through Karl Polanyi and Norbert Elias to Barrington Moore, Jr. In an essay that is actually about Britain, Moore states well the essence of the argument:

> Creditworthiness came to epitomize the desired moral qualities of the busi-
> nessman as the use of credit became more and more an important aspect of
> business life despite suspicions and hostilities that survived from an agrar-
> ian era. A creditworthy man was a dependable man, especially in repaying
> his debts. He displayed all the new – that is, non-aristocratic – virtues of
> thrift, prudence, and steady application to work. Outwardly he gave no sign
> of emotionally or financially distracting ties and expenses. His house, fur-
> niture, horse and carriage should be of good quality, but definitely not
> showy. Above all there should be no signs of a taste for champagne and
> sexual variety. (1998: 25)

This pithily makes the connection between 'respectability', the 'civilizing'
of behaviour and creditworthiness. In the early stages of the growth of
capitalist economies, credit was local and relatively personal. As many
English novels of the eighteenth and nineteenth centuries depict, people
(including local bankers) often found themselves in financial trouble from
having helped out friends and acquaintances who proved less reliable
than they seemed. In Britain, the danger diminished during the nineteenth
century through legislation and through the growth of national and
central banking institutions. In the USA, credit remained for longer less
well developed and more local.[2]

Max Weber recorded many concrete illustrations of the constraints
imposed by the market in America during his 1904 visit. In perhaps the
nearest he ever came in his writings to telling a joke, he recalled a story
told him by a German doctor who had set up practice in a Midwestern
town. One of his early patients made a remark that puzzled him. Just
before lying down to undergo his medical examination, he announced,
'Sir, I am a member of the – Baptist Church in – Street'. Not understanding the relevance of this information to the man's medical condition, the
doctor asked an American colleague what its significance might be. The
American smiled, and explained that the patient was telling the doctor
that he need not worry about his fee being paid (Weber, 1946: 304).
Weber commented:

> Admission to the local Baptist congregation follows only upon the most
> careful 'probation' and after closest inquiries into conduct going back to
> early childhood (Disorderly conduct? Frequenting taverns? Dance? Theatre?
> Card Playing? Untimely meeting of liability? Other Frivolities?). . . .
> Admission to the congregation is recognized as an absolute guarantee of the
> moral qualities of a gentleman, especially of those qualities required in busi-
> ness matters. Baptism secures to the individual the deposits of the whole
> region and unlimited credit without any compensation. (Ibid.: 303)

Thus it was crucial that membership of a sect provided a certificate of an
individual's moral standing, and especially his business morals. In this

respect, membership of a 'sect' was of much greater value than membership of a 'church', into which a person is born and which 'lets grace shine
over the righteous and unrighteous alike'. By extension, expulsion from
one's sect for moral offences could mean financial and social disaster,
through loss of credit and social standing. Beyond that, however, precisely
which sect one belonged to was largely irrelevant: 'It does not matter
whether one be a Freemason, Christian Scientist, Adventist, Quaker or
what not. What is decisive is that one be admitted to membership by
"ballot", after an *examination* and an ethical *probation*' (ibid.: 307).
Furthermore, Weber observed that by the late nineteenth century, the
function of certifying the social respectability and financial trustworthi-
ness of members was becoming secularized: it was increasingly fulfilled
not just by religious sects, but also by a wide variety of clubs and frater-
nal societies to which members were admitted by ballot.[3] Weber did not
list them, but he was no doubt thinking of associations found in most
towns, like Rotary, Odd-Fellows, Foresters and so on, as well as the more
elite and exclusive social clubs of the great cities. He noticed that many
middle-class American men, especially outside the biggest cities and
outside areas of recent immigrant settlement, wore lapel pins denoting
their membership. It was an outward sign of an inner constraint to the
maintenance of respectability, particularly in business.

Norbert Elias, in whose discussion of civilizing processes in Europe
such prominence is given to the doings of courtiers, is often seen as standing in opposition to Max Weber's stress on the discipline imposed on
bourgeois tradespeople by market relationships. This is a misunderstanding. Although he argued that historians and sociologists had previously
overlooked the significance of the 'courtization' of warriors as an earlier
phase in the growth of the social constraint towards self-constraint, he did
not argue that self-restraint was uniquely severe in courtly circles, nor that
it is *exclusively* from the cultural legacy of those circles that the pattern
of restraints in modern society is derived. In fact, in many asides comparing the constraints of life at court with those found in middle-class
professional and commercial society, Elias acknowledged the latter to be
the more compelling. For one thing, it was only towards their peers that
court people needed to subject themselves to great constraint, and far less
towards their social inferiors inside and outside the court.

> The masking of spontaneous impulses . . . did not have the same form and
> structure in the framework of court society as it has in the pacified middle
> classes that are brought up to earn their living by work, or in all the other
> strata of industrial societies whose members are subject to the constraints
> of work and career. In court society the armour [of self-constraint] was not
> yet as all-embracing and automatic as in these working societies, since the

greater inequality of people – the subjection, dependence and submissiveness of the lower-ranking, particularly the poorer strata – always opened a broad social field to court people in which affective impulses of all kinds could be openly expressed. (2006a: 258)

In middle-class professional and commercial society, the occupational functions – competition for capital and wealth, the acquisition of professional skills, success in business – are far more central to social existence and esteem, and through the occupational sphere people of all classes are far more closely bonded to each other. Professional and commercial people in the nineteenth century were shaped above all by the necessities of careers demanding regulated work and the subjection of the affects to routine; overall, the pressures upon them were more demanding than those upon courtiers. But the aspects of sociability once so central to the existence of the courtier – ornamentation and furnishing of a house, visiting etiquette, the rituals of eating and the rest – were now relegated to 'private life' and no longer shaped so directly or intensely. They received their impress more indirectly, as a function of occupational situations and interests (2006a: 123–6).[4] Thus Elias was by no means out of step with Weber in contending that the spreading web of economic interdependence exerted growing 'pressure towards foresight and self-constraint' (2000: 379–82), foresight including rationalization and the advance of the threshold of shame and embarrassment.

Arguably, Elias uncharacteristically accepted too uncritically the sociological orthodoxy about the constraints of the market and the connection between creditworthiness and 'respectability'. For one thing, as Newton (2003) has argued, the development of banking and more impersonal institutional arrangements for credit probably diminished the strength of the specifically 'civilizing' pressures that they exerted. But, in any case, even at the earlier stage, the connection between respectability and creditworthiness was at least two-way. The dependence of a person's credit standing on his or her respectability was at least as much the result of the prior development of very strong social codes as the codes were of the power of credit.

Elias's line of thought was taken up and developed with particular reference to American history by Thomas Haskell (1985). His concern was to explain the connection between the spread of market relationships and the 'rise of humanitarian sensibility' – an aspect of what Elias referred to as the widening of circles of mutual identification – and especially the anti-slavery movement. How was it that market relationships apparently characterized by the pursuit of self-interest were nevertheless associated with a shift in the conventions of moral responsibility, notably towards slaves? After reviewing the opinions of Marxists, Weber and Foucault, Haskell drew on the theory of civilizing processes: 'What altered cognitive style in a "humanitarian" direction was not in the first instance the ascendancy of a new class, or the assertion by that class of a new configuration of interests, but rather the expansion of the market, the intensification of discipline . . . [and] the power of market discipline to inculcate altered perceptions of causation in human affairs' (1985: 342). Changed perceptions could effect changes in feelings, just as much as emotions influence perception. Incongruous as it may seem, observed Haskell,

> the boundaries we observe today between good and bad manners could prove to be seamlessly interwoven both with the 'capitalist' conventions that authorize the individual to adopt a comparatively high level of aggressiveness in economic affairs and with the 'humanitarian' conventions that inhibit us from taking pleasure in (or even remaining indifferent to) the agony of others. (Ibid.: 548)

There is an enduring paradox here, which Haskell met head on. The rules of the nineteenth-century marketplace apparently sanctioned unrestrained self-interest – unrestrained because of the widespread belief that the laws of supply and demand automatically transmute each individual's self-interest into the greater good of the greater number. If that were indeed true,

> no one need be concerned with the public interest. Once this lesson with its time bomb of anti-traditional implications was incorporated into common sense, the very possibility of moral obligation was put in doubt; the burden of proof henceforth rested on those who wished to deny that 'everything is permitted'. (Ibid.: 549)

This very idea has been more or less influential throughout American history, never more so than at the beginning of the twenty-first century. Haskell contends, however, that the burden of proof was mitigated by the market itself. Implicitly echoing Durkheim's dictum that 'not everything that is in the contract is contractual',[5] Haskell points out that the marketplace is not a Hobbesian war of all against all, and that 'many holds are barred'. Success in business requires not just shrewdness and pugnacity, but also restraint, and market discipline taught people two things: first, to keep their promises; and second, to attend to more remote consequences of their actions (ibid.: 550–1).[6]

About the first of these there need be little dispute: keeping promises is much in line with what Weber argued. People constrained to keep their promises came to assume that countless others similarly constrained could be trusted to keep their promises. Yet,

> The norm of promise keeping (observed often in the breach, as all norms are) is so basic to the form of life that prevails today that we take it for

granted, forgetting how recently it came into being and at what cost, in terms of instinctual [*sic*] renunciation, this stage of the 'civilizing process' was attained. (Ibid.: 551)

Haskell points out that breach of promise between individuals was beyond the scope of royal law in the Middle Ages; and even in the eighteenth century, when state-formation processes had greatly advanced, contract law by no means formed so large and dominant an element in common and statutory law at the time of Blackstone's *Commentaries on the Laws of England* (1765–9) as it became later. Contracts are both promises and 'recipes, for . . . new ways of acting on the world, new recipes for producing desired events', and the explosion of contract law in the century between 1770 and 1870 is a measure of the 'increasing frequency of recipe usage and the burgeoning fund of recipe knowledge available to the merchants, manufacturers, artisans and improving farmers of England and America in these years' (ibid.: 556).[7]

The recipes provided by the burgeoning law of contract are also the basis for Haskell's contention that the market taught people to attend to more remote consequences of their actions. This echoes Elias's stress on the significance of lengthening 'chains of interdependence'. Yet, while the significance of these legal developments must be acknowledged, it appears to me that this second prong of Haskell's thesis is more problematic than that concerning trust and promise-keeping. As he himself pointed out, the belief that the laws of supply and demand automatically transmute the pursuit of self-interest into the common good might be taken to imply that no one need concern him- or herself with questions of the public interest. In other words, while markets may have led to a concern for reputation, integrity and respectability in one's dealings with the people with whom one dealt directly, faith in what Adam Smith famously called the 'hidden hand' of the market may equally have absolved one of any need to consider the wider repercussions of one's activities. That very strand of thought has always been to a greater or lesser extent influential in American business and politics, and at times the hidden hand has seemed to be identified with the hand of God.

The issue is blurred by the tendency of sociologists and historians from Max Weber onwards to refer to 'the market' as if markets were all of a piece. But markets, besides being mechanisms for the allocation of resources, are also structures of power – widely different structures, moreover, in which the distribution of power chances varies greatly.[8] It therefore seems unlikely that different markets will impose exactly the same patterns of constraint on all the people who do business within them. Indeed, that was implicitly recognized in the American political system before economists had fully conceptualized different market structures:

federal 'anti-trust' legislation in the late nineteenth and early twentieth centuries was designed to impede the abuse of monopoly power by the 'Robber Barons' of the Gilded Age, but it was also not unconnected with the unease that was felt during the Progressive era about the extravagant and sometimes 'immoral' lifestyle of the super-rich.

Later, from the 1920s and 1930s onwards, economists were to conceptualize different market power structures in a series of models or ideal-types:[9] perfect competition, imperfect competition, oligopoly and monopoly. Weber's discussions of the constraints imposed by 'the' market appear to be concerned chiefly with small businessmen trading in perfect or near-perfect markets; and Elias and Haskell, among many others, have followed him in that respect. A perfect market is one in which – among many other technical conditions – there are many buyers and sellers, none conspicuously more powerful than the others, so there is no possibility of collusion and no single trader can exert much influence over price. Here, in the helplessness of the producer to affect the price at which he can sell, lies some affinity with the Calvinist doctrine of predestination with which, since Weber, discussions of the rise of capitalism have been entangled (Goudsblom, 1977: 189–90). The model of perfect competition has great emotional appeal, because it is the economic counterpart of the classic political model of liberal democracy, in which equal and well-informed individuals form their political opinions independently of anyone's power to manipulate them. Both models have diminishing reality-adequacy in the modern world.

Such a market structure will be conducive to maintaining a reputation for personal integrity and promise-keeping, but whether and how it is conducive to attending to the more remote consequences of one's actions is a more open question. It is easy to see how the necessity of maintaining a reputation for integrity and respectability in one's local community and among the people with whom one directly traded would give rise to strong pressures towards conformism. That is especially clear in relation to standards of honesty in commerce, and perhaps to the avoidance of personal extravagance ('champagne'), but in regard to other matters not directly linked to trading ('sexual variety', for instance), the standards to which conformity was demanded did not arise directly from the exigencies of the economic mesh itself. They arose from broader social standards, whose dominance originated, for example, in widespread religious conventions; the link to the commercial world arose from the fact that in a world of numerous small traders, if one's customers or suppliers disapproved of one's morality, they could wreak great damage on one's business.

But such markets are not conducive to very elaborate forms of foresight and long-term strategy towards a complex world at a distance. They are more likely to result in the assumption that the unknown competitors, customers and suppliers far away down chains of market relationships are much the same as the people with whom one immediately deals; and if one conforms to the fairly simple rules that ensure a reputation for integrity and respectability in one's local community and among one's immediate customers and suppliers, that is as much as one can do to ensure one's prosperity and survival in the wider and anonymous marketplace.

This simple logic may retain some force in rural and small-town communities, which still account for a larger proportion (at least geographically) of America than of most other advanced industrial countries. But today, few businesspeople in big cities and major corporations are operating in perfect markets. The power ratios between buyers and sellers may be very unequal. Rather than being at the mercy of impersonal market forces over which they have no control, rival businesspeople know exactly against whom they are competing. (Between rival firms, it is true, the power ratios may be more even, and competitors may hold each other in check.) Economists use complex models of game-playing to understand and predict the behaviour of small numbers of competitors in such oligopolistic and near-monopoly markets. People who run vast multinational corporations do have to peer down long chains of consequences; they have to plan complex strategies and seek to have long-term foresight. But there is little evidence that the corporate super-rich are subject to the kinds of market constraint upon their personal morality and rectitude that Weber depicted. A taste for champagne and sexual variety may be tolerated as long as it is associated with growing shareholder value. The actions and reactions of governments or powerful rivals do have to be taken into account, but weaker players – such as small suppliers (perhaps in other countries) – as well as wider consequences (which economists call externalities) such as pollution and environmental degradation can safely be ignored.

At the beginning of the twenty-first century, even the capacity of markets to enforce standards of basic honesty appear to be called in question by a series of scandals involving major American corporations.[10] Senior executives were found to have pursued personal gain by means of false accounting, false statements to share markets and false public relations to inflate stock prices. In such organizations, the values being absorbed appear to be deception and the ruthless pursuit of competitive survival. It remains to be seen whether such scandals presage a longer-term trend to the corruption of corporate organizations as the key emergent social form of the modern world. They are enough, however, to prompt a serious reflection on the world since the collapse of the communist bloc. The faults of the USSR and other communist countries convinced many that a strong state was in itself wrong, and that civil society should be stronger and the state weaker. Today we can see that *both* a strong civil society *and* more effective states (and international organizations) capable of enforcing appropriate means of market regulation are essential to protect societies against depredations of the kind involved in such scandals.

The overall burden of this argument is the need for a certain caution about the effects of market constraint. There is no doubt that the experience of farmers and tradespeople has left its stamp upon American social character, particularly given the relative weakness of the influence of a dominant 'good society' or of warrior elites that have left a strong mark in many other countries. It helps to entrench a habit of plain dealing and a high degree of everyday civility in face-to-face interaction – 'have-a-nice-day' manners. Whether it fosters a concern with more remote consequences of one's actions – an awareness of externalities and seeking to deal with them for the general good – is more debatable. There is some psephological evidence that American voters who most fervently adhere to 'small-town values' are also those who reject personal responsibility for the more remote consequences of their own activities, for instance, on the world's environment. This is not to deny the broad validity of the argument that longer chains of interdependence force 'more people . . . more often to pay more and more attention to more other people',[11] but that operates in tandem with another Eliasian idea: functional democratization – that is, the power ratios along the chains of interdependence must also be becoming relatively more equal. In markets, that does not appear to be the case.

Not so many Americans are now small independent businessmen, even if there remains a social legacy from when more of them were. On the other hand, the expansion of big business is part of a broader trend towards large-scale organizations of many types. Most Americans now work in such large-scale organizations, the constraints imposed by which may in recent decades have left a greater imprint on the American habitus than markets of the classic type now do.

The constraints of organization

Charles Perrow, the distinguished sociologist of organizations, has pointed out that while Americans celebrate individualism and entrepreneurship, well over 90 per cent of the American workforce today works for someone else, in return for a wage or salary. In 1800, only about 20 per cent did so. Moreover, in excess of half of all gainfully employed Americans work for organizations with 500 or more employees; in 1800, the corresponding figure was nil (2002: 1). True, the particular workplace where people are employed may be much smaller, but along with many other such units it forms part of and is *controlled by* some much bigger organization. Those organizations include government agencies (federal, state and local) and big voluntary-sector organizations (churches, school systems, charities), but among them the large capitalist corporation is especially prominent. Among the corporations, in turn, although industrial businesses typically remain the biggest on average, the large service-sector corporations are catching them up.

The level of affluence enjoyed by Americans would not be possible without large organizations, and yet Perrow is 'troubled' by several consequences of their scale and dominance that are at odds with the national we-image of individualism and entrepreneurship. These consequences include: the centralization of surpluses and concentration of wealth and power; externalities; the promotion of the 'structural interests' of the organization; and the 'absorption of society' and the socialization of employees and customers to the needs of the organization.

Wage dependence – the fact that most employees work for their organization for fixed wages – tends to result in the concentration of surpluses at the top within the organization, and the wider effect is the concentration of wealth and power in society as a whole. 'The accumulation of wealth and power through large organizations', writes Perrow (2002: 16), 'is the modern device for generating inequality.' This is clearly evident at the beginning of the twenty-first century, when economic inequality in American society is growing spectacularly (see chapter 10 below).

Large organizations, lightly regulated, are able to pass off onto the rest of society the costs of some of the consequences of their activities – consequences that economists call 'externalities'. Such obvious external effects of industrial production as dirt and pollution have been discussed by economists since the nineteenth century: the factory chimney pumping out smoke caused increased cleaning costs, but not to the owner of the factory. Other familiar externalities include the exhaustion of natural resources, workplace accidents and industrial diseases, the costs of rectifying and treating which all typically fall on a wider social entity than the perpetrating firm. Perrow lists several more examples: 'the externalities of urban overcrowding, the failure to smooth production resulting in boom-and-bust cycles and layoffs, and some of our military adventures to secure investments and markets abroad' (ibid.: 16). The common feature is that, since these costs are not included in the price of the goods and service produced, they are borne by everyone, not just those who buy the goods and services.

The economists' concept of externalities is closely connected to the sociologists' notion of unintended or unforeseen consequences of social action. But externalities may be neither unforeseen not unintended – all that is necessary is that an organization can get away with not meeting the cost. Or, more cogently, any single firm or organization may contend that it cannot assume responsibility for such external costs because its competitors are not assuming them; any single firm or organization would therefore be placed at a competitive cost disadvantage in the market. The only way out of this dilemma is for governments to enforce regulations requiring *all* competitors to follow the same rules. This has often been the case in the past with legislation on employment law or health and safety at work, to prevent the exploitation and endangerment of workers. The federal system has often served to make such measures less effective in the USA than in many other advanced economies. In the case of the major externalities of the modern world, such as environmental pollution and global warming, effective regulation would have to be worldwide – difficult enough at the present stage of development of international institutions, and even more difficult when the world's most powerful country does not recognize the necessity.

More immediately relevant to the effects of large organizations on social habitus, Perrow contends that they develop 'structural interests' of their own; they become collective actors or agents in their own right, with needs and collective preferences of their own. Increasingly, they socialize people to fit their needs. 'From working in organizations, we get organizationally friendly habits of the heart and organizationally friendly cognitive patterns of the mind, stemming from unobtrusive controls over, and extensive socialization of, personnel and even customers' (ibid.: 13). Furthermore, it became apparent in the second half of the twentieth century that large organizations tend to 'absorb society'; that is, they 'wittingly and unwittingly absorb the functions performed by smaller autonomous units of society such as families, kinship networks, local churches, and small governmental units and businesses, weakening those parts of society that are not governed by an employment contract' (ibid.: 15).

It is debatable, as Perrow concedes (ibid.: 6–7), whether all these effects are characteristics not of large organizations as such but of the form of *capitalism* in which large organizations flourish. But, he points out, many of the worrying features of big economic organizations are replicated by big non-economic organizations: 'Big churches and federal governments also centralize power, socialize employees to bureaucratic values, "deskill" them unnecessarily, and generate their own "externalities" . . . that are shifted on to a fragile environment or fragile groups within the polity' (ibid.: 2).

Moral alarm at these trends is not new. In the decade after the Second World War, when a particularly strong spurt in the growth of large organizations became evident, there appeared (besides Riesman et al.'s *The Lonely Crowd*, already mentioned) famous books by Vance Packard (*The*

Hidden Persuaders, 1957), and William H. Whyte (*The Organization Man*, 1956). Both were concerned with aspects of the capacity of large organizations to 'socialize' employees and customers – Packard with manipulation of the public by big business and the media, and Whyte with the absorption of workers' whole identity into their employing organizations. Half a century later, on the other hand, Richard Sennett drew attention to the deleterious human consequences of its becoming less likely that people had a job for life within the same organization, and how the increasingly common pattern of having to switch frequently between quite different forms of employment led to 'the corrosion of character' (1998), the loss of a person's public identity.

Setting aside any question of the morality or desirability of these tendencies, however, it should be acknowledged that the effects of large organizations on the people they employ have some of the characteristics of a civilizing process. That is to say, a common thread in these arguments is that modern organizations impose an increasing social constraint towards self-constraint, including more demanding standards of emotion management. The lingering positive value-connotations of the word 'civilization' (see p. 5 above) may obscure this basic fact, because organizations are seen to promote such qualities as 'conformism' towards which an ideological disapproval is widely shared. But that does not refute the proposition that such qualities are the outcome of 'civilizing' pressures.

A specific instance concerns negotiating skills, which modern organizations require to a very demanding standard. As Mastenbroek (1999) has pointed out, the development of negotiating techniques is a neglected facet of the long-term civilizing process. In medieval and early modern Europe, negotiations frequently broke down in violence. Negotiators were advised not to show their true emotions, to stay cold and calculating. In contrast, in the age of modern organizations, Mastenbroek (1999: 66) cites advice for negotiators as involving tactics such as:

• voice your demands with consideration for the interests of others;
• be friendly without giving in;
• design creative solutions while holding on to your interests;
• be assertive without forcing your way.

In other words, negotiators are expected to be able to handle a more flexible and differentiated form of self-control reminiscent of the 'informalization' phases in the development of manners in general. But such skills, into which organizations socialize their members, are also redolent of Riesman's 'other-directed' personality type, and of the avoidance of boat-rocking by 'organization man'.

Overall, Stokvis (1999) appears to be right in speaking of a modern 'commercial civilizing process', but its roots appear to lie more in the social constraints towards self-constraint imposed by large-scale and hierarchical organizations than in any stemming directly from the marketplace, as classical discussions from Weber onwards tended to imply.

The question then remains whether and why any of these consequences of large-scale organizations are more distinctively characteristic of American society than of other advanced industrial capitalist societies. Perrow pays special attention to the nineteenth-century American textile and railway industries in describing the development of big organizations of the modern type. The 'Lowell model' of textile manufacturing was, for instance, associated with highly standardized products and inflexibility, in contrast to the 'Philadelphia model' of flexible networks of small firms. But textile factories and railway networks were growing at the same time in Europe too. Were there any differences? In a valuable discussion, Perrow (2002: 16) offers an explanation that is very much in line with the arguments being made in the present book. The peculiarity of American history, he suggests, is that it permitted less regulation of the pursuit of wealth and power, and that pursuit took place 'over a socially and culturally unencumbered landscape'. In Europe, older elites – the landed classes, nobility, church and state bureaucracy – saw a new capitalist class as rivals for power, and feared large organizations would be beyond their control. They therefore imposed limits on the accumulation of capital, because they had the strength to do so. It was often members of such older social formations who sponsored measures to protect workers' rights – factory health and safety legislation, holiday entitlements, unemployment and old-age pensions. There is no need to assume that *all* their humanitarian sentiment was motivated by fear of the rival power of the new capitalists.

In the United States, in contrast, corresponding older social formations were weaker and had less power to place restrictions on capital. The colonial gentry and their successors, such as what we have called the New England *Bildungsbürgertum*, did not sufficiently monopolize any power resources to raise serious obstacles, even if they had the inclination. The southern quasi-aristocracy of planters probably had the inclination – hostility to capitalism was widespread in the ante-bellum South – but their power was broken in the Civil War. In consequence, while American citizens have commonly continued to fear *large government*, fear of *large private organizations* has not been so widespread. Despite intermittent enactment of (for example) anti-trust legislation, and its even more intermittent enforcement, few effective measures were taken to impede the growing size and power of organizations. Over the last quarter of a century, with the fashion for the privatization of government activities with the aim of reducing the scale of 'big government', they have often been handed over to other big and not dissimilar, but private, organizations. Organizational growth has generated great inequality. And, whatever impediments Europeans may initially have put in the way of these trends, those impediments have increasingly been undermined by the sheer scale of American global power, bringing with it the 'American model'.

Conclusion

Looking back over chapters 3, 4 and 5, it can be seen that the changes in social standards of behaviour and feeling that are central to Elias's theory of civilizing processes followed a broadly similar course in America to those which he and subsequent scholars have observed in Europe. It would have been surprising had they not, give that the first European settlers brought with them to America the 'mental outfit' of seventeenth-century Europe, and that from this starting point the two continents have remained in close contact and reciprocal influence ever since.

At every stage, however, commentators have seen American society as internally more egalitarian than European, and sought from this to account for distinctive features they saw in American habitus. Yes, there have been quasi-aristocracies in America, and emulation of the manners of higher strata by those who seek to climb the social ladder is evident there just as it is in Europe. But in America no single status elite has attained the kind of monopoly position seen in many European countries in the past.

Relative equality of social status – or at least the widespread assumption that America was a land of opportunity in which all could rise through their own efforts – was reflected in Americans taking for granted at a fairly early stage that standards of social behaviour applied to all, irrespective of social class. One would not, for instance, find that a manners book written in nineteenth-century America gave as a reason for acquiring skill in boxing – the 'gentlemanly art of self-defence' – the need to be able to 'knock down' a member of the lower orders who insulted a lady in the street, as a British book recommended ([Anon], 1859: 191–3). Rather, an American would be expected to be able to wreak vengeance on a culprit of any class, and not necessarily with only his fists. As so often, though, such generalizations do not apply in the South during slavery and its long aftermath, which followed the descendants of slaves into the cities of the North. The association of functional democratization with a widening of the circle of mutual identification – an idea that Tocqueville anticipated in his thesis about the 'softening of manners' as social conditions become more equal – seems well attested through American history, as long as the excluded outsiders are always remembered as exceptions. The relative informality and egalitarian style of everyday manners in America are widely assumed to be the product of an egalitarian society.

But that is to tell only half the story. To present equality as the rule and inequality as the exception diminishes the importance of the excluded exceptions in the process of forming the egalitarian style of social intercourse *against* those who were excluded from being real all-American people: slaves and their descendants, the 'Indians' and various immigrant groups who have not immediately fitted in easily. Criminals, 'socialists' and, recently, Hispanics have been seen as posing dangers from within; dangers from without have included the former colonial power (and its internal Tory sympathizers) in the early days of the Republic, through to communists and terrorists in recent decades. The fears generated by these perceived threats from within and without have exerted powerful pressure towards conformity to an American standard style, and helped forge strong we-feelings. But factually there has always been a very wide economic gap between the richest and poorest Americans, and in recent decades economic inequality has increased very rapidly. It will be interesting to see whether and how this comes to be reflected in *decreasing* circles of mutual identification. It may be that in America at the present day, as in several European countries in the past, an empire helps to sustain *all* Americans in we-feelings of superiority over the rest of the world, thus impeding the development of we- and they-feelings *within* American society.

One thing that has changed gradually in the force field of reciprocal influence between Europe and America is that the dominant part in model-setting has passed to the United States; in line with its assumption of economic, political and military supremacy, its cultural dominance has increased too. That America should have become the model-setting centre for the world *outside* is paradoxical in view of there not having been any single model-setting centre *within* the USA.

American society has remained more like a social and cultural marketplace, and indeed the market has in many respects been the central institution imprinting itself on American people in a less regulated and qualified way than was often the case in Europe. Yet markets, including labour markets, are also structures of power. Markets and large-scale organization, while on the one hand generating inequality, at the same time exert very considerable pressure towards standardization, conformity and adherence to rules.

6

Violence and Aggressiveness

Although the Americans have in a way reduced egotism to a philosophical theory, they are nevertheless extremely open to compassion. In no country is criminal justice administered with more mildness than in the United States. Whilst the English seem disposed carefully to retain the bloody traces of the dark ages in their penal legislation, the Americans have almost expunged capital punishment from their codes.

Tocqueville, *Democracy in America* (1961 [1835–40]: II, 199)

Tocqueville's usual prophetic insight may seem to have deserted him when he commented upon the compassion and mildness of Americans' feelings in the 1830s about crime and justice. Now the USA shares with the People's Republic of China and the feudal kingdom of Saudi Arabia the distinction of being one of the world's last principal bastions of judicial execution. More generally, Tocqueville's remark hardly accords with how the rest of the world tends to perceive America at the beginning of the twenty-first century. America is seen as a society with an astonishingly high rate of murder and other crimes of violence; a country where an obsession with the use of guns is elevated to an article of national faith; and where life – other people's – is held cheap (unless it be the life of an unborn foetus); where the circle of compassion – how 'other people' are defined – is narrow, as exemplified both in an extraordinarily high prison population within the USA and in the fact that the US Army of Occupation in Iraq after 2003 did not even keep any record of the number of Iraqis killed.

This perception is of course an unfair and unbalanced stereotype. Like most stereotypes, it contains just sufficient a small kernel of truth for it to grow like a snowball. A large proportion of American citizens feel as much distaste for that kernel of truth as do so many outsiders.

Figure 6.1: Window stickers, Homestead, PA, May 2001
Photograph by Pieter Spierenburg.

Why Tocqueville's observation now rings hollow raises a multitude of problems. It is not just the matter of capital punishment, which he specifically mentioned, but of whether the USA is in some more general sense 'a violent society', more violent than other comparable countries. To begin to answer that question, a distinction has to be drawn between long-term trends in violence on the one hand, and the absolute level of violence at any point in time on the other. Very broadly speaking, the *trends* in the long-term graph of violence have been similar in the USA and other Western countries, but actual *rates* of at least some forms of violent crime have tended to be higher in America. How is that to be explained?

Long-term trends in violence

Murder rates per 100,000 of the population are often taken as an index of levels of violence in a society generally. This is an oversimplification, and trends in lesser forms of interpersonal violence should also be taken specifically into account. But for comparative purposes, homicide – including manslaughter or unintentional homicide – is at least a *relatively* clear and unambiguous index, because recording it is likely to be a little more reliable than statistics of the many other forms of violence,

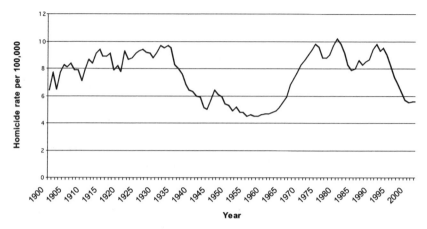

Figure 6.2: Homicide rate per 100,000 population
Sources: US Department of Commerce and Bureau of the Census (1975); US
Census Bureau, with corrections for 1900–32 from Eckberg (1995: 13).

the definitions of which both differ widely from one legal system to
another and change over time within particular jurisdictions. The relia-
bility of crime statistics is in general open to criticism, yet from a mass of
accumulated evidence, a reasonably consistent picture emerges.

Contrary to widespread popular belief, the long-term trend of homicide in Western societies has been downwards. Accumulating historical
data from England, Belgium, the Netherlands, Scandinavia, Germany,
Switzerland and Italy, Eisner (2001, 2003) shows that in Europe murder
rates are much lower than they were several centuries ago. Estimates for
the late Middle Ages range from 20 to 40 homicides per 100,000 population, in contrast to rates of between 0.5 and 1 per 100,000 in the mid-
twentieth century. The decline has not, however, traced a smooth curve.
There have been fluctuations, with strong upward spurts at certain
periods. The most recent such surge lasted from the early 1960s to the
early 1990s, when the downward trend was reasserted. It is now clear that
trends in the United States are much the same as in Europe (see figure
6.2).[1] This general pattern, which many criminologists now relate to
Elias's theory of civilizing processes, is remarkable. As Eisner (2005: 8)
has commented: 'Despite all the differences in political and social arrangements between the US and Europe, there appears to exist a staggering
commonality as regards the ups and downs of homicide rates.' The most
recent upward spurt in homicide rates began in the early 1960s, and came
to an end on both sides of the Atlantic in the early 1990s.

Both the long-term pattern of decline and the periodic upsurges stand
in need of explanation.

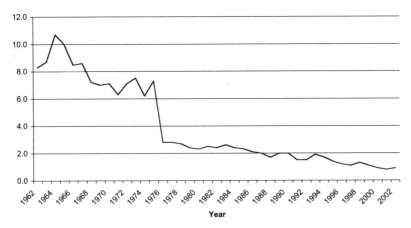

Figure 6.3: Percentage of all known murders arising from 'romantic triangle'
Sources: Stearns (1989: 161); US Census Bureau.

Among the first to notice the long-term downward trend of violence, French historians advanced what they called the *violence au vol* thesis (Spierenburg, 1996: 64). They contended that the feudal code of honour led to a preponderance of violent crime, but the transition to a market-based commercial society led to a shift towards the dominance of property crime. In effect, this is a corollary of the discussion in chapter 5 of the constraints more generally imposed by markets. When applied to America, the thesis has some appeal in helping to account for the persistence of higher levels of violence in the South, where slaveholding and its long aftermath may be thought to have served to some extent as a functional equivalent to European feudalism (see chapter 4). In his classic studies, Gurr (1981: 341–2) attributed the long-term decline more generally to a broader 'cultural change' in Western society, which he described as a 'growing sensitization to violence', coupled with 'increased internal and external controls of aggressive behaviour'.

One small sign that this is true of the USA as well as elsewhere is the decline in the proportion of all known murders attributed to jealousy and the 'romantic triangle'. Murders stemming from this kind of passion have been consistently higher in the South, with other regions showing rates around two-thirds of those in the South (Stearns, 1989: 161). But the trend in the nation as a whole has been steadily downwards ever since such statistics were first compiled in 1962 (see figure 6.3). Stearns (ibid.: 154–7) sketches the persistence to some extent until the 1970s of ambivalence towards the culpability of men – usually men – who killed their spouses's lovers. By the 1890s most states had rejected or curtailed the unwritten law that excused such killings on grounds of passion-induced insanity.

Significantly, however, that often went along with the enactment of laws criminalizing adultery. That is a clear case of the state claiming a monopoly of the legitimate use of violence, through eliminating the need for private vengeance by exacting punishment itself. Nevertheless, the defence of justifiable homicide persisted to some extent: for example, Texas permitted the killing of the lover if the couple were discovered still *in flagrante delicto*, although emotion must be fresh, and there must not be any element of planning and calculation.[2] As late as 1977, Georgia forbade the defence of justifiable homicide in an interestingly worded ruling: 'In this day of no-fault, on-demand divorce, when adultery is merely a misdemeanour . . . any idea that a spouse is ever justified in taking the life of another – adulterous spouse *or* illicit lover – to prevent adultery *is uncivilized*. This is murder' (quoted by P. N. Stearns, 1989: 156; my emphasis). Among other things, this suggests how changing attitudes to violence are linked to the processes of informalization discussed in chapter 3, and again illustrates how more apparently 'permissive' conventions often require more, not less, demanding standards of emotion management.[3]

The connection of all this with Elias's theory of civilizing processes is obvious.[4] To reiterate briefly, Elias's argument is that longer chains of interdependence, arising from the growth of trade and markets as well as the increasing scale and effectiveness of state apparatuses among other processes, increase the 'social constraint towards self-constraint' and towards greater habitual foresight. More habitual self-constraint over impulsive action goes hand in hand with the 'advance of the threshold of repugnance'; and that applies to anticipating in more complex ways the embarrassment that will arise from the reaction of other people not just if one misuses one's knife, fork or handkerchief, but also if one succumbs to violent impulses. What is more, it is suggested that longer chains of interdependence – and especially more even power ratios between the links – are associated with a 'widening circle of mutual identification'. Thus, it is argued, the pleasurable excitement that our ancestors experienced in the spectacle of burning heretics, public torture and executions came to be impeded by shame and repugnance, and came normally to find expression in only 'refined' and indirect forms. One prominent component of this transformation of the impulses of aggressiveness and cruelty identified by Elias is the transfer of emotions from direct action to spectating, a shift towards visual pleasures (2000: 170). That is illustrated by the rise of modern sports (Elias and Dunning, 1986; Dunning, 1999). The rules of many sports circumscribe the kinds and extent of violence that can be used, and the pleasure of spectators arises from the 'mimetic' character of the contest on the field.

For criminologists and historians of crime (notably Garland, 1990; 2001; Johnson and Monkkonen, 1996; Eisner, 2001; 2003: 87), the theory of civilizing processes has become a prominent component of their explanations of the long-term decline of homicide rates. Yet, however neatly the theory may predict the decline in 'romantic triangle' murders, its implications for homicides overall are not so clear-cut. The thesis about more extensive webs of interdependence exerting greater social constraint towards self-constraint applies more directly to 'impulsive' than to 'instrumental' violence.[5] Even if habitus changes in the direction of people's having a greater habitual capacity for controlling their aggressive and potentially violent impulses, why should the instrumentally rational use of violence decline? While the central thrust of the process is towards a specific type of conscience-formation, producing feelings of guilt and repugnance with regard to any pleasurable use of violence, is it not true, on the other hand, that increasing pressures towards competition, achievement and the demand for foresight actually facilitate the use of violence in an instrumental way?[6] Indeed, Spierenburg provocatively remarks that 'It would be an exercise in purging moral judgements from our scholarly view if we asked ourselves whether it is possible to commit a "civilized" murder' (1996: 69). But the distinction between 'expressive' and 'instrumental' – or 'affective' and 'rational' – violence is not dichotomous, rather a continuum; and, as Elias (2006a: 101–2) contends, rationalization is itself a process of emotional change.

Be that as it may, much historical research appears to support the notion that the spreading web of interdependence is linked to the downward trend in homicides overall. It was formerly conventional wisdom that industrialization and urbanization produced social chaos and rising levels of crime, but the opposite may rather be the case: that they 'were, rather, stabilizing forces that drove down crime' (Brown, 1991: 130). From England, and notably from Lane's detailed studies of nineteenth-century Boston and Philadelphia (1967; 1979), it would appear that 'the apparent increase of problem behaviour of all sorts . . . was not "real" but "official", the product of stricter standards more strictly enforced' (Lane, 1979: 119).[7] The increasing constraint towards self-constraint arose not just from more effective policing and administration in the cities, but also from the increasing discipline demanded in the industrial and bureaucratic workplace and in the classroom (Brown, 1991: 130). Besides, if Lane is right in attributing the pacification of the nineteenth century to more effective policing and administration, those forces will serve both to inculcate self-constraints over impulses to affective violence and *simultaneously* to deter instrumental violence.

Why, then, if such 'civilizing' changes in habitus constitute the fundamental trend, do most countries seem periodically to suffer upswings in violence? Why indeed did there appear to be a more or less simultaneous upturn in many countries in the 1960s? These questions serve as a reminder that nothing about civilizing processes is 'inevitable'; they can build up momentum, yet remain fragile when confronted by counter-vailing forces. In particular, Elias warned that if the level of danger and insecurity in a society rose again, if its internal pacification was called in question, then people's fears could burst through the veneer of self-constraints.[8] Several sorts of circumstance can in principle have such results. First, there is the effect of warfare, which tends to legitimate indi-vidual violence (Gurr, 1981: 320); this would appear to fit the case of mid-nineteenth-century America, where violence began to increase during the period of rising tension leading up to the Civil War, and continued in its aftermath into the 1870s. Second, many studies have investigated the connection between changes in crime rates and the cycle of economic prosperity and decline (ibid.: 328–30). High unemployment has often been associated with rising crime, sometimes with rising violence; but no simple pattern has been found that holds for all countries and periods, or for trends in violent versus property crime. Third, it would be wise not to dismiss out of hand the effects of the stresses of the initial phases of rapid urbanization and industrialization, nor to overgeneralize from local studies such as Lane's, well-founded research though they were. Circumstances vary. In some countries and periods, rapid industri-alization and urbanization have indeed been accompanied by high levels of crime and violence. While Lane, and more broadly Elias, may be right that the underlying long-term effect of larger-scale and more effective administration is 'stabilizing' and 'civilizing', in the shorter term the rapidity of economic growth is often associated with demographic changes that outstrip the capacity for social integration. Gurr concluded from a good many studies that, for instance, in nineteenth-century America, while the trend in violent crime among Anglo-Americans was falling, that was not true of various groups of immigrants, who in response to the opportunities presented by America's booming economy were arriving in its cities in large numbers. Meanwhile, nineteenth-century Germany provides a reminder that the *depopulation* of rural areas by rapid migration to the cities can equally be destabilizing, leading to upturns of crime and violence in the economically depressed country-side (ibid.: 337; Johnson, 1995).

There remains the puzzling question of why so many Western coun-tries more or less simultaneously witnessed a marked upturn in the graph of violent crime from around 1960. In the case of Britain, Dunning and his colleagues (Dunning and Sheard, 1979: 288–9; Dunning et al., 1988: 242–5) tentatively offered an explanation that introduces an interesting qualification into the theory of civilizing processes. They speculated that functional democratization, as one of the central components of the civilizing process, produces consequences which are, on balance, 'civilizing' in its early stages, but that when a certain level has been reached it produces effects which are decivilizing and promote disruptive conflict. Functional democratization has perhaps proceeded far enough for the demands of outsider groups to be expressed strongly, but not far enough – in Britain at least – to break down rigidities which prevent their demands being met fully.

Lane too invoked the principle of 'relative deprivation' in the USA; people in the past may have been much poorer in absolute terms, but 'they were not continually reminded, in living colour, about the lifestyles of the rich and famous . . . and they did not watch the majority of their fellow citizens move ahead of them along routes they despaired of following' (1997: 343). Compatible with this is Brown's interpretation of the effects of the advent of 'post-industrial' society. The upturn, he considers, was at least partly the effect of increasing unemployment and weak social security, associated with an increasing process of social exclusion and the division of American society into the protected and the unprotected strata (1991: 132). That is in turn consistent with Loïc Wacquant's (2004) studies of the black ghettoes of Chicago in the 1980s and 1990s, where he found evidence of a 'true decivilizing process'[9] in which *less* demanding standards of emotion management and impulse-control can be observed in successive generations. There, the increasing division between the protected and unprotected strata is seen in what Wacquant calls 'social *de*differentiation' – the withering away of the organizational fabric (civic, religious, welfare and commercial) of ghetto neighbourhoods, and the disappearance of stable working-class black American households. It is seen too in the *de*pacification of everyday life, and in the 'informalization' of the ghetto economy – that is, the loss of conventional forms of employment and welfare and their replacement by drug-dealing and other illegal activities on a large scale. Together, these processes probably produce a dual effect, increasing the propensity for *both* instrumental *and* impulsive violence. That is, in such a situation, people may resort to means such as armed robbery to obtain what they cannot gain by legal means; but at the same time an increased level of danger and insecurity in everyday life is likely to be associated with more impulsive violence too. As Eisner (2005: 13–14) has pointed out, most of the increase in homicide rates during the 1960s–90s period was due to an increase in young men killing other young men, usually in public spaces rather than in private disputes. Brawls in bars and in the streets, drug-related fights and turf wars between gangs contributed most to the upswing – not just in the USA, but in Europe too. Some of this may be seen as a return to honour and vengeance killings of a kind that may have been thought archaic in modern societies.

The retreat from 'penal welfarism'

More particularly in America, these processes have gone hand in hand in a vicious spiral with the social retrenchment of the state, which increasingly provided (in Wacquant's phrase) not a social safety net but, rather, a penal dragnet. At the start of the twenty-first century, about 2 million people were in prison out of a total US population of around 290 million. That represents approximately 0.7 per cent of the population, compared with 0.12 per cent in England and Wales, which have the highest rates of imprisonment in the EU. The American prison population underwent a fivefold increase in the three decades after 1972, when the population as a whole grew by just over a quarter. In all countries, young males form a large part of the prison population, but in America young *black* males are vastly over-represented. Among young men born between 1965 and 1969, 3 per cent of whites but a staggering 20 per cent of blacks had served time in prison by their early 30s (Pettit and Western, 2004). The risk of imprisonment was negatively highly correlated with levels of education. Pettit and Western found that nearly 60 per cent of black high-school dropouts born in 1965–9 had been imprisoned by 1999. Compared with males born just 20 years earlier, in 1945–9, the risk of imprisonment had doubled for both racial categories. Earlier still, in the 1930s, the USA had rates of imprisonment not greatly different from those of European countries (Tonry, 2004: 22).

Quite why the American penal system responded in this extreme way to the upsurge in violence that was the common experience of many countries from the 1960s to the 1990s is still very much debated among penologists. Some facts are clear. One is the length of sentences imposed: more than half of American prisoners are currently serving sentences of more than six years, whereas in most other countries fewer than 5 per cent serve sentences longer than one year (ibid.). The alarm of respectable citizens at the upsurge in homicide and the apparent prevalence of 'crime' undoubtedly played some part in bringing this about. In response, there were widespread public demands for stricter sentencing. Public discussion of 'a punishment to fit the crime' tends to focus on the worst cases in each category – a 'minority of the worst'. In response, judges (who in the USA are more integrally a part of the political system than in most European countries) impose longer sentences; and legislation for rigid sentencing rules in any case reduces the scope that judges have to exercise discretion. The result is a system designed to deal with monsters, but which swallows up hordes of minor criminals. An extreme case is California's 'three strikes and you're out' law, where a third conviction, even for a relatively minor felony, results in life imprisonment without parole. Unlike the eighteenth-century British practice of hanging people for stealing a pocket handkerchief, this policy has the disadvantage that the economic cost of permanently imprisoning so many people will most likely force its abandonment in the end.

Even though the graph of homicide turned down again in the 1990s throughout the Western world, there seems to be a cultural lag: the moral panic shows little sign of abating, with as yet no return to the 'penal welfarism' predominantly concerned with rehabilitation that prevailed through the twentieth century until the 1970s (Garland, 1985). These trends are particularly extreme in the USA, but can also be seen to a lesser extent in some other countries. Writing from an Eliasian perspective, Pratt (2002) has gone so far as to refer to a 'breakdown of civilization'. Explaining changes in the penal system is, however, secondary to explaining the overall international trends in crime to which they were essentially a response.

The late twentieth-century reaction

Into the long-running discussion of the effects on violence of a transition from industrial to post-industrial society, Gurr introduced that hardy perennial of American sociology, changing values. Episodes of social disorder, in his view, occur when major social crises coincide with a change of values:

> [Industrial societies were] dominated by a self-confident middle class convinced that prosperity in this life and salvation in the next could be achieved through piety, honesty and hard work. All authorities spoke with the same voice. The institutions of public order were effective because they reinforced the dominant view. They did not merely punish those who transgressed. They were missionaries to the under class . . .

In contrast, post-industrial society was marked by an ethic of 'aggressive hedonism', which he described as:

> a mutation of Western materialism, stripped of its work ethic and generalized from material satisfactions to social and sexual ones [in coexistence with] a sense of resentment against large impersonal organizations or indeed any external source of authority that might restrain them from 'doing their own thing'. (Gurr, in Graham and Gurr, 1979: 369–70)

The problem with arguments of this kind is not so much that 'values' do not change – they do – but rather that to treat them as though they were an independent variable does not do much to advance sociological explanation: the question is *why* values change. Gurr was probably right about the steady and consistent 'civilizing' pressure that a 'self-confident middle class' exerted on the lower orders in Victorian times. Their 'missionary' activities, in the form of 'civilizing campaigns' to pacify, educate and clean up the poor, have been studied in many countries (Mennell, 1998: 125–9). And, as De Swaan (1988) shows in detail in five countries, the pressures of interdependence between rich and poor in growing cities went along with a widening of the circle of mutual identification between the better and worse off, and to *collective* solutions being sought and implemented in, among other things, better education, public health and social security.

The late twentieth century witnessed a widespread turning away from such collectivist solutions, and in some respects a diminution of mutual identification,[10] a trend that was particularly strong in the USA and UK, both of which politically adopted a combination of free-market neo-liberalism and social conservatism. David Garland (2001) has put forward a complex interpretation in which changing values are treated not as an independent variable but as closely interwoven with structural changes. Together, changes in structures *and* values go a long way to explaining *both* the upsurge in crime and the socio-political response to it.

A good point at which to break into the spiral process is to consider the effects of what is often known as 'consumer capitalism'. It has no exact starting point, but in the post-war period more and more new products became widely available, as business continually sought to identify new markets. At the same time, the growth of the mass media fuelled relative deprivation: 'through television, today's ghetto children . . . see what they are deprived of in every programme and commercial' (Meyrowitz, 1985: 133, quoted by Garland, 2001: 86). Moreover, the new consumer goods were everywhere, ready for theft. All countries began to experience sharp upturns in property crime. Of nothing is that more true than the motorcar. The car also made possible an increasing geographical separation between the prosperous and the poor. Again in most Western countries, people began to commute longer distances from home to work. In America, a minority of the 'protected strata' began to live in 'gated communities' (Blakely and Snyder, 1998), as part of a more general 'white flight' into the suburbs.[11] At the same time, the same business logic increased the proportion of the deprived and excluded: they were the 'groups who could not easily be turned to profitable use' (Garland, 2001: 79). From the late 1970s, the USA and Britain led the way towards labour markets becoming more precarious. The lifetime security of a full-time job in industry or the public sector became more exceptional, and greater 'flexibility' became the norm. 'Flexibility' is a euphemism for having to change jobs more frequently, to retrain, to relocate, to work part time, to experience reduced security and fewer benefits such as health insurance and retirement pensions. Western labour markets, especially those of the USA and Britain, have become increasingly polarized:

[W]hile the best-qualified strata of the workforce could command high salaries and lucrative benefits packages, at the bottom end of the market were masses of low-skilled, poorly educated, jobless people – a large percentage of them young, urban, and minority – for whom continuous unemployment was a long-term prospect. These new wage patterns, which by the 1980s were reinforced by increasingly regressive tax structures and declining welfare benefits, reversed the gains of the last half century. (Ibid.: 82)

And why were tax structures becoming more regressive and welfare benefits declining? Another twist in the spiral is that the process of economic polarization also fostered the formation of new class interests and sensibilities. Again in Garland's words:

Broad social classes that had once supported welfare state policies (out of self-interest as well as cross-class solidarity) came to think and feel about the issues quite differently. . . . [I]mportant sections of the working and middle classes [came] to see them as being at odds with their actuarial interests, and as benefiting groups that were undeserving and increasingly dangerous. (Ibid.)

This whole process, in short, is a complex of what Elias (1978: 17–30, 163) called 'compelling forces', which all parties caught up in it experience as inescapably carrying them along, and it has a strong element of the self-fulfilling about it. In this light, the 60 per cent probability of a black male high-school dropout born in 1965–9 having served time in prison appears a little less surprising.[12]

From the early 1990s, the graph of violence in many countries turned downwards again. Brown (1991: 153) put an optimistic spin on this, attributing it to the coming 'Information Society', placing his faith in high technology increasing the effectiveness of crime prevention and the criminal justice system; in an expanding prison population taking the hard core of criminal out of circulation; in community self-help leading to the strengthening of neighbourhoods; and, above all, in a more effective education system that would bring about a 'self-imposed renewal of social discipline'. Yes, perhaps; or perhaps not. As yet, the decline in crime has not been associated with a reversal in the other intertwining strands in the compelling spiral process.

Is America peculiarly violent?

In America specifically, the 1960s were marked not just by rising crime rates but also by racial conflict, uprisings in the urban ghettoes and by a

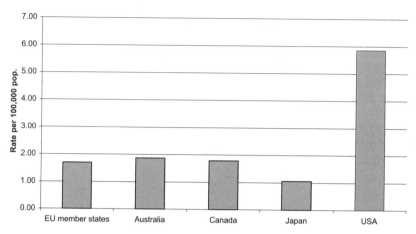

Figure 6.4: Comparative homicide statistics, 1998–2000
Source: Barclay and Tavares (2002: 3, 10). Cf. Beeghley (2003: 48ff.).

series of political assassinations. Alarmed by all of this, the federal government established a National Commission on the Causes and Prevention of Violence under the chairmanship of Dr Milton Eisenhower. In the research to which this gave rise, however, the key question was not so much why the USA, like so many countries, had witnessed a short-term upturn in violence, but whether in longer-term historical perspective America had consistently had a higher level of violence than other comparable countries. In other words, even if the USA has experienced upturns and downturns in the graph of violence that run roughly parallel to those in other countries, are there characteristics of American society that cause a secular upwards displacement in the graph: that America is, and even perhaps always has been *pro rata* more violent than other Western societies?

A snapshot of comparative homicide rates for the years 1998–2000 is shown in figure 6.4. It can be seen that the USA had much higher murder rates than Australia, Canada, Japan and the then 15 member states of the European Union – all countries that might reasonably be considered comparable economically, socially and politically with the USA. It is especially striking that Canada, here as in many other respects, resembles a modern European social democracy more closely than it does the giant neighbour on which it abuts to the south.[13] Within the EU, the highest rates were recorded in Northern Ireland, in the aftermath of three decades of low-intensity civil war; but at 3.1 per 100,000, that was scarcely more than half of the American rate. Luxembourg and Austria, with rates of 0.87 and 0.90 respectively, had the lowest rates among EU countries.

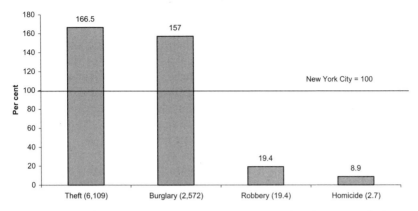

Figure 6.5: London crime rates (per 100,000) compared with New York City, 1990
Source: Zimring and Hawkins (1997: 6), based on data from the FBI (1990) and London Research Centre (1993).

Elsewhere, certainly, there were countries with higher rates than the USA. Russia, for example, had a rate of 20.52, and Estonia, Latvia and Lithuania – the three Baltic states that were formerly part of the USSR – also recorded rates higher than America. As for South Africa: with an astonishing 54.25 homicides per 100,000, it was almost ten times as murderous as the USA. It is safe to say, however, that these countries – all of them having endured phases of extreme social upheaval and instability – are not ones to which most Americans would wish to have to look for favourable comparisons.

So, even though murder rates have been falling in the USA, as in other countries, since the 1990s, its *comparatively* high rate of killings must significantly contribute to the popular fear that has driven the compelling spiral mentioned above, including 'white flight' and diminishing support for penal welfarism. There is, however, one notable feature of these statistics that has not yet been mentioned: as Zimring and Hawkins (1997) demonstrated, although by longstanding habit Americans speak of crime and violence as nearly synonymous, in fact the problem is *not crime*. Zimring and Hawkins show that the incidence of non-violent crimes like theft and burglary is often actually lower in the USA than in comparable countries. Figure 6.5 gives a small flavour of their evidence: it shows that in 1990 Londoners were more than half again as likely to suffer theft or burglary as were New Yorkers. America's problem is the exceptionally high rates of *interpersonal* violence. The implication seems to be that a larger proportion of Americans are especially prone to expressive or impulsive homicide.

A cultural 'strain of violence'?

A question much debated is whether there is something in American 'culture' that predisposes its people towards a higher level of violence than is seen in other comparable countries. Three volumes by Richard Slotkin (1973; 1985; 1992) constitute the most ambitious attempt to map a persistent mythology of 'the frontier' running through American literature and culture from colonial times to the twentieth century. Myths, argues Slotkin, have long-term practical effects on how people live:

> The mythology of a nation is the intelligible mask of that enigma called the 'national character'. Through myths the psychology and world view of our cultural ancestors are transmitted to modern descendents, in such a way that our perception of contemporary reality and our ability to function in the world are directly, often tragically, affected. . . . [M]yths reach out from the past to cripple, incapacitate, or strike down the living. (1973: 3, 5)

Closely bound up with the myth of the frontier is what Slotkin calls 'the myth of regeneration through violence'. This can be traced to the earliest stages of European colonization in North America:

> The first colonists saw in America an opportunity to regenerate their fortunes, their spirits, and the power of their church and nation; but the means to that regeneration ultimately became the means of violence, and the myth of regeneration through violence became the metaphor of the American experience. (Ibid.: 5)

The first victims of the myth were the native Americans; but in Slotkin's account people have continued to die in consequence of the power of the myth, now embodied in the image of the 'gunfighter nation' (1992). In between, says Slotkin, no historian who lived in the nineteenth-century heyday of the real frontier 'saw as much significance in it as the theorists of a post-Frontier historiography, Frederick Jackson Turner and Theodore Roosevelt' (1985: 16).[14] Slotkin contends that it is less the reality of frontier life than the myth that has left an enduring legacy in present-day levels of violence:

> [T]he conception of America as a land of unlimited opportunity for the strong, ambitious, self-reliant individual to thrust his way to the top has blinded us to the consequences of the industrial and urban revolutions and to the need for social reform and a new concept of individual and communal welfare. (1973: 5)

Slotkin's thesis was based largely on the study of cultural products, from literature and art to films. More conventional historical research appears to support it. Richard M. Brown, in the preface to his book *Strain of Violence*, wrote that 'repeated episodes of violence, going far back into our colonial past, have imprinted upon our citizenry a propensity to violence' (1975: vii). 'Our history', he continued, 'has produced and reinforced a strain of violence, which has strongly tinctured our national experience.' Brown paid particular attention to regional variations in traditions of violence, especially the conservative vigilante tradition of the South and West. In a remark redolent of the Vietnam era when the book was written, but still pertinent a generation later, Brown commented that 'for an increased understanding of Lyndon B. Johnson's role as a protagonist of America's violent intervention in Vietnam, it is instructive to consider his central Texas homeland where the ethic of violent self-defence – so notable in Johnson's foreign affairs leadership – had become a behavioural norm' (ibid.: viii, 236–99).

Explanations based on the influence of some free-floating and abstract 'cultural trait' – such as 'strain of violence' or the 'myth of regeneration through violence' – always seem a little weak unless it can be shown, first, why the cultural trait has a strong appeal; and, second, how the cultural trait becomes institutionalized and concretely enacted in the practices of social life. Both are possible in the case of the myth of the frontier.

The Western myth as a form of romanticism

The long-lasting appeal of the frontier, and its apparently greater significance for those who came later than for those who lived through it, may make sense if it is seen as one instance of a romanticism associated with the tightening of social constraints. Elias wrote at length (2006a: 230–85) about 'aristocratic romanticism' in sixteenth- to eighteenth-century France. Why did poetry evoking a past rural idyll, tales of wandering knights and novels about nymphs and shepherds appeal strongly to members of a court society? The feeling of estrangement from the land, of being torn from their native soil and of longing for a vanished world resonated with their actual experience: the growing and more effective power of the central royal government stripped all the nobility of their former territorial autonomy, and for the upper ranks their existence now centred on life at court, with its intense constraints. They had been deracinated and deprived of their former social functions. Another example is the German bourgeois romanticism of the nineteenth century, reaching its pinnacle in Wagner's music dramas. In *Lohengrin*, *Tannhäuser*, *Tristan* and *Parsifal* there is again the glorification of medieval knighthood, and in *Die Meistersinger* of the free, autonomous medieval guilds. Again, this phase of romanticism arose

> precisely when the German bourgeoisie's hopes of a greater share of power had been broken and the pressures of state integration in conjunction with those of industrialization were increasing. It is, in other words, one of the central symptoms of romantic attitudes and ideals that their representatives see the present only as a decline from the past, and the future – as far as they see the future at all – only as the restoration of a better, purer, idealized past. (Ibid.: 238)

It is no accident that, on a lower plane of cultural creation than Wagner, the Wild West novels of Karl May were immensely popular in late nineteenth-century Germany (Ridley, 1983: 30–41). In America itself, the beginnings of romanticism can be seen in Jefferson's hatred of the cities and dream of an agrarian republic (White and White, 1962). But, if Elias's interpretation of romanticism is valid, the social basis of the appeal of the myth of the frontier may better be sought – as well as in the more pacified and administered West *after* the closing of the frontier – in the vast migration into the fast-growing cities and in the imposition of industrial and bureaucratic discipline.

No duty to retreat

The institutionalization of the frontier myth in law and social practice is laid out by Brown in his book *No Duty to Retreat* (1991), tracing the divergence between English and American common law on the question of when a person was allowed to kill another in self-defence. For centuries, the common law of England has required a person who is threatened with attack, death or bodily harm, to retreat – indeed to flee from the scene – in order to forestall violence, if such flight can be safely made. Only when cornered, when one has one's 'back to the wall', is one allowed to kill in self-defence. In contrast, 'In America a gradual legal revolution reinterpreted the common law to hold that, if otherwise without fault, a person could legally stand fast and, without retreating, kill in self-defence. This was a right to stand one's ground with no duty to retreat' (Brown, 1991, Preface).

The doctrine emerged in the frontier states, but by the early twentieth century it was more generally recognized that the English 'duty to retreat' was 'inapplicable to American conditions' (Wharton, 1907, quoted by Brown, 1991). The difference in 'conditions' amounts to the fact that England, even in the Middle Ages, was relatively stably settled, with state and judicial authorities who claimed a monopoly of the legitimate use of violence: there was, at least in principle, somewhere to retreat to. On the American frontier, first in the Appalachians and then moving west, there were at least for a time no effective authorities nearby from whom to seek protection. Such social conditions were factually ephemeral; if they had long-term consequences, it was because, as Slotkin argued, myths from the past continue to affect people's perception of contemporary reality. Through such myths the frontier can be argued to have left a mark that was enacted in law: in 1921, in the case of *Brown v. United States*, Justice Oliver Wendell Holmes upheld the principle of there being 'no duty to retreat'. In a letter after the case, Holmes wrote: 'a man is not born to run away' (Brown, 1991: 32).

The principle could be seen in action very clearly in the South, where the old honour code persisted strongly into the twentieth century, where almost no 'fair fight' was likely to result in a conviction, and where (as Lane, 1997: 150, dryly comments) there was something approaching a 'duty to advance'. The honour code was also democratized, especially in the West. In Europe and the Old South, the duel had been socially exclusive, connected with a 'gentleman's code', and fought with swords or single-shot pistols.[15] The repeating revolver, perfected a decade or two before the Civil War, and the associated role of the gunfighter helped to create something of a socially different character in the post-bellum West: the classic 'walkdown' gunfight depicted in countless Westerns. From Owen Wister's *The Virginian* (1998 [1902]) to Fred Zinneman's *High Noon* (1952), the gunfight became fixed 'in the popular mind of America' (Brown, 1991: 48). And not just in the popular mind, but also in the legal system. For Oliver Wendell Holmes, 'no duty to run away' was 'a deeply felt philosophy of behaviour with the authority of a moral value – one that . . . grew out of American conditions' (Brown, 1991: 36). In Brown's view:

> [It helps to] explain why the American homicide rate has been so much higher than that of England during the nineteenth and twentieth centuries. It also helps to explain why our country has been the most violent among its peer group of industrialized, urbanized democracies of the world. The attitude of no duty to retreat has long since become second nature to most Americans and has had a deep, broad impact with a significant, although often intangible, effect upon our foreign relations and military conduct. . . . It is an expression of a characteristically American way of life. (Ibid.: Preface)

The suggestion is that myths and cultural traditions from a very different earlier stage in the development of American society have entered into the habitus – second nature – of (many) Americans today. It seems a strong

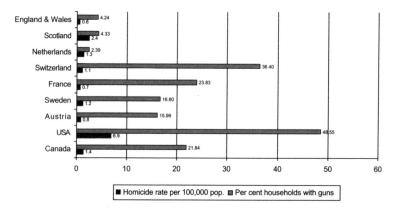

Figure 6.6: Homicide rates and percentage of households with one or more guns in USA and eight other industrial countries (1990s)
Sources: Gun ownership: Block (1998: 4), based on data from the 1996 International Crime (Victim) Survey; homicides (most recent years available): Krug et al. (2002).

argument, but are there alternative explanations for America's comparatively high rates of violence?

The gun culture

The widespread ownership of firearms in the USA may offer an explanation for why the level of lethal violence is so much higher there than in comparable countries – and, paradoxically, an explanation that does *not* depend on Americans on average being 'more aggressive' or 'more impulsive' in their habitus or personality makeup. It could be argued that similar incidents of everyday conflict and 'aggression' are simply much more likely to have lethal outcomes when guns are available. The sort of drunken brawl that in a European country probably results in cuts and bruises will, where there is a greater chance that participants are able to pull out firearms, more probably result in fatalities.

In 1996, a comparative survey of the ownership of firearms showed that a far larger proportion of households in the USA owned a gun than in eight other industrial countries (see figure 6.6). Very nearly half of all American households owned guns. If we except the special case of Switzerland,[16] where military regulations require men to have a gun in their possession, the American figure is more than twice that in the next highest countries, France and Canada. In all the countries illustrated in figure 6.6, the commonest reason given for owning a gun was hunting animals; the incidence of hunting-gun ownership is higher in rural areas

and small communities than in very large cities.[17] McDowell (1995) estimated that in the mid-1990s, while about half of all American households
owned at least one gun, most of these were suitable for hunting or target
practice; about 10–20 per cent of households owned defensive guns.

In a sense, then, the prevalence of firearms might seem to offer a 'material' rather than a 'cultural', still less a 'psychological', explanation for
America's high level of violent death. Unfortunately, that interpretation is
highly questionable.

First and most important, international homicide rates are not closely
correlated with rates of gun ownership. Despite the prevalence of guns,
Switzerland has a low homicide rate, and France, Canada, Sweden and
Austria, the next nearest rivals to America in gun ownership, have very
much lower homicide rates than it does.

Second, from the standpoint of the theory of civilizing processes, the
preponderance of hunting weapons is not just to be set aside as of no significance. While it is generally accepted that farmers need to kill pests and
predators for commercial reasons, hunting – the killing of animals for
sport and enjoyment – is different. Elias pointed out that the threshold of
repugnance had gradually advanced not just in relation to the suffering
and death of human beings, but also of animals. He mentioned the
Midsummer's Day custom in sixteenth-century Paris of burning alive a
dozen or two cats for the entertainment of the king and populace (2000:
171–2; cf. Darnton, 1984). The growth of feelings of repulsion to cruelty
towards animals has been traced by Keith Thomas (1983) and in subsequent research (Tester, 1991; Franklin, 1999). Certainly hunting is not
extinct in Europe, and certainly a great many Americans would share feelings of distaste for hunting; the fact remains, though, that hunting with
guns is a vastly more popular pastime in America than in Europe. This is
one sense in which there is a 'gun *culture*', so that the sheer number of
guns does not provide a purely 'material' alternative to 'cultural' accounts
of American violence.

Third, the geographical distribution of high murder rates within the
USA also shows that gun ownership is not in itself an adequate explanation. Nor, in itself, is the 'frontier thesis' by which Slotkin sets so much
store in this context. Lane (1997: 349) points out that neither recency of
settlement nor a history of Indian wars is necessarily associated with high
present-day levels of violence: for instance, neither Minnesota nor South
Dakota has been noted for its violence. Rather, 'the most casual glance
at the map of murder across modern America will show that . . . the
highest murder rates are those in the South, followed by western places
largely settled, often via Texas, by ranchers and other migrants from the
Confederacy' (ibid.: 350). While not dismissing the frontier legacy out of
hand, Lane places greater emphasis on the legacy of the South. The

southern code of honour and its democratization – its permeation into all ranks of society – can be seen as arising out of the institution of slavery on the Chesapeake fringes as early as the seventeenth century. Lane expresses the contrast between the habitus of the North and the South very clearly. In the North:

> An evolving sense of middle-class respectability . . . led young men as they grew older and got steady jobs to abandon physical responses to frustration or insult. In some a sense of personal dignity was deeply engrained by parental or religious training, beyond the reach of sticks and stones as well as words, preventing overreaction to assault from outside the confident inner self. [In contrast,] in the South the daily need to assert personal dominance, first of all over slaves, demanded that even the most successful live by the code and handle their own affairs without calling in the law. (Ibid.: 351)

This code, and a low rate of conviction for homicide arising from any kind of quarrel, reinforced each other. And while any violence by blacks against whites was savagely punished, violence against blacks – whether by whites or other blacks – was not. Since the apparatus of the state offered little protection, disputes had to be settled directly, often through fighting at the slightest provocation. This Southern inheritance, Lane and others argue, is one reason among others for homicide among black Americans having been at times as much as eight or ten times as high as among whites. The short fuse of many poor inner-city young black men may stem in part from this historic source.

Meanwhile, the fraction of Americans who own defensive guns is growing, apparently reflecting an increase in the number of people who have lost confidence in the capacity of the state to protect them – thus replicating in modern form the circumstances that led to the southern syndrome in the first place. Even if they never actually use them for defensive purposes – and how often they do so is disputed – those who own such guns apparently gain powerful symbolic reassurance from them. That contributes to the passions deployed in political debates about gun control. Opinion polls consistently show that a majority of Americans wish to see the gun-control laws strengthened, but 'the passion and the money are on the other side' (ibid.: 346). At the beginning of the twenty-first century, the power and money of the gun manufacturers and the passion of those like the National Rifle Association (NRA) who celebrate guns appear for the time being to be rolling back restrictions on gun ownership.[18]

In the long debate among historians of the gun culture and its origins, it has until recently been axiomatic that gun ownership has always been very widespread: 'the gun culture in America is as old as the first British settlements' (ibid.: 344). Apart from Quaker Pennsylvania, every colony 'at least theoretically' required that able-bodied free men own a musket as members of militias. This basic assumption has been challenged by Michael Bellesiles in his controversial book *Arming America* (2003). On the basis of a study of probate records, which apparently show relatively few firearms being handed down through inheritance, Bellesiles argued that gun ownership was exceptional in the seventeenth, eighteenth and early nineteenth centuries, even on the frontier, and that guns became a common commodity only with the industrialization of the mid-nineteenth century, with ownership concentrated in urban areas. As it happens, that coincides very clearly with the point at which homicide rates in the more settled parts of America, including the great cities such as New York, soared out of line with rates in comparable parts of Britain (Lane, 1997: 344). Some minor errors were, however, found in Bellesiles's research, and as a result of the controversy he was forced to resign his academic position and the book was withdrawn.[19] It is safe to say that these consequences would not have followed had the book been about the history of stamp-collecting in America.

Did democracy come too early?

These various elements of an explanation for the consistently higher levels of violence that have persisted in the USA in comparison with Western Europe and other similar countries should not be seen as separate 'factors'. Rather, as Spierenburg (2006) points out, it is essential to take a long-term perspective on them as an overall figuration in which people's habitus is connected with wider balances of power in the society as a whole. Following Elias, Spierenburg stresses that, in what became France and in most other parts of Western Europe, there had taken place over many centuries gradual processes of centralization, eventuating in the concentration of the means of violence in fewer and fewer hands, and ultimately in the establishment of a relatively effective monopoly apparatus in the hands of kings. Gradual it may have been, but the struggles among a warrior elite were bloody, as more and more players were deprived of their capacity to wage war independently of the central ruler. The process was in its final stages when European colonization of North America began. Once stable and effective royal monopolies of violence had been established, as they were in general by the late seventeenth and the eighteenth centuries, the people's aim in subsequent struggles – most spectacularly in the French Revolution – was not to challenge or destroy the monopoly as such, but rather to 'co-possess' the monopoly (as Spierenburg terms it). In other words, the aim was to assert a more broadly based control over those who exercised the monopoly, to democratize it.

In North America, however, 'there was no phase of centralization before democratization set in', and Spierenburg ventures to suggest that 'democracy came to America too early'.[20] He hastens to add that that is not a value judgement, but a rhetorical statement, by which he means:

> [T]he inhabitants did not have sufficient time to become accustomed to being disarmed. As a consequence, the idea remained alive that the very existence of a monopoly of force was undesirable. And it remained alive in an increasingly democratic form: not [as in medieval Europe] of regional elites carving out their private principality, but of common people claiming the right of self-defence. . . . Local elites and, increasingly, common people equated democracy with the right of armed protection of their own property and interests. (2006: 109–10)

Spierenburg acknowledges that it would be an oversimplification to suggest that the transition from struggles to destroy the monopoly apparatus to struggles to co-possess it did not take place at all in the USA, but 'the best one can say is that the majority of the population wanted it both ways': they 'accepted the reality of government institutions but at the same time they cherished an ethic of self-help' (ibid.: 110). That helps to explain the continuity of private militias and vigilante movements through much of American history (Bellesiles, 2003; Brown, 1975). 'Today', remarks Spierenburg, 'the idea that individuals cannot and should not rely on state institutions in order to protect their homes is alive and well. Members of the Michigan Militia explicitly say so in [Michael Moore's 2003 documentary film] *Bowling for Columbine*' (ibid.).

Lynching and vigilantes

Lynching – when private citizens usurp the function of the courts by killing a person without due process – is next only to the use of private armies against the forces of the state as a paradigmatic instance of a breach of the state's monopoly of the means of organized violence. The trend of lynchings between 1882 and 1970 is shown in figure 6.7.

These are official figures, gathered from 1882 onwards, but they need to be treated with a certain caution. 'Lynching' means the killing, by a group of people (usually described as a 'mob'), of someone 'for an alleged offence without legal trial, especially by hanging' (*OED*); but the term is now sometimes used in a much looser sense to include the *random* killing in the street by a mob, of victims not accused of any specific offence and selected simply on the basis of some visible characteristic, usually skin colour.[21] The distinction is clear in principle, but in compiling statistics may not always be easy to apply in practice to every marginal instance. Be that as it may, the graph in figure 6.7 shows an interesting pattern. The

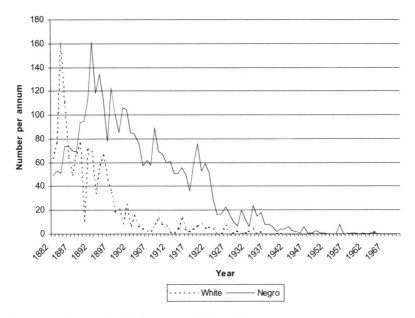

Figure 6.7: Persons lynched, by race, 1882–1970
Source: US Department of Commerce and Bureau of the Census (1975: 422).

victims of lynching in the USA were by no means exclusively blacks. In the Midwest and West many white people died in this way too, but white deaths peaked in the 1880s, a decade earlier than those of blacks. In the South, until the abolition of slavery, it had of course been perfectly legal for a slave-owner to kill his slave if he wished, so the practice was to some extent hallowed by tradition.[22] Nevertheless, the peak of black lynching did not come immediately after the Civil War or Reconstruction, but in the 1890s, and it tailed off only slowly through the early decades of the twentieth century (Brundage, 1993). Garland (2005a) characterizes these as 'public torture lynchings', involving publicity, crowds, ritual and abnormal cruelty. They have cast a long shadow: Messner et al. (2005) demonstrate that county by county in the South, there is a high correlation between the incidence of lynching in the past and that of homicide at the present day.

Zimring (2003: 90) presents a detailed analysis of regional distribution of incidents, drawing on data from a 1919 report on the 30-year peak period of lynchings, between 1889 and 1918.[23] They show that 88 per cent of all lynchings took place in the South, 7 per cent in the Midwest and 5 per cent in the West, while only nine killings occurred in the north-eastern states, less than half of 1 per cent of the total for the nation. As many as 73 per cent of the victims were blacks and many others were native Americans.[24] Of course, incidents of mob violence have occurred in many other countries, but, remarks Zimring:

> What distinguishes the saga of lynching in the United States from most other examples of mob violence in Western history are the volume of killings, the length of the period lynching was practised in the United States, and its linkage to racial repression. Rather than a series of unconnected episodes of group violence, lynching in parts of the United States was a regularly occurring event that was the expression of an institutional social structure that generated repeated lynchings for many decades. (2003: 90)

Yet how is the peak of lynching to be explained? Of course, accusations of rape and lesser sexual offences were frequently involved. But psychological explanations in terms of black male lust or white male sensitivity to it in the South cannot account for the timing. As Lane points out, 'White women had often been routinely and calmly left alone on plantations full of black men, notably during the Civil War – why the sudden upsurge in concern more than twenty years later?' (1997: 153). And why did it gradually decline in the twentieth century? The answer appears to lie in the political and social conflicts that the post-bellum South underwent. Poor whites, notably sharecroppers – suggests Lane – feared that rich plantation-owners would mobilize the votes of their black tenants to dispossess them; and, meanwhile, the rich whites feared an inter-racial alliance of the dispossessed. These fears declined as sharecropping was put on a legal basis, and as the black population was systematically deprived of its right to vote. The decline in lynching coincided with the completion of the legal and political subjugation of the blacks. As C. Vann Woodward (1974) pointed out, the 'Jim Crow laws' enjoyed a 'strange career' in the sense that they began to spread most widely several decades after the Civil War.

Underlying this explanation of trends in the South, and indeed the incidence of lynching in the Midwest and West as well, is a broader consideration: the relative weakness on the ground – in various areas and periods – of the forces and apparatus of legal government. That is reflected not just in lynching but also in a wider and, as Richard Maxwell Brown has argued, distinctively American tradition of vigilantism. Brown points out (1975: 22) that, violent though the British Isles (notably Ireland and Scotland) were in the seventeenth and eighteenth centuries, there was no tradition of groups of residents taking the law into their own hands; that was 'repugnant to the British approach to law and order'. In contrast: 'Vigilantism arose in response to a typical American problem: the absence of effective law and order in a frontier region. It was a problem that occurred again and again beyond the Appalachian Mountains. It stimulated the formation of hundreds of frontier vigilante movements' (ibid., 1975: 22).

Before the Civil War, almost every state or territory west of the Appalachians had well-organized vigilante groups. They were typically socially conservative, aiming 'to re-establish in each newly settled frontier area the community structure of the old settled areas along with the values of sanctity of property and law and order', and represented 'the contradictory coupling of lawlessness in behalf of lawfulness' (ibid.: 22, 21). From the earliest such movement, in the Back Country of South Carolina in 1767–69 through to the 'vigilance committee' in San Francisco in 1856, they were typically under the control of the frontier elite, acting in its defence 'against the threatening presence of the criminal and the disorderly' (ibid.: vii).[25] On the other hand, it was not uncommon for vigilantes to slip their leash, and for conflicts and vendettas between them and their opponents to give rise to more rather than less violence and disorder. (In that respect, their story is not wholly unlike that of mafia in nineteenth-century Sicily, which originated in private militias recruited by landowners (Blok, 1974).) And, as America became an urban, industrial society after the Civil War, the character of vigilantism changed to reflect the tensions of the new society, its targets including 'Catholics, Jews, Negroes, immigrants, labouring men and labour leaders, political radicals, advocates of civil liberties, and nonconformists in general' (Brown, 1975: 23).

Brown thus interprets vigilantism as originating to fill a vacuum created by the weakness and remoteness of the governmental apparatus for the maintenance of law and order. The decline of lynching and vigilantism is one facet of 'the taming of warriors' in an American context. It signifies a growth in the effectiveness of the governmental monopoly of organized violence, and in a sense a greater trust in government: with the rise of the Jim Crow laws, dominant groups trusted government – once blacks were deprived of political power – to act in what they perceived as the interests of their local community.

Digression on the Second Amendment

In resisting regulation, the mass-membership National Rifle Association rests its case on the Bill of Rights, specifically the Second Amendment, which states that 'A well-regulated Militia, being necessary to the security of a free State, the right of the people to keep and bear arms, shall not be infringed.' How that provision, added to the Constitution in 1791, is to be interpreted in the very different society of today is the nub of political controversy about guns.

Historians and lawyers – as well as politicians and voters – have differed in their interpretation of the purposes that lay behind the Second Amendment, and about its relevance today. A meticulous study by Uviller and Merkel (2002) of the historical context in which the amendment was framed, however, demonstrates beyond reasonable doubt that those who framed it intended that the right to bear arms be indissolubly tied to a 'well-regulated militia'. Their study focuses on the militia to which the amendment refers, its meaning for citizens towards the end of the eighteenth century and its legal and political basis. While it is certainly true that there was at the time a strongly held belief that private citizens had a right to possess arms, the constitutional provision for a 'well-regulated militia' can only be understood in relation to the equally widespread distrust of standing armies. The authors of the *Federalist Papers* had to invoke the insecurity of the frontier to overcome the possibility that a standing army might actually be forbidden under the Constitution, and the Bill of Rights as a whole represents a series of safeguards that proved necessary to gain the states' approval of the Constitution. Only a tiny professional army, little more than a frontier force, existed for most of American history. A 'well-regulated militia' made up of ordinary citizens was an acceptable alternative to any larger standing army. But, as Uviller and Merkel show, those who framed the amendment meant the emphasis to be on *well-regulated*; after Shay's Rebellion they certainly did not intend to promote the spontaneous appearance of armed groups, nor to provide constitutional protection for what was to become the American tradition of lynching and vigilantism. Furthermore, it was intended that the federal government would write the regulations, and as early as 1792 the Militia Act began a long process of transforming the volunteer militia of the kind that had fought at Lexington and Concord into a National Guard not only under the control of but also *armed by* the federal government.

The National Guard soon became an institution quite unlike the citizen militia mentioned in the amendment; and since a militia no longer exists, Uviller and Merkel contend that the Second Amendment is as 'silent', dead and inoperative as is the Third Amendment which prohibits the billeting of soldiers in people's homes without the consent of the householder. No one now disputes that the Third Amendment relates to an eighteenth-century custom that simply no longer exists, but the Second remains the centre of controversy. The Supreme Court could in principle rule that, in the absence of a 'well-regulated militia', the Bill of Rights no longer imposes any limits on the state's monopoly of the means of violence – but that is inconceivable in the foreseeable future, given the charisma attaching to gun ownership that makes the USA peculiar among modern industrial states.

It is important to recognize, however, that the persistence of such widespread and relatively unregulated ownership and use of guns in America today is not being attributed to the persistence of a 'cultural tradition', conceived of as some free-floating body of ideas. It is, rather, that the opinions of some influential and powerful people, widely shared in the late

eighteenth century, became enshrined in quite concrete institutional provisions that continue to shape the power ratios underlying political discourse to this day. There is a strong contemporary 'cultural tradition' in
favour of much more stringent gun control, but it shows no sign of being
able to surmount the obstacles posed by the Second Amendment *and* the
multiple jurisdictions of the federal Constitution that are a living legacy
from two centuries ago, *as well as* the strong current of public opinion
and interest groups that continue to support that legacy.

Capital punishment

The argument that 'democracy came too early' to America is equally relevant to understanding the persistence of capital punishment in America.
Spierenburg has also demonstrated the connection between state-formation processes and the rise and decline of capital punishment in Europe.
In *The Spectacle of Suffering*, he argued that executions and other punishments carried out under the public gaze, which became institutionalized in the course of the later Middle Ages, 'first served to seal the transfer
of vengeance from private persons to the state' (1984: 202).[26] In the
emerging states of Western Europe, authorities were preoccupied until
well into the sixteenth century with maintaining a highly unstable and
geographically limited monopoly of violence. Into the early modern
period, displays of physical punishment were still considered indispensable to the bolstering of authority. The pleasurable excitement spectators
experienced at witnessing executions and tortures may become more
comprehensible when it is realized that such events were directly linked
to people being forced to relinquish direct action for vengeance through
the vendetta or the lynch mob.

Spierenburg's book pits Elias's theory against that of Michel Foucault.
In his well-known book *Discipline and Punishment* (1977), Foucault
depicted the transition from public executions in the eighteenth century
to incarceration in the nineteenth as a rather sudden *rupture*. Spierenburg,
in contrast, demonstrates from the archives that the process was far more
gradual. Some mitigation of the more extreme, mutilating punishments
can be detected from the early seventeenth century. In most Western
European countries, executions were removed within prison walls during
the nineteenth century, and abolished in the twentieth. But over the whole
of that period there is clear evidence of a gradual but eventually acceler-
ating increase in sensibility towards the suffering of the victim: '[T]he
spectacle of punishment, even if it was inflicted upon the guilty, was . . .
becoming unbearable. By the end of the eighteenth century some of the

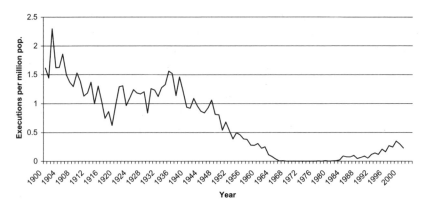

Figure 6.8: US rate of executions, per million population, 1900–2001
Sources: US Department of Commerce and Bureau of the Census (1975); US Census Bureau; Espy and Smylka (1994).

audience could feel the pain of delinquents on the scaffold. . . . [I]nter-human identification had increased' (Spierenburg, 1984: 184).

Echoing Elias, Spierenburg (ibid.: 204) argues that psychological controls were largely confined to the context of a person's own group. During the early modern period, the mutual dependence between social groups increased and, in consequence, the context of psychological controls widened and an increase in mutual identification took place.

At first glance, capital punishment appears to be yet another instance of 'American exceptionalism'. Indeed, several leading American students of the problem of capital punishment (Zimring, 2003; Whitman, 2003; Steiker, 2002) have explicitly linked its persistence to distinctive characteristics of American culture. Yet, as David Garland (2005b) has argued, until the last three decades of the twentieth century America followed much the same trajectory as the rest of the world. Tocqueville was not wrong: in some respects America was in advance of Europe. Michigan abolished the death penalty in the 1840s, long before any European nation, and in the northeastern states executions were, at an early stage, hidden from the public gaze and removed to within prison walls (see Masur, 1989).[27] Later, supposedly more humane methods of killing – the electric chair, the gas chamber, lethal injections – were introduced in the USA, while hanging continued in Europe and the Commonwealth countries (as indeed did beheading in France). Yet, as figure 6.8 shows, although capital punishment declined steadily in America, as in Europe, through the twentieth century and came close to being abolished between the 1960s and 1980s, there was then a resurgence in America that was not seen in Europe. Early in the twenty-first century, a renewed decline is apparent. As Garland notes, it is not easy to see how this pattern of change can be explained by a constant, namely an 'American culture' assumed to stretch back to roots in the earliest stages of European settlement. So how is it to be explained? Once again, Spierenburg's provocative hypothesis that 'democracy came too early' appears to be relevant; or, at the very least, the political structures of American democracy have subtly constrained the workings of an underlying civilizing process that would not otherwise have been radically different from that seen in Europe.

It should first be noted that, in Garland's phrase (2004), 'the cultural shadow of the death penalty is longer in the USA than elsewhere and quite disproportionate to its penological importance'. For, in fact, in relation to the number of murders, few people are sentenced to death and even fewer actually executed. Roughly speaking, there are about 15,000 arrests for homicide each year, but only about 150 death sentences are passed, and fewer still are carried out (usually only after repeated appeals and legal arguments lasting a decade or more). Furthermore, there is no single 'American culture' when it comes to capital punishment. The states vary widely in their legal provision for the death penalty, in their sentencing practices and in their propensity actually to carry out the sentence. As Garland (2004) summarizes the position:

> States like New Hampshire have the law on the books but don't impose death sentences; states like New York or New Jersey impose sentences but have not carried out an execution since the 1960s; states like California or Pennsylvania frequently impose death sentences and execute a few of them; and states like Texas or Oklahoma or Virginia have the law, impose sentences, and carry out frequent executions. Then there are twelve states, along with Puerto Rico and the District of Columbia, in which capital punishment does not exist.[28]

There is a clear geographical pattern in this variation. The states that have abolished the death penalty are concentrated in the northern USA; below them come the 'mixed states' that may have the death penalty but rarely if ever carry it out; and then in the South are the states that carry out the bulk of executions. Zimring (2003: 89–118) has demonstrated that there is a strong positive correlation between the geographical distribution of judicial executions now and that of extra-judicial lynching a century ago. 'Those parts of the United States where mob killings were repeatedly inflicted as crime control without government sanction are more likely to view official executions as expressions of the will of the community rather than the power of a distant and alien government' (2003: 89). In other words, executions are most common in those parts of the country where it was truest to say (once more in Spierenburg's words) that 'the idea remained alive that the very existence of a monopoly of force was unde-sirable' (2006: 152). Another continuity is that black males are statisti-cally greatly over-represented among those executed, just as they were the principal victims of lynch mobs.

That the death penalty represents a sharing of the monopoly between the state and the people at large is symbolized by two distinctive features of American practice. First, and uniquely, the *jury* rather than the judge has been deemed to have responsibility for sentencing in homicide cases. Secondly, in recent decades legal sanction has been given to 'victim state-ments' in court – in other words, relatives of the deceased are entitled to make emotional pleas to the jury for vengeance (or, less commonly, for mercy). Both of these practices have in the past been rigorously disallowed in most other Western countries, although several of them have recently begun to copy the American model of allowing victim statements.

The system, as Garland (2004) again notes, 'is strikingly democratic and sensitive to public opinion'. And therein lies the most obvious con-trast with the countries of Europe and the Commonwealth. When the death penalty was abolished in those countries in the latter half of the twentieth century, public opinion polls generally showed clear majorities in favour of its retention. As was so often the case in previous phases of civilizing processes in Europe in earlier centuries, standards of behaviour and feeling changed first among minorities in the higher strata, and were then slowly accepted and adopted by the majority in the lower strata. What was true of table manners also went for judicial executions. The rel-evant power ratios made it possible for a more liberal elite initially to defy and subsequently to lead public opinion, and the process has by now con-tinued to the point where the death penalty is regarded as a breach of international law. Its abolition is a condition of membership of the European Union, and EU member states are forbidden to extradite sus-pects to the USA unless the American authorities give binding undertak-ings in advance that they will not seek the death penalty.

But the internal power ratios are very different in the USA. There is a good deal of evidence that, if the matter were left in the hands of the members of the US Supreme Court and Congress, the death penalty would have been abolished there too. Indeed, in the 1960s the Court did come very close to effectively abolishing it; even though homicide laws are mainly a matter for state jurisdictions, the Court's interpretation of the constitutional prohibition of cruel and unusual punishments and rulings on judicial procedures meant that no executions took place anywhere in the USA between 1968 and 1976 inclusive. Where America differed from Europe was that in the USA abolition produced a backlash in public opinion on a scale far larger than the occasional emotional outbursts by right-wing politicians and newspapers in Europe. The Supreme Court responded to this by reversing many of its earlier rulings, and executions rose again, peaking in 1999 at about the same level as that seen in the early 1950s. In the early years of the twenty-first century, the Court cautiously began once more to impose some restrictions, such as forbidding the execution of juveniles and the mentally retarded. The decline also owes something to the advent of DNA evidence, which has demonstrated how frequently wrong convictions have led to this most irreversible of punishments.

The issue of the death penalty, very much like that of gun control, became entangled in the 'culture wars' that have characterized American politics since the 1960s. The actual number of executions that takes place is tiny in relation to the number of murders that occurs each year, but executions are nevertheless of great symbolic importance for the increasingly polarized conflict between advocates of two different ways of life, associated with different social standards of behaviour and feeling. Garland (2004) has characterized the battle over capital punishment as a 'constrained civilizing process', because of the obstacles encountered when elites attempted to lead public opinion in the direction of abolition. The phrase is not quite right, because all or most facets of civilizing processes in Europe and elsewhere have also been marked by conflicts and resistance; it is an oversimplification to see civilizing processes in Europe, whether of table manners or the use of violence, as a simple and smooth process of the 'trickle-down' of upper-class models of behaviour and feeling leading to their passive adoption by the lower orders. With the quibble that '*relatively more* constrained civilizing process' might be a better term, it can nevertheless be acknowledged that the constraints appear to be greater in the USA.

Yet again, it must be stressed that the constraints are not in any abstract sense merely 'cultural'. It comes down to the fact that politicians, especially from the southern execution states, cannot allow themselves to be seen as 'soft' on capital punishment if they wish to retain their seats in legislatures. And in most states judges and public prosecutors are elected: they are part of the political system; they too have elections to lose if they are perceived to be too lenient. The case of capital punishment once more shows the significance of there not having been in America any single central model-setting elite to the extent that has often been seen in European countries. Compared with most other developed countries, in America a different balance is struck between the responsiveness and the autonomy of elites, both of which are essential for the functioning of democracy.[29] Tocqueville had already perceived this when he warned against the 'tyranny of the majority'. Viewed from America, the capacity of political leaders in Europe to defy, or at least to go out in front of, public opinion may appear 'undemocratic' and 'elitist'. Viewed from

Europe, the inability or unwillingness of American political leaders to do so may appear not as 'democratic' but as 'populist' or even 'cowardly'. In neither case is it a matter merely of 'attitudes' or 'culture'; it is also a question of prevailing balances of power. And the two facets – 'culture' and 'power' – are inseparable and reciprocally reinforce each other.

Conclusion

In its homicide rates and capital punishment, the USA appears to be out of step with other democracies of the developed world at the beginning of the twenty-first century. On examination, however, it is evident that trends in the USA are not so radically different from other countries as they first appear. Although the absolute *level* of homicides is very much higher than in comparable countries, the underlying long-term *trend* in homicides has been downwards since the nineteenth century, with an upturn from about 1960 that has more recently gone into reverse. Similar trends are evident internationally. Executions too declined in the USA through most of the twentieth century and came close to abolition, but then staged a comeback in response to a conservative backlash in public opinion, in which capital punishment came to be a key symbol in America's internal 'culture wars'.

The imprint of history is evident in the ways that the USA differs from other democratic countries. The monopolization of the means of violence by the state has been less complete, and its legitimacy more open to dispute in political debate, than in most other countries. But, more especially, the legacy of the South – of slavery, of a planter aristocracy, and their aftermath – can be seen to the present day. In the South, both before and long after the Civil War, only violence by blacks against whites was consistently, and savagely, punished. Many quarrels between whites were left to be settled according to the honour code, while much white violence against blacks and black violence against blacks was ignored by the putative monopoly apparatus of the state. The legacy was transmitted to the parts of the West that were largely settled from the South. Not only do they have elevated murder rates, but there is a high correlation between the states that have accounted for most of the executions in recent decades and the incidence of lynchings a century earlier, with blacks over-represented among the victims of both. Equally, it has been argued that the 'hair-trigger' resort to violence among black males in the urban ghettoes is the consequence of their growing up in communities where the forces of 'law and order' could not be relied upon to provide any alternative to violent self-defence. It is a subject for further research and debate to what extent that trait derives from the lack of protection encountered in the rural South in the more or less distant past, or from the withdrawal of the forces and support of the state from urban ghettoes in the more recent past.

According to Elias, consistent and relatively gentle pressures are more effective than punishments that are draconian but unpredictable in tilting the balance between external constraints and self-constraints, towards self-constraints carrying greater weight in the steering of conduct, so that more demanding standards of emotion management are internalized and come into play more 'automatically'. It may be recalled that Jefferson believed that Americans 'could be restrained from wrong and protected in right, *by moderate powers* confided to persons of [their] own choice and held to their duties by dependence on [their] own will' (see p. 29 above). That same view seems to have been put into practice in those states from which Tocqueville drew his conclusion – quoted in the epigraph to this chapter – that nowhere was 'criminal justice administered with more mildness than in the United States'. But that was certainly not true everywhere, and not all American prisons to this day have a reputation for the mildness of their regimes. In recent decades the prison population has greatly increased, and reliance on incarceration alone, simply to take offenders out of circulation, is unlikely to be the most effective way of exerting steady and consistent 'civilizing' pressure.

From time to time in discussions about the high level of violence in the USA, people ask whether Americans are in some sense 'more aggressive' than the citizens of similar countries. But that is to turn a sociological into a psychological question, a question of the personality attributes of individual people. In the past, when scholars attempted to account for 'cultural' differences between the people of different countries or different periods in history, they often referred to child-rearing practices and the 'personality' outcomes that they produced and reproduced. In the case of America, a good deal of attention was paid to how children are taught to handle aggression. Margaret Mead, in *And Keep Your Powder Dry* (1942: 138ff.) – significantly alluding to the 'gun culture' in its very title – saw it as characteristically American that children were encouraged and trained to 'stand up for yourself', for example in the school playground.[30] They were taught not to let themselves be bullied, and not to run to Mummy to help them out. Parents were equally afraid of their child being either a coward or a bully or both. The ethic of standing up for oneself was, according to Mead, qualified by a sense of fair play, and children were taught not to pick on people smaller than themselves. But young Americans had to show they 'had what it takes'. This ethic is plainly consonant with the legal doctrine of 'no duty to retreat'.

Yet child-rearing practices explain little in themselves. It is no more than a truism that it is through socialization from childhood onwards that the standards of behaviour and feeling prevalent at any time and place are transmitted to the next generation. The practices change in conjunction with changing standards and changing social structures. As the Stearnses (1986: 241) demonstrated, the standards for the emotional management of anger and aggressiveness in American child-rearing have changed over time, and changed in a direction broadly as predicted by the theory of civilizing processes. They propose a rough periodization. In the seventeenth century, parents showed little specific concern with children's anger as such, and there is evidence of considerable anger in adult relations for example with neighbours, but emphasis was placed on the necessity of 'breaking the will' of the child. Disapproval of anger increased in the eighteenth and early nineteenth centuries, but from about the mid-nineteenth century the Stearnses note an ambivalence about anger: while parents attempted to discipline and control their children's anger, they also approved of an appropriate channelling of anger, especially among males. A strong assertiveness in the business sphere, for instance, was considered necessary. Finally, since about 1940, a more uniform disapproval of anger is apparent, with some fluctuations in the degree of permissiveness (consonant with the cycles of informalization and reformalization mentioned in chapter 3). These trends were related to the more extensive networks in which people were entangled:

> In the more complicated society developing in the eighteenth century, the new sort of personality was more adaptive. Economically, the society relied on people to be assertive rather than submissive and passive. But people now frequently interacted in larger groups, often where they were not known to others. In such situations, uncontrolled rough-and-tumble anger could be a serious problem. It was important that people develop inner controls. Thus some sense of self as possessing control and initiative was useful and adaptive, as might not have been the case before. (Stearns, 1988: 57–8)

Thus there is no point in trying to treat 'social', 'cultural' and 'psychological' facets of civilizing processes as if they were separate 'factors' linked by billiard-ball causality. They all have to be seen in terms of a whole figuration of interconnected changes. Central to understanding figurational changes are not just the chains of interdependence which – with local and temporary reversals – bind more and more people together, but also the key balances of power within those webs of interdependence. Sometimes it seems relevant to try to separate the 'cultural', 'economic' or 'political' constraints that figurational interdependence exerts on people, but that can be misleading. It is often said that in America the market played a greater part in the formation of social character, and the state less, than in Europe. Indeed, as discussed in chapter 5, the spread of market relationships did have great significance. Yet in the end the effects of market relationships, or any other particular forms of interdependence, cannot be understood without considering state-formation processes, especially the formation of a relatively effective monopoly of the means of violence. What the state does *or does not do*, and how relatively effectively *or ineffectively* it does it, set the context and implicit rules for all forms of social interdependence. Chapters 7–9 of this book will therefore be concerned with the formation of the American state and how it resembles and differs from the experience of Western Europe. It will draw on the various strands of Norbert Elias's account of state-formation in Europe, first in relation to the consolidation of American national territory and then with internal aspects of the process and its consequences.

7

And Wilderness is Paradise Enow:
From Settlements to Independence

The state-society that became the United States of America was not exclusively an evanescence of the human spirit but, like other states elsewhere, arose out of a long-term process of state-formation that involved contests – frequently violent contests – between many rival groups of human beings.

There is an enormous literature on American political development, but most of it is slanted rather towards nation-building than state-formation, towards the construction of a sense of shared national identity rather than internal pacification and the forging of an effective monopolization of the means of violence.[1] Of course, the two can by no means be entirely separated. 'We-images' and especially 'we-feelings' are important, notably today when the USA has become the world's one super-power. Yet while there is no doubt that the formation of we-identities in the course of nation-building is an important facet of state-formation processes, it is subsidiary to the central feature of the formation of a state in the sense in which Weber defined it: 'an organization which successfully upholds a claim to binding rule making over a territory, by virtue of commanding a monopoly of the legitimate use of violence' (1978 [1922]: I, 54). Establishing such a monopoly involves, on the one hand, securing and extending the boundaries of a territory, to a considerable extent by means of the use of violence against external opponents; and, on the other, it involves the internal pacification of the territory. Elias's thesis (to quote it again) is that internal pacification also, in the long term, comes to be embodied in a more pacific habitus: 'if in this or that region, the power of central authority grows, if over a larger or smaller area the people are forced to live at peace with each other, the moulding of affects and the standards of emotion management are very gradually changed as well' (2000: 169; translation modified).

At first glance, state-formation in North America may appear to have an entirely different starting point from the corresponding process in Western Europe. For one thing, by the time European settlement on a significant scale began in North America, the precursors of several of the states which constitute Europe today – England, France, Spain, Portugal, The Netherlands, Sweden, though not Germany or Italy – had already assumed something like their present territorial shape through processes that had begun centuries earlier in the Middle Ages. Internally, they already had relatively well-developed state apparatuses, and, with necessary provisos about the prevalence of civil wars in seventeenth-century Europe, most of the settlers came from internally relatively pacified states. Yet, on closer inspection, there are interesting similarities beside the differences between North America and Western Europe. In particular, competition for territory – between rival groups of European settlers, between rival groups of indigenous people, and between Europeans and the indigenous population – was as essential a feature in North America as it had been and continued to be in Europe.

Towards the end of the first millennium AD, Western Europe had reached a stage of extreme fragmentation characterized by a high degree of local political and economic autarky (see above, p. 14). Gradually the balance between centrifugal and centripetal forces tilted, earlier in some regions than in others, and there set in a two-sided process of internal pacification on the one hand and violent contest for territory on the other. Slowly a pattern emerged of larger, more effective, and politically and economically more interdependent territorial states. It could be said that there had been a steady increase in the typical size of the 'survival unit' (Elias, 1991: 178–9) in which Europeans lived – meaning the social unit to which people looked for most of their basic needs of food, shelter, sexual partners and (above all) physical protection. The very earliest European settlers in North America would have grown up in fairly large survival units. In Western Europe, localities were, by today's standards, still relatively self-sufficient, but nevertheless increasingly bound together by a web of trade, administration, law and law-enforcement. In the early seventeenth century, the population of England (with Wales), one of the best integrated of European states at the time, was between four and five million. Some of the early settlers were seeking refuge from religious persecution or civil strife, but moving to a place of greater physical safety was hardly their primary motive. The new settlements began in circumstances that dictated a high degree of autarky. Given their dangerously unreliable supply lines across the Atlantic and the remoteness of established authority in Europe, they were thrown back on their own resources economically, politically and militarily. They were all too aware that they were not migrating to an unpopulated land devoid of human threats.

Autarky, but not *terra nullius*

Early Puritan settlers in New England thought of themselves as undertaking an 'errand into the wilderness' (Miller, 1956).[2] Their errand, in the sense of a journey commanded by God, was primarily religious and undertaken for their own spiritual benefit, not for that of the inhabitants of the land to which they journeyed. Elsewhere, the first English settlers had less elevated errands: the first Virginians 'spent their early days digging random holes in the ground, haplessly looking for gold instead of planting crops' (Loewen, 1995: 90). In both cases, the wilderness was also in their minds: their settlements were remote from their European homelands and isolated from them by voyages that were long in both distance and duration. But in a more objective sense they were not embarking on life in a wilderness. The land was populated by people whom Europeans then called 'Indians'.

The Indians had already transformed the landscape, by repeatedly burning the undergrowth, and by clearing and planting fields. The hunting plains Indians who provided the Hollywood stereotype of the Indian in the twentieth century were only ever a minority: in the eastern regions of North America, the Indians were chiefly agriculturalists living in settled communities. The Europeans generally settled among them, sometimes seizing their fields. In the case of Plymouth Plantation, the site was chosen because of its harbour, fresh water and cleared fields planted with corn – in fact it was a deserted Indian village whose population had recently been wiped out by disease (ibid.). The susceptibility of the indigenous population, here as elsewhere in the Americas, to infections unwittingly introduced from Europe facilitated European settlement in its early stages – a sick and subsequently much reduced population could offer less resistance.

Yet the surviving indigenous people were organized in settled communities with varying degrees and types of political organization, and the incomers always recognized that fact. Here a contrast with Australia is instructive. When in 1788 they established another European fragment society in the newly charted southern continent, the British regarded Australia as *terra nullius*, an empty land. Like the North American Indians, the aborigines had transformed the landscape through their use of fire (Goudsblom, 1992: 31–3), but because they were nomadic hunters rather than sedentary farmers (and because the population was relatively sparser) they were not organized in anything that eighteenth-century Europeans could recognize as state-like territorial units. The Europeans never entered into relations of close interdependence with the aborigines in the way they did with the Indians. In North America, the technological gap between the indigenous population and the first settlers was not so great. Indeed, at the very start, the settlers were more dependent on the Indians. The story is well known of how, in 1587, when the supply ship belatedly reached Virginia, the first English settlement at Roanoke was found deserted; it is most probable that the surviving settlers had sought food and refuge among the Indians, and were simply absorbed into Indian society. Still more familiar is the story of the 'first Thanksgiving' when, after the Indians of Massachusetts had helped the Plymouth settlement to survive the winter and imparted their knowledge of how to grow food in this environment, both sides are supposed to have sat down together to eat and to celebrate the first harvest.[3]

At first, then, the power ratio between settlers and Indians was relatively even. It did not long remain that way. The settlers had a monopoly of firearms, and even if the Indians later acquired guns and powder from European sources, the settlers retained an immense advantage. From an early stage, the indigenous population began to withdraw westwards in the face of the European advance. Thomas Jefferson and John Adams both remembered that in their childhood they had seen Indians in Virginia and Massachusetts. Yet long before that, relatively few of the European settlers would commonly have had direct dealings with Indians. Darcy Ribeiro, contrasting the pattern of white settlement in Latin America with that of the 'Anglo-Americans' in the North, asserts:

> Confronted with the Indian, the colonist of North America as a rule behaved with the Anglo-Saxon attitude of avoidance and repulsion. As long as there was no ecological competition for territory and for Europeanization of the landscape, the colonists allowed the Indian his tribal existence, exchanging pelts for tools. Above all, he avoided the redskin. The few whites who penetrated deeper into the country and lived with the Indians quickly became encultured as Indians, because there was no social space for mixed forms, who were viewed by the settlers of the coast with the greatest repulsion. When competition did start, they faced each other like two autonomous, opposed entities. . . . The attitude of avoidance and refusal to mingle, to assimilate, and live together, was less proper to the spirit of generous tolerance of cultural differences than to the spirit of apartheid and segregation. (1971: 355)

In line with Ribeiro's view, Stannard relates this 'spirit of apartheid' to the belief common in seventeenth-century Europe and shared by such intellectuals as Locke and Leibniz that there existed hybrid human/animal species; mutual identification, he contends, extended neither to animals nor to those, like the Indians, who were not categorized as fellow humans (1992: 226). This belief, he argues, had self-fulfilling consequences:

> What in fact was happening in those initial years of contact between the British and America's native peoples was a classic case of self-fulfilling prophecy, though one with genocidal consequences. Beginning with the false prejudgement of the Indians as somehow other than conventionally human in European terms (whether describing them as living 'after the manner of the Golden Age' or as 'wild beasts and unreasonable creatures'), everything the Indians did that marked them as incorrigibly non-European and non-Christian – and therefore as *permanently* non-civilized in British eyes – enhanced their definitionally less-than-human status. (Ibid.: 230)

But in my view this is to give undue causal weight to intellectual ideas in the everyday behaviour and attitudes of early settlers. Stannard, in any case, hedges his bets by citing Elias for evidence of 'violent manners [and] brutality of passions that characterized urban Europe', thus recognizing that the breadth of mutual identification with animals and with fellow *European* human beings was by modern standards low there too (ibid.: 59, 298n.). So how did the extent of mutual identification differ between Europe and North America, and between North America and Latin America? For one thing, the number of white settlers in proportion to the native population in Latin America always remained much smaller, and interbreeding in consequence much more common (an empirical confirmation, if it were needed, of membership of a single species). The white population in North America grew far more rapidly, permitting a much higher degree of endogamy (even though the male population continued to exceed the female in the USA until the late nineteenth century).

Rather than fall back on weak and ultimately untestable cultural explanations, it is more fruitful to look at the pattern of interdependence, and the consequent power ratios, between settlers and Indians. Karen Kupperman's detailed study (1980) of early contact between the English and the Indians is revealing.[4] She shows that in the late sixteenth and early seventeenth centuries many people in England believed that their society was 'rapidly changing for the worse, that all the old social controls and supports were breaking down'; they especially 'feared the tearing down of distinctions between people', and many early descriptions of the Indians 'held them up as an example of a society that had not lost its social moorings as English society had done'. Kupperman stresses that the differences between the settlers and the indigenous inhabitants in everything from technology to manners and beliefs about the natural world were initially less than they tend to appear in retrospective view. European observers with the closest knowledge of the indigenous societies tended to portray Indian individuals and cultures with respect; 'far from charac-terizing the Indians as sub-human brutes who lacked government, eye-witness writers did not have the least doubt that the Indians were organised in a civil society' (ibid.: 47). Certainly, some of the English could be profoundly 'racist' (to use the term anachronistically). The crucial point, however, is that Kupperman's study demonstrates that the sense of innate European superiority tended to be least among those who had most frequent and intense direct contact with Indians. This finding is consistent with one of the major propositions of the theory of civilizing processes: that mutual identification is associated with interdependence, especially relatively equal interdependence (and thus relatively even power ratios) between groups of people. The circle of mutual identifica-tion should be expected to widen as interdependence increases and becomes more equal. What in fact happened in North America, of course, was the opposite. The technological gap between the settlers and the Indians widened, and the balance of population shifted rapidly against the Indians. Settler reliance on Indians diminished rapidly. All these con-tributed to a steady tilting of the power ratio against the Indians. Fairly soon, setting aside minor considerations like the peltry trade, the interde-pendence between the settlers and the Indians was reduced almost to the purely ecological level of the contest for territory.[5]

Population

The balance of power between Indians and settlers was to a certain extent a function of the balance of population. Although many other develop-ments played their part, the power ratio between the two could scarcely but be affected by the rapid decline of Indian and rapid growth of settler numbers.

There are no firm figures for the indigenous population of North America before the arrival of European settlers. Estimates made by twen-tieth-century scholars have varied greatly. For a long time, an estimate of about 1 million was widely accepted. Since the 1960s, however, figures as high as 18 million have been advanced. On balance, a pre-contact popu-lation of between 4 and 7 million now seems a reasonable estimation (Krech, 1999: 93). Even starting from this estimate, the rate of decline in the indigenous population was drastic and sustained. Elsewhere in the world, populations ravaged by epidemics have recovered; yet in North America regional declines of 80 per cent or more between contact and the nadir that the Indian population reached in the late nineteenth century were not untypical.

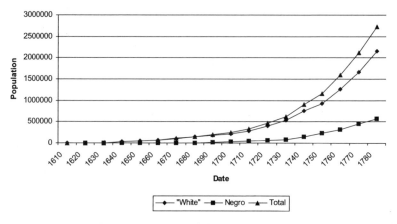

Figure 7.1: Estimated settler population of the thirteen colonies, 1610–1780
Source: US Department of Commerce and Bureau of the Census (1975).

The undoubted decline of the indigenous population, no matter how hard it is to quantify exactly, stands in strong contrast to the rapid growth of the European settler population. As figure 7.1 demonstrates, the white population of the region that comprised the original 13 colonies rose from 350 in 1610 (confined to the first colony, Virginia) to more than 2 million in 1780. The growth of the Negro population is shown separately; since slave labour represented a resource to the colonists, even if Negroes were not much used in fighting, they can, for purposes of assessing the power ratio vis-à-vis the Indians, be added in to the total population. It can be seen how quickly the colonial population came to outnumber the indigenous. Although English colonization began seriously only in 1607, when the Spanish Empire had already taken shape and developed for more than a century, numbers increased rapidly. The Spaniards and the French sought to ensure that only their own citizens, and good Catholics among them, were allowed to settle in the Americas. France, like England, was a late starter in North America, but the numbers of French settlers in the regions it claimed never approached those of the British colonies. The English authorities made no attempt to control migration to the new colonies. They attracted settlers of diverse religious conviction and none. Nor did the London government oppose the substantial migration of non-British people during the eighteenth century – to that is owed such early minorities as the Pennsylvania 'Dutch' – and it positively encouraged the slave trade. And besides, as Merrill Jensen (1997: 25) wrote, 'the government looked upon the colonies as places to send undesirables, the unemployed and convicts, and tens of thousands . . . were sent to America'.

Figure 7.2: George Henry Broughton, *Pilgrims Going to Church* (armed)
Source: Toledo Museum of Art, Toledo, Ohio.

In assessing the balance of population between the colonists and the original inhabitants, it has also to be borne in mind that a substantial proportion of the 4–7 million pre-Columbian population – if we accept that as a probable range for North America as a whole – lived well out of direct contact with the British colonies of the eastern seaboard (Ubelaker, 1988: 291). Nevertheless, even if the tribes of the seaboard and the Appalachians were soon outnumbered, they played a substantial part in the earlier stages of American state-formation. In Virginia, violent conflicts between Indians and white settlers had occurred from the beginning. The presence on board the *Mayflower* of Miles Standish, hired as military leader, shows that before they landed at Plymouth Rock the 'Pilgrim Fathers' had no unrealistic expectation that relations with the continent's existing inhabitants would be always peaceful. Yet, three centuries later, Lipset (1963) could write about the formation of American national identity without mentioning the native Americans at all.

Early phases of the American state-formation process

One striking difference between state-formation processes as they unfolded in Western Europe and North America was their speed: many of the phases of the European process find an echo in North America, but there they follow upon each other in more rapid succession. Phases of North American development that took place in the seventeenth and eighteenth centuries are in some respects equivalent to phases through which Western Europe passed much earlier. What has to be compared is *the structure of underlying social processes*, sometimes at chronologically widely separate periods, rather than making synchronic comparisons at a specific point in history.

The North American elimination contest (1): consolidation of the eastern seaboard

The colonists who came to the eastern seaboard in the seventeenth century had grown up in burgeoning commercial state-societies, and brought with them the mental furniture of early modern Europe. Yet the territorial elimination contest that was played out in North America in the first century and a half of white settlement resembled in many ways that which had unfolded over a period of several centuries in medieval Europe. In the Middle Ages, the connection between land, the means of violence and overall political power had been so direct and uncomplicated that the struggle for territory formed the simple centrepiece of state-formation processes. By the seventeenth century, commercial wealth and administrative structures had begun to complicate the relationship: land remained the pre-eminent, but not the only, power resource. In North America, land was abundant – provided that the indigenous population could be kept at bay – and the colonies' survival and expansion rested above all on acquiring it. The quest for land ran as a leitmotif through American history for the best part of three centuries.

It is important to recognize that the competition for territory is not driven primarily by any 'aggressive' habitus on the part of the people involved. Speaking of medieval Europe, Elias argued that, given the initial condition of a society with numerous power and property units of relatively equal size, there was a very high probability that under strong competitive pressures the tendency would be towards the enlargement of a few units and finally towards monopoly (2000: 264). The competitive pressure derived from the particular way in which warrior lords are socially interdependent with each other. The constant violent conflicts over land were in no way simply the 'result' of people's aggressive motivation. On the contrary, the feudal magnate *had* to fight with neighbours to extend his territory. In some abstract philosophical sense, a magnate with, for the time, an unusually pacific outlook was 'free' to choose merely to try to hold onto his existing domains and avoid conflict with his neighbours. Yet the consequences of such a course of action were perfectly plain: anyone who declined to compete, merely conserving his property while others strove to increase theirs, necessarily ended up 'smaller' and weaker than the others, and was in ever-increasing danger of succumbing to them (ibid.: 219). Each knew that if his neighbour acquired more land – even if from a third party rather than from himself – the increased economic and military resources it brought meant inevitably that the balance of power between him and his neighbour was tilted to his own disadvantage, and it was extremely probable that sooner or later his domains would be invaded, his army defeated, his lands absorbed by the more powerful neighbour and he and his family killed.

By the early modern era, European states had achieved a far more complex level of social organization than in the high Middle Ages, and power resources had therefore become more diversified. In the age of mercantilism, governments were aware of the significance of trade in creating the wealth of a nation, and therefore of the naval and military means of controlling trading routes and opportunities. Yet, as the Physiocrats continued to stress in the mid-eighteenth century, land could still be seen as the fundamental source of wealth, and control of terri-tory – very obviously in North America – underlay the growth of national trade.

The American elimination contest differed from that of medieval Europe in at least one very important way. The territorial struggle in North America was driven as much by rivalries between the various estab-lished states back in Europe as it was by local conflicts.[6] In that respect, it was somewhere intermediate along a continuum between the endoge-nously driven battles between numerous local warlords in early second-millennium Europe and the largely exogenous race for territory in Africa between European colonial powers in the nineteenth century. In the sev-enteenth century, England, France, Spain, Sweden and The Netherlands all established settlements in North America. The Swedes who settled in the Delaware River area in 1637 are often forgotten; after some years of conflict with the Dutch for control of the area that later comprised Philadelphia and New Jersey, they were eliminated as an independent player in the continent following their defeat at Fort Casimir in 1655. The Dutch lasted longer. They established a settlement on Manhattan Island in 1612, and they developed trade links with the Indians up the Hudson valley. New Amsterdam was formally established in 1626. In the wider New Netherland territory, including Long Island, there were both Dutch and English towns, and both sent members to the representative assem-bly summoned by Pieter Stuyvesant in 1653–4. The outbreak of the Second Anglo-Dutch War (1665–7) – a conflict between two great com-mercial powers in Europe – sealed the fate of the independent Dutch set-tlements. In 1664, Stuyvesant surrendered New Amsterdam, which became New York and stayed so apart from a brief interval when the Dutch regained control in the course of the Third Anglo-Dutch War (1672–4). By the end of the seventeenth century, the English could claim to rule a consolidated strip of land along the entire eastern seaboard, between the vicinity of Maine and that of Georgia. The strip was not wide – rarely more than 200 miles. Nor was the territory internally wholly pacified, although government was gradually becoming more effective. The 'rebellion' of Nathaniel Bacon against the royal Governor's authority in Virginia in 1676 was just one among many incidents in the unruly life of the early colonies. At just the same time, in Massachusetts in 1675–6, the colonists defeated the Wampanoag and Nipmuck Indians in 'King Philip's War', the last extensive war between whites and Indians on the eastern seaboard (though far from the last in North America, and far from the last skirmish).

The development of colonial government

The stage of relatively great local economic and political autarky in the European colonies of the eastern seaboard was brief. The precariousness of life for the settlers in the very earliest colonies, in any case, disguises the fact that they found themselves where they were not by accident but in consequence of organization, direction and capital on a scale that could only have been provided, at that date, by the commercial states of Western Europe (Tilly, 1990). Settlements were not established directly by European governments, although their growing naval and merchant fleets helped to make transatlantic settlement possible. Rather, the colonies were established either by companies or by rich individual proprietors under royal charter (or, in the case of the Dutch West India Company, with the sanction of the United Provinces). Virginia, Massachusetts Bay, New Netherland and (much later, in 1732) Georgia were founded by companies. Maryland, Pennsylvania, Delaware, New Jersey and North and South Carolina were founded by rich proprietors, either alone or in partnerships. Connecticut, Rhode Island and New Hampshire began as offshoots of Massachusetts, while the settlements in Maine formed part of Massachusetts from 1691 until after the War of Independence. The organization required to found Massachusetts is partly obscured by the tiny origins of the Pilgrims' slightly earlier settlement at Plymouth Plantation, which was absorbed into Massachusetts in 1691. In fact, the scale of planning and capital that the Massachusetts Bay Company had to provide is evident in the landings at Salem in 1629 and 1630. About 400 people, with supplies and animals, arrived in 5 ships in 1629, to be followed in June 1630 by more than 1,000 in 11 ships. Besides Salem, the towns of Boston, Charlestown, Dorchester, Lynn, Medford, Roxbury and Watertown were founded immediately, and numbers of both people and towns rose rapidly. John Winthrop, named as first Governor by the Company, already faced a fairly considerable task of government.

Thinking of the problem that confronted an early medieval ruler like Charlemagne, Norbert Elias wrote that 'the strength of the centrifugal tendencies towards local *political autarky* within societies based predominantly on a barter economy corresponds to the degree of local *economic autarky*' (2000: 207). In other words, if remote territories claimed by a central ruler could in practice only be ruled by delegating their government and defence to a subordinate who was granted sufficient land to fulfil these functions autonomously from the central ruler, then there was a considerable chance that the subordinate would not long remain subordinate: the resources granted to enable him to rule in the name of the king could equally well enable him to rule in his own name. Of course, England and the other countries of Western Europe were by the seventeenth century far from predominantly barter economies (although the American colonies remained dependent on barter to a remarkable degree until after the Revolution), and had developed considerable administrative, fiscal and military apparatuses. Even so, those apparatuses were still not adequate to provide day-to-day government in scattered settlements 3,000 miles away on the far side of the Atlantic. In practice, both proprietors and companies appointed governors for their colonies, who set up what were, in effect, private governments. Perhaps if an analogy with the era of Charlemagne seems too far-fetched, the incipient dynamics of the situation could be compared to the later phase in the development of France, the so-called 'figuration of the competing princes' in the fourteenth and fifteenth centuries, when regional apanages granted by kings for their younger sons to rule became in following generations the basis for resurgent centrifugal tendencies undermining the central power of the king (Elias, 2000: 289–302).

Whether or not the royal government back in London thought about the problem in quite those terms, by the later seventeenth century it was taking a considerable interest in American colonies that were now growing rapidly in population and prosperity. 'The Crown', succinctly remarks Gordon S. Wood, 'began to take back what it had so freely given away to private individuals and groups at the beginning of the century and to assert greater control over the government of the colonies' (in Schlesinger, 1993: 18). From the 1660s onwards, many of the original charters were revoked, and the private governments placed under royal jurisdiction. The charter of the Massachusetts Bay Company, for instance, was revoked by Charles II in 1684. The most extreme move in this direction occurred the following year, when his brother and successor James II attempted to place the northeastern colonies within the framework of a single Dominion of New England, on the model of the centralized viceroyalties of imperial Spain. That collapsed with James's own exit in the Glorious Revolution of 1688–9. Nevertheless, by the time the proprietors of the Carolinas sold out to the king in 1729 and the trustees of Georgia surrendered their rights to the crown after only 20 years in 1752, nearly all the colonies had become royal provinces with royal governors. The exceptions were Pennsylvania and Maryland, which technically remained in the control of their founding proprietorial families until the Revolution, and the two small New England chartered colonies of Connecticut and Rhode Island. These too, however, now had to function more closely within the framework of British law and authority.

At the same time, royal control did not run very deep in colonial society. Even after most of the settlements had been transformed into crown colonies, defence – that most central function of states – was normally left largely to the colonists themselves. In the mid-eighteenth century, contingents of the royal army were permanently stationed only in the most vulnerable locations, in comparatively new colonies like South Carolina and Georgia and at strategic points such as New York (Williams, 1960: 318). The legislative assemblies of the colonies also exerted some check on royal power. The first, that of Virginia, had been established as early as 1619. Under royal government, the pattern was that the upper house of each of the bicameral legislatures was nominated by the governor, but the lower house was popularly elected. In spite of the governors retaining the right to veto legislation, their veto (like that of the crown itself in Great Britain) had in practice to be exercised with increasing restraint.

One of the key trends running through the long-term processes of state-formation in Western Europe is the transformation of private monopolies of force and taxation into public monopolies. Elias described this as a process 'in which control over the centralized and monopolized resources tends to pass from the hands of individuals to those of ever-greater numbers, and finally to become a function of the interdependent human web as a whole, the phase in which a relatively "private" monopoly becomes a "public" one' (2000: 276). Nothing better shows the accelerated character of American state-formation and its complex similarities to and differences from Europe than the relationship between private and public monopolies.

Although Elias, whose primary focus of attention was the French state, spoke of the French Revolution as being a decisive event in this process (ibid.: 312–13), its origins lie much further back in time, and its rate of progression differed considerably between countries. The development of royal absolutism in France, Spain and the Habsburg lands can be seen as a consolidation of monopolies of a 'private' character, reaching its pinnacle in the age of Louis XIV (1643–1715), who is apocryphally said to have claimed that '*L'état c'est moi*'. The depersonalization and institutionalization of the exercise of power had begun far back in the Middle Ages when the expansion of the territory under the control of one magnate made it impossible for one man to exercise all the functions of rule personally. Yet even the immense and complex apparatus at the apex of which stood Louis XIV remained in important ways 'private'. It was still essentially an extension of the royal household, an administration of the sort that Max Weber (1978: II, 1006–69) labelled 'patrimonial bureaucracy'. There remained no distinction between the public and private revenues and expenditures of the king.

England, later Great Britain, diverged rather earlier from the path that was leading to an absolutist regime on the French or Spanish model. Even under Queen Elizabeth, Parliament had become a greater constraint on royal power than were its counterparts in France. The early Stuarts, under whom the first permanent English settlements in North America began, may have aspired to absolutism at home, but made no attempt to impose it in the colonies. Charles I's conflicts with Parliament culminated first in his attempt to govern (and tax) without it, and then to the Civil Wars (1642–51), his beheading and the interregnum of the Commonwealth (1649–60). The outcome was a permanent shift in the balance of power between the monarchy on the one hand and the major landowning aristocracy and gentry and mercantile interests on the other. In his brief reign (1685–8), James II embarked on many policies (including, as noted above, in North America) that could be and were interpreted as a reassertion of aspirations to absolutism, but his overthrow in the Glorious Revolution reconfirmed the shift that had taken place in the central power ratio in the English state. While the monarch's political preferences did not cease to be of negligible significance in government for more than a further century, the Hanoverian kings who succeeded to the throne on the death of Queen Anne in 1714 cannot be represented as absolutist. The role of Parliament and of cabinet government steadily increased during the eighteenth century, and factions among the aristocracy and gentry gradually assumed the role of political parties (not yet *mass* parties) between which political office alternated peacefully. These developments may be said to have led not just to political but also to cultural differences between England and France (Mennell, 1996a: 102–33).

This sequence of stages in state-formation processes in England (or Great Britain, after the union of England and Scotland in 1707) forms the background to the early stages of state-formation in British North America. Because of the stages reached on one side of the Atlantic, the actions of the crown in bringing the colonies on the other side under royal jurisdiction in the late seventeenth and early eighteenth centuries may be interpreted – with rather more confidence after the Glorious Revolution – as part of the process of transforming private into public monopolies. But it is an ambiguous question, complicated by the role of the locally elected or appointed legislative assemblies. Given the political and religious sympathies of many of the earliest settlers during the reigns of James I and Charles I, and given the centrality of the struggle between kings and Parliament through most of the seventeenth century, it is hardly surprising that assemblies were established at so early a stage in the history of the colonies. When serious disagreement eventually arose between the crown and the colonies, Parliament itself provided the precedent for members of the assemblies claiming a better right than the royal governors to represent the public interest. While they were by no means yet modern democratic regimes based on universal suffrage, the colonies had already moved further in that direction than the 'home country'. But what precipitated the final breach was not an absolutist impulse to suppress incipient democracy, but rather the unforeseen consequences of the joint success of Britain and its colonies in consolidating their hold over the whole eastern seaboard.

The North American elimination contest (2): The French, the Indians and the crisis of British rule

It is possible to imagine a course of events in which the American colonies remained part of the British Empire – that indeed remained Benjamin Franklin's goal until the very eve of the War of Independence (Morgan, 2002) – and it is often said that it was only a brief loss by the British of naval supremacy to the French that precipitated the surrender at Yorktown in 1781. But this book is not an exercise in counterfactual history.[7] Considering the growing size and prosperity of the colonies and the technology for communication and ruling at the time, most historians have thought it likely that sooner or later a breach would have come about. While it cannot be said that the sequence of events which did in fact lead to the independence of the United States of America was 'inevitable', the series of four 'French and Indian Wars' that followed the consolidation of the eastern seaboard under British rule and their aftermath clearly formed part of a 'compelling process' driven by territorial competition between the states of Europe in Europe *and* in North America.[8]

One of the summary trends that Elias shows to run through the course of state-formation in Western Europe is that as the number of *internally* relatively highly pacified states diminished in number and increased in territorial size, the scale of wars *between* them increased. From the Middle Ages until the mid-nineteenth century, France and England were almost invariably on opposing sides. By the early modern period they were no longer seriously competing actually to take territory *from each other* in Europe, although after 1714, when the Elector of Hanover became also King George I of Great Britain, Britain was more directly involved in the still endemic wars in Germany. But Britain and France were locked in a worldwide maritime and colonial rivalry as part of a struggle for pre-dominance in Europe. The consolidation of English rule along the eastern seaboard and the gradual extension of the frontier of trading and settlement westwards towards and beyond the Appalachians during the late seventeenth and eighteenth centuries led to battles with the French, who were moving down from Canada in the interior. Fighting flared up in North America particularly during each of the successive European wars. 'King William's War' (1689–97) corresponded to the war waged in Europe by the Grand Alliance against France over the succession to the throne of England. 'Queen Anne's War' (1702–13) was the American counterpart of the War of the Spanish Succession in Europe. And 'King George's War' (1744–8) was a transatlantic branch of the War of the Austrian Succession. The French and British colonists, with their respective Indian allies, launched steadily more ambitious raids on each other's settlements. The cycle of colonial violence came to a head in the fourth of the series, the Seven Years War (1756–63), known in America as *the* French and Indian War (in the singular).

In the Seven Years War, Great Britain and Hanover were allied with Frederick the Great of Prussia against an alliance consisting of Austria, Saxony, France, Spain and (for part of the time) Russia and Sweden. Ostensibly, the war broke out in Europe over the province of Silesia, which Prussia had seized from Austria in 1740. After many vicissitudes, which need not concern us here, the Prussians were victorious, and the war resulted in no territorial changes in Europe. In long-term historical perspective, the significance of the Seven Years War lies less in the battles between the European great powers in Europe than in the struggle between Britain and France over colonial possessions in other continents. For it was at this time that Britain, notably under the military leadership of Robert Clive, established its clear ascendancy over the French in India. The outcome was the same in North America, but with unforeseen consequences that made the triumph prove to be only short term.

The notional distribution of territory in North America between Britain, France and Spain at the outbreak of the Seven Years War is shown in figure 7.3 – 'notional', because the map gives the false impression that there were clear borders of the kind that appear on a modern map between territories that are unambiguously subject to one jurisdiction rather than another. In the mid-eighteenth century, there were borderlands rather than borders, in which French, British and indigenous groups mingled, traded and fought. There was an enormous imbalance between the populations of the British and French colonies – that of the colonies of the eastern seaboard was already of the order of 1.5 million, while only 50,000 or so French settlers are thought to have constituted the colonial population of Canada. Outside these heartlands, various groups of Indians

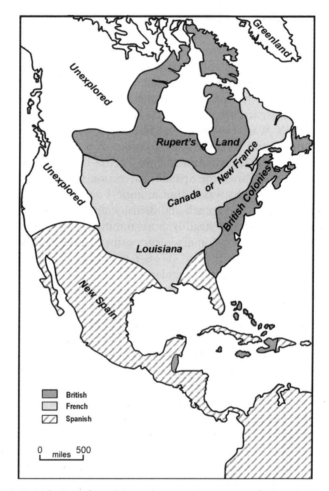

Figure 7.3: British, French and Spanish possessions in North America, 1750

remained forces to be reckoned with. Nevertheless, the French had heavily fortified the approaches to the St Lawrence River, and they had begun constructing a line of forts with the aim of impeding the British colonists' expansion into the Ohio valley and, ultimately, of laying claim to the whole Mississippi valley and linking up Canada with New Orleans, thus encircling the British colonies.

Hostilities in America actually broke out in 1754, two years ahead of the Seven Years War as it is viewed from Europe. It was not a war *just* about land. To European states in the age of mercantilism, commerce and manufactures were equally the means to national wealth and power. Immediate issues between the British and French in North America included claims to fishing rights off the Gulf of St Lawrence, and the control of fur trading in the interior. But if land and commerce were now analytically separable power resources, in North America they were in practice still fused: the competition for control of territory was still paramount. The war began badly for the British side. In 1754 the Governor of Virginia sent a force under the young George Washington first to negotiate unsuccessfully with the French over their intrusion into land claimed by the British in the Ohio Valley, and then to attempt to expel them from the strategic site at the fork of the Ohio, where modern Pittsburgh now stands, and where the French had erected their Fort Duquesne. The following year, a larger military force under General Edward Braddock, commander-in-chief in North America, was routed near Fort Duquesne by the French and their Indian allies, and Braddock himself was killed. Subsequently, the tide turned. In 1758, British forces captured the fortress of Louisburg which controlled access to the St Lawrence; in 1759, forces under General James Wolfe defeated the French army at Quebec; and in 1760, Montreal fell to General Jeffrey Amherst. The Treaty of Paris which concluded the Seven Years War in 1763 also marked the end of French power in Canada, which was ceded to Britain along with all lands east of the Mississippi hitherto claimed by France. Florida was also ceded to Britain by Spain.

Parallel with the elimination contest among European powers in North America, but thoroughly intertwined with it, was a similar contest among indigenous peoples. In the 'French and Indian' wars, the French fought in alliance with Algonquians, the British with the support of most of the Iroquois. The Iroquois, in particular, conducted themselves from an early stage as an independent power in their relations with the white settlers, allying themselves first with the Dutch and then, fairly consistently, with the British. But this formed part of their own striving for hegemony over other indigenous peoples in a vast region to the west of the seaboard colonies. The League of the Five Nations (Mohawk, Onondaga, Cayuga, Oneida and Seneca) was formed in the early years of the sixteenth century in the middle of what was to become New York State (Fenton, 1998). Much later, in the early eighteenth century, a sixth tribe, the Tuscaroras, who had migrated to New York from North Carolina, was formally admitted. At about that same time, in response to problems arising from contact with the whites, the Iroquois instituted a Confederacy that was responsible for external relations, while the institutions of the League in effect remained the apparatus of internal rule. The Iroquois were noted for their elaborate system of government, involving the election of delegates to represent the various lineages on the council of the League, and modes of decision-making that required a high degree of consensus before all the nations were committed to any collective action. (Indeed, one reason for qualifying statements about their alliance with the British is that some factions of the Iroquois did from time to time fight with the French.) It has in fact been argued that the Iroquois system of consensus-promoting checks and balances had a major influence on the formulation of the US Constitution.[9] But their high level of internal pacification was combined with bellicosity towards external rivals. During the seventeenth century, they defeated the Huron and other tribal groupings to their west, and by the time the Confederacy was formed they were the dominant power between the Mississippi in the west and the white coastal settlements in the east, and roughly from the St Lawrence in the north to the Tennessee in the south. In particular, they effectively held the balance of power between the French and the British, opposing the expansion of French settlement southwards. At the end of the Seven Years War, the British were thus militarily indebted to their Iroquois allies, and this was to have unforeseen consequences.

The standard histories of the American Revolution dwell especially on the issues and events connected with the slogan 'no taxation without representation'. At the end of the Seven Years War, Britain had acquired vast new territories and in seeking to control them faced a considerable problem of overstretch. It was no longer realistic to leave the defence of the entire North American territory largely to the colonial militias with the support only of small detachments of the royal army at strategic locations. The posting there of a large standing army, however, posed two problems. For one thing, the entire idea of standing armies was relatively new in the eighteenth century, and their development was associated more with the absolutist monarchies of the continent than with the parliamentary regime of landowners and merchants that Britain was becoming. Whatever the merits of the army for fighting foreign wars, a standing army as a potential agent of oppression at home had been viewed with suspicion in England since the Civil Wars, and the suspicion was inevitably shared by the North American colonists. Secondly, standing armies had to be paid for by raising revenue, and the attempts of the London government to tax the colonies led to steadily increasing resentment through the 1760s and early 1770s. Certainly 'no taxation without representation' was the kernel of the discourse through which the Revolution was justified by its leaders (and its supporters back in Britain), and there is no need to retell the story in any detail here.

In the background is another consideration, however, which although well known has been paid less attention. By royal proclamation in 1763, the British government reserved the Ohio valley for the Indians – among whom their allies the Iroquois were the dominant power. They drew a line on the map between white and Indians, without the means to police and enforce it.

> In the years just preceding the war for independence, the frontier regions
> between British colonists and tribal Indians rocked in turmoil. . . . Garrisons
> stationed in western forts were withdrawn to control eastern urban rebels,
> and squatters known as 'settlers' rushed to occupy lands for which they had
> only the most tenuous pretensions of right, when they had any at all.
> Deputy Superintendent George Croghan declared in 1769 that 'there were
> between four and five thousand [settlers], and all this spring and summer
> the roads have been lined with wagons moving to the Ohio'. (Jennings,
> 2000: 216)

Theodore Roosevelt recognized the significance of this. In *The Winning
of the West*, he pointed out that 'the Ohio Valley and the other western
lands of the French had been conquered by the British, not the
Americans', and argued that the British wished 'to keep woodland and
prairie for the sole use of their own merchants, as regions tenanted only
by Indian hunters and French trappers and traders'. He described the
American Revolution as 'fundamentally a struggle between England . . .
and the Americans, triumphantly determined to acquire the right to
conquer the continent', and pointed out that, had they not won that right,
'we would certainly have been cooped up between the sea and the mountains' with the Alleghenies as the western frontier (1995 [1889–99]: II,
374–5). Among modern historians, Francis Jennings in particular has
argued that the American Revolution must be seen as a conflict over the
control of conquests and, if he is right, this underlines the parallels
between the continuing elimination contest in North America and that
which had unfolded much earlier in Europe. The colonists were also colonizers; while resisting the imperial ambitions of the British government,
they were consciously seeking to create their own empires. This theme
could scarcely be as prominent as 'no taxation without representation' in
the rhetoric of the Revolution, but leaders such as Jefferson never made
any secret of their vision of the immense possibilities offered by westward
expansion. The opportunities for enrichment were irresistible:

> Though the crown made an effort to preserve 'crown lands' for the Indians,
> it was unable to prevent some of its own officials from the common rapac-
> ity. . . . Governor Lord Dunmore launched war against the Shawnees in
> 1773 to open their territory to immigrants from Virginia who would have
> to buy from him. Mostly, however, crown officials acquired rights quietly
> that they hoped to cash in when times became quieter. . . . The
> Revolutionaries, however, were in a hurry. (Jennings, 2000: 216)

That tells a story startlingly reminiscent of the problem faced by aspirant
central rulers in a feudal Europe with a pre-monetary economy.

After independence, any impulse to reserve western lands for indigenous
peoples was diminished. Besides, under the Articles of Confederation, the

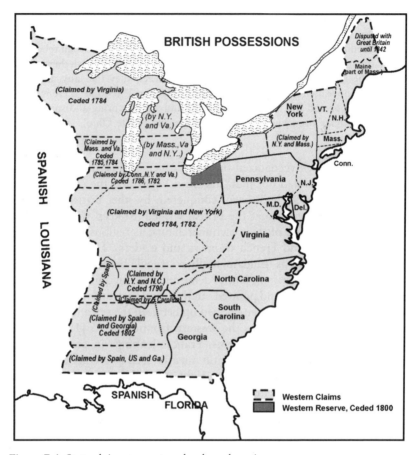

Figure 7.4: State claims to western lands and cessions

government of the United States was extremely weak. In the absence of a central monopoly apparatus, stirrings of rivalry and territorial competition between the states of the new Union were clearly evident. Explaining the background to the drafting of the new Constitution in 1787, Isaac Kramnick writes:

> As a result of this vacuum of power at the centre, the thirteen states were beset by rivalries, general confusion and numerous variations and duplications. They acted, in short, like the sovereign and independent states they assumed they were. Seven of the thirteen states, for example, printed their own money. Many passed tariff laws against neighbouring states. Nine of the thirteen had their own navies, which often seized ships of other states. The states continually argued over their boundaries and their claims to land in the western territories. (1987: 20)

Maps of the period show parallel stripes of land running westward to the Mississippi from the Appalachian boundaries between the states of the eastern seaboard, each stripe claimed by its respective state (see figure 7.4). Is it too fanciful a counterfactual speculation to think that the imperatives of the 'monopoly mechanism' could have come into play and initiated a different sequence in the North American elimination contest, in which the states of a little more than nominal union fought it out amongst themselves for the western territory? In the event, after the adoption of the Constitution, rather than the original states expanding ever westwards, new states were created and admitted to the Union, beginning with Vermont (which had briefly been an independent republic) in 1791, Kentucky in 1792 and Tennessee in 1796. By the time of the Civil War, a majority of the states had been created by, rather than being participants in the creation of, the federal government.[10] The great cataclysm of the Civil War can, however, serve to remind us that alternative and earlier scenarios of inter-state conflict over the western lands might not have been inconceivable.

Conclusion

In this chapter, the earlier phases of the formation of the American state have been traced from the first European settlements to the War of Independence and its immediate aftermath. The aim has been not to moralize about the motives, the 'aggressiveness' or the limited scope of mutual identification of the participants, but to focus on the underlying dynamics of a long-term process in which motives and perceptions were at least as much the product as the cause of events. In the territory of what became the USA, there took place an 'elimination contest' not unlike that which had unfolded in Western Europe several centuries earlier, but which was driven in part by competition between European colonial powers that had themselves already reached a later stage of state-formation processes. The next chapter will deal with the process of westward expansion in the nineteenth century to the formation in turn of an American overseas empire at the end of the nineteenth century and in the twentieth.

8

But Westward, Look, the Land
is Bright: From Frontier to Empire

Whenever one looks at an historical process *a posteriori*, knowing what was the final outcome, it is difficult to perceive the uncertainties at each stage, the range of alternative outcomes that might have been. In retrospect, it may be hard to imagine how there could be any outcome other than a USA stretching from Atlantic to Pacific and between what are now the Canadian and Mexican borders. By the 1840s it already appeared inevitable to a good many Americans. Justifying expansion into Texas, Mexico and Oregon, the Jacksonian journalist John L. O'Sullivan wrote in 1845 that it was 'by right of *manifest destiny*' for the United States 'to overspread and to possess the whole of the continent which Providence has given us', both for 'the development of the great experiment in liberty and federative self-government entrusted to us' and for 'the free development of our yearly multiplying millions'. If the phrase was new, the idea had been steadily forming for half a century. Thomas Jefferson (see p. 42 above) had from an early stage had his eye on expansion into the 'free land' to the west. And in 1812, just nine years after Jefferson had doubled the national territory through the Louisiana Purchase, John Quincy Adams wrote to his father:

> The whole continent of North America appears to be destined by Divine providence to be peopled by one nation, speaking one language, professing one general system of religious and political principles, and accustomed to one general tenor of social usages and customs. For the common happiness of them all, for their peace and prosperity, I believe it is indispensable that they should be associated in one federal Union. (Quoted in Remini, 2002: 44)

Yet destiny had not always been quite so manifest. Looking back to the period between the Declaration of Independence and the adoption of the

Constitution, John Adams wrote in his diary: 'no-one thought of consolidating this vast continent under one national government' (quoted by Kramnick, 1987: 18). So to what extent was the continental USA 'inevitable' or 'accidental', and how far was it the outcome of conscious plans or of unintended processes?

Manifest destiny and latent dynamics: a necessary theoretical digression

Here an illuminating comparison can again be made with Elias's study of state-formation, starting the best part of a millennium earlier, in the region that eventually became France. Elias showed how unavoidable was a violent 'elimination contest'; but he also repeatedly stressed that this did not mean that a high probability was attached to any particular outcome of the struggle. It was highly likely that a large state would emerge somewhere in the general region of modern France, but there was nothing at all certain about its eventual boundaries: the regional diversity between the north and south, between *langue d'oc* and *langue d'œil* among other things, might well have resulted in separate northern and southern states emerging. Above all, the whole weight of Elias's narrative goes to show how uncertain it long remained that the Paris kings would emerge as final victors and monopolists. And the *a posteriori* perspective leads one far too easily to imagine that the participants at each stage foresaw the outcome, that they had a long-term strategy or plan, which, in the end, they succeeded in implementing. Nothing could be further from the truth. Early French kings may, for all we know, have occasionally entertained daydreams of restoring their rule over the old west Frankish region. Their successors eventually expanded beyond the boundaries defined by the Treaty of Verdun in AD 840, although the eastern boundary of the French state was not finally (as it now appears) settled until 1945. At any rate, if early rulers did indeed have such grand *dreams*, it was nothing so ethereal that guided their military endeavours against their rivals: they just fought the next battle. There was no grand *plan*; instead, writes Elias: 'To some extent the same is true of the French kings and their representatives as was once said of the American pioneer: "He didn't want all the land; he just wanted the land next to his"' (2000: 312).

That is not to say, however, that the overall territorial expansion of the USA was as unplanned as that of France centuries earlier.[1] It is not just the probability of alternative outcomes that changes in the course of a process of social development, but also the foreseeability and plannability of such outcomes. This is – yet again – a function of changing power ratios between the groups of people whose interests and intentions are interweaving to produce the process. We have already noted that, without being blind to very important contrary movements, Elias sees one of the broad trends in the development of modern industrial societies as being towards 'functional democratization', by which he means that on the whole the power ratios within society – between, for instance, social classes, men and women, rulers and ruled – have become *relatively* less unequal. An important consequence of this dominant (if partial) trend is illustrated in Elias's series of 'game models' (1978: 71–103). Generally speaking, the more relatively evenly balanced are the power ratios between players, the more prevalent will be unforeseen outcomes that are not planned or intended by anyone. Elias illustrates the point at its simplest by reference to a basic two-person game like chess. Even when only two players are involved, a rather different situation emerges if, for whatever reason, their strengths in the game gradually become more equal. Two things diminish: the stronger player's ability to use his or her own moves to force the weaker to make particular moves, and his or her ability to determine the course of the game. The weaker player's chances of control over the stronger increase correspondingly. But, as the disparity between the players' strengths is reduced, the course of the game increasingly passes beyond the control of either. As Elias explains:

> Both players will have correspondingly less chance to control the changing figuration of the game; and the less dependent will be the changing figuration of the game on the aims and plans for the course of the game which each player has formed by himself. The stronger, conversely, becomes the dependence of each of the two players' overall plans and of each of their moves on the changing figuration of the game – on the game process. The more the game comes to resemble a social process, the less it comes to resemble the implementation of an individual plan. In other words, to the extent that the inequality in the strengths of the two players diminishes, there will result from the interweaving of moves of two individual people a game process which neither of them has planned. (Ibid.: 82)

A principle that is true in even a simple two-person game becomes still more evident in Elias's subsequent multi-person games, in which more players form more complex networks of interdependence with each other. The more players there are, the more likely it is that their moves will interweave to produce a game process that none of them has planned; and, furthermore, the likelihood is markedly increased the more relatively equal become the power balances between the players.

How does this relate to the question posed above? How far was the continental USA 'inevitable' or 'accidental', and how far was it the outcome of conscious plans or of unintended processes?

The most obvious part of the answer is that, whatever processes of functional democratization may have been in train *within* American society, the power ratios between the United States and its neighbours have steadily changed *in the opposite direction*. That is, the USA, like the proverbial pioneer, has over a prolonged period become more powerful in relation to the people who held 'the land next to its'. The result has been that, while the 'accidental' remained important in providing opportunities for expansion, the process overall came over time *more* to resemble the implementation of the stronger party's plans, and *less* a social process that no one had planned or intended. This can be seen if we now return to the historical events that marked US territorial expansion.

The balance between the planned and the unplanned in US territorial expansion

Certainly Jefferson and other American leaders in the late eighteenth century, like other less exalted farmers, looked in expectation at the rich lands to the west. But it was not a vision of the Pacific Ocean that guided their military and political activities in the short term. Like the medieval French kings depicted by Elias, they just fought the next battle and seized the next opportunity.

The interweaving of interest and opportunity can be seen most spectacularly in the Louisiana Purchase of 1803. As has often been noted, it was ironic that President Jefferson, the proponent of minimal government, should so decisively have exercised the powers of the federal government – his opponents said he had exceeded them. Buying all the remaining territory claimed by France in North America – about 800,000 square miles – virtually doubled the national territory. The present state of Louisiana is only a small fraction of what Jefferson bought. The French lands then known as Louisiana extended from the west bank of the Mississippi and Missouri roughly to the watershed of those rivers in the high Rockies. It was a wedge-shaped tract with fairly loosely defined boundaries, at its widest in the north and tapering southwards to New Orleans, with Spanish (later Mexican) land to its west (see figure 8.1). The events leading to the Louisiana Purchase were really a hangover from the European great power politics that – as we have seen in chapter 6 – played such a part in the colonial phase of American state-formation.

Although it never seriously populated it, France had claimed control of the region since the late seventeenth century. But in 1763, following its defeat in the Seven Years War, France ceded Louisiana west of the Mississippi to its ally Spain in order to prevent it from falling into the

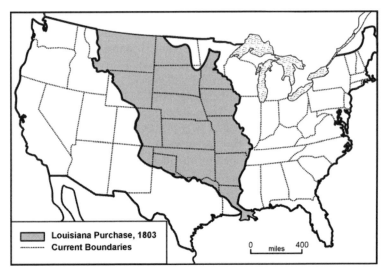

Figure 8.1: The Louisiana Purchase, 1803

hands of Britain, as did the lands to the east of the great river. In 1795 the young United States had signed a treaty with Spain to guarantee American navigation rights on the Mississippi; export trade through New Orleans was vital for the then American western lands between the Appalachians and the Mississippi. In 1801, however, Napoleon induced a reluctant King of Spain to transfer Louisiana back to France. (The king did so on condition that France did not further cede the land to a third party, a condition that was broken within two years, but which showed some percipience on his part in view of what happened to the remaining Spanish territory once the USA had acquired Louisiana.) Fearing that access to the Caribbean was under threat, Jefferson instructed Robert Livingston and later James Monroe to negotiate in Paris the purchase of New Orleans and western Florida. Napoleon's reluctance was undermined by Livingston's threat of a rapprochement with Britain; simultaneously faced with defeat in the slave rebellion in Santo Domingo led by Toussaint L'Ouverture, Napoleon decided to concentrate his forces in Europe and to sell off the whole of Louisiana. Going beyond their original instructions, Livingston and Monroe seized the chance, correctly anticipating Jefferson's agreement. The purchase price was $15 million. The Senate gave its consent to the treaty by 24 votes to 7 in October 1803. Jefferson immediately dispatched Lewis and Clark on their famous expedition of 1804–6, in which they not only explored the newly acquired territories but also continued west to the Pacific through the Oregon country, to which Spain and Britain – and now by implication the USA – had laid claims.

The Louisiana Purchase came out of the blue to most Americans. The opportunity that arose out of a fleeting historical conjuncture in international politics was seized by a handful of key players at the pinnacle of the US government. They may indeed have been aware of a strong current in public opinion in favour of indefinite westward expansion, but that was quite inchoate, and in the still-fledgling United States of 1803 it was probably broadly still true that (in John Adams's words) 'no-one thought of consolidating this vast continent under one national government'. The Purchase itself, however, helped to precipitate a change in popular perceptions. After the acquisition of such a vast additional territory, westward expansion need no longer be imagined to rest solely on individual pioneers nibbling at small parcels of land to establish squatters' rights; exercising the power of the federal government could gobble up huge mouthfuls of land. That was to become increasingly apparent. In 1803, territorial rights under international law had been gained through an entirely peaceful diplomatic transaction (including diplomatic threats) by a country that was not then militarily very strong.

But military power would come to play a more prominent part. This can first be seen in the complicated sequence of events leading to the incorporation of Florida into the Union. Florida had been settled by the Spaniards in the sixteenth century, but it became a British territory in 1763 at the end of the Seven Years War (along with the French territories to the east of the Mississippi). Under the Treaty of Paris which ended the War of Independence, however, it reverted to Spain in 1783. There was some ambiguity about whether Florida constituted part of the Louisiana Purchase, and in 1810–12 President Madison seized two areas of West Florida. Raids into Georgia and Alabama by Seminole Indians from Florida in 1818 led Madison to authorize General Andrew Jackson to invade Florida to punish the Seminoles; he not only did that, but also seized the Spanish town of Pensacola and executed two British men for having armed the Seminoles and encouraged their raids.

These events threatened to cause a major diplomatic crisis between the USA and Britain. That the matter was subsequently settled peacefully and greatly to the Americans' advantage is usually credited to the skill of John Quincy Adams, who was then Secretary of State (Remini, 2002: 54–6). The upshot was that Spain agreed to sell its indefensible territory of Florida to the USA in exchange for a settlement of the boundary (ill-defined since 1803) between Louisiana and the remaining Spanish territories in the south and west of the continent. Negotiations eventuated in the Adams–Onís Treaty of 1819, which made the USA finally a transcontinental power. The agreed boundary ran northward from the Gulf of Mexico along what is now the eastern boundary of the state of Texas, zigzagging to the 42nd parallel (now the northern boundary of California,

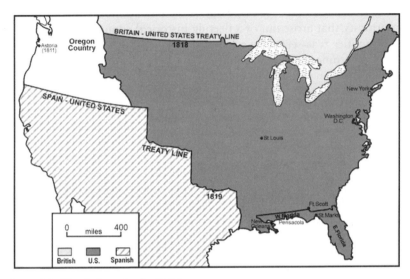

Figure 8.2: North America in 1819

Nevada and Utah), and then due west to the Pacific (see figure 8.2). Spain (finally) renounced its claim to the Pacific Northwest, and the USA (temporarily, as it proved) its claim to Texas.

Spain in the early nineteenth century had long been declining in power; Britain decidedly was not. After the War of 1812, there was no resort to military force in Anglo-American relations. Nevertheless, tensions persisted, especially about the boundary with Canada. For one thing, it was long remembered that a large proportion of the 100,000 loyalists (about 3–4 per cent of the US population) who fled abroad during and after the War of Independence had found refuge in Canada; this coloured attitudes on both sides until the mid-nineteenth century. Between the Great Lakes and the Pacific, the boundary had been left undefined. In 1818 a joint commission reached an amicable settlement. Under it, the 49th parallel became the recognized boundary between the Lake of the Woods and the watershed of the Rockies, while the land between the Rockies and the Pacific – later known as the Oregon Country – was to be jointly occupied for ten years; the agreement was to be renewed for further periods if both countries consented.

In 1845, President Polk proposed to terminate the agreement with Britain over the Oregon Country, and to claim the whole of the Pacific Northwest for the USA, up to the boundary with Russian Alaska (54° 40' N.). But his eyes were mainly on California, and in 1846 agreement was reached with Britain that the 49th parallel boundary now be extended westward across the Rockies to form the frontier between what became

British Columbia and the State of Washington. The remaining territorial development in that region was the USA's purchase of Alaska from the Russians in 1867; a dispute with Canada over the Alaskan panhandle was settled in 1903.

As late as the end of the nineteenth century, leading Americans such as Theodore Roosevelt, Henry Cabot Lodge and James C. Blaine were still hankering after the annexation of Canada. Indeed, it was a plank in the Republican platform in 1896, though it was dropped in the following election. By 1900, relations with Britain were on the whole good, but the balance of power between the two nations was tilting (it has been noted in the discussion of manners in chapter 3 how British travellers were coming to view America and things American with greater respect) and there was also an element of realpolitik in attitudes to Canada: 'With America's new power and confidence, Canada, indefensible against American land attack, came to be seen as a useful hostage to British behaviour' (Zimmerman, 2002: 450; see also pp. 22, 30).

American relations with Britain over Canada, and with its other neighbours, are not to be thought of purely as a series of bilateral power ratios. Trials of strength between any two powers can generally be understood only within a wider latticework of multipolar relations. Thus, that an amicable settlement of the Canadian border to the Rockies and a satisfactory *modus vivendi* over the Oregon Country were reached in 1818 owed much to the fact that Britain had an interest at the time in cementing relations with the United States. In Europe, Britain was preoccupied with opposing the aspirations of the so-called Holy Alliance (Russia, Prussia and Austria) to restoring monarchies overthrown in the Napoleonic period. Under the auspices of the Alliance, France had recently invaded Spain and restored King Ferdinand VII, and the next step appeared to be an attempt to restore Spanish control over the newly independent republics of South America (Remini, 2002: 52–3). That would clearly benefit neither Britain nor the USA, and they had a common interest in avoiding conflict with each other at that juncture.

The role played by diplomacy in establishing the borders of the conterminous USA is not, however, enough to establish any startling contrast with Elias's account of equivalent processes in medieval and early modern Europe. True, Elias placed most emphasis on wars between European neighbours, but he acknowledged the part that even then was played by diplomacy, with inter-dynastic marriages often cementing the settlements reached. But war and diplomacy are not separate things – as Clausewitz so famously observed, 'war is the continuation of politics by other means', and the converse is also true. More precisely, war and diplomacy are functional equivalents in relations between states, and they are not mutually exclusive equivalents. Who gained the hand of many a princely daughter was settled as much by military strength as by goodwill between families; and, like dynastic marriages, the purchase of land may appear more peaceful and civilized than conquest by force of arms, yet mostly rested on the potential force behind it. The proportions of force and diplomacy depend largely on the power ratios between players in any particular situation. This principle can be seen clearly in the next important episode in the territorial growth of the USA: the annexation of Texas and a substantial part of Mexico.

Mexico had gained its independence from Spain in 1821. Neither it nor the colonial power before it exercised much control over sparsely populated Texas, and by the early 1830s around 30,000 US immigrants had moved into the territory. By 1836 they had established effective independence from the Mexican government, and petitioned the United States to be admitted to the Union as a slave state (Mexico had abolished slavery in 1829). There was an outcry from abolitionists, whose objections were stated by John Quincy Adams among others, and the admission of Texas was rejected by Presidents Jackson and Van Buren. For a decade, the Texas Republic was tenuously independent. The British preferred that it stay so, as a means of blocking the further westward expansion of the USA; their preference served only to make annexation more attractive to the Americans. In 1845, under President Polk, Texas was finally annexed. At this point it was good tactics for Polk to reach the 1846 settlement with Britain about the border with Canada, because that cleared the decks for the war with Mexico over the disputed southwestern boundary of Texas that had just broken out.

The outcome of the Mexican War (1846–8), which saw the US army rout the Mexicans and occupy Mexico City, was that the American claim to all the land north of the Rio Grande was conceded. Under the 1848 Treaty that ended the war, the USA gained the lands that were to form the states of California, Nevada, Arizona, Utah, the western parts of Colorado and New Mexico, and the southwestern corner of Wyoming (see figure 8.3).[2] At this time, the notion of 'manifest destiny' was very much in the air, and many Americans (including Polk himself) were disappointed that US advantage was not pressed further. The land acquired in fact corresponded to that which the US had offered to buy from Mexico before the war, and the purchase price was paid. But this was hardly a market-clearing price freely agreed; the result was made possible by war, and war was made attractive by the self-evident imbalance of power between the two countries. Many Americans felt uneasy about it at the time. Ulysses S. Grant recorded his unease as a young officer during the Mexican War.

> Generally the officers of the army were indifferent whether the annexation [of Texas] was consummated or not. For myself, I was bitterly opposed to

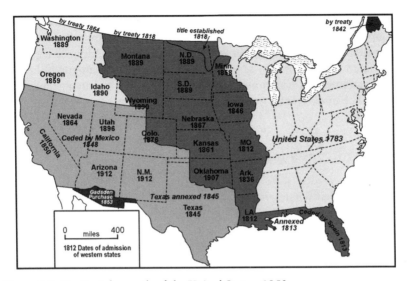

Figure 8.3: Territorial growth of the United States, 1853

the measure, and to this day regard the war which resulted as one of the most unjust ever waged by a stronger against a weaker nation. It was an instance of a republic following the bad example of European monarchies, in not considering justice in their desire to acquire additional territory. (Grant, 1994 [1885]: 37)

'Poor Mexico! So far from God, and so close to the United States.'[3]

'Accident', or historical conjuncture, played a part in each stage in this process of territorial growth, but it is also clear that with each successive stage in the process the probability of the final outcome increased, because as its territory grew the power ratio between the USA and its neighbours tilted in its favour. Unlike in the European Middle Ages, when, as Elias pointed out, a magnate's power vis-à-vis his neighbours was (at least in the early stages of state-formation) related to the size of his territory in a quite direct way, other considerations such as its rapid economic growth also came into play in increasing the power advantage of the USA. But territorial growth remained highly significant in a way that, by the nineteenth century, it certainly could no longer be *within* Europe; for one thing, westward expansion was itself one driving force in American industrial growth.

With the increasing power advantage of the USA, two things also increased: the *probability* of the final outcome of a transcontinental USA, and the extent to which that became more explicitly the intended *goal* of the US government. Both arose from the structure of a gradually unfolding long-term process; there is no reason to believe that America's behaviour differed – for reasons of national ideology and culture, for example – from that which any other state would have followed in similar circumstances. That can be seen even in the case of the Monroe Doctrine, enunciated in 1823; it may seem in retrospect to be a dramatic once-and-for-all statement of a national ideological principle, but its meaning and significance underwent a gradual change as American power grew.

'Sovereignty' as a function of power ratios

It is curious that what came to be known as the Monroe Doctrine, a cornerstone of American foreign policy throughout the nineteenth and twentieth centuries, very nearly began life as a joint declaration by the USA and Britain. In 1823 both countries were concerned that Spain and its European allies were about to attempt to reassert Spanish rule over the Latin American colonies, nearly all of which – with the principal exceptions of Cuba and Puerto Rico – had gained de facto independence. British Foreign Secretary George Canning proposed a joint declaration opposing all future colonization in Central and South America. At first, President Monroe, with the agreement of his predecessors Jefferson and Madison, was inclined to accept the British proposal. However, his Secretary of State, John Quincy Adams, strongly opposed a joint declaration (he said that it would make America 'come in as a cock-boat in the wake of the British man-of war' [Remini, 2002: 60]), and he had his way. Monroe's message to Congress in December 1823 was the joint work of Monroe and Adams. The 'Doctrine' stated that Europe and the Americas had different political systems, and that the United States would not interfere in European affairs. The USA furthermore recognized the existing European colonies and dependencies in the Western hemisphere, but asserted that the hemisphere was closed to future colonization, and that were any European power to seek to control or oppress any of the new nations of Latin America, the United States would take that as a hostile act against itself.

At the time, though, the declaration attracted relatively little attention; it is easy to forget that the USA was not then a major military power, and Monroe and Adams were both aware that American intervention in Latin America would only have been possible with the support of the British navy. For good reason, ten years later the USA did not oppose British acquisition of the new colony of the Falklands Islands. The Monroe Doctrine only gradually came into its own, at first nearer to home where America had a more credible power advantage. President Polk invoked it in the 1840s, warning Britain and Spain off from any claims in California and Oregon. More decisively, at the end of the Civil War the American threat of force precipitated the collapse of the French adventure of a puppet empire in Mexico. Only in 1895 was the doctrine deployed against Britain, by President Cleveland's administration, with reference to a long-standing boundary dispute between British Guiana and Venezuela. The British could still shrug off the use of the Doctrine in this context as 'a novel prerogative', but shortly settled the boundary by diplomatic means (Jeffers, 2000: 313–16).

By the turn of the century, America was building a substantial navy of its own, and in 1904 President Theodore Roosevelt added the so-called 'Roosevelt Corollary' to the Monroe Doctrine. Also known as the 'Big Stick Policy', this was an assertion of the USA's right to police the hemisphere.[4] Given that the unruly and economically ill-managed states of Latin America were quite likely to provoke intervention by European creditor nations, the USA claimed an exclusive right to intervene in their affairs, and did so frequently throughout the twentieth century. Only when the power ratio between the USA and its hemispheric neighbours to the south had become very unequal could the Monroe Doctrine be taken to mean that the USA was 'practically sovereign' in the Western hemisphere, carrying with it the right to use force in the territories of lesser sovereignties. But that is to run ahead of the story.

The major gains in the territory legally claimed by the USA were embodied in treaties with the European powers and Mexico, reached with varying degrees of sabre-rattling and actual use of force. The same treaty-making power of the federal government was then employed in relations with the various Indian tribes who might have been under the impression that they themselves had some legal claim to the land. The Senate had to ratify the Indian treaties, which could be taken to imply that the tribes were independent and sovereign states just like the European powers. In fact, from the earliest decades after independence, the USA never viewed the tribes in that light (Remini: 2002: 90–1). It did not need to. The power ratio between Indians and European settlers shifted steadily against the earlier inhabitants from shortly after the beginnings of European colonization, and violence characterized relations with the Indians – treaties or no treaties.

The fate of the Iroquois – key players in their own right in the earlier elimination contests – is emblematic. In the War of Independence, most of the Iroquois sided with the British, that option presenting their last hope of resisting encroachment by white settlers. The consequences of defeat were disastrous for them. Those who survived were widely scattered, many of them seeking refuge in Canada or trekking west to the Wisconsin region. Those who remained in New York State were made subject to American law (Lane, 1997: 74–5). The westward migration of the Indian peoples was to become a pattern (see figure 8.4). Some of it

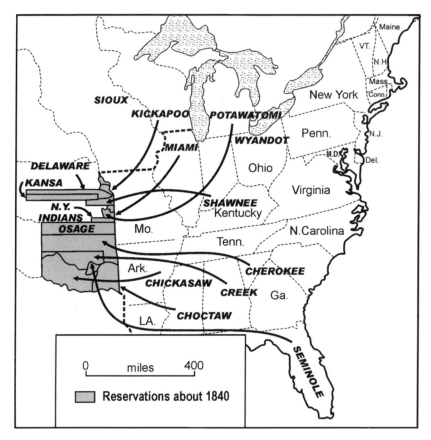

Figure 8.4: The removal of the eastern Indians, 1840

was simply a response to the westward encroachments of white settlers, but some of it was the intentional result of US government policy.

The most notorious instance is the expulsion of the 'Five Civilized Tribes' from the southeastern states in the 1830s under the presidency of Andrew Jackson (ibid.: 75–7). The Cherokee, most prominent of the five tribes, had also sided with the British in the War of Independence, and continued their resistance to the new US government for some time afterwards; Jackson, from much earlier in his career, had always viewed the Indians as easily manipulated by the British or Spanish against American interests (Remini, 2001). By 1820, however, the Cherokee had adopted a system of government modelled on that of the United States. But at about the same time, gold was discovered in their tribal lands in northern Georgia, and the government of that state began a long struggle to expel them. The US Supreme Court ruled in the Cherokee's favour in 1832, but the ruling was ignored, and in 1838 federal troops were used to drive out the five tribes westward 300 miles towards Indian Territory (later Oklahoma), along what became known as the Trail of Tears; about 4,000 of the 20,000 people perished on the forced march. Between independence and the closing of the frontier at the end of the nineteenth century:

> The Indian nations entered into 800 treaties with the Unites States. . . . The United States Senate refused to ratify 430 of them, even though the government charged the Indians with having to live up to the terms of those treaties. Even more tragically, of the 370 treaties that were ratified, the United States proceeded to violate provisions in every one. (Inouye, 1992)

It is hard not to moralize in the face of such figures. Yet, taking as detached a view as possible, it is probable that, while the United States had the military and administrative means to tip the balance of power still more decisively against the Indians, even towards the end of the nineteenth century its military and administrative apparatus would have been inadequate (had there been the political will) to tilt it in the other direction and resist the pressure of the westward movement of white people in search of land.

The frontier

Fixing the external boundaries of a growing national territory proceeded hand in hand with the internal settlement of the land by subjects of the United States. There can be no disputing the fact that westward expansion was central to the history of the United States. It was noted in chapter 6 (pp. 137–8 above) that, as a lasting image in American culture, the frontier has underpinned a form of romanticism. But the present chapter is more concerned with the consequences of the frontier as a factual social process.

Controversy has raged ever since Frederick Jackson Turner – writing shortly after the 1891 US Census showed that the frontier had at last been 'closed' by the spread of unbroken settlement from Atlantic to Pacific – delivered his celebrated lecture, 'The Significance of the Frontier in American History', in 1893 (1947 [1920]: 1–38).

The Turner thesis

Turner may be said to have anticipated by almost half a century key elements of Norbert Elias's theory of civilizing processes, and by the best part of a whole century the consequent discussions of decivilizing processes. To see this, one has to make allowance for a very different vocabulary. When Turner wrote about 'civilization', he used the word in the accustomed nineteenth-century sense redolent of 'progress'. Nor did he use any of the other concepts by which we would now characterize Elias's insights. Nevertheless, he clearly postulated a connection between, on the one hand, the intertwined processes of state-formation and the control of violence and, on the other hand, the moulding of the culture, social character and habitus of the people who live within a state. And he saw that differences in the environment and the historical experience of the United States had given a cast to that connection different in important ways from that found in Western Europe.

In Turner's view, the development of the states of the eastern seaboard was in many respects not dissimilar to what could be seen in Europe, notably 'the evolution of institutions in a limited area', such as the rise of representative government, the development of more complex organs of government, and the rapid division of labour in the rise of manufacturing industry. In this respect, he did not depart drastically from the 'germ theory' of Herbert Baxter Adams and the Johns Hopkins School (see p. 2 above), who, playing down the extent to which America's social institutions represented a new beginning, sought to trace their roots back to European soil (Adams, 1882: 8). Turner, however, pointed out that *both* the organism (or 'germ') *and* the habitat in which it lives play their parts in evolutionary processes. He contended that the existence and expansion of the frontier from the earliest settlements to the 1880s had introduced a decisively different 'evolutionary' influence. The kernel of his argument runs:

> [W]e have . . . a recurrence of the process of evolution in each western area reached in the process of expansion. Thus American development has exhibited not merely advance along a single line, but a return to primitive conditions on a continually advancing frontier line, and a new development for that area. American social development has been continually beginning again on the frontier. This perennial rebirth, this fluidity of American life, this expansion westwards with its new opportunities, its continuous touch with the simplicity of primitive society, furnish forces dominating American character. (Turner, 1947: 2–3)

Turner traced the steady drift of 'the frontier' westward from the eastern seaboard in the seventeenth century to the Rocky Mountains and beyond in the nineteenth. In fact, he distinguished three phases of the advancing frontier: the traders' frontier, the miners' and ranchers' frontier and the farmers' frontier. French colonization, he pointed out, had been dominated by its trading frontier, but English colonization by the much greater

numbers who pushed forward the farming frontier (ibid.: 13). Both the
brilliance of his insight and an unwitting blindness can be seen in the contrast he drew between frontiers in America and in Europe:

> In the case of most nations . . . development has occurred in a limited area;
> and if the nation has expanded, it has met other growing peoples whom it
> has conquered. . . . The American frontier is sharply distinguished from the
> European frontier – a fortified boundary line running through dense popu-
> lations. The most significant thing about the American frontier is that it lies
> *at the hither edge of free land*. (Ibid.: 2–3; my emphasis)

A more accurate way of formulating the difference between America and
Europe would have been to say that the power ratio between the USA and
its neighbours in the interior – principally the Indians, after the elimination of the French – was far more unequal than that typical in Europe,
where, in general, expanding states eventually came up against other
states of roughly comparable strength. But this more nuanced conceptualization is already implied in Turner's remark that '[t]he trading frontier,
while steadily undermining Indian power by making the tribes ultimately
dependent on the whites, yet, through its sale of guns, gave the Indians
increased power of resistance to the farming frontier' (ibid.: 13).

Turner (ibid.: 22ff.) listed a number of specific ways in which the experience of the frontier fed back into American society in the more settled
east. First, the frontier had 'promoted the formation of a composite
nationality for the American people'. It diluted the predominantly English
character of the eastern seaboard. 'In the crucible of the frontier . . . immigrants were Americanized, liberated, and fused into a mixed race, English
in neither nationality nor characteristics. The process has gone on from
early days to our own' (ibid.: 22, 23)

Second, the advance of the frontier had decreased America's dependence on England for supplies – as distances westward increased, it
became impractical to rely on transatlantic shipments, and eastern cities
began to compete with each other to supply the needs of the frontier
lands.

Third, more especially after Independence, it was legislation to meet
the necessities of the westward-moving frontier that did most to develop
the powers of the central government. Apart from the great issue of
slavery, legislation was enacted for railways and many other forms of
internal improvements, and above all for the sale and disposal of public
lands. The very fact that the unsettled lands had been vested in the federal
government proved crucial in tilting the power ratio from the states
towards the federal government.

Fourth, it also proved significant that federal attempts to make the
public land a source of revenue, and to lease it gradually in parcels in

order to create a more compact pattern of settlement, consistently failed. The hunger of the frontiersmen for land was too intense. John Quincy Adams admitted defeat: 'My own system of administration, which was to make the national domain the inexhaustible fund for progressive and unceasing internal improvement, had failed.' His successor as President, Andrew Jackson, 'formally recommended that all public lands should be gratuitously given away to individual adventurers and to the States in which the lands are situated' (both quoted in ibid.: 26). 'A system of administration', Turner pithily commented, 'was not what the West demanded; it wanted land.' He drew a contrast with what he described as 'the European system of scientific administration'. But while more recent scholarship has viewed the settlement of North America as just one instance of a more general 'Great Frontier' (Webb, 1952; McNeill, 1983) of European expansion into so-called 'free land' in many parts of the globe from 1500 onwards, Europe itself had not experienced anything closely comparable with America's western frontier. The eastward drift of German colonists during the Middle Ages had been relatively organized, with groups settling in villages under the authority of church and nobility, and – apart from the more dramatic incursions of the Teutonic knights – it was gradual and (for the times) relatively peaceful (Gerhard, 1959: 209–29, esp. 218–28). And that all happened too early for the term 'scientific administration' to spring to mind. The nearest comparison in the nineteenth century was with the expansion of Russia eastward across the Siberian vastness of Asia (see Lincoln, 1994). Between 1861 and 1914, five million peasants migrated to Siberia, where they were able to acquire landholdings on average about four times as large as those in European Russia. Even so, relative to the land area involved, the numbers were not huge and, more crucially, they settled almost entirely in regions in which the Tsarist government already had some presence (Mikesell, 1960: 67, 73). Nevertheless, they demonstrated impulses towards innovation, independence, self-reliance and rude democracy that 'cast fears into the hearts of their rulers' (Billington, 1969: 79; see also Gerhard, 1959: 223–8). A more striking contrast, because nearer at hand, is between the American frontier and the westward expansion of Canada. This indeed might be what Turner had in mind in speaking of 'European . . . scientific administration'. In Canada, the framework of law and order was put in place under the authority of the federal government *before* the arrival of large numbers of settlers. Indeed, the Royal North-West Mounted Police (an armed force modelled on the Royal Irish Constabulary rather than on the unarmed county constabularies of Great Britain) was created in 1873 'for the specific purpose of ensuring a non-American type of development in the prairie west'; they 'maintained much tighter control of western settlements, and the six-shooter never became the symbol of Canadian freedom' (McNaught, 1969: 146, 176). In further consequence, Canadian treaties with the plains Indians were honoured, and even if in the longer term the system of reserves provided a far from perfect social solution, in the short to medium term the prairies were opened up for farmers far more peacefully than happened south of the border. This outcome owed much to the fact that the pressure of numbers of settlers pressing west was less than in the USA, but also much to the Canadian Constitution having been consciously designed to tilt the balance of power between the provinces and the Dominion government much more in the centre's favour than that between the states and federal government of the USA.

Fifth and most famous of the consequences of the frontier that Turner discerned for American society was its promotion of 'rugged individualism': '[T]he frontier is productive of individualism. Complex society is precipitated by the wilderness into a kind of primitive organization based on the family. The tendency is anti-social. It produces antipathy to control. The tax-gatherer is viewed as a representative of oppression' (1947: 30). How prescient that sounded in the 1990s, with the rise of extreme right-wing militias and the bombing of the Federal office building in Oklahoma City.

Sixth, and in Turner's own opinion most important, frontier individualism had from the beginning promoted 'democracy'. By that, he mainly meant the extension of the franchise. The first generation of frontier states after Independence all had wide suffrages, and he believed that this had forced the eastern states – and even Europe – to follow suit (ibid.: 30, 243–68). Turner, however, also entered a note of warning:

> So long as free land exists, the opportunity for a competency exists, and economic power secures political power. But the democracy born of free land, strong in selfishness and individualism, intolerant of administrative experience and education, and pressing individual liberty beyond its proper bounds, has its dangers as well as its benefits. Individualism in America has allowed a laxity in regard to government affairs which has rendered possible the spoils system and all the manifest evils that follow from the lack of a highly civic spirit. (Ibid.: 32)

If even Turner could enter such a reservation, later writers, less sympathetic than he to the romanticization of the pioneer, underlined how individualism undermined the civic spirit. Lewis Mumford, noting how on the frontier 'social man could become an "individual"', spelled out how that was linked to what would later be called environmental depredation: 'uninfluenced by peasant habits or the idea of an old culture, the work of the miner, woodman, and hunter led to unmitigated destruction and pillage . . . backwoods America turned the European into a barbarian' (1957 [1926]: 26).

Decivilizing processes on the frontier?

A central part of Turner's thesis was that over a long period elements of the American population were returning to conditions of greater autarky, to much higher levels of danger in everyday life, and thus – in Elias's terms – to a continuous source of *de*civilizing pressures. To quote one of Elias's most important *obiter dicta*:

> [T]he armour of civilized conduct would crumble very rapidly if, through a change in society, the degree of insecurity which existed earlier were to break in upon us again, and if danger became as incalculable as once it was. Corresponding fears would burst the limits set to them today. (2000: 532*n*)

The pattern of people's fears responds to changes in the dangers they face. Changes in people's fears are in turn likely to be associated with wider changes in their typical behaviour, emotions and beliefs. Elias thinks of civilizing processes as involving a change in the balance between external constraints and self-constraints, the balance tilting over the generations towards the latter in the steering of behaviour in the average person. 'External' constraints include both natural forces and constraints imposed by interdependence with other people. The lengthening chains and more extensive networks of interdependence, through which people exert more demanding but more indirect constraints over each other, play a principal part in the tilting of the balance. Now, if these chains break and the networks shrink as Turner contended they did for people on the frontier – if people are 'precipitated . . . into a kind of primitive organization based on the family' – the pattern of external constraints will be changed.

It follows that the operation of self-constraints will not remain unchanged if changes take place in the pattern of external constraints. There are two broad reasons for this. First, calculation of the external constraints always plays a part in the steering of conduct and, if the calculations suddenly or gradually yield different outcomes, behaviour will change. (To put it more directly, at the margin people's behaviour will change if they discover they can get away with pursuing their advantage in ways that were not worth the risk before.) Secondly, however, behaviour will change still more if the calculations become more difficult, if the changes become more 'incalculable', if life is lived in face of greater uncertainty and unpredictability. It is quite likely that the greater fears corresponding to higher levels of danger will produce in some people, or perhaps eventually all, behaviour that may be described as 'more emotional' or 'more impulsive', in which the gradually acquired apparatus of self-constraints is undermined. On the face of it, many of these conditions would appear to have been met for white settlers on the frontier. They lived in scattered homesteads in relatively self-sufficient small groups.

They were more at the mercy of natural forces – fire, flood, wild beasts – than they would be in a city. Far from medical help, minor injuries and infections were more likely to be fatal. Violence from human enemies, white or Indian, was a greater threat outside the daily beat of the forces of 'law and order' within the boundaries of an organized state. Fears rise when control of natural forces and social events declines. Rising fears make it still more difficult to control events, notably to stand back from an escalating and self-perpetuating cycle of violence – such as that between whites and Indians – and, through a detour via detachment, find the means to bring it under control. That makes people still more susceptible to wish fantasies about means of alleviating the situation.

But is all this true of what actually happened on the frontier?

In bringing Turner's frontier thesis and Elias's theory of civilizing and decivilizing processes to bear on each other, their very different uses of the words 'civilization' and 'civilized' once more raise problems. Turner still thought in the uncritical nineteenth-century way about 'civilization' advancing into regions hitherto characterized by 'savagery'. Although the 'primitive conditions' of the frontier had left their mark on the settlers, and that in turn had made a large imprint on American culture and (what we would now call) habitus more widely, he did not perceive any general collapse of civilized standards on the frontier.

In that, he was right. Decivilizing pressures (in Elias's terms) were always in tension with quite strong civilizing pressures too. One reason was that those who moved west were not *tabulae rasae*: they had, by and large, been raised in more settled and (again in Elias's technical sense) more civilized circumstances. They took with them a vast inheritance of knowledge, beliefs and feelings into which they had been socialized and enculturated in the more settled East (or Europe).[5] In most people, most of the time, this inheritance precluded any abrupt abandonment of 'civilized' self-constraints in their – usually temporary – return to 'primitive conditions'. A second reason is that although the first generation of their offspring might indeed be raised amidst a relatively high and incalculable level of danger, internal pacification of territory by the forces of the state and economic development of many sorts were rarely more than a generation behind the first settlers in their movement west. (Figure 8.5 shows the area of land within incorporated states and the extent to which it lagged behind the total territory of the USA.)

Land hunger stoked the head of steam driving the westward movement, and farmers constituted much the largest element in the migrating population. Ahead of them, over the centuries, had moved the fur-trappers, followed by some other traders, and then miners and ranchers. The pastoral heyday in the West was relatively brief: the cowboy era lasted only two or three decades after the Civil War, even if it lasted long enough

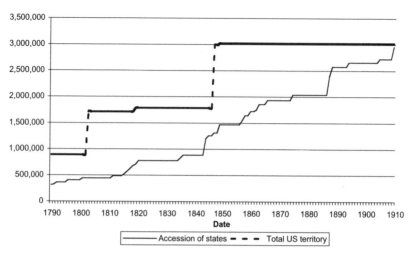

Figure 8.5: Territorial area of the conterminous USA, 1790–1912
Source: US Department of Commerce and Bureau of the Census (1975).

for the Cain and Abel theme of conflict between ranchers and farmers to be recalled in so many Hollywood westerns.

As in the Bible, Cain won. And it is a characteristic of agricultural settlements almost everywhere, and in almost every era, that they have needed relatively strong protection from the dangers posed by other human beings – the destruction of crops, the theft of stored harvests, attacks by brigands or outlaws. It is a basic feature of agrarian society that:

> [Farmers] lived a life that was (comparatively) productive and vulnerable. Warriors, on the other hand, were unproductive and destructive but ready to fight. Innocuous as it is, this formulation conveys something that is essential to the structure of military–agrarian societies. Given the peasants' productivity and vulnerability and the warriors' powers of destruction and readiness to fight, a combination of the elements of productivity and armed force turned out to be well nigh inevitable for both groups. The warriors needed the peasants for food, the peasants needed the warriors for protection. This unplanned – and, in a profound sense, fatal – combination formed the context for the great variety of mixtures of military protection and economic exploitation that mark the history of the great majority of advanced agrarian societies. (Goudsblom, 1996b: 58–9; see also Goudsblom, 1992: 57–8)

'The function of warriors', comments Goudsblom, 'was to fight against other warriors.' Thus do we so often see the US Cavalry galloping across the silver screen to drive off the attacking Indians, and the US Marshals and county sheriffs using their guns to protect the peaceful farmers. If the element of economic exploitation is unusually unobvious in the relation between farmers and warriors in the American West, it is because the real coercive component in this particular figuration was experienced by the previous occupants of the abundant land. And rapid internal pacification meant that the underlying use of the means of violence could quite soon be once more hidden behind the scenes of social life. At any rate, the more lurid manifestations of what we might call 'frontier decivilizing processes' did not happen on the farming frontier, or certainly not widely or for very long. Ray Allen Billington (1903–81), one of Turner's most distinguished students, pointed out that most of the settlers 'had some wealth, for the frontier was no place for the penniless',[6] and that '[i]n their new homes a few succumbed to the vagrant habits of the squatters and began the drifting that predestined failure, but far more persisted until neighbours thickened about them and the transition to civilization began' (Billington, 1977: 56). To understand 'the frontier process', Billington – who continued to use Turner's nineteenth-century terminology – said it was necessary to ask 'whether they succumbed to barbarism or perpetuated the culture they had known in the East'. Much as the vocabulary grates on modern ears, the underlying question is valid, and Billington's answer to it was balanced and reasonable. He concluded that nearly all the settlers were determined to transfer the cultural institutions of their homelands to their new communities and that, although the majority were people of small learning, most pioneer settlements contained an educated group which assumed the functions of leadership. Nevertheless, their ambitions were rarely fully attained, since every effort to create carbon copies of eastern seaboard or European patterns of life was doomed by social and economic conditions on the frontier. Reiterating the central point of Turner's thesis, Billington contended: 'Both these environmental conditions and the determination of the pioneers to duplicate accustomed patterns help to explain the unique western culture that did emerge' (ibid.).

On the other hand, in a fine study of surviving memoirs of fur-trappers at the extreme forward edge of the traders' frontier in the Rockies in the period 1825–45, Billington produces some vivid evidence of their lowered threshold of repugnance in relation to eating, drinking, sex, violence and cruelty (ibid.: 19–50). This appears to be the effect of adaptation to a situation of extreme danger and the extreme measures necessary to survival. They faced the dangers of freezing winters in the mountains, of grizzly bears and rattlesnakes, and (even though many of them took wives from tribes such as the Crow) especially of hostile Indians.

The mountain men had to adjust themselves completely to the wilderness world about them. Their primitive existence revolved about three things: beaver, buffalo, and Indians – or, as they would have phrased it, fur, meat and ha'r, or their own scalps. To secure fur and meat, they had to risk their ha'r; to keep their ha'r, they had to develop forest skills superior to those of their principal antagonists, the Indians. Of the red men with whom the trappers carried on a constant battle, the Blackfeet of the Three Forks country were most feared; it was understood in the mountains that when a trapper saw a Blackfoot or a Blackfoot saw a trapper, shooting started at once. Yet even such friendly Indians as the Crows could never be completely trusted, for few could resist stealing a carelessly watched horse or pouncing on an unwary white man. Constant vigilance and superb skill were necessary just to stay alive in such a country. (Ibid.: 27–8)

If the term 'decivilizing process' is considered too contentious, an alternative way of describing what was happening would be to say that such men in such an environment had to reacquire skills that would have been 'second nature', essential to survival, for all human beings in the long millennia when hunter-gatherer societies were the sole form of human social organization, but which had since been lost to most people living in the commercial, agrarian and industrial society that the USA had become by the nineteenth century. The kind of constant vigilance needed to survive in the mountains was a polar opposite to the kind of vigilance that Elias (2006a) depicts as necessary for social survival by aristocrats in French court society. Both situations demanded foresight, but for the courtier, an extreme curbing of the impulses was necessary, whereas for the mountain trapper (more like the medieval warrior), a capacity for the unrestrained venting of impulses was essential. Billington speaks of the trapper Edward Rose, who had joined the Crow: 'A fellow trapper saw Rose lead his tribesman to victory against a Blackfoot war party in 1834 then whip his followers into a bloody frenzy as they hacked off the hands of the wounded enemy warriors, pierced their bodies with pointed sticks, and plucked out their eyes' (1977: 29–30).

These accounts date from a period when the trapping frontier was nearing its end. They describe an extreme situation. But in long-term perspective they are rather interesting. The extremes of violence and cruelty in combat that they depict are reminiscent of Elias's account of *Angriffslust* – the 'joy in attacking' – among early medieval warriors in Europe. And the element common to both of these otherwise very different times and places is the very high everyday level of danger. The ability to give unrestrained vent to aggression had survival value in both instances. Equally, it became a liability on the more complex battlefields on which organized armies came to fight. By the seventeenth century, battles were lost by commanders who were too impulsive (Elias, 2006a: 210–11). If Nevins and Commager (1992: 179) are right, many of the USA's defeats in the War of 1812 provide an American parallel, for they blame 'a frontier dislike of training and discipline'. This point is of a piece with Spierenburg's argument (discussed in chapter 6 above) that 'democracy came too early' in America, so that the legitimacy of the state holding a monopoly of the means of violence was less firmly established than in Europe.

The frontier as continuing state-formation

The classic status of 'The Significance of the Frontier' and the other writings in which Turner elaborated his thesis is beyond dispute, although the 'frontier hypothesis' has remained the subject of controversy among historians for more than a century. Until the 1920s it was the dominant interpretation of American social development. Then, in the 1930s and 1940s, it was the target of extensive criticism.[7] After a period of more evenly balanced debate and detailed research to test particular aspects of the original hypothesis, controversy flared up again in the 1980s, notably following the publication of Patricia Nelson Limerick's brilliant book *The Legacy of Conquest* (1987).

The criticisms levelled at Turner in the mid-twentieth century can be roughly grouped under four heads.

First, a vagueness and inconsistency were found in his use of key concepts such as 'democracy', 'individualism' and even 'frontier'. These faults were accentuated by the sheer brilliance of Turner's writing, with its tendency towards rhetorical overstatement.

Second, the same rhetorical overstatement led to the accusation that Turner was a 'monocausalist' – that he believed the frontier explained everything distinctive about American society. Critics pointed out that many other processes needed to be given due weight: the rise of capitalism, class conflicts, slavery and a whole series of other power struggles. Some opponents (such as Hacker, 1933), indeed, in advocating interpretations in terms of class struggle, came close to adopting a rival form of monocausalism. A careful reading of Turner shows clearly that he was in fact well aware of other forces besides the frontier shaping the character of American society. He gave close attention to the role of 'sections' in American history – the slaveholding society of the South as well as the commercial society of the Northeast and the West (Turner, 1932). And Limerick (1995) conceded that Turner himself had also developed a counter-thesis in which industrialization and urbanization played as important a part as the frontier.

Third, as for Turner's stress on the frontier's role as a crucible in which immigrants were 'Americanized' and a composite American nationality formed, it was convincingly pointed out that most immigrants from Europe were assimilated in the cities, and even as early as 1870 only 10 per cent of foreign-born Americans were farmers. Moreover, only a small proportion of the population could ever have directly experienced life on the frontier – otherwise it would not have been a frontier, however defined – and as the total population of the USA grew, 'it was the experience of an ever shrinking portion'. David Potter, who in his book *People of Plenty* emphasized economic abundance as the greatest force in shaping American social character, pointed out that more people became rich by moving to the city than ever did by going West (1954: 159). On the other hand, notes Hofstadter, 'the experience of growing up in a dynamic and rapidly developing rural environment, common to most parts of the country . . . was widely shared throughout our history' (1969: 123, 125).

Fourth, perhaps most complicated was the debate about whether the frontier promoted 'democracy' in America. It was alleged that the frontier interpretation promoted intellectual isolationism, exaggerating the uniqueness of American 'civilization' through a relative ignorance of Europe and its history (Hayes, 1946). More especially, it blocked recognition of the growth of democracy on both sides of the Atlantic as a process common to the rise of modern commercial industrial societies (Wright, 1930; 1934). That was compounded by Turner's very American tendency to identify 'democracy' with egalitarianism (Hofstadter, 1969: 126). Besides, the Spaniards had 'had the run of the whole hemisphere', so did abundant land promote individualism and democracy among *them*? No. Nor was the westward movement of the southern slaveholding plantations marked by the rise of vibrant democracy. Which, according to George W. Pierson (1942), showed that a one-sided environmental explanation is inadequate, and that the cultural inheritance brought by settlers from Europe, or from the eastern seaboard, was at least as important. On the other hand, by following Tocqueville in perceiving participation in a web of local institutions and voluntary associations as fundamental to democratic life, Elkins and McKittrick (1954) were able to draw conclusions about an 'organic connection' between the frontier and the basis of American democracy relatively favourable to Turner's view. Noting that sociological studies in the 1950s showed that such participation was at its most vigorous in new suburban communities, they found similar vigour in the historic new communities on the western frontier, especially in the Old Northwest, where there had been a higher proportion of small towns compared with the more wholly rural southern frontier.

In the most recent phase of debate about frontier history, some of these older issues have been recast in the light of subsequent research. In *The Legacy of Conquest*, Patricia Nelson Limerick very cogently undermined the image of the self-reliant and individually responsible pioneer, at any rate on the farming frontier. Even the dietary self-sufficiency of settlers had been greatly exaggerated: *The Legacy of Conquest* begins by citing the recollections of a Virginian woman, Nannie Alderson, who married and went to live in Wyoming in the 1880s. She remembered that 'everyone lived out of cans', and outside every farm in the 1880s stood a great mound of empty food cans, steadily growing from year to year (1987: 17). The consumption of canned food is evidence of the long chains of interdependence stretching back east (although the fact that the garbage collectors never called is a reminder that differences remained between life in the West and the East). Limerick also showed vividly how the supposedly self-reliant pioneers fell into the habit of blaming everyone but themselves when things went wrong. Farmers encroached on areas of semi-aridity, and felt betrayed when rains proved inadequate. Mechanized farming caused dustbowls. Where crops did not grow, weeds were introduced that did. The promoters of farming or mining on the frontier were often blamed for failure. Increasingly, so was the federal government:

> Blaming nature or blaming human beings, those looking for a scapegoat had a third, increasingly popular target: the federal government. Since it was the government's responsibility to control Indians and, in a number of ways increasing into the twentieth century, to control nature, Westerners found it easy to shift the direction of their resentment. Attacked by Indians or threatened by nature, aggrieved Westerners took to pointing accusingly at the federal government. In effect, Westerners centralized their resentments much more effectively than the federal government centralized its powers. (Ibid.: 44–5)

The way the federal government controlled, or failed to control, the disposal of the vast nationalized resource of the public lands is central to understanding the West. The federal government promoted railways and colleges through grants of land, but much of the rest was gained by whoever made the first claim. The concept of 'property', Limerick pointed out, was actually very complex. Who owned mineral rights under farmland or grazing? Who owned wild animals or timber? Even water resources were often gained by first claim, a monopoly that could be used to control a wide territory. The sources of conflict were obvious.

The rhetoric of heroic independence, says Limerick, has begun to sound anachronistic in our own complex times of global interdependence – but in fact 'the times were always complex'. 'There is nothing wrong with human interdependence', she wrote in words reminiscent of Norbert Elias, 'it is . . . a fact of life' (ibid.: 78).

> A recognition that one is not the sole captain of one's fate is hardly an occasion for surprise. Especially in the American West, where the federal government, outside capital, and the market have always been powerful factors of change, the limits on personal autonomy do not seem like news. And yet humans have a well-established capacity to meet fact of life with disbelief. In a region where human interdependence has been self-evident, Westerners have woven a net of denial. (Ibid.: 95–6)

Nowhere is the denial more evident than in what Limerick called 'the idea of innocence'. One of the virtues of the 'new Western history' has been its capacity to deal with multiple points of view. And a characteristic of the 'white' point of view has been blindness to motives other than the most innocent. The dominant motives are seen as improvement and opportunity rather than to 'ruin the natives and despoil the continent': '[P]ersonal interest in the acquisition of property coincided with national interest in the acquisition of territory, and those interests overlapped in turn with the mission to extend the domain of Christian civilization. Innocence of intention placed the course of events in a bright and positive light' (ibid.: 36).

Turner and the Turnerians undoubtedly wrote their history too much from this point of view. It is a valuable corrective to see the process from multiple points of view, and Limerick portrays the West as not so much an advancing line of settlement along which 'civilization' overcame 'savagery', but rather as a borderland where there was continuing cultural contact and assimilation between English-speaking Americans, the Indians and Hispanic elements. The latter, a strong element in the history of the Southwest, were especially invisible in Turner's original essay. Limerick went too far, however, for she rejected Turner's entire notion of the frontier *process*, seemingly because she believed that it – or indeed any notion of developmental process – was inseparable from outdated notions of 'progress' and of 'civilization' versus 'savagery'. That is to throw the baby out with the bathwater. From an Eliasian point of view, one of the great virtues of Turner's thesis – whatever its defects – was that it was very much cast in processual terms. Limerick has been criticized for portraying an almost static image of an unchanging West of timeless borderlands (Adelman and Aron, 1999). That is paradoxical, for the title of her book was *The Legacy of Conquest*, and conquest itself is a social process. Limerick, as she herself admits, took her clues from the present, just as Turner did from his own time (1987: 31). The problem with writing history from whatever happen to be the dominant values of the day is that it leads to moralizing, and moralizing reduces the shelf-life of the product (Elias, 2006a: 33–4). Conquest – the acquisition of territory by force – is morally less palatable to people at the turn of the twenty-first century than it was a century or two earlier, let alone in the Middle Ages. That is irrelevant to understanding conquest as a structured social process that has occurred constantly, at least since the beginnings of agriculture about 12,000 years ago, to the accompaniment of bloodletting that is repulsive to Western people nowadays (Goudsblom, 1996b).

Whatever happened through the mingling of cultures, what certainly did advance was a line of effective American conquest. The frontier process was one of continuing state-formation, using the term in its Weberian and

Eliasian sense rather than in the constitutional sense of the admission of new states to the Union. Much of what is glimpsed through a silver screen darkly is in effect a folk memory of a process of internal pacification that was unfolding in the West in the decades after the Civil War. Richard Maxwell Brown (1991: 41) sets the cowboy era of the post-bellum Wild West in context as a 'Western Civil War of Incorporation'. From the Hollywood image, it would be difficult to see that anything more was involved than many local quarrels between gun-slingers. Brown, however, argues that America was a strongly politicized nation after 1860, and the political and ideological allegiances of the gunmen were important. Many of them strongly identified with the Union or the Confederacy, with the Republicans or the Democrats. Brown distinguishes between 'incorporation' and 'resister' gunfighters. Examples of the former are Wild Bill Hickok and Wyatt Earp, and among the latter was John Wesley Hardin. The process of incorporation 'resulted in what should at last be recognized as a civil war across the entire expanse of the West – one fought in many places and on many fronts in almost all Western territories and states from the 1860s and beyond 1900 into the 1910s' (ibid.: 44). The Western Civil War of Incorporation comprised several different kinds of conflict besides this echo of the Civil War in the more familiar sense. Apart from the insurgent Indians, gradually forced by military pressure and economic encroachment into reservations, the process impinged on the traditional ways of life and livelihood of the Hispanos of the Southwest, who hit back through the activities of *bandidos*. Moreover, in the mines, mills and logging camps on what Brown calls the 'wageworkers' frontier' of the West, conflicts between corporate industrialists and workers often resulted in strikes that culminated in violence between trade unionists and paramilitary and military forces. Government usually brought its growing strength to bear on the side of capitalism.

The process of incorporation was also a conflict of values. Below a relatively small elite of business and professional people and skilled craftsmen was a mass of unskilled and poor, who adhered to traditional social values of family and community:

> [T]hose who resisted the dominant trend of society were often, in line with traditional values, strongly prone to combat and violence. They were not offended by disorder, for in the accepted reality of their lives tumult was as likely as not to be the norm and was easily squared with their social values, which the more cosmopolitan citizenry in the growing towns and cities saw as antiquated and harmful. Comfortable with turbulence, the recalcitrant had little interest in or sympathy for the incorporation process stressing the aggregation of wealth, the consolidation of capital, and the centralizing of authority at the local, the state (or the territory), and the national levels. . . . [T]he incorrigible disorder and violence of the outlawed and alienated was

met with the ultimately successful violence of vigilantes and local officers of the law. (Ibid.: 45–6)

Brown's concept of a 'Western Civil War of Incorporation' as a direct aftermath of the more familiar Civil War is controversial. His political interpretation perhaps distracts attention from something more fundamental: the relative absence of a monopoly of violence. But a process of incorporation was certainly in train. It was no other than an American manifestation of the processes of the taming of warriors and of internal pacification that are defining components of any process of state-formation. And, arguably, Turner saw that very clearly. That he did so is obscured for us by his use of 'civilization' in the complacent sense of his own time, as something static that Europeans and Americans had definitively achieved, but which then underwent a process of geographical 'advance'. He painted too pretty a picture of what was in most respects not a pretty scene. But then our perception and feelings are conditioned by the advance of the threshold of repugnance towards violence during a further century of 'civilization' in the more technical sense that is employed in this book.

What, then, remains of Turner's celebrated frontier thesis? Even his 'sharpest critics have rarely failed to concede the core of merit to his thesis', said Richard Hofstadter (1969: 119), and that has remained so in the most recent phase of the debate. Despite the manifold qualifications that need to be made in the light of a century's further historical research, it is still true that for two and half centuries, the American people shaped their lives with the vast interior of the continent before them.[8]

> Their national existence up to Turner's day had been involved with conquering, securing, occupying, and developing their continental empire. It is hard to believe that this process of westward settlement, so demanding, so preoccupying, so appealing to the imagination, so productive of new and rich resources for the economy, could have been carried on for so long without having some effect upon their politics and diplomacy, the pattern of their nationalism, their manners, literature, and their habits and institutions. (Ibid.)

The question of whether Turner exaggerated the significance of the 'closing' of the frontier at the end of the nineteenth century remains. He began his essay by pointing out that between the 1880 and 1890 censuses, the frontier, and the supply of free land, had disappeared for the first time since the beginning of European settlement. Critics up to and including Limerick have emphasized how arbitrary it was, following the US Bureau of the Census, to proclaim that the frontier had disappeared simply because there were in 1891 no regions with a settled population of fewer than two people per square mile. That is right: complex long-term social processes like those associated with the frontier rarely have an absolute end point, any more than they have absolute beginnings.[9] Yet it was not unreasonable for Turner to anticipate profound consequences for American society. No matter when the frontier was 'closed', land did gradually become scarcer, and that has rarely been without significance in agrarian societies. In European history, the eleventh century AD offers a distant precedent. As the margin of effective cultivation was reached in a feudal society, it became more and more difficult for all members of the knightly class to secure a fiefdom of their own. Not only did social competition intensify, but landless knights embarked on military adventures to conquer new territory: the Normans conquered England and Sicily, and were prominent among the Crusaders who established the short-lived Latin Kingdom of Jerusalem, and casually inflicted longer-lasting damage on their fellow Christians in the Byzantine Empire as they proceeded to the Holy Land (Elias, 2000: 214–20). Thus it is perhaps no accident that America began to acquire its first overseas empire in the decade that it declared its internal frontier closed.

Beyond manifest destiny: the beginnings of an American empire

Ever since Frederick Jackson Turner published his famous paper, most debate among historians and social scientists has been about the consequences of the so-called 'closing of the frontier' for the *internal* development of American society. But Turner himself foresaw that it might also have implications for the USA's *external* relations:

> That these energies of expansion will no longer operate would be a rash prediction; and the demands for a vigorous foreign policy, for an interoceanic canal, for the revival of our power upon the seas, and for the extension of American influence to outlying islands and adjoining countries, are indications that the movement will continue. (1947: 219)

In the 1890s, the USA began to compete with the European powers, not to settle its own North American borders but to acquire overseas dominions (Zimmerman, 2002). The ambition to build a canal across the Panama isthmus, to facilitate trade and military deployments between Atlantic and Pacific, had implications beyond engineering the secession from Colombia of the new state of Panama. The USA had, since the Civil War, become a major world economic power. It looked to protect its trade routes from possible rivals, and built a navy third in size after those of

Britain and Germany. The Hawaiian Islands, an independent Polynesian monarchy, lay athwart the great circle route from California and the canal to China and the Far East. American missionaries turned traders proved adept at insinuating themselves into the Hawaiian political structure, and at the second attempt – the first was vetoed by President Cleveland – they persuaded the USA to annex the islands. Almost simultaneously came the Spanish–American War of 1898, triggered by Spain's brutal attempt to suppress a rebellion in Cuba. The USA ruled Cuba only until 1902, when it was granted a limited form of independence,[10] but it kept Puerto Rico on grounds of its strategic location in relation to the eastern end of the canal. As a more or less accidental by-product of the war, the USA found itself a colonial power in the Philippines (Go and Foster, 2003), where its rule began with the task of suppressing a rising by Filipino freedom fighters. As in the case of Hawaii, Guam, Midway and various other Pacific islands, the decision for annexation was driven by the competition with other world powers in which the USA was now ineluctably caught up. Specifically, it was feared that Japan might annex Hawaii, and Germany the Philippines.

These decisions were debated heatedly; many Americans (notably Mark Twain and Carl Schurz) felt uneasy at ruling any territory that did not become fully integrated into the USA, and whose inhabitants were not accorded the full democratic rights of American citizenship. That the advocates of annexation won is one small sign of the flaws in the 'emanation of the human spirit' or 'expression of fundamental values' interpretation of American political development, and of the strength of the model of a 'compelling process' Elias developed through his study of Western European history.

The sense of an inherent conflict between the democratic rhetoric of the era of the War of Independence on the one hand and the emergence of America as a world power on the other has endured. The USA's belated intervention in the First and Second World Wars, and the debate over the League of Nations, all reflect that. And during the Cold War, there remained a constant need to justify the conflict by presenting it as a battle between a free and an unfree world.

Most Western historians place the blame for the great falling out between the two wartime allies squarely on the shoulders of Josef Stalin, who not only snuffed out the democratic regimes of half a dozen countries in Central and Eastern Europe, which, thanks to the Yalta agreement, found themselves on the wrong side of the Iron Curtain, but who was also beyond dispute one of the great mass murderers of history. There is another, minority, viewpoint articulated by such critics as Noam Chomsky and Gore Vidal, who blame the onset of the Cold War on President Truman's reneging on the Yalta agreement by beginning the process of incorporating West Germany into the emergent Western alliance (Vidal, 2002).

But it scarcely matters who is right about the historical details. In the historical big picture, the years immediately after VE Day were a classic illustration of how victory over one enemy brings the victor face to face with another powerful rival, and potentially (in accordance with the principle of the monopoly mechanism) into a bigger and better round of an elimination contest. Such processes have been familiar since antiquity: Thucydides (1972: 49ff.) began his account of the Peloponnesian Wars by recounting how a dispute over the small city of Epidamnus had brought Corcyra into conflict with Corinth, then Corinth with Athens, and so on until – after their joint victory over the Persians – there broke out the great war between Athens and Sparta. The stand-off between the USA and the USSR, which endured for more than three decades, did not result in direct conflict between the two great powers for each other's territory; the hotter parts of the Cold War were to be found in a series of peripheral wars fought mainly by their proxies. In spite of the superficially grave threat of nuclear annihilation, mutually assured destruction (MAD) actually produced a period of global stability that was conducive to prosperity in the Western world.[11]

It was the economic failure of the Soviet empire that brought about its collapse in 1989–90, and for once in the course of human history a struggle left the victor as the overwhelmingly dominant power in the world, there no longer remaining a further rival to be confronted – at least for the time being. It has been calculated that in 2002 the USA, with about 5 per cent of the world's population, created and consumed about a third of Gross World Product; and by 2005 its military expenditure was very nearly as much as that of all the other countries of the world combined. This degree of predominance is without precedent in world history, and its maintenance has become an explicit goal of US government policy (see United States Government, 2002).

The Dubya Addendum

After the events of 11 September 2001, President G. W. Bush announced what we may call the Dubya Addendum to the Roosevelt Corollary to the Monroe Doctrine, extending beyond the Western hemisphere the USA's self-proclaimed right to intervene in other states. In a speech at West Point on 1 June 2002, he stated that 'our security will require all Americans to be . . . ready for pre-emptive action when necessary to defend our liberty and defend our lives'. The 'Big Stick' was now to be used against any state anywhere. In effect, this amounts to an attempt to embark on the establishment of a world state – a statement that may appear startling unless it is read in the light of Weber's definition of a state as an organization successfully upholding a claim to a monopoly of the means of violence. The final 'internal pacification' of the world is indeed an attractive dream, but those who have dreamed of an eventual world government have generally imagined it under the auspices of the Charter of the United Nations rather than under the USA as one country among many. The unilateral exercise of the monopoly by the USA is deeply problematic. The objections that anti-imperialists made to America's acquisition of its first colonies a century ago apply *pari passu* today. Weber, after all, spoke of a monopoly of the *legitimate* use of the means of violence, meaning that the central apparatus first *claims* that only it has a legitimate right to exercise force, and (with luck and beneficent government) that legitimacy in due course also comes to reside in the minds of its subjects. How are the 95 per cent of the world's population who are not US citizens to exercise any democratic constraint upon American policy? And if they do not, how long will an effective US monopoly survive?

Conclusion

The theme of chapters 7 and 8 has been the long-term operation of what Elias called the monopoly mechanism, traced through a sequence of elimination contests that resulted in the formation of the national conterminous territory of the USA. Though differing in detail and in timing from the equivalent process studied by Elias in Western European history, what unfolded in North America also shows strong underlying similarities, in its various stages from the earliest European settlements to the beginnings of the USA's present dominant position in the world.

Such long-term processes emerge from the interweaving of countless people's plans and intentions, but overall their course is not planned. Chance and 'events' may play too great a part for specific outcomes at each stage of development either to be foreseen or effectively intended, even when the broad direction of the process is well established. The process instead comes to exert compelling forces over those people, groups and states caught up in them, so that at each stage people often feel there is only one possible response to the emergent situation confronting them. Their actions seem more the product of the process than the process of their actions. It has, for instance, been said that Britain acquired its empire in a fit of absent-mindedness, and much the same may go for America's. Nevertheless, the American national experience has been consistently (and over a longer period than Britain's) of the power ratios between itself and its potential opponents tilting steadily in its favour. And thus, in contradiction of what seem to have been Elias's expectations for modern societies in general, the element of the planned and intended in the USA's expansion – while never complete – has tended to increase.

There remains the question of what effect this national experience has had on American habitus. Elias, not just in *The Civilizing Process* but also in many more of his books and essays, pointed to the ways in which the particular history of a country's state-formation processes left its mark on its character. In the case of the USA, it is the history of westward expansion and the experience of the frontier that has, since Turner, been most discussed as a source of a lasting social psychological legacy. As a romantic myth, it may indeed continue to be influential, although as with any myth one still has to investigate the social basis of its appeal. In this chapter, some caution has been expressed about the direct effects of the frontier experience as a factual social process. One conclusion we may tentatively suggest is that Turner's rugged individualism may owe less to the specifics of the frontier than to the more general American experience of accumulating power chances of all kinds. The sovereignty of the individual, like the sovereignty of countries, depends upon power ratios being skewed in their favour. That was the central experience of the frontier: most individuals were accumulating wealth under the protection of government, and their power advantage over potential enemies was steadily increasing. After the national territory was consolidated, Americans' experience of the world at large followed a similar trajectory. This has imprinted itself in the form of most Americans' intense nationalism and the sense of 'American exceptionalism'. Or, to put it in another way, they have exceptionally strong 'we-feelings'. This is not unique: it has also been found in other imperial powers, persisting for example in France and especially Britain, in spite of their now diminished power position in the world. Because it rests on highly unequal favourable power balances, such intense national pride is generally associated with a weak capacity for collective reflexivity: in other words, it makes it difficult for citizens of such powerful countries to see themselves as others see them, as one country among many (albeit weaker) others.

9

Integration Struggles

Processes of state-formation are Janus-faced. One face is the external struggle for the acquisition of territory through warfare and other means, described, as it worked out in North America, in chapters 7 and 8. The other face consists of the concomitant processes of internal pacification, stabilization and integration of a territory. The two faces are inseparable because of what Goudsblom (2001: 104) has called 'the paradox of pacification'. He quotes the old adage that 'if you want peace, prepare for war', but remarks that it is equally true that if you want to wage war with some chance of winning, you have to see to peace within your own ranks. State-formation involves the organization of violence, and the paradox arises from the civilizing constraints that that organization entails. 'Organized violence is generally far more effective than unorganized violence. To be effective, however, it requires a high degree of internal pacification. Those who participate in exercising it must not fight each other' (ibid.)

There is, however, a double paradox here. For processes of internal pacification and integration do not necessarily proceed smoothly. If successful, eventually they usually produce new and more effective forms of social organization within which people live peacefully together. In the short term, nevertheless, processes of integration very commonly bring with them 'integration struggles';[1] when hitherto relatively autonomous people and groups are forced into closer dependence on each other, the level of conflict initially often rises rather than diminishing. In American history, the greatest such struggle was the bloody Civil War, the outcome of which, in the successful integration of the conflicting sections of the USA, was long in doubt. But other less dramatic integration processes have given rise to a variety of other conflicts and political cleavages. One example that has run through much of American history is the relations between the cities and the countryside.

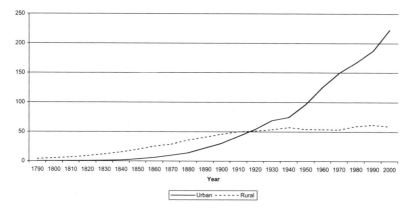

Figure 9.1: Population in (legally defined) Urban and Rural Territories
Sources: US Department of Commerce and Bureau of the Census (1975); US Census Bureau (2002).

Urbanization and resentment of the city

The cities of the eastern seaboard – albeit small by today's standards – were key nodes in the development of American society from early colonial times. And as Wade (1968: 190) observed, when in 1800 the farming frontier barely extended beyond the Appalachians, there were towns in the Ohio valley and as far west as St Louis, Denver, San Francisco and Seattle which were already growing to regional prominence before the westward expansion was complete. He quoted a remark from 1884: 'The city stamps the country instead of the country stamping the city. It is the cities and towns which will frame state constitutions, make laws, create public opinion, establish social usages, and fix standards'. More recently, Monti (1999: 24–5) has remarked: 'We are a bourgeois people who made an urban world.' Yet it is very easy to forget how recently the USA became a predominantly urban society. Figure 9.1 shows the growth of population resident in urban and rural areas over the 200 years from 1790 to 1990, although it needs to be interpreted with some caution. In the *Historical Statistics of the United States* (US Department of Commerce and Bureau of the Census [1975]), on the one hand, the 'urban' population includes all people living in incorporated townships with 5,000 or more people – and after 1950, villages down to 2,500 are included as urban, provided that they are incorporated as municipalities. On the other hand, the various incorporated municipalities that together constitute a conurbation are counted separately. This legal definition does not accord with either everyday or social scientific understanding of what constitutes urban life. With these reservations, it is none the less striking that a majority of Americans did not come to live in urban areas, as thus defined, until the 1920s. In the 1990s, the Bureau of the Census defined a series of Metropolitan Statistical Areas (MSAs) which, although more realistic for most practical purposes, are difficult to compare with the long-run historical data series. In 2000, about four-fifths of Americans lived in 256 metropolitan areas with populations of 100,000 or more.[2]

What life in small communities meant for the life of most people in America in the first half of the nineteenth century has been well stated by Peter Dobkin Hall:

> [T]he culture of America before 1850 was local and familial. Most Americans lived in towns and villages of less than 2,500 inhabitants which produced the greater part of the food, clothing, shelter, and intellectual and welfare services consumed by their citizens. These goods and services were produced and consumed primarily within the context of the family: of the 7.7 million Americans in the workforce in 1850, 4.9 million operated family farms; the remaining 2.8 million (with the exception of a few hundred thousand who worked on the railroads and a handful of large-scale industrial establishments) worked in homes and family businesses. . . . The sources of information, identity, and ambition were local or regional: people read local newspapers and received their career training locally, usually through the family-controlled system of apprenticeship; although many·were seeking their fortunes in the West and in the growing cities, most people lived out their lives in the places where they had been born. (Hall, 1982: 2)

Such communities were often emotional pressure cookers: the close bonds of family and community solidarity often coexisted with the bonds of hatred and vendetta. When durable and effective monopolies of physical power have not yet formed, or have broken down, some of the strongest interdependencies that bond people are those that arise from exposure to the danger of physical violence (Elias, 1974: xx).

A romantic nostalgia has long attached itself to the idea of a good old way of life in small communities. Thomas Jefferson famously glorified the rural way of life and denigrated the city,[3] but this trait has by no means been confined to America. In the late nineteenth century the German sociologist Ferdinand Tönnies formulated the contrast between *Gemeinschaft* (community) and *Gesellschaft* (association), a static polarity between the supposed solidarity and harmony, warmth and cooperation of the past and the impersonality and conflict of life in urban-industrial society. But, before large and eternal conclusions are drawn about the habitus to which small communities give rise, an important caveat must be entered. Elias (1974) pointed out that the static use of the concept 'community', as if it signified the same kind of entity at all stages of social development, is highly misleading. Life in a small isolated farming community in earlier centuries, particularly where the process of state-formation was not yet well advanced, was very different from life in a small farming community today. Present-day communities may be physically remote, surrounded by prairies or mountains, but in highly differentiated societies they are integrated into far-spreading webs of interdependence – markets, transport, communications, and organizations social, political and economic – that did not exist in earlier phases of social development. They are 'small towns in mass society', penetrated by 'the agencies and culture of mass institutions', and thus can no longer be understood – if they ever could – in terms of 'a dichotomous difference between urban and rural, sacred and secular, mechanical and organic forms of social organization' (Vidich and Bensman, 1968: vii).

Certainly a greater range of functions had to be met from within a local community that was more loosely connected to a less differentiated society and a relatively less durable state. But it is the degree of differentiation and integration in the wider society, rather than the size of the local community as such, that principally shapes the civilizing pressures that shape people's habitus. As Elias explained:

> As the bonds between first producers and last consumers become longer and more differentiated and the decision-making machinery becomes an affair of many levels with many feedbacks, private and public aspects of people's functions and lives become more highly and more firmly differentiated. Commodities and services are provided by means of long chains of interdependent and hierarchically ordered specialised occupations, with a strongly *impersonal and public* character even if they retain the form of a private enterprise. The functions of this type of occupation *for their occupants*, in other words, have to be increasingly subordinated to their functions *for others* – to their impersonal functions within this wide and far-flung nexus of functions. (1974: xxvii)[4]

Yet life in small towns and communities has imprinted itself on the American habitus. Its influence may persist today more through the force of romantic political and cultural traditions than through its congruence with present-day social realities. (Here we are back to Frederick Jackson Turner and the image of the self-reliant frontiersman – tempered, however, by the reality that any community that largely ate out of cans was factually by no means self-sufficient, and was connected by chains of interdependence to the food-packing factories of Chicago and much else beyond – see pp. 204–5 above.) It can probably be seen in the body of American public opinion opposed to stronger gun-control laws: the romantic folk memory of a past when people *had* to defend themselves has become linked to a moral belief that people *ought* to continue to do so even within the framework of a much more highly developed state-society. It probably also contributes to the paradox that people hostile to 'big government' are also quite likely to favour government intervention in what others would regard as matters of private morality. As Elias (1974: xxvii) pointed out, it is characteristic of communities in less differentiated societies that public and private functions are less distinguishable. This was very likely especially true in what Page Smith (1966) called 'covenanted communities', the numerous towns across America founded by people of the same ethnic and religious background. The cultural lag of nostalgia for a supposedly simpler and better life may thus help to sustain the strongly moralizing campaigns of the contemporary Christian Right on issues such as homosexuality and abortion.

Again, these should not be seen abstractly as conflicts between free-floating 'cultural traditions'; they are, rather, the product of an endlessly growing web, weaving people of very different backgrounds and beliefs into closer unplanned interdependence with each other – an interdependence that none of the various parties may initially want.

Immigration

The United States is a nation of immigrants. It has been estimated that fewer than a third of today's population have roots going back in America before 1800; the rest are descended from people who were themselves also immigrants, mainly from the British Isles before and shortly after independence.[5] The flow of newcomers from other parts of the world has been an important factor in American territorial expansion and economic growth. But, despite any such benefits, one aspect of American history is a continual series of established–outsider struggles, in Elias's original and most literal sense referring to relations between longer-resident groups and newcomer groups (see above, pp. 18–20). Even before independence, some English-speaking residents of Pennsylvania expressed fears and resentments about the influx of German-speaking 'Pennsylvania Dutch' immigrants (Morgan, 2002: 72–9). The provenance of each successive wave of mass immigration over the last two centuries has varied, but as long as they remained near the bottom of the hierarchy of employment, education and living standards, each ethnic group – Irish, Jews, Chinese, Poles, Italians, Latinos – has been despised by more established groups, typically two-front strata who were themselves still striving for further ascent up the social ladder. That is to say, they were typically stigmatized as dirty, morally unreliable, promiscuous, impulsive, disorderly, drunken, prone to gambling, irreligious, not

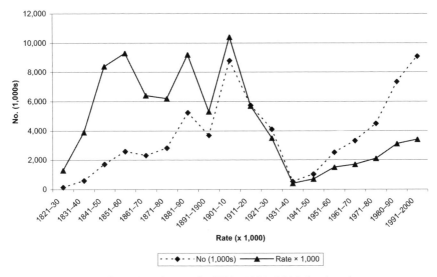

Figure 9.2: Rates of immigration to the USA, 1821–2000, by decade
Sources: US Department of Commerce and Bureau of the Census (1975); US Census Bureau (2002): table 5.

respectable, or any permutation of such qualities. The fear of being 'swamped' (as it has often been put) by supposedly less 'civilized' newcomers is a recurring theme. As figure 9.2 shows, even during the peak period of immigration in the first decade of the twentieth century, newly arrived migrants never amounted to more than about one person per annum for every 100 members of the existing population. The foreign-born proportion of the total resident population hovered around 14 per cent during the six decades from 1860 to 1920 (see figure 9.3). That is a substantial outsider element for established groups to come to terms with, but it is markedly lower than the corresponding figures for Canada and Argentina just before the First World War, which were 22 and 30 per cent respectively (Higham, 1968: 96). On the other hand, figures for the country as a whole do not tell the whole story, for in some localities, the proportion of foreign-born residents was at times far higher; in the 1860s, more than half of the population of Chicago, Milwaukee and St Louis was foreign-born.

'Nativism' became a powerful political force in nineteenth-century and early twentieth-century America. Nativism had a strong appeal 'for artisan and manual workers who associated immigrants with a new and threatening America – an America of increasing urban poverty, of factories and railroads, and of rising prices and abruptly changing markets' (Bailyn et al., 1992: II, 563–4). In the 1840s and 1850s they formed semi-secret organizations like the Order of United Americans, banding

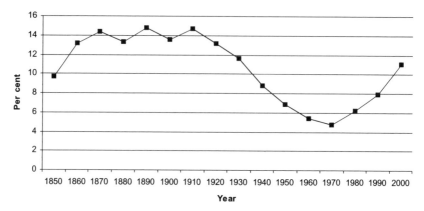

Figure 9.3: Foreign-born proportion of US resident population, 1850–2000
Sources: US Department of Commerce and Bureau of the Census (1975); US
Census Bureau (2002): table 41.[6]

together to protect native-born workers. Then and later, many trade
unions excluded immigrants because immigrants desperate to find work
acted as strike-breakers, thus making it more probable that they would
indeed be willing to break strikes (and also thus providing Robert
Merton [1968: 475–90] with one of his most famous examples of a 'self-
fulfilling prophecy'). The mid-1850s saw the upsurge of a short-lived
nativist political party, formally named the American Party, but always
remembered as the 'Know-Nothings' (because members were supposed,
if asked about its organization, to say they knew nothing). It gained very
widespread support, especially in the Northeast, in 1854–6, and
although it soon faded it played a significant part in the collapse of the
old Whig Party and the rise of the Republicans immediately before the
Civil War.

Nativist movements also had strong quasi-religious elements: they were
associated with anti-Catholicism, sabbatarianism and the temperance
movement. The latter two are typical of established groups' claim to
higher standards of self-restraint as a sign of their social and moral superiority over the outsiders; nativist sentiment played some part even as late
as 1918 in the adoption of the Eighteenth Amendment to the Constitution,
which inaugurated the ill-fated venture of Prohibition (Mennell, 1969).
Catholicism, too, was then seen as more lenient, more morally permissive
than the various strands of nonconformist Protestantism hitherto dominant in America. In the middle of the nineteenth century, anti-Catholicism
was to a large extent an expression of hostility to the Irish immigrants; not
until the 1890s, and then dramatically in the decade 1901–10, did the 'new
immigration' from largely Catholic Southern and Eastern Europe overtake

the formerly dominant Northern and Western European sources of sub-stantially Protestant immigrants. In the 1920s, severe restrictions were imposed on new immigration, causing new arrivals to plummet, as figure 9.2 has shown.

Yet the sheer scale of immigration over the half century after the Civil War made it increasingly difficult to sustain the old predominantly White Anglo-Saxon Protestant (WASP) we-image of Americans as a whole. More inclusive we-images began to emerge, still with religious undertones but no longer specifically Protestant or even Christian. It is not an acci-dent that the pledge of allegiance to the flag dates from this period.[7] A first version was published in the juvenile periodical *The Youth's Companion* on 8 September 1892: 'I pledge allegiance to my Flag and the Republic for which it stands; one nation indivisible, with liberty and Justice for all.' The words 'the flag of the United States of America' were substituted for 'my Flag' in 1924, and the pledge was officially recognized by the United States government in 1942. In 1954 Congress inserted 'under God', so the pledge has since then read:

> I pledge allegiance to the flag of the United States of America and to the Republic for which it stands, one nation under God, indivisible, with liberty and justice for all.

Immigrants do not remain immigrants. Successive waves, successive ethnic groups, have gradually become assimilated.[8] That has come about through intermarriage and by successive generations of migrants achiev-ing economic success and organizing themselves to exercise political power. In other words, the power ratios between the established and a succession of outsider groups gradually become relatively more equal. This process has been reinforced by the unparalleled diversity of the sources of immigration into the USA; in contrast to other major immi-gration destinations like Canada and Australia where, until relatively recent decades, migrants from the British Isles were predominant, or Argentina where Italians were similarly prominent, the USA has for long drawn people from most parts of the globe, even if different sources have been more or less prominent at different periods. The diversity of immi-grants has also been such that no single group was large enough to alter pre-existing relationships; and, in America, ethnic groups had to compete with (and were often played off against) each other. 'Accordingly, the immigrants have never been arrayed solidly against the native population on economic issues, and no political party has ever captured the whole "foreign vote"' (Higham, 1968: 98).

Although the metaphor of the melting pot is a hallowed one in American thought, it conveys too uncomplicated an image of a never-failing production line. So far, indeed, over many generations more and more people have been poured out in the mould of 'Americans'. Among those of European descent, *objective* ethnic differences in education, occupation, family and community have been in long-term decline. At the same time, for many people a *subjective* identity as 'hyphenated Americans' (Italian-, Irish-, Jewish- and so on) has, if anything, grown in importance. Alba has argued, on the basis of detailed survey data, that this does not represent a revival of ethnic division, but rather a '"symbolic ethnicity", a vestigial attachment to a few ethnic symbols imposing little cost on everyday life' (1990: xiii). Furthermore, he detected the emergence of a latent, implicit and broader ethnic group that he called 'European Americans', based on ancestry from anywhere on the European continent, and 'with its own myths about its place in American history and its relationship to the American identity' (ibid.: xiv). Even if few Americans explicitly think of themselves as 'European Americans', this development is not insignificant in a period when the USA has received large numbers of immigrants from Latin America and Asia.

Towards the end of the twentieth century, the graph of immigration once more took a sharp up-turn.[9] There was an influx of newcomers from many parts of the world, including notably Asians and Latin Americans. In the decade 1991–2000, the absolute number of (legal) immigrants actually exceeded that in the previous peak decade of 1901–10, although because the total population of the USA was almost four times as great in 2000 as it had been in 1901, the *rate* of immigration in relation to the established population was only one-third of that reached a century earlier. In 2000, the proportion of foreign-born residents was approaching that of 1930, but was still lower than the peaks in 1890 or 1920. Once more, some Americans expressed fears that the melting pot was becoming choked, that, for instance, Spanish might overtake English as the principal language spoken in the southwest of the USA – such a sensitive issue that the question was raised whether for the first time it should be constitutionally specified that English was the official language of the United States, something hitherto so obvious as not to need stating. Perhaps more worrying was the emergence of the doctrine of multiculturalism, which, going beyond tolerance of ethnic cultural differences, in its most radical forms championed separatism rather than integration (ironically, there were even a few self-appointed black spokesmen in the 1980s and 1990s who rejected such integration as had been achieved since the 1960s). As Schlesinger complained, this form of multiculturalism 'belittles *unum* and glorifies *pluribus*' (1992: 17). He was particularly alarmed at the damage the doctrine was doing to school curricula:

> The militants of ethnicity now contend that a main objective of public education should be the protection, strengthening, celebration, and perpetua-

tion of ethnic origins and identities. Separatism, however, nourishes prejudices, magnifies difference and stirs antagonisms. The consequent increase in ethnic and racial conflict lies behind the hullabaloo over 'multiculturalism' and 'political correctness', over the iniquities of the 'Eurocentric' curriculum, and over the notion that history and literature should be taught not as intellectual disciplines but as therapies whose function is to raise minority self-esteem. (Ibid.)

Yet, although it is always possible that the melting pot will eventually cease to smelt, the advent of multiculturalism and separatism is more likely a symptom of the dynamics of established–outsider relations during a period of high immigration than a significant cause of a possible failure of the assimilating process. In fact, despite economic arguments that the immigration in the late twentieth and early twenty-first century has included too high a proportion of the relatively unskilled and unqualified (Borjas, 2000), there has been little clamour – compared with that which prompted the restrictions of the 1920s – for a reduction in immigration. One reason may be that because new immigrants acquire US citizenship and voting rights relatively soon after their arrival,[10] politicians are wary of alienating potential supporters at the ballot box.

Growth of the means of ruling

American political thought has contained a strong current of ambivalence bordering on squeamishness towards the growth of an effective state apparatus. The American distrust of centralized government was (as noted in chapter 1 above) expressed notably by Jefferson, who has been persistently influential ever since the age of Enlightenment. In his writings he took too much for granted that a peaceful, 'civilized' society is simply the outcome of consciously enlightened political institutions, and that all humans can be governed and govern themselves by reason. The immediate consequence of this belief seems to be that from the start internal pacification was taken too much for granted – at least by Jefferson and his numerous intellectual descendants – and seen too much as a one-sided product of Americans' peaceful and reasonable habitus rather than both pacification and habitus being the outcome of a two-way process over time. Jeffersonian rhetoric against 'big government' has remained very audible in American public life to the present day. Nevertheless, willy-nilly, it has come about.

Police forces

The distrust that citizens have felt towards distant government authority, combined with their trust in themselves and their neighbours in local
communities, is seen in the organization of policing throughout the
USA.

In increasingly urbanized and industrialized societies, police forces
came into existence in effect to take over the functions of enforcing law
and order hitherto performed, on the one hand, by the military and, on
the other, by members of a community at large. Military forces came to
be seen as concerned almost exclusively in the functions of attack and
defence in relation to meeting and making threats external to the state territory, and were deployed in support of the civil power only in exceptional
circumstances. In some countries this process of differentiation out of the
military was quite direct, as can be seen, for example, in the French *gen-
darmerie* and the Italian *carabinieri*, which remain quasi-military armed
forces of the national state, alongside other police forces of a less military
character (see Emsley, 2004). In contrast, American police forces emphatically did not develop directly out of the military, even though it remains
true that they did in effect assume some of the functions that the army or
militias had previously met when necessary (Monkkonen, 1981).
American police were modelled not on the centralized French, Italian,
Prussian or Russian models, but on the British. Both the United States
and, to a lesser extent, Britain have retained decentralized systems of
policing.[11] One major difference is that American police have always been
armed, whereas police in Great Britain have never routinely carried
firearms.[12]

The Metropolitan Police, created in London in 1829, served as the
model for the first American force, set up in New York in 1844. Boston,
Philadelphia and other cities quickly followed.[13] The emphasis was on
preventing crime through regular foot patrols, and at first there were no
detectives. Discipline was to be maintained through a quasi-military
command structure, although decentralization was taken to extremes,
authority often being delegated to wards and neighbourhoods. This
reflected the well-established confidence in the 'community', and a
matching distrust of 'government' and 'the state', the same pattern that
underpinned the vigilante tradition in America: 'the same citizens who
might distrust punishment power in the hands of a distant government
authority trust themselves and their neighbours' (Zimring, 2003: 109).
While decentralization of policing was certainly consistent with the ideological objective common to nineteenth-century Britain and America of
keeping the constabulary close to the people, it created acute problems
of control, as police became enmeshed in neighbourhood and city poli-

tics. The anxiety to prevent the police from becoming a tool for the extension of central governments' intrusion in private and commercial life made them susceptible to becoming corrupted as the tools of local political and ethnic interests. More seriously still, crime did not respect the boundaries between the plethora of police jurisdictions. In the USA by the early twentieth century, this problem led to the creation of state police forces and a number of federal agencies, notably the Federal Bureau of Investigation (FBI), rather than to the integration and coordination of city forces within a wider framework. The outcome was a highly decentralized system with around 20,000 separate policing agencies in the country as a whole. The effect seems to be that there are considerable geographical variations in policing, but that overall America is a highly policed society, because local forces may pay attention to minor offences (for example jay-walking) that are deemed too trivial for forces (for instance in Britain) covering bigger territories and subject to more centralized setting of priorities.

At the time of writing, there are signs that under the provisions of the Patriot Act, passed by Congress in the immediate aftermath of the attacks on New York and Washington on 11 September 2001 and in the context of the so-called 'war on terror', centrally coordinated mass surveillance of citizens, of the kind Americans have habitually dreaded, may be coming about; but it is too early to draw any firm conclusions about that.

Growth of the civil apparatus of ruling

Military and police forces have a direct and obvious connection with any government's claim to a monopoly of the legitimate use of violence. Less obviously, so has a government's civil service. The civilian bureaucracy administers the laws of the land, always including the effective levying of taxation and then a huge range of other matters down to (for example) ensuring that people are not cruel to animals and that they observe prohibitions on smoking in designated places. But enforcement of the full range of a state's internal laws and regulations always rests in the last resort on the means of violence, no matter how rarely they are actually employed.

Although a promising start had been made to the creation of a federal civil service in the first quarter of the nineteenth century, 'the election of Andrew Jackson, with his contempt for educated expertise and his distrust of large-scale organizations, curtailed the development of efficient administrative practices and a trained civil service' (Hall, 1982: 228). Jackson is generally credited with fostering the 'spoils system', which has continued to undermine the adequacy of the government apparatus in the USA to the present day. Despite the long-term growth of the federal bureaucracy, its higher reaches have never attained the degree of political independence that was achieved in Britain through the Northcote–Trevelyan reforms, which were fully implemented by 1870. In the USA, many civil servants are appointed not for their expertise but on the basis of clientelism or cronyism. European civil services are sometimes criticized *either* for being insufficiently expert *or* for being unrepresentative of and unresponsive to the people at large. The British civil service was in the past often mocked for being dominated by a 'cloistered elite' (Wakeford, 1969) of gentlemanly amateurs, who were educated in the English public (i.e. private) schools and at Oxford and Cambridge, where they often read traditional subjects like classics (the relevance of classics to ruling a country in the modern world being questioned). The French elite, on the other hand, has been criticized not for its lack of specialized expertise – which it is seen as having acquired in abundance at the *grandes écoles*, notably the École Nationale d'Administration (ENA) – but rather for the contempt that it shows, in its expertise, for public opinion; Pierre Bourdieu (1996) described it as a 'state nobility'. The American bureaucracy suffers from both criticisms at once, lack of expertise *and* unrepresentativeness. The spoils system feeds back into a lack of confidence in and hostility to the growth of government, fostering the perception that 'they're in it for what they can get out of it'. That in turn may be reinforced (in spite of a tendency in public opinion to distrust big government more than big business) by the fact that at the higher levels, officials are commonly recruited for their business background. At its worst, this spiral culminates in a scepticism about the whole notion of there being such a thing as the 'public interest'. In sum, as noted in chapter 4, there has never been anything in America corresponding to the *Amtscharisma*, the prestige of public service, found in many European countries. The relative weakness in America of the ideal of an independent and politically neutral civil service, whether at federal or state level, is seen in such matters as a returning officer – responsible for ensuring the integrity of an election – being at the same time involved in actively campaigning for one of the candidates.

Yet, none the less, the public-sector bureaucracy has grown in the USA as it has in other countries. Even if legal differences and problems of definition make precise international comparisons difficult in this area, an upward long-term trend is a common characteristic of industrial societies. The number of civilians employed by the US federal government in relation to the total American population is shown in figure 9.4. It must be emphasized that this graph shows only *federal* civilian employees, and if those employed by the states and by cities and other local authorities were included, the percentage would be considerably higher, although the overall trend would probably be not very much dif-

Figure 9.4: Civilian employees of the federal government in relation to total US population
Sources: US Department of Commerce and Bureau of the Census (1975); US Census Bureau (2002).

ferent. With those caveats, it can be see that government civilian employment shows a long-term upward trend, with some decline towards the end of the twentieth century. Shorter-term trends appear to correspond to political events. Wars appear to give impetus to administrative growth. Periods of peace, as in the 1920s and after the Second World War, see some decline. The most dramatic leap in the graph is associated with President Franklin D. Roosevelt's New Deal measures to counteract the Depression in the 1930s, followed immediately by the Second World War. Then the post-war decline is reversed by an upward blip in the Vietnam era. An era of a general ideological preference for smaller rather than bigger government, together with the end of the Cold War, may help to explain the downward trend in the 1990s, although that may again be reversed in connection with the so-called 'war on terror'. Civilian employees of the federal government as a proportion of total population rose from 0.06 per cent in 1816 to a peak of 1.27 per cent in 1981; its decline to 0.95 per cent in 2001 is exaggerated by the very rapid increase in US population, especially through immigration, in the 1980s and 1990s.

Tax, money and credit in state-formation

In late eighteenth- and nineteenth-century America, the development of financial institutions was widely viewed with the same kind of ambivalence or hostility as standing armies, gun control, centralized police forces and government bureaucracy. The monopolization of the means of violence, stressed Elias (2000: 268), was inseparable from the monop-olization of the means of taxation, and nowhere are people likely to view with enthusiasm the growing power of authorities to extract tax from them. But in America, suspicion extended more broadly than simply to the institutions related directly to taxation. There was some kind of latent recognition that the growth of a money-based economy is inter-woven not just with the formation of a more effective state apparatus, but also with changing modes of social interdependence and social con-straint.

In his account of state-formation in Western Europe, Elias looked back as far as the ninth century when, outside certain enclaves and in most of the vast territory that had once been part of the Roman Empire, long-dis-tance trade, towns of significant size and monetary exchange had virtu-ally disappeared. In their place stood innumerable small feudal territories that were largely autarkic, both economically and politically. Within these territories, tiny proto-towns simply formed part of the cellular structure of society at large: in them, as on a manor, commodities were largely pro-duced and consumed in the same place. But that began to change. With the exchange of products down longer chains – longer both geographi-cally and in terms of the specialization of labour – and with wider markets, there was also a greater need for the growth of money as a unified standard of exchange. Gradually, a slow long-term shift in the *balance* between the barter and monetary sectors of the economy came about (ibid.: 222).

Now, this process had already gone quite a long way in Europe by the time European settlement of North America began. The American colonies did not begin their financial development from anything like the level of ninth-century Europe. Yet barter played a surprisingly prominent part in economic life in the colonial period and beyond, at least outside the main towns – and the colonies were predominantly rural societies. Barter was referred to as 'country pay' (Bryson, 1994: 82; Larkin, 1988: 36–9). Direct exchange of goods and services imposes severe limits on the extent of trade: it depends on the 'double contingency' of a person who has X and wants Y encountering a person who has Y and wants X. Capital and credit are required if the person who has X and wants Y is nevertheless prepared to exchange his X for Z, and to hold Z until he or she happens upon a person with Y who wants Z. Using money obviates that problem, provided that parties to the transaction have confidence in money retaining its value – and that ultimately depends on the effective-ness of governments in enforcing laws of 'legal tender', punishing people if they do not accept the government's coins (or, later, notes).

In the colonial era, the balance between the barter and the monetary sectors of the economy had probably tilted backwards compared with

Britain at the same date. No doubt that owed something to the geographical dispersion of settlement and the questionable capacity of colonial governments to enforce their writ everywhere. But it was also in part the consequence of the London government allowing very little British specie to circulate in the colonies. This was the age of mercantilism, and thus of the belief that the wealth of a nation was enhanced by retaining as much bullion as possible within its own shores (America did not count as its own shores). In consequence, even in the monetary sector of the economy, American businesses kept their accounts in pounds, shillings and pence, but for actual transactions they had to rely on whatever coins were available. These might include Spanish doubloons and reals, French sous, Portuguese Johannes, and Dutch dollars, as well as a variety of home-minted coins such as the fugio. Traders had to know the exchange rates between these various currencies (Bryson, 1994: 81; Larkin, 1988: 38). After the Revolution, the United States dollar was adopted as the standard currency, but foreign coins were not finally withdrawn from circulation until 1857.

Although the supply of coinage was more important then than now – the US government issued only coins, not notes, until the Civil War – the shortage of specie was only part of a general problem of illiquidity in the colonial and early federal period. Trade on a significant scale and over any considerable distance required credit, and there were few if any banks before independence. A commercial banking system developed in the first half of the nineteenth century, but was not very effective in mobilizing long-term (as opposed to working) capital for industrial and mercantile enterprise. Before the Civil War, such few investment banks as existed were more concerned to channel European investment into schemes promoted by entrepreneurs in their own cities – Boston, Philadelphia, New York – than with mobilizing domestic capital and deploying it more widely (Hall, 1982: 242). With the outbreak of the Civil War, European investors were 'not eager to bet on the North', and so the US Treasury took steps 'to mobilize the capital of the Union, to get it out from under mattresses and out of private investment into the yawning coffers of the state' (ibid.: 243). The government for the first time issued its own paper money, the 'greenback' (Goodwin, 2003), and created a national banking system by chartering a network of 'national' banks which enjoyed a monopoly over the distribution and redemption of the national bank notes. Crucially, the notes were legal tender, and redeemable at face value at any bank in the country, not just – as in the case of ante-bellum paper – at the particular bank that had issued them. After the Civil War, what may again be called the longer chains of interdependence created by a national banking system permitted many facets of American life – not just business, but trade unions, political movements, social and cultural associations – to be organized on a national scale in a way that they had not been before (Hall, 1982).

The second emergency measure taken by the Treasury during the Civil War was to encourage the Philadelphia investment banker Jay Cooke to create a national market in government bonds, selling them directly to the public, not just to bankers. That greatly extended the government's lines of credit. But why was it necessary to use a private individual like Cooke, rather than the government's own central bank? Because there *was* no central bank. And that takes us to the greatest political struggle concerning finance and its role in state formation.

The central figure in the story is the first Secretary of the Treasury, Alexander Hamilton, whose grasp of finance and economics appears astonishingly modern in comparison with most of the other Founding Fathers. Under the Articles of Confederation, the Continental Congress had had few powers, and none over taxation. In its having to *request* necessary funds from the states, the federal government then 'more closely resembled the present-day United Nations than it did the modern US government' (Gordon, 1998: 13). The new Constitution changed that drastically. Hamilton established the system of tariffs that was (along with sales of public land in the course of westward expansion) to be the federal government's principal source of revenue right up to the First World War. He also introduced excise duties, including one of 25 per cent on whiskey which, in 1794, led to a rising of farmers west of the Appalachians who were heavily dependent on the sale of the whiskey they distilled. That was the first direct challenge to federal authority. It was quickly suppressed, its leaders being pardoned, thus demonstrating both the government's authority and, for present purposes, also the inseparability of the means of violence and the means of taxation. Later, in the 1790s, after Hamilton's tenure, still more taxes were introduced, contributing to the growing unpopularity of the Federalist party and the success of the Jeffersonians. J. K. Galbraith (quoted by Gordon, 1998: 43) remarked that while eighteenth-century Americans objected to taxation without representation, they objected equally to taxation *with* representation.

Another aspect of Hamilton's policy was of still greater significance for the construction of the American federal state. He established a national debt and a national central bank to manage it, both in the face of great political opposition. His model was unashamedly the Bank of England and the British national debt. Even at the beginning of the twenty-first century, many people still view a national debt with suspicion, as something a little immoral, as if it were just the same as individuals running up debts they cannot repay. While there are technical issues about the relationship between the size of national debt and a government's budgetary surplus or deficit, no economist now regards a national debt as anything but essential; there are fundamental differences between a private person's debts and those of an effective state, which are fundamentally backed by its power of taxation. Even so, it was a little provocative of John Steele Gordon to entitle his book about the US national debt *Hamilton's Blessing* (1998). Hamilton recognized that the vast growth of the British national debt in the century or so since the foundation of the Bank of England had played a key part in making Britain a commercial, industrial and military power in the world. A central bank performs several functions. It holds the government's funds and provides a means of transferring them from one part of the country to another. It is a source of loans to the government and to other banks, and, through its control over the sale of government bonds, it regulates the money supply and imposes discipline on other banks, preventing them from printing money irresponsibly without adequate backing in holdings of bonds. Above all, Hamilton recognized that:

> [T]he greatest problem of the American economy at this time was a lack of liquid capital, which is to say, capital available for investment. Hamilton wanted to use the national debt to create a larger and more flexible money supply. Banks holding bonds, he argued, could issue bank notes backed by them. He knew also that government bonds could serve as collateral for bank loans, multiplying the available capital, and that they would attract still more capital from Europe. (Ibid.: 27)

That came true: within a few years of the chartering of the Bank of the United States, American bonds achieved the highest international 'credit rating' (to use a modern term anachronistically).

After another political battle, Hamilton also succeeded in his aim of taking over into the national debt the debts that the individual states had accumulated in the course of the War of Independence. There were economic reasons for this, such as associating these debts too with the security provided by the federal government's control of the most reliable source of tax income, the tariffs. But there were also political reasons, connected with the more consciously directed aspects of state-formation, for extinguishing as much state paper as possible and replacing it with federal bonds. The state debts were largely held by prosperous businessmen, merchants and farmers, whose 'loyalties lay mainly with their respective states and the cosy local societies in which they had grown up' (ibid.: 29–30). Although they had in general supported the creation of the new Union, Hamilton suspected their support would fade if self-interest dictated it. If they held a large share of their assets in federal bonds, self-interest would become a factor in their continuing to uphold the Union.

But Hamilton's understanding of finance was well ahead of that of most of his contemporaries, and he – and his legacy – faced great and continuing opposition. John Adams wrote: 'Every dollar of a bank bill that is issued beyond the quantity of gold and silver in the vaults represents nothing, and is therefore a cheat upon somebody' (quoted in ibid.: 28). Jefferson was a formidable opponent of the Bank: he referred to 'the tribe of bank-mongers, who were seeking to filch from the public their swindling, and barren gains' (letter to Adams, 24 January 1814). In 1811, the charter of the Bank of the United States was not renewed when it expired. Certainly, ideas and sentiments – misunderstanding and distrust of the fiduciary principles of banking, fear of the power of bankers, hostility to the role that a central bank could play in the expansion of the powers of government – played a part in this outcome. And the institutional effects of such sentiments, if not the sentiments themselves, persisted over two centuries. 'Anyone who doubts the influence of great men on history', writes Gordon, 'should consider how Jefferson's intense, even irrational hatred of banks has affected the history of the United States.'

> The savings-and-loan crisis of the 1980s, 160 years after Jefferson's death, had its origins, in a very real sense, in Jefferson's passion.[14] For that passion, articulated by one of the most articulate men who ever lived, greatly strengthened a fear of powerful financial institutions in his political heirs. This led to laws that favoured many small (and thus weak) banks over a few large ones. Even today, when thousands of banks have merged and banking across state lines has finally become possible, the United States still has more banks than all the rest of the industrialized world put together. (Gordon, 1998: 35–6n)

But it is generally a mistake to treat ideas as a free-floating causal force in history and social development. In 1811, as so often, practical economic and political interests were also in play. In the two decades since the Bank of the United States had received its charter, more than 100 state banks had been created, and they chafed under the discipline of the federal bank. And the BUS was a competitor too: the state banks were eager to become depositories of government funds, as this would allow them to expand their issue of bank notes and thus their loan business (ibid.: 46).

One immediate consequence of the abolition of the BUS was to jeopardize the defence of the realm during the War of 1812. The costs of the war soon faced the federal government with a fiscal crisis, along with rapid inflation and many bank failures. The storm was weathered, but in 1816 President Madison quietly approved a charter for the second Bank of the United States, which closely resembled the first. Yet even that did not last. When Andrew Jackson became President in 1829, he used the tariff surplus to repay the national debt. He saw it as a way of ridding the country of paper money – still viewed as in some way not 'real', and not quite honest – and of undermining both the Eastern financiers and the emerging capitalist class in general. In 1833 Jackson destroyed the second bank by withdrawing government deposits from it and placing them instead with the state banks.

In a classic instance of unintended consequences, however, this encouraged the state banks – freed from the discipline of the BUS – to print paper money irresponsibly, triggering a bout of speculation and inflation that Jackson eventually had to quell with the Specie Circular of 1836. This stipulated that the government itself would not accept payment in paper currency. Its effect was to precipitate one of the deepest and most prolonged economic depressions in American history. Nevertheless, the USA endured without any central bank until the creation of the Federal Reserve Board under President Woodrow Wilson in 1913. By then, the need for such an institution had become inescapable. The Federal Reserve acts as an instrument of economic management for the federal government, holds the reserve accounts of and makes loans to commercial banks (thus exercising the discipline that the BUS had once initiated), and has the sole right to issue the Federal Reserve bank notes (commercial banks having lost the right to issue their own currency notes). Once again, practical social and economic exigencies overcame a cultural tradition of hostility to central authority and regulation.

The breakdown: the Civil War and its aftermath

Compelling processes of economic and political integration can precipitate conflicts leading to their opposite. In the Civil War, the USA underwent a process – temporary, as it proved – of disintegration.

The compromises that emerged from the debates at Philadelphia in 1787 reflected the Founding Fathers' recognition that the former colonies had not hitherto been at all closely integrated with each other. That is seen in the balances struck in the Constitution between states' rights and the powers of the federal government, as well as in the checks and balances between the branches of government. The interpretation of these compromises remained in dispute, no more so than in the Nullification Crisis of 1832 when South Carolina claimed the right to nullify a federal tariff law; federal military intervention in the state was only narrowly avoided. The Constitution's silence on the question of slavery is, however, the most eloquent evidence of the low level of integration of the states with each other. Many of the signers were already uneasy about the morality of slavery, but silence was at the time both expedient and possible. Why that was so was later stated with characteristically terse insight by Ulysses S. Grant:

> In the early days of the country, before we had railroads, telegraphs and steamboats – in a word, rapid transit of any sort – the States were each almost a separate nationality. At that time the subject of slavery caused little or no disturbance to the public mind. But the country grew, rapid transit was established, and trade and commerce between the States got to be so much greater than before, that the power of the National government became more felt and recognised and, therefore, had to be enlisted in the cause of this institution. (1994 [1885]: 660)

Until the middle of the eighteenth century, there was relatively little coastal trade between the tidewater settlements; they were largely self-sufficient and their main trade was in commercial products across the Atlantic. When in 1736 Virginia gentleman William Byrd II corresponded with a friend in Massachusetts, his letter travelled via London. This lack of what Grant called 'rapid transit' diminished swiftly in the decades before the Civil War. Post offices spread widely throughout the USA in the 1820s, although only in 1861 was a coast-to-coast telegraph link established (Brown, 1989: 44, 12–13).

A subsidiary reason for the signers' ability to sidestep the issue of slavery was that at the time there were still slaves in the North, although far fewer – no more than 10 per cent of the national total, New York and New Jersey having the largest share within that. Vermont abolished slavery in 1777, before its admission to the Union, and the other northern states followed suit in the late eighteenth and early nineteenth century, which served to make slave-ownership a more clear-cut line of division between the sections.

This is not the place to retell the political and legal history of the growing tension between a 'free' North and a slave-owning South, nor of the eventually unsuccessful compromises through which some leaders hoped to reconcile the continued existence within one country of what others increasingly perceived as two incompatible ways of life. That the Civil War *was* about two incompatible ways of life is now clear, although in its early stages some ambiguity remained. At first, Lincoln emphasized the preservation of the Union rather than slavery as the main issue. His caution was dictated initially by the necessity of preventing the secession from the Union of Maryland, Kentucky and Missouri, the slave-owning border states where Confederate sympathies were strong. It was also pursued in the hope that the southern states would eventually accept the *gradual* emancipation of the slaves in return for federally funded compensation; during the first year, the conflict only slowly metamorphosed in people's minds and on the reality of battlefields from being an internal insurrection to being an out and out war (McPherson, 1990). In the later years of the war, emancipation became as central to Union war aims as it had been to the political and legal conflicts that preceded the war.

At the most obvious level of the surface of politics, an immediate effect of the secession of the Confederate states, and with it the withdrawal of southern members from Congress, was a decisive shift in the balance of power in Washington. To say that the South had held a stranglehold on federal politics during the 72 years between the adoption of the Constitution and the outbreak of the Civil War might be a little too colourful. It is a fact, however, that for more than three-quarters of that period the President had been a slaveholding southerner; after the war, no southern resident was elected President until Lyndon Johnson in 1964.[15] In Congress, 23 of the 36 Speakers of the House and 24 of the 36 Presidents Pro Tempore of the Senate had been southerners; for half a century after the war, none was. Before the war, 20 of the 35 Justices of Supreme Court had been southerners, and they had been in a majority throughout the period; only 5 of the 26 justices appointed in the five decades after the war were from the South (McPherson, 1990: 12–13). The disappearance of the southern legislators now permitted Congress to enact a flood of legislation that mobilized Union resources for the war and also facilitated the economic growth of the North. Higher tariffs – previously blocked by southern cotton interests – directly promoted industrial growth. A national banking system was created to repair at least some of the damage caused by the southern-dominated Jacksonian Democrats' destruction of the central bank, and the national debt (once paid off by Jackson) rose dramatically to finance the war. To encourage small farmers and increase agricultural production, the Homestead Act offered free lands to settlers in the public domain. Land grants were also used to promote internal improvements, notably the transcontinental railway (completed in 1869) and the establishment of 'land-grant colleges', many of which, during the following century, evolved into notable universities. As so many adult males went away from productive work to fight in the army, another measure with long-term consequences was the creation of a bureau to encourage immigration under labour contracts (Foner, 1988: 21). After the war, the American economy grew extremely rapidly, but the South's share of national income and wealth was greatly reduced. In 1860, the South accounted for about 30 per cent of the national economy, and per capita income (including slaves in the total population) in the region was two-thirds of that in the North; in 1870 these figures had declined to 12 per cent and two-fifths respectively, and they did not recover during the nineteenth century (McPherson, 1990: 11–12; cf. O'Brien, 1988).

This shift in the economic balance was not immediately mirrored on the battlefield. As is well known, the Confederates for the most part outgeneralled the Union armies, especially in the eastern theatre, during the first half of the war. These early successes had diplomatic consequences, which serve as a reminder that the dynamics of this complex struggle were not quite entirely determined by forces within America. In Britain, the dominant world power of the time, public opinion was divided in its sympathies, but recognition of the Confederate government would appear to have been fairly narrowly averted by the diplomatic skills of Charles Francis Adams and especially by the news of decisive Union victories at Gettysburg and Vicksburg on 4 July 1863.[16] Had recognition been granted, and had the British more actively aided the Confederate cause, the course of the war might have been different.[17] In the end, however, the weight of Union industrial output and manpower proved decisive.

Subsidiary power struggles within the two conflicting sides were also significant. Foner (1988: 11–18) refers to the 'Inner Civil War' in the South, between the large-scale plantation owners of the Tidewater plain and the white 'yeoman' farmers of the hill country inland, where slavery was insignificant. The Confederate government was seen as acting (including taxing) principally in the interest of the planters, and there was fairly considerable Union sympathy among the small farmers, with not insignificant numbers of men from areas like east Tennessee volunteering to fight in the Union armies. In the most extreme case, the mountainous northwest of Virginia seceded from the state in 1861 and was admitted to the Union as the new state of West Virginia in 1863 (in circumstances the legality of which Virginia has never accepted). Within the plantation belt, too, the power of the slaveholders was coming under challenge. As an institution, slavery was beginning to disintegrate before the Emancipation Proclamation, let alone Appomattox. Thousands of slaves who were within reach of Union territory made good their escape, fleeing north of the Mason–Dixon line or into areas of Virginia, Tennessee and Louisiana that were captured early in the war. Even in the heartlands of the Confederacy, the absence of so many fighting men from among the whites was associated with widespread reports of insubordination among black slaves on plantations left in the charge of women and old men (Foner, 1988: 3).

The North too was transformed by the war. The economy boomed; factory production spread, and with it grew an industrial working class; cities like Chicago grew rapidly; integrated railway and telegraph systems tied far-flung localities more closely together. Above all, the war – and the legislation enacted to prosecute it – accelerated the formation of an industrial bourgeoisie, and tied the interests of this class firmly to the Republican Party and the national state (ibid.: 21). But there were divisions in the North too. Emancipation was to remain an article of faith for the Republican leadership for many decades, but this did not always go hand in hand with a belief in racial equality, and among the lower orders racial resentments sometimes boiled over into violence.

Reconstruction

Conventionally, the term Reconstruction is applied to the period 1865–77. The process may, however, be said already to have begun during the Civil War. In 1863, provision was made to re-establish governments in newly occupied states where 10 per cent or more of the population had taken the oath of allegiance to the Union. Even before Lincoln's assassination, Republicans in Congress had criticized his moderate and lenient plans for the reincorporation of the secession states, on the grounds that they did not include provision for the social and economic reform of the South. In 1865–6, several states had already adopted new 'black codes', designed to maintain white supremacy and a continuing supply of cheap labour by imposing severe restrictions on the civil rights of the blacks. Violent riots by whites against blacks occurred, with the acquiescence of local authorities, in New Orleans (among other cities in the South) in July 1866, and the army had to restore order. Under Lincoln's successor Andrew Johnson, who continued the moderate policies with far less political aptitude, the conflict between Congress and the executive became acute – Johnson's impeachment famously failed by one vote – and, after a decisive victory for the Radical Republicans in the 1866 elections, Reconstruction was pressed forward under Congressional leadership. Military governors were appointed. The Freedmen's Bureau was created with the tasks of protecting and educating the emancipated slaves. Courts and judicial procedures were revised, schools established and taxation reformed. By 1870 all the former Confederate states had been readmitted to the Union. But their new Republican governments were coalitions of blacks, 'carpetbaggers' (northerners who had come south for the purpose), and what were called 'scalawags' (southerners who sympathized, or at least collaborated, with the forces of Reconstruction). For a time in the first half of the twentieth century, opinion among historians of the period – not untainted by assumptions of black racial inferiority on their own part (Foner, 1988: xx) – was that the carpetbagger regimes were a cesspit of corruption, the product of northern opportunism and vindictiveness. More recent scholarship suggests that they were no more corrupt than governments throughout the Union, and stresses the leading part played in the reforming governments by the blacks themselves. The most serious failure of Reconstruction was the absence of any attempt at land reform; without that, the poverty of most blacks persisted and became an obstacle to their sustaining their rights of citizenship. What is indisputable, though, is that the majority of the white population in the South regarded these governments as alien impositions, and that Reconstruction served to deepen racial hatred and political bitterness. Terrorist secret societies like the Ku Klux Klan and the less well-known Knights of the White Camelia deployed violence and intimidation and, in spite of the vigorous use of the army against them under President Grant, persisted for decades. Reconstruction came to an end in 1877 when Rutherford B. Hayes, fulfilling promises made as part of the compromise that helped him emerge victorious from the disputed presidential election of 1876, withdrew the army from the South, and honoured a pledge not to interfere in the administration of elections there. The one-party political system that arose proved to be one more bequest from the Civil War and Reconstruction that lasted in the South until the 1960s or 1970s.[18] The 'Jim Crow' laws passed in the closing decades of the nineteenth century reintroduced elements of the black codes that had helped to trigger Radical Reconstruction in 1867, and lynchings of blacks rose rapidly to a peak in the 1890s, remaining high until the 1920s. These outcomes recall Tocqueville's metaphor of the kite: 'the destinies of the world unfold through the consequences, but often the contrary consequences, of the intentions which produce them, like a kite that flies by the opposing forces of the wind and the string' (1971 [1893]: 43). The goal of Reconstruction had been to set in train a process of social and political integration, not just of the Confederate states into the Union, but also of blacks into American society; yet for the former slaves and their descendants over the next 100 years the wind generally proved stronger than the string. In effect, the struggle between North and South, in particular between elites differing considerably in their habitus (see chapter 4), continued for another century. Ironically, after the overtly racist regimes of the South were broken in the 1950s and 1960s, not only was the South more fully socially integrated into the Union, but the political balance of power swung somewhat away from the North in favour of the South.

Post-bellum national integration

Other processes of national integration were unfolding through the conflicts of the decades following the Civil War. The rapid spread of railways, together with the telegraph and other means of 'rapid transit', made possible the articulation of many forms of organization – economic, political, social, educational and cultural – on a national scale for the first time. There were many strands. The wartime growth of the federal bureaucracy, together with the large number of veterans entitled to federal pensions, created a considerable constituency of people with a direct interest in maintaining the authority and taxing powers of the national government (Foner, 1988: 23). After the war, a more effective civil service gradually took shape, despite the spoils system and political conflicts impeding reform (Skowronek, 1982: 177–211). On both sides of industry, too, the scale and scope of national organization increased. The American Federation of Labour (AFL), always seen as a relatively elite grouping of craft unions, was founded in 1886. The Gilded Age is associated with the emergence of massive corporations dominated by the so-called Robber Barons – the Vanderbilts, Fricks, Stanfords, Morgans, Rockefellers – especially in such sectors as railways, steel, coal, oil and banking. This period marks the first great spurt of the plutocratization of American politics, which has continued – with fluctuations – to the present day (Phillips, 2002). Railways especially were identified with massive corruption, with legislators granting them land and public assets (Foner, 1988: 461ff.). The Grant presidency saw the beginnings of the symbiosis of the Republican Party and big business. Yet at the same time, the activities of the 'trusts' or cartels were often so blatantly against the public interest that Jacksonian suspicions of banks and big business were revived, and not only among Democrats. The Sherman Anti-Trust Act was passed in 1890, but trust-busting was rarely pursued with vigour except under Theodore Roosevelt (1901–9), and in the long term did not impede the organization of business on a national scale. At the same time, professional, academic and cultural associations were organized at a national level: the American Medical Association's founding in 1846 antedates the Civil War, but the American Bar Association was formed in 1878. Many scholarly bodies were founded in this period too, such as the American Historical Association in 1884 and the American Economic Association in 1888.

Hall makes the case that, more than independence or the Constitution or, for that matter, the Civil War, it was these private corporations and associations that socialized individuals to a 'national outlook'. His stress on the emergence of nationally minded elites, however, needs qualification. As has already been argued in earlier chapters, compared with some other countries, notably Britain and France, the USA did not develop a single well-integrated model-setting elite concentrated geographically in the capital city. In that respect, the experience of the USA perhaps more closely resembles Germany during the *Kaiserreich* (Elias, 1996). In another respect, however, it markedly did not follow the same track as Germany. In both cases, unification of the national territory was gained, or regained, on the battlefield – in Germany's case, shortly after the American Civil War, through the Prussian–Austrian War of 1866 and the Franco–Prussian War of 1870. But, while in Germany that consolidated the political power and prestige of a military elite and a military ethos, this did not happen in the USA.

A central ambivalence: the armed forces

From the vantage point of today, when military expenditure plays such a significant part in the US economy, it may seem strange that for much of its history a large proportion of its citizens viewed the very existence of a standing army with grave distrust. This was one of the key issues in the debates about the Constitution.

It has to be borne in mind that the standing, professional, army was a relatively newly invented institution at the time of the War of Independence. The military historian John Keegan has observed that the replacement of crowd armies by armies with a professional nucleus was one of the most important, if complex, processes in European history. In the first half of the seventeenth century Prince Maurice of Nassau and King Gustavus Adolphus of Sweden were important pioneers in the training and disciplining of professional troops, but the process cannot be attributed to a few key individuals: it was, rather, a response in many countries and over a long period to the increasing scale and complexity of warfare.

> Whatever its origin – whether it was, like the British army, forged by civil war from a bumpkin militia, or, like the Russian, hammered out of a conscripted serfdom by foreign mercenary officers – the standing army which emerged in most European states during the seventeenth century stood alone and apart, both among the other components of the state's apparatus and in the experience and imagination of the people it policed. Over no other group of subjects did the state exercise so rigorously, so minutely, so continuously its power. (Keegan, 1976: 174–5)

That was why standing armies were viewed with such suspicion, especially in Britain where after the Civil War and the Restoration the incipient development of an absolutist monarchy had been reversed and a parliamentary regime was very gradually emerging (Elias, in Elias and Dunning, 1986: 26–40). A large and highly disciplined standing army acting in strict obedience to an absolutist monarch (or, indeed, to the landowner-dominated early parliamentary regime) was always potentially an instrument for the subversion of liberty and the dominance of the central government. Thus in Britain throughout the eighteenth century and most of the nineteenth century, it was mainly the volunteer and part-time county militias who, when necessary, were called out in support of the civil power. The professional army *per se* was relatively small and to a great extent deployed abroad in the emerging empire (which was how, especially from around 1760 onwards, the Americans came to share with some fervour the general British dislike of standing armies, since many of them came to see the British forces as a foreign army of occupation). One reason, however, why the British state was able to make do most of the time with only a small professional army was that Great Britain is an island, and it was internally already relatively highly pacified by the late eighteenth century. The main threats to British national security came most literally from overseas, and the Royal Navy was its principal bulwark – as Alexander Hamilton noted in *The Federalist* number 8 (Madison et al., 1987 [1788]: 117). Navies are much less easily used as instruments of internal repression than are armies (Elias, 1950; Mills, 1956: 175). But, as Hamilton spelled out in *The Federalist* number 24, the geographical situation of the infant United States was very different: its potential overseas enemies – Britain and Spain at that stage – would pose a threat mainly through alliances with the Indians of the interior. Even without foreign intervention, the volunteer militias would be inadequate for coping with the Indians:

> Previous to the Revolution, and ever since the peace, there has been a constant necessity for keeping small garrisons on our Western frontier. No person can doubt that these will continue to be indispensable, if it should only be against the ravages and depredations of the Indians. These garrisons must either be furnished by occasional detachments from the militia, or by permanent corps in the pay of the government. The first is impracticable; and if practicable, would be pernicious. The militia would not long, if at all, submit to be dragged from their occupations and families to perform that most disagreeable duty in times of profound peace. And if they could be prevailed upon or compelled to do it, the increased expense of a frequent rotation of service, and the loss of labour and disconcertation of the industrious pursuits of individuals, would form conclusive objections to the scheme. It would be as burdensome and injurious to the public as ruinous to private citizens. (Hamilton, in Madison et al., 1987: 191)

So a 'permanent corps in the pay of the government' would indeed amount to a standing army in time of peace, but, asked Hamilton, could anyone seriously believe that it would be prudent for there to be a constitutional ban on standing armies? It would leave the frontiers of the new Republic 'naked and defenceless'.

Although standing armies were not forbidden under the Constitution, a prejudice in favour of relying mainly on part-time militias persisted. The Continental Army had been disbanded in June 1784 after the Treaty of Paris, and a small force of only 700 men was recruited to push federal authority beyond the Appalachians (Skelton, 1992: 4). Under the Articles of Confederation, all officers below the rank of general were to be nominated by the states; only generals were to be appointed by the federal government, but there *were* no generals. The force trebled in size to deal with Shay's Rebellion in 1786, but when Washington became President fewer than 1,000 soldiers were again on active service under federal authority. When the Constitution came into force, officers had to swear to uphold it and took oaths of allegiance to the President, but otherwise controversy continued throughout the 1790s – intertwining with wider debates about the scope of federal authority vis-à-vis the states – over the character, size, organization, functions and even necessity of a permanent army. Recruitment grew in the face of Indian troubles, but not dramatically; during the near-disaster of the War of 1812, the number of Federal troops eventually exceeded 40,000, but reverted to the authorized strength of about 12,000 after the peace in 1815 (see figure 9.5). With the exception of an upward blip at the time of the Mexican War, what Andreski (1968) called the *military participation ratio* (MPR) – military numbers as a proportion of the population – did not increase dramatically until the Civil War, and indeed tended to fall.[19]

Nevertheless, something that had an important bearing on the distrust many Americans felt towards standing armies happened during the early decades of the Republic: there gradually emerged an officer class largely detached from politics, after the period of the Revolution and its immediate aftermath when men such as Washington and Hamilton had been both political and military leaders. The reorganization of 1802 which abolished Hamilton's post of Inspector-General of the Army also established the United States Military Academy at West Point. Skelton points to parallels between the development of the officer class and that of the legal and medical professions in the same period:

> [L]awyers used law magazines to develop a group image that distinguished law from politics and stressed the objectivity and social utility of the calling. The tension between regulars and citizen-soldiers had its analogue in the struggle of the orthodox medical profession against such irregular practices as . . . homeopathy. Among physicians as well as officers, the emphasis was on professional education, internal standards, and a scientific approach to their field of responsibility as a means to distinguish themselves from their rivals and justify their existence before a sceptical public. (1992: 359–60)[20]

The detachment of officers from politics was shaken by the Civil War, and by Reconstruction, when generals discharged essentially political functions in the post-bellum South, but was re-established relatively quickly afterwards. Once more, the ideology of professionalism among the officers of the regular army – encapsulated in William Tecumseh Sherman's celebrated rejection of the temptation of political office – played its part. But that ideology was not a free-floating 'cultural influence'; its strength has to be understood from its being a principal means by which some at least of the regulars sought to distinguish themselves as professionals from the amateurs of the militias. From Reconstruction to the end of the nineteenth century there were political battles between protagonists of the state militias – their case bound up with the wider issue of states' rights – and those who advocated an efficient professional federal force (Skowronek, 1982: 85–120). The militias, or 'National Guard' in each state, were reformed and expanded as state police forces for riot control to confront the wave of industrial unrest in the period, yet in all but a few states they remained firmly part of the political patronage system. The champions of the regular army wished to create a General Staff on the European – notably Prussian – model, with the professionals forming the nucleus of an organization structure of expansible units into which recruits (and the militias) could be efficiently incorporated in times of need.

Political constraints, however, led to the decline in numbers of soldiers on active service to fewer than 30,000, a tiny force deployed mainly on the western frontier. It was not until after the war with Spain that Elihu Root, Secretary of War under Theodore Roosevelt, succeeded in creating a General Staff, bringing each state's National Guard under federal super-vision, and significantly increasing the established strength of the regular army. Even so, in the years up to the First World War, not only did the issue of the regulars versus the militias continue to simmer, but within the army the Chief of Staff and the Adjutant-General – each with allies in Congress – were embroiled in a contest for control of the army, and Congress passed legislation to limit the powers of the new General Staff (ibid.: 212–47). This episode in effect represented a second front in resis-tance to the emergence of a clear monopoly of control over the principal means of violence. The principle of checks and balances extended even to military management.

Just how relatively small were the federal armed forces can be seen in figure 9.5, which shows the number of military personnel (including the navy and marine corps, and latterly the air force, as well as the army) between 1789 and 2001. During that period, the USA became a far bigger country both territorially and in inhabitants. Its population grew from about 4 million to nearly 300 million – a 75-fold increase – and figure 9.5 therefore shows military personnel as a percentage of total population. This measurement, of fighting men per head of the general population, is particularly appropriate to the issue of the potential utility of armed forces as a means of internal repression. The peaks in the graph obviously coincide with wars – the War of 1812, the Mexican War, the Civil War, the Spanish War, the First and Second World Wars, the Korean War and Vietnam. All since the Civil War have been fought overseas: none of the subsequent steeples represents an army enlarged to quell rebellion or to suppress internal disorder.

In peacetime, throughout the nineteenth century military personnel on active service amounted to around 0.1 per cent, one in a thousand, of the

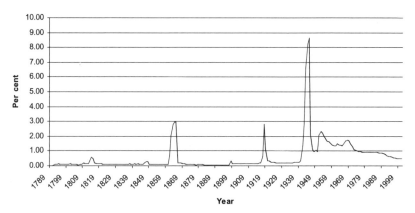

Figure 9.5: US military personnel on active service as percentage of population, 1789–2001
Sources: US Census Bureau (2002); US Department of Defense (2002).

population. By comparison, the British normally had much the larger army as well as navy – numerically and proportionately – until after the Second World War. (Of course, in the nineteenth century, the UK was not only a greater world power than the USA, but until 1856 it had the larger population. France, as a land power, had an army bigger than either the USA or the UK.[21])

Deployment of the armed forces in support of the civil power

In the pacified and populous parts of the USA, the army was thus for many decades scarcely a visible presence. In the *process* of internal pacification, of course, the army was often quite visible, especially from the Cherokee 'Trail of Tears' in 1838 to the subsequent pacification of the plains Indians tribes in the later decades of the nineteenth century. It was also continually deployed in support of the civil power in the former Confederate states during Reconstruction, especially in face of what was, in effect, a rival military force: the Ku Klux Klan.

Reconstruction came to an end in following the disputed presidential election of 1876, and the army was withdrawn from the South. It was not to stay long in its barracks, however. The following year, the 'Great Strike' – a nationwide railroad strike – marked the beginning of two decades of labour violence 'unparalleled in any other industrial nation' (Skowronek, 1982: 87). A collapse of civic order seemed to threaten, first in the cities of the East and then moving westwards, as the state militias proved unreliable (ibid.: 99–100). Although the number of regular troops available in the eastern states was small, they gained widespread admiration for the efficiency and disinterestedness with which they helped to restore order. Yet the old distrust of anything approaching a federal monopoly over the organized means of violence came to the fore again in 1878, when Democrats in Congress succeeded in severely restricting the routine use of troops as a posse by federal marshals confronting civil unrest. At a day-to-day level, the exercise of federal authority within states was hobbled, although the President's own prerogative to deploy troops remained (ibid.: 102–3). In 1894 Grover Cleveland used it to send regulars into Chicago – against the wishes of the Governor of Illinois – to break the Pullman strike, and seven men were killed (Jeffers, 2000: 293–309). The use of regular troops in these circumstances might be taken to bear out the historic fear of a standing army as a threat to civil liberties, even if such incidents have been few and far between. But the argument is invalidated when it is remembered that the National Guard – the supposedly benevolent citizen militias – posed at least as great a threat. As late as 1957 it was the National Guard that was deployed by Governor Orville Faubus in Little Rock, Arkansas, to prevent nine black pupils being admitted to the Central High School in pursuance of the Supreme Court's 1954 ruling in *Brown v. Topeka*; and again in 1970 it was Ohio National Guardsmen who shot and killed four people in a protest against the Vietnam War at Kent State University. In the Arkansas case, President Eisenhower immediately 'nationalized' the militia – brought them under federal command – and thus demonstrated that in the last resort it is the federal government, not the states, which controls the monopoly of the legitimate use of the means of organized violence. The use of this power is, however, rare – it is encountered more commonly in face of a major natural disaster than in a breakdown of order.

The military–industrial state

During the Cold War decades numbers in the armed forces remained roughly five to ten times higher in relation to total population than before the Second World War, a substantial break with American tradition.[22] C. Wright Mills was one of the first social scientists to draw attention to the changed power position of the military in American society after the Second World War. 'Since Pearl Harbour', he wrote, 'those who command the enlarged American violence have come to possess considerable autonomy, as well as great influence, among their political and economic colleagues' (1956: 198). Furthermore, he argued, 'the military has become enlarged and decisive to the shape of the entire economic structure; and, moreover, the economic and the military have become structurally and deeply interrelated, as the economy has become a seemingly permanent war economy; and military men and policies have increasingly penetrated the corporate economy' (ibid.: 215). Mills's thesis was eloquently developed by ex-soldier President Dwight D. Eisenhower in his last address to the nation before he left office in 1961, when he spoke of the 'military–industrial complex':[23]

> Until the latest of our world conflicts, the United States had no armaments industry. American makers of ploughshares could, with time and as required, make swords as well. But now we can no longer risk emergency improvisation of national defence; we have been compelled to create a permanent armaments industry of vast proportions. Added to this, three and a half million men and women are directly engaged in the defence establishment. We annually spend on military security more than the net income of all United States corporations.
>
> This conjunction of an immense military establishment and a large arms industry is new in the American experience. The total influence – economic, political, even spiritual – is felt in every city, every Statehouse, every office of the Federal government. We recognize the imperative need for this development. Yet we must not fail to comprehend its grave implications. Our toil, resources and livelihood are all involved; so is the very structure of our society.
>
> In the councils of government, we must guard against the acquisition of unwarranted influence, whether sought or unsought, by the military–industrial complex. The potential for the disastrous rise of misplaced power exists and will persist.
>
> We must never let the weight of this combination endanger our liberties or democratic processes. We should take nothing for granted. Only an alert and knowledgeable citizenry can compel the proper meshing of the huge industrial and military machinery of defence with our peaceful methods and goals, so that security and liberty may prosper together. (Eisenhower, 1961: 1035–40)

Other sociologists of the time (Janowitz, 1960; Rose, 1967: 134–51) sought to rebut Mills's thesis about the confluence of military, economic and political power, but any conclusion was premature. A longer perspective is needed on such a long-term process, and Eisenhower's warning may seem more prescient at the beginning of the twenty-first century than in the middle of the twentieth. One thing is clear: the nature of the danger posed by a powerful military establishment has changed since the founding of the Republic. The fears that Mills and Eisenhower expressed may have been lineal descendants of the fear of standing armies that the authors of *The Federalist* sought to assuage. But they are not the same as the simple fear that a standing army under government control would lead to soldiers on the streets as direct instruments of political repression. *Within* the United States, the means of violence have not gone away, but they are normally confined to barracks, as they are in any other modern internally pacified state. But the fear that the intermeshing of military, political and economic interests might subvert democratic politics and (through the ever more widely pervading mass media) manipulate public opinion stems from something new and complicated.

One might indeed conjecture, in the light of Elias's theories, whether the post-war militarization of American society has also witnessed the emergence of a new 'good society' of military officers. That is not to suggest that people in the lower echelons will look to the military caste for models of how to handle their knives and forks. Something more important may be taking place, something akin to the militarization of popular habitus that Elias (1996) traced in Wilhelmine Germany: a revival of the code of 'honour' and its penetration into elements of the lower strata. In Germany, he argued, that went along with a national sensitivity to all forms of humiliation, coupled with an assertive triumphalism and, nevertheless, great status insecurity. (Not everything that goes on at the level of habitus is conscious; internal conflicts abound.) The instrumental manipulation of national we-feelings thus became a highly effective instrument in the toolkit of the ruling apparatus. The fears expressed from Eisenhower onwards testify both to the danger and to the continuing American tradition of distrust of big government, big armies, and over-powerful authority.

Conclusion

Underlying the various aspects of American social development discussed in this chapter has been a single theme: the largely unplanned social processes that produce longer chains of interdependence. As more and more people are thrust together, they typically resent their enchainment. The result is conflict: integration struggles are contests in which some or even most parties seek to resist their integration into larger and more encompassing forms of social organization. In America, these integration struggles can be seen in rural resentment of the towns, in race relations and the reception of immigrants, in resistance to government bureaucracy, in battles over the development of banking and finance, and most spectacularly in the Civil War. Despite resistance in the short term, however, the exigencies of new forms of interdependence in the long run generally result in the formation of larger structures and institutions. At this level of generality, all this is consistent with the conclusions reached by Norbert Elias on the basis of his studies of European social development (and indeed with the insights of earlier writers, notably Karl Marx and Herbert Spencer). More problematic, however, is the connection that

Elias made between lengthening chains of interdependence on the one hand and mutual identification on the other. The light that American social development throws upon that problem is the central concern of the next chapter.

10

The Curse of the American Dream

What is commonly called the 'American Dream' is the belief that, through individual hard work and determination, American citizens from even the humblest origins can achieve prosperity and social esteem for themselves, their families and descendants. The belief rests on the perception that the social structure of the United States is open and egalitarian, posing fewer obstacles to the talented and ambitious rising socially and economically than they would have encountered in many other countries, especially in the Old World. Such a social structure gave people every incentive to exercise strict self-discipline: it exerted a social constraint towards self-constraint. The 'American Dream' thus had a strong affinity with the Protestant ethic and with the spirit of capitalism discussed in Max Weber's famous essay; Weber, after all, drew heavily on Benjamin Franklin's advice to his readers to be thrifty, to work hard, to waste no time and constantly to pursue self-improvement.

The American Dream undoubtedly inspired generations of Americans, and helped to attract waves of new immigrants. It has left its mark on American politics. In 1906 Werner Sombart famously asked *Why Is There No Socialism in the United States?*, and an important part of his answer (1976 [1906]: 116–17) was that the plentiful opportunities for working people to achieve success through their own individual efforts made it less likely that they would band together to pursue collective advantage through socialist trade unions and political parties of the kind that were then arising in Europe.[1] It seems fairly clear that most Americans think in terms of what David Lockwood (1966) called the 'ladder image' as opposed to the 'conflict image' of society. In twentieth-century Europe at least, surveys found that, on the whole, middle-class people tended to see society as providing a ladder of opportunity up which, by individual effort, they had the chance to climb in the course of their careers. Manual workers, such as those working on an assembly-line, tended on the other hand to have little confidence that they could raise their standard of living through individual effort, and sought rather to improve their lot collectively through unions and parties that represented them in conflict with employers. In contrast, a striking finding reported by Ely Chinoy (1955) in a study of American automobile workers in the 1950s was that a very high proportion of them either aspired to start their own business and become their own boss, or had actually attempted to do so. Even if they had failed before, many retained the ambition to try again. In Europe, the two images of society corresponded to a real difference in the life-chances of working- and middle-class people, but in America working-class people too tended to adhere to what in Europe was a middle-class vision.

The American Dream is a key national myth that has certainly contributed something to Americans' strong we-feelings – their fierce national pride and identification with their country. To call something a myth is not to say that it is necessarily or wholly false; for their power, myths typically require a proportion of truth content, some measure of congruence with reality. The Dream might appear to be consistent with Norbert Elias's thesis that in the course of social development longer chains of interdependence are generally associated with functional democratization, which in turn promotes a widening circle of mutual identification among people. But it has never been widely argued that the USA is a land of *equality* (except before the law); on the contrary, the vertical ladders have become ever more extended. The Dream rests at most on *equality of opportunity*, or at least on the knowledge that in the past some Americans have been able to rise from log cabin to White House, or from poverty to vast wealth. Is there a sufficient measure of reality-congruence to sustain the Dream?

Equality and inequality in America

It has sometimes been argued that, although the USA is an *unequal* society, it is not *stratified* into classes. That is to say, in contrast to the way most Western European countries were seen in the past, society in the United States did not resemble a layer cake, with clear lines marking one layer off from the next. Even if the ladders from the bottom to the top of American society were very long, they were at least continuous. The social psychologist Roger Brown argued that 'life in the United States is organized by socio-economic status, organized as a *continuum* of positions rather than as a *set* of classes' (1965: 106, my emphasis; see also Kingston, 2000). There was certainly a prestige ranking of occupations, and fathers' occupations were the principal determinant of differences in styles of life between families. But occupational rankings formed a continuum, and there were no discontinuities in style of life sufficient to indicate a structure of clear-cut boundaries between well-defined classes (Brown, 1965: 133). In other words, even if there was consciousness of superiority and inferiority between widely distant parts of the continuum, there were no breaks, no insuperable barriers of social distance at specific points in the hierarchy, across which Americans could simply not acknowledge each other and interact in a reasonably egalitarian way. Brown's view of mid-twentieth-century America is consistent with Tocqueville's or Martineau's observations on the relative ease of social encounters in the USA, and with the horror felt by nineteenth-century British travellers at the equality of respect accorded to menial servants (see chapter 3 above). Of course, as Brown observed (like Tocqueville and Martineau), this was not the whole picture: race survived as a caste-like element alongside this rather benign view of inequality in the USA.

Nor can social prestige be divorced from wealth and income. Long-term trends in economic inequality before the twentieth century can be inferred only somewhat impressionistically. Broadly speaking, the early Republic was composed largely of farmers, tradespeople and professionals, among whom differences of income and wealth were by later standards relatively modest, although besides the great slave-owners there were some extremely wealthy people before the Civil War (Pessen, 1980). Certainly, many large fortunes were made in the course of industrialization, particularly from the Civil War onwards. Household income surveys, in the USA as in other countries, date only from after the Second World War, but research by Thomas Piketty and his colleagues (Piketty and Saez, 2003; Atkinson and Piketty, 2007) on tax records has permitted more accurate estimates for the past century. In most countries, no more than 10 per cent of the population paid progressive income tax before the war, so the data are most representative of the top decile of incomes. Piketty and Saez found that changes in the proportion of US national income accruing to the wealthiest are in fact most apparent not in the top 10 per cent but in the top 1 per cent of taxpayers. Their share follows a U-shaped trajectory. It fell steeply about the time of the First World War, recovered some ground in the 1920s, but then fell sharply again with the Great Crash of 1929 and the subsequent Depression. From this period until the mid-1970s, inequalities of income in the USA were not greatly different from those observed in other countries, and indeed the concentration of wealth in the top percentile was less unequal in the USA than in the UK (Wolff, 2002: 32–3). But from then onwards, incomes in the top percentile rose very steeply, reaching a share not far short of that in 1913. The same happened to slightly lesser degree in the UK and Canada, but *not* in France (Piketty, 2003) or Japan.

How is this to be explained? First, in the USA, as in other countries, the richest part of the population used to derive the bulk of their income from the yields on investments and from business profits, with earned income contributing very little. Their investment income suffered a severe setback from the effects of wars and depression, and the introduction of progressive income taxes in most countries prevented the share accruing to owners of capital from recovering during the decades of prosperity after the Second World War. What accounts for the top percentile's share of US income in 2000 almost regaining its 1913 level (nearly 17 per cent compared to 18 per cent) is a dramatic increase in very high *earned* incomes – salaries and remuneration packages paid to those who manage great corporations. In other words, the top percentile is more than ever composed of the *working rich*. According to Perucci and Wysong (2002), the ratio between the remuneration of chief executives of American corporations and that of their average employee rose from 45:1 in 1973 to 326:1 in 1997. Compared with Europe or Japan, 45:1 was already extremely high, but the later figure helps to justify Frank and Cook (1996) speaking of a 'winner-takes-all' society.

At this level, the distinction between wealth and income blurs, because vast earned incomes are ploughed into investments. By the turn of the new millennium, the top 5 per cent of Americans owned more than half the wealth of the entire country, with the top 20 per cent owning over 80 per cent.

What then of the other end of the spectrum? The number of very poor people is growing as a consequence of such processes as the decline of traditional manufactures and well-paid and secure manual employment, itself linked to globalization, with such jobs coming to be performed much more cheaply in developing countries. Thus in America, more people are having to make their living in poorly paid part-time and short-term jobs, particularly in the service sector. Poverty of the sort once associated in the public mind with poor black communities is coming to affect increasing numbers of white people too. The problem, of course, is how to define 'poverty', when Americans in the bottom percentiles of income in their own society are still vastly better off than the average person in many countries of the world. Even so, real incomes in the lower deciles of American society have been stagnating or even declining in the early twenty-first century. In 2005, the bottom 20 per cent of Americans had incomes of between nil and $13,478 per annum, and the next two deciles (from 20 to 40 per cent) had incomes in the range of $13,478–$25,847 (Johnston, 2005), which does not compare particularly favourably with other industrial democracies. Some increase in social inequality is nevertheless evident internationally.[2]

The underclass in American society is growing, and yet, as Michael Harrington noted as long ago as 1962, these 'other Americans' often seem

at most semi-visible. They come, like much else that evokes embarrassment, to be hidden behind the scenes of social life. This is in part a matter
of geographical separation in cities; recall Tom Wolfe's *Bonfire of the
Vanities* (1988), where the tragicomic plot hinges on a member of the corporate rich taking the wrong turning off the freeway and panicking to find
himself in a black ghetto. In part, it is also a matter of invisibility in the
dream-conserving mass media.

These trends raise once again a question encountered earlier in the
book: to what extent are they the outcome of the plans and preferences
of governments or other powerful groups, and to what extent are they an
unintended, unplanned, blind but compelling process? Although the
decline in the value of investments appears to have been an *unintended*
consequence of war and depression, from Roosevelt's New Deal to
Johnson's Great Society progressive taxation equally appears to have been
intended to curb what had become politically unacceptable gross inequalities. Why, then, did the trend go into reverse? Economic theory can be
deployed to represent growing inequalities as 'inevitable' and 'rational'.
Top corporate management, it has been contended, has become a general
skill rather than one limited to particular industries and enterprises, and
reaches its own level when sold in a world market. Yet the astronomic
remuneration found at the highest levels in the USA has not been copied
in most other countries, not even in the UK to anything like the same
extent. (There is, apparently, no connection between high executive pay
and company performance, except that the wider the pay differentials, the
lower the commitment of the less well paid [Pfeffer and Sutton, 2006].)

At the other end of the scale, in a global economy, businesses – it is
argued – will inevitably engage the cheapest labour anywhere in the
world, and 'old-fashioned' attempts by trade unions in the USA and other
rich countries to protect their members' wage levels, pension rights,
working hours and other conditions of employment merely serve to
increase 'inflexibility' and decrease 'competitiveness'. And tax cuts for the
rich, it is argued, lead to more rapid growth and wealth formation, constituting 'an incoming tide that will lift all boats'. These attitudes are not
equally acceptable in all countries. There appears to be an historically
grounded difference between the market- and parliament-orientated
Anglo-Saxon state-societies and the countries of continental Europe,
which relied from the seventeenth century on a more authoritarian, but
also more caring, state.[3] (Japan also fits more into the latter category.)

Looking at these processes through the lens of Elias's theory,
Wilterdink (2000) contended that the decrease in socio-economic inequality in Western societies during the larger part of the twentieth century was
connected with the strengthening of networks of interdependence at the
national level. He hypothesized that the increase in inequality evident

since about 1980 was connected to the strengthening of *international* interdependencies and a corresponding weakening of the ties of interdependence *within* nation-states. Alderson and Nielsen (2002) present data confirming the link between the growth of inequality in particular countries and the rate of growth of inward and outward flows of foreign direct investment that they have experienced. But that appears to be only part of the explanation; political and institutional differences are also important in explaining variations between countries. Or, to put it another way, the key internal power ratios within each country have to be taken into account; the narrowing of economic inequality went along with more even balances of power between upper and lower strata in many countries. Those balances appear to be tipping back in favour of the more privileged, and global interdependences are increasingly interwoven with countries' internal power ratios. Research by both economists and sociologists continues; it is clear, though, that the degree of socio-economic inequality has implications for social cohesion within nation-states, and particularly for the viability of the American Dream.

The American welfare state

One distinctive feature of inequality in America is the relatively low level of transfer payments – social security, unemployment pay, health insurance and so on – made under government auspices to the socio-economically disadvantaged. One measure of this can be seen in figure 10.1, which shows that in 1998 the proportion of GDP spent on these purposes in America was about half of that in Sweden (which, however, is notably high).

These figures do not by any means tell the whole story. It is tempting for foreigners to interpret them as showing the comparative underdevelopment of the 'welfare state' in America,[4] and then to explain them by referring to the 'attitudes' of American public opinion. America is seen as lagging behind other Western democracies in the development of collective provision, and that is often laid at the door of 'ideology'; a dominant 'rugged individualism' has given rise to a lower degree of 'mutual identification', including less sympathy felt by the better off towards the less well off. That view is greatly undermined by the fact that, as the economist Jacob Hacker (2002) has shown, if the US figures are adjusted by adding in spending by corporations on health care and pensions for their employees (spending that the government regulates and also facilitates through tax concessions), then America's 'welfare state' expenditure is about as large in relation to GDP as other countries'. Nor can the USA be accused of historically having dragged its feet in the development of other

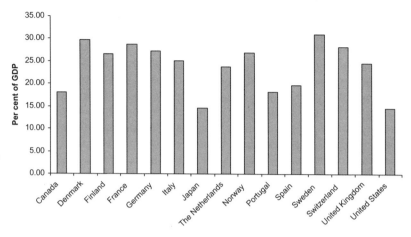

Figure 10.1: Public social expenditure as proportion of national GDP, 1998
Source: OECD: <http://www.oecd.org/dataoecd/43/14/2087083.xls>, accessed 11 May 2004.

forms of collective provision such as compulsory schooling and public health investments.

As in some of the other subjects discussed in this book, such as manners and violence, it appears that the USA has followed the same general long-term direction of development as Western Europe, but that political and institutional circumstances (and, yes, perhaps, to a degree that is difficult to determine, 'ideology' too) have given collective provision in the USA some distinctive features, a flavour of its own.

Abram de Swaan's classic *In Care of the State* (1988) provides a framework for seeing this in perspective. A study of the long-term development of collective provision in five countries (USA, UK, France, Germany and the Netherlands), it combines in an original way ideas from Elias's theory of civilizing processes and from rational choice theory.[5] De Swaan's basic premise is that, for the wealthy, the poor have always been both a threat and a resource. Where pacification was incomplete, as at times and places in feudal Europe or more recently in the course of the westward expansion in America, it could be seen rather clearly that the poor represented both a danger and an opportunity to more powerful groups. They (especially, but not solely, beggars and bandits) posed a threat of physical attack upon persons and property. Simultaneously, they constituted a resource for use as workers and as soldiers in power struggles among competing elites. Later too, the poor were seen both as a threat to public order and public health, and as a reserve of potential workers, recruits, consumers and political supporters.

The interdependence between the rich and the poor, the strong and the weak, has always been rich in 'externalities' (see pp. 115–17 above). The external costs and benefits of poverty affected the elites collectively. Separately, no single powerful person or faction could ward off the threat from the poor, nor exploit the potential benefits they represented as a resource. That could only be achieved collectively, and here the familiar problem of the 'free rider' arises: 'any joint effort on the part of the rich to control the "externalities" or to exploit the opportunities the poor offered, might also benefit those among the established ranks who had not contributed to it' (De Swaan, 1988: 3). To the established groups in society, the problem of poverty thus represents a problem of collective action, and a major thesis of De Swaan's is: 'The dynamics of the collectivizing process in poor relief, health care and education stem largely from the conflicts among the elites over the creation of collective goods and the distribution of costs among them' (ibid.: 3). In earlier centuries, vagrancy and rural banditry created a paradox of collective action for villages and towns in the absence of regional or national authorities. No single community could afford to adopt the needy: any that did so would be overwhelmed by people flocking from afar. Rejected everywhere, therefore, vagrants became a common threat to harvests and food supplies.

The succession of measures adopted to deal with this problem can be seen as a process of the collectivization of risk, spreading it to successively wider collectivities. At the time that the English settlement of North America began, the Elizabethan Poor Law of 1601 had made it incumbent upon each parish to levy a tax on local property-owners to support its own poor – that is, those born in the parish. Similar measures are found in other European countries. In a more mobile society, however, that proved an increasingly impractical policy. A distinction began to emerge between the 'deserving poor' – the sick or aged whose poverty was no fault of their own – and the able-bodied poor. The solution to the problem of the latter that suggested itself in one form or another in each of the countries De Swaan studied, including colonial America, was the workhouse. In principle, each parish was to place its own poor in such an institution, putting them to work to produce the means of their own support. Workhouses never were in practice self-supporting, but they paved the way for centrally regulated poor relief. Once the predicament of the poor appeared amenable to remedy, and the vagrant poor to moral regeneration, the established citizenry could afford a sense of identification with the paupers, and a symptomatic genre of moralistic literature sprang up during this phase.

A further characteristic phase of development in most of De Swaan's countries during the early stages of industrialism was that of workers' mutualism – that is, friendly societies and formal networks of mutual aid formed among working people themselves. (In America, mutual aid through church- and synagogue-based networks was comparably important.) However, the very solidarity that sustained them could only survive in small homogeneous enclaves – among workers in a single small community or a single factory – and by their nature these were vulnerable to cumulative risks when an epidemic or unemployment struck many members at once. New, more encompassing modes of mutual identification grew: nationalism in the process of competitive state formation, class consciousness out of the clashes between workers and employees. Both contributed to the establishment of nationwide social security arrangements.

The pioneering enactment of accident, sickness and disability insurance by Bismarck's government in the newly unified Germany

> reveals many essential traits of the social laws which other countries were to adopt in the next half-century. His was an effort at state-building, quite self-consciously designed to strengthen the new German state apparatus and to improve its ties with the industrial working class whose Marxist leaders at the time proclaimed it to be 'without a fatherland'. (Ibid.: 187)

The measures were thus pushed through against the opposition of the workers' movement, indeed with the (unfulfilled) objective of undermining it, and with the support of employers' interests. A quarter of a century later in Britain, the introduction of pensions and national insurance was also the product of an activist government eager to secure working-class votes, although this time the political complexion was Liberal and the new provisions had the support of the trade union movement.

Arguably, and contrary to widespread perception, the beginnings of an American welfare state antedate both the German and British measures. For remarkably generous pensions had been created for veterans of the Union armies after the Civil War (Skocpol, 1992; De Swaan, 1988: 204). Gradually, they were extended beyond those who suffered injuries and disablement in the war, so that almost anyone who had fought for the Republic could claim, and there were benefits for orphans and widows too. The growth of the scheme owed a great deal to clientelist intervention by politicians on behalf of their constituents. It is estimated that by 1890 about two-thirds of northern white Americans over the age of 65 were receiving pensions. Blacks, and those who had fought for the rebels, were excluded. So were post-Civil War immigrants, although the political machines to some extent provided support for them, with the gaining of loyal votes as the motivation (Merton, 1968: 126–36). But the veterans' schemes were curtailed as a result of the Progressive movement's campaign against political corruption early in the twentieth century, and what social security there remained was for the most part archaic local charitable provision.

There was little further social security legislation until the 1930s, apart from provision for industrial injuries compensation and pensions for 'worthy widows' (shades of the notion of 'the deserving poor' in Victorian England). The power of employers to obstruct any new taxes that would add to their costs was, if anything, reinforced by the main skilled trade union federation, the AFL, which viewed state intervention with a suspicion almost equal to the employers'. The main structural problem, however, was then – and to some extent remains – that many areas of social provision are not a federal but a state responsibility. The consequence is that the individual states are in a position in relation to each other not unlike parishes under the Elizabethan Poor Law: any unit that makes more generous provision than its neighbours will attract potential beneficiaries to it, and if it levies higher taxes to pay for them, it will give potential employers and taxpayers an incentive to locate themselves elsewhere.

The widespread belief in the duty to provide for oneself and one's family, and the expectation that if one did so one's children had a very high chance of becoming members of the property-owning rather than the working class, also no doubt inhibited in America the sorts of social welfare that were developing in European countries. Such faith was shaken by unemployment reaching 25 per cent and the widespread poverty of the Great Depression; it was then, under the New Deal, that there was a dramatic change of direction. Political realignments made possible a nationwide, compulsory system of old-age pensions and unemployment insurance. Some cautious extensions followed: surviving spouses and dependants were brought within the old-age pension scheme in 1939, disability benefits followed in 1956, and health insurance for the elderly (Medicare) and for welfare recipients (Medicaid) came in 1965 under Lyndon Johnson. Social security grew rapidly as a share of GNP in the 1960s and 1970s. Since then, attempts have been made to curtail it, but even under the Reagan administration and its successors (as under their counterparts in other countries, such as the Thatcher and Blair governments in Britain), the effect has been if anything to curtail the rate of growth rather than the actual size of expenditure on collective welfare provision.

It is easy to attribute recent trends in America to the election of 'right-wing' governments and the resurgence of 'individualism' in public opinion. But that cannot be the whole story, for the 'rightwards' drift in policies towards the 'welfare state' appears to be internationally widespread. That suggests that a more general structural process may be at work. One element would appear to be bound up with the globalization of the world economy and with the increasing salience in the long-established industrial economies on 'high-tech', knowledge-based employment. The poor within these countries – the uneducated, lacking technical skills and perhaps also civilized (in the technical sense) social skills – are losing their value as a resource, but they continue to represent a potential threat to the more prosperous. That in turn has fostered a realignment in the perception of class interests on the part of strata that would once have favoured collective provision, feeding into the 'rightwards' drift in politics. The same point has been made before, in chapter 6 above, in accounting for the 'decline of penal welfarism' and the surge in America's prison population.

There is some evidence that public opinion in the USA is less sympathetic than that in Western European countries towards the government assuming a collective responsibility for such matters as seeking to maintain full employment, guaranteeing a decent standard of living for the unemployed, or providing a basic income for everyone (Lipset and Marks, 2000: 289), although a good deal rests on how the questions are phrased. Noble (1997: 3) asserts that public opinion surveys regularly show strong support for a range of social welfare programmes. He argues that the American pattern owes more to the structure of American political economy, notably the power ratio between business and labour, decentralized government, and racial cleavages. His argument seems to apply particularly well to the problem of health care in the USA.

Health care in America

The 'problem' has nothing to do with the *quality* of medicine: America has probably the finest doctors, hospitals and medical technology in the world. The problem is what it costs. In 2005, health care costs totalled $1.9 trillion (that is, 1.9×10^{12}), thus consuming about one-sixth of the entire US economy – almost double the average for the OECD countries (*Economist*, 2006a). In 2005, the average American spent about $6,280 per annum on health care, but the 'average' American is hardly relevant in this instance. For the system depends on private medical insurance, sold by insurance companies either directly to individual people or to corporations which provide insurance for their employees. People who have secure employment in financially sound companies have been well looked after. About 78 million of the elderly, the disabled and the poor are covered by Medicare and Medicaid. But, in 2005, that left about 46 million American residents (about 15 per cent of the population) without any insurance cover, and an estimated further 30 million seriously underinsured, totalling about a quarter of the population.[6] The USA is the only OECD country that does not guarantee universal health coverage. Yet, in practice, about 60 per cent of the total cost of health care is met by government, not just through Medicare and Medicaid but through tax subsidies to companies that provide cover for their employees.

This has much wider social implications than merely the health status of poorer Americans. The point is that, for a very significant part of the population, bad as illness may be in itself, it can also have catastrophic financial consequences for a family's entire standard of life. For them, it is a major source of fear and danger. As Elias argued, fear and insecurity undermine normal 'civilized' constraints across the board: to quote him again, if danger became as incalculable as it once was, 'corresponding fears would soon burst the limits set to them today' and 'the armour of civilized conduct would crumble rapidly' (2000: 532). And if it crumbles among the unprotected strata, fears will also rise among members of the protected strata – as was noted in chapter 6 in connection with violence.

The central problem of health care was remedied more than half a century ago in most other advanced countries, through various forms of nationally organized health services or health insurance. Over the decades, many attempts have been made in the USA to find some equivalent arrangement that would be politically acceptable. But the insurance companies and the doctors prosper immensely from the status quo, and have always raised the cry of 'socialized medicine'. Doctors, provided that they are not overly concerned with issues of social exclusion, can indeed point to the merit of the market, that levels of remuneration well in excess of those found in other countries give enormous incentives for medical research and innovation, for very able people to enter the medical profession in America, or indeed for doctors to migrate there from abroad. The upshot is that the relevant power ratios within the American political system have so far prevented reform (Starr, 1982).

Yet the present system did not, as it would be easy to assume, arise directly from an ideological preference for private over public provision. It took hold as an unintended consequence of wage controls adopted to control inflation during the Second World War, which led corporations to use health cover as a means of competing for scarce labour. By the early twenty-first century, for old-established major corporations, the costs of providing health cover (including 'legacy' costs of providing for their pensioners too) were proving a serious threat to the viability of their business. This has been one factor in the decline in competitiveness experienced by such stalwarts of the American economy as General Motors, US Steel and the airlines. America's semi-privatized welfare state more or less worked for several decades after the Second World War, but only because there was a stable corporate order providing economic security for workers (Krugman, 2005). That stability was crumbling by the late twentieth century for a good historical reason. Peter Drucker (1969) pointed out that the great corporations that had dominated the US economy for the best part of a century were the product of the last great spurt of technological innovation, and that the next great spurt – the digital and information revolution that was only beginning when he wrote – would produce another crop of great corporations. But the speed of change is now much greater than in the past, so that the turnover of corporations is too fast to give workers the expectation of a whole lifetime's career and consequent security from any employer. Moreover, newer arrivals on the corporate scene, such as the supermarket giant Wal-Mart, maintain their competitiveness by (among other things) not providing their employees with health insurance and pensions on the model of older companies. These constitute good reasons to detach health insurance and pensions from employment.

In a book chiefly concerned to take a long-term perspective on American society, it may seem out of keeping to dwell at such length on an area of contemporary political controversy like health care. Yet, as a case study, it is highly significant as one field in which America seems more than other countries so far to have withstood the compelling force of De Swaan's long-term 'collectivizing process'. Whatever the merits of the state not becoming a monopoly provider of *health services*, the costs of encouraging competition in the sale of *health insurance* are known to be high. The cheapest way of providing health insurance for all is via 'community rating' schemes, where all members – young and old, rich and poor, healthy and sickly – are charged the same rate, thus spreading the actuarial risk across the whole community. If competitors are allowed to 'cherry-pick' the lowest-risk customers by offering them lower charges, then the average cost to the remaining higher-risk people is increased and, at the margin, some will not be able to afford cover (Light, 2006). That is why the 'adamantly pro-market' *Economist* (2006a) concluded that in the longer term America 'may have no choice other than to accept a more overtly European-style system'. Nevertheless, opposite forces are also at work. Nathan Glazer (1998) has noted a trend towards the American welfare state model becoming less exceptional, as other countries attempt to scale back their expenditure. Elements even of American health care are being emulated in Europe. Light attributes that to the influence of American management consultants, but there are broader structural forces too: globalization is putting the states of the world in a position analogous to that of the states of the Union, or of parishes under the Elizabethan Poor Law: if their provision is more generous than their neighbours, it may attract migrants (a good thing if extra labour is needed) but at the same time help to make their economies uncompetitive in global markets.

One final paradox: De Swaan's proposition that, to the rich, the poor always represent both a threat and a resource now applies to the USA's position in the world as a whole. American business has certainly been quick to recognize low-paid workers in other parts of the globe as a valuable resource; and, especially since 11 September 2001, America has equally certainly seen the world beyond its shores as a source of threat. It will be interesting to see whether, in the longer term, the USA will succumb to the logic of De Swaan's collectivizing process: that is, build collective institutions to harness the resources and minimize the threat. In the short term, it has done the opposite.

Social mobility in America

'Most Americans', commented *The Economist* in 2004, 'see nothing wrong with inequality of income so long as it comes with plenty of social mobility: it is simply the price paid for a dynamic economy.' What, then, is the basis of the American Dream in the facts about social mobility in American society?

For purposes of assessing 'equality of opportunity' and the relative 'openness' of a society (or conversely the degree of class closure that prevails in it), sociologists and economists focus principally on intergenerational mobility; that is, they attempt to measure the probability that children will end up in a higher (or lower) paid and more (or less) socially prestigious occupation than their parents achieved. It is sometimes argued that the chances of downward mobility, of offspring falling into a lower social group than their parents occupied, is a better measure of openness or meritocracy than is upward mobility. In a growing economy, and particularly where the proportion of non-manual occupations is expanding in comparison with manual ones, short-range upward intergenerational mobility across a significant social line of distinction like the manual/non-manual one may not be a measure of underlying openness or the reward of any exceptional individual merit, but merely of 'automatic' promotion resulting from changes in the occupational structure. Thernstrom's careful study (1964) of working-class social mobility in a small New England city in the nineteenth century showed that the bulk of upward movement was of this short-range kind. But it was enough to sustain confidence in the American Dream.[7] For it is a well-established sociological finding that people experience the discontentment of 'relative deprivation' (Runciman, 1966) more through their comparisons of small inequalities among people nearby and not very different from themselves than through resentments of the vast differences between themselves and the topmost strata remotest from them.[8]

Broadly speaking, though, the rapid growth both of the economy and of the population of America at large does appear to have been associated in the nineteenth century with at least some spectacular instances of long-range upward mobility – Andrew Carnegie to give just one example – as well as a large amount of shorter-range mobility. Towards the end of the century, in the Gilded Age, there were symptoms of the formation of a plutocratic elite sharing some of the marks of a European-style aristocracy (see chapter 4), but closure did not succeed or persist strongly into the early twentieth century. What, then, happened to social mobility in the early twenty-first century?

There is a large and technical literature on rates of social mobility in industrial societies, which I shall not attempt to summarize in any detail here. A major study by Erikson and Goldthorpe (1992) suggested that rates of mobility fundamentally differed little between Europe and America. A more recent comparison of eight countries by Blanden et al. (2005) seems, however, to show that the United States and Britain (the two countries where economic inequality increased most dramatically in the late twentieth century) now have *lower* rates of intergenerational mobility than do Canada, the four Scandinavian countries and West Germany. Mobility in Britain has actually fallen. The expansion of higher education since the 1980s has disproportionately benefited children from affluent families, and there is a strong relationship between parental income and educational attainment. For the USA the picture is slightly different: '[P]arental income leads to a less marked advantage in terms of education, but this educational advantage is worth more in the labour market in the US than in other countries.' There is also a racial dimension, with black families showing markedly more restricted mobility than whites. The idea of the USA as the land of opportunity persists, but 'clearly seems misplaced' (ibid.: 7). *The Economist* (2004) commented that 'the United States risks calcifying into a European-style class-based society', probably an overdramatic conclusion that managed to be simultaneously unfair both to America and Europe, but nevertheless posing an interesting question about the future of the American Dream. The question is: how much *actual* social mobility (and over what range, long or short) is necessary to maintain the plausibility of popular belief in the Dream? Will the *real* and measurable increase in economic inequality, together with a *possible* decline in actual mobility, eventually exert pressure towards a greater reality-congruence of popular perceptions?[9]

Conclusion: Upwards identification, not mutual identification?

For the moment, a fervent belief in the American Dream still appears to be extremely widespread among residents of the USA. It forms part of national identity and is a component of popular 'patriotism'; to that extent it may be consciously fostered by elites to distract attention from growing inequality ('patriotism is the last refuge of a scoundrel', as Dr Johnson observed). At any rate, a belief that the USA is a land of equality of opportunity where everyone has a chance to succeed through individual effort helps to promote a strong sense of identification with the nation. But is this a two-way, *mutual* identification, of the kind that Elias's theory seems to predict will be the outcome of growing ties of interdependence and *relatively more equal* balances of power? Possibly not. The identification may be asymmetrical rather than mutual. For the other side of the coin, what we may call the curse of the American Dream, is the widespread belief that people who do not succeed in rising or bettering themselves through their individual efforts have only themselves to blame. In the past, this extended to a belief in the inherent inferiority of those who remained at the bottom of the social hierarchy, notably the blacks. Even today, attitudes sometimes verge on that: such people are *undeserving*. There remains a preponderance of African Americans among the very poor, and, as noted in chapter 6, the last three decades of the twentieth century saw an increasing resort to the 'penal dragnet' rather than a social safety net. To the extent that the poor can be blamed for their plight, there is less need to do much *collectively* for them. This has not been an historical constant; in the periods of the New Deal and the Great Society a very different attitude gained ascendancy. But in recent decades, it has seemed on the whole that the bulk of Americans 'don't care about inequality' (Glazer, 2005). The economists Alesina et al. (2001) conclude that:

> Americans redistribute less than Europeans for three reasons: because the majority of Americans believe that redistribution favours racial minorities, because Americans believe that they live in an open and fair society, and that if someone is poor it is their own fault, and because the political system is geared towards preventing redistribution.

Nathan Glazer accepts that race, in particular the identification of 'the poor' with the blacks, is central to the difference between Europe and America in attitudes to redistribution. Redistributive programmes 'are not seen as programmes for "us" and "people like us", but for those who are different and less deserving, particularly blacks' (2005: 5). Where Glazer may be wrong, at least in the longer term, is that this will remain a transatlantic difference. For there are signs that in Britain (Goodhart, 2004) and some other European countries, ethnic diversity resulting from the large-scale immigration of recent decades is undermining the sense of there being a single, homogeneous national community, and consequentially reducing the willingness of citizens to pay progressive rates of tax to ameliorate the condition of the less fortunate.

Finally, two more general points related to the theories of Norbert Elias which provide the guiding thread of this book.

First, Elias recognized that processes leading to the closer integration and interdependence of people and groups could have contrary consequences. In the short term, they can lead to conflict, various forms of integration struggles, and hostility rather than mutual identification. In the longer term, however, as previously noted, he tended to associate longer chains of interdependence with a trend towards functional democratization – relatively more equal balances of power between people and groups – and with increasing mutual identification. This assumption may need to be qualified. For the greater part of human history, the lengthening of interdependencies went hand in hand with growing inequality (Goudsblom, 1996c); it was perhaps only within competing national states – the subject of Elias's study – that it led to a diminution of power differences, a tendency that is now being undermined by globalization.[10] Furthermore, it appears that the resulting identification may be asymmetrical. The American Dream appears to give rise to 'upwards identification' by the less well off, but large parts of the better off do not reciprocate the identification.

Second, the relation of the American Dream to the actual facts of equality, inequality and social mobility in the USA today raises questions about the reality-congruence of popular beliefs. How many people have to experience cognitive dissonance, and how strong a cognitive dissonance, before popular perceptions change? So long as a sense of relative deprivation is generated mainly by comparisons with the lot of people fairly close and similar to oneself, perhaps a more macroscopic picture of gross inequality has little effect. The concept of reality-congruence, introduced here, will be central to the next chapter, which is concerned with American religiosity.

11

Involvement, Detachment
and American Religiosity

Religion . . . never has in itself a 'civilizing' or affect-subduing effect. On the
contrary, religion is always exactly as 'civilized' as the society or class which
upholds it.

Norbert Elias (2000: 169)

The *Washington Post* reported on 27 August 1999 that Vice-President
Gore, subsequently the unsuccessful candidate in the disputed presidential election of 2000 and known as one of the most scientifically minded
of leading American politicians, had refused 'to take a clear stand on
whether public schools should be required to teach evolution and not creationism'. That is a striking testimony to the persistence of strong literal-
ist, fundamentalist, supernatural beliefs in the USA. It is, in particular, a
symptom of a predominantly populist politics which makes it dangerous
for politicians to deny folk beliefs and leaves great power in the hands of
the ignorant. Surveys show that only one in ten Americans believes in
Darwinian evolution.[1] In most other advanced Western countries, scientists and politicians would denounce creationism – belief in the literal
truth of the biblical account of God creating the universe in seven days –
and would carry the authority to convince most people.

Today, it may seem anachronistic to oppose science and religion to each
other in such a direct way. The heyday of that debate was Victorian
England, when churchmen defended Genesis, denied the validity of
Darwin's theory of evolution and were trounced by his champions,
notably T. H. Huxley. Today, many distinguished scientists practise a religion – but theirs are usually the more intellectualized religious beliefs that
do not contradict modern science.

Of course, in every country, there are small defiant minorities who hold to beliefs, including the Creation, at odds with modern scientific knowledge. The fact that in the USA they remain vocal and sufficiently numerous not to be easily dismissed with ridicule is perhaps a symptom of a relatively weak elite monopolization of the means of orientation, paralleling the relatively weak monopolization of violence.[2] It may also be regarded as echoing the false polarity of 'liberty' versus 'government' that has endured in American thought since the early years of American independence, and that aspect of the frontier spirit that Turner described as producing 'antipathy to control . . . intolerant of administrative experience and education, and pressing individual liberty beyond its proper bounds' (1947 [1920]: 30, 32; see also p. 197 above). Paraphrasing Tocqueville on the 'tyranny of the majority', we may discern in it a tyranny of the well-organized minorities.

My concern in this chapter is principally with religion as a means of orientation, its cognitive function for people in helping them make sense of the world. Besides orientation, religion manifestly serves other functions for people, especially in meeting emotional needs such as consolation in times of distress. The cognitive and affective aspects of religion cannot, however, be entirely separated. For many Americans, the connection between the two appears to differ somewhat from the dominant pattern in Europe.

Viewed from Europe, where there has been a marked trend towards secularization in most countries for well over a century, the enduring religiosity of the USA is perplexing. Religion has been succinctly defined as 'the invocation of the supernatural' (Wilson, 1982: 154). And even at the highest levels in the USA, rhetoric is deployed about a personal God who actively gives direction through prayer. Presidential prayer meetings are publicized, especially at times of international crisis. The question is whether the rhetoric of religion in politics is a veneer, or whether it does indicate the actual role of religious thinking in policy-making. It may simply be that the boundaries between what Pierre Bourdieu called 'fields of discourse' are drawn differently in the USA. It goes without saying that the natural sciences in the USA are no less reality-orientated than anywhere else. It may even be true that the proportion of political leaders in other Western countries who privately adhere to religious beliefs is no smaller than in the USA. But religious belief is regarded in Europe as largely a private matter – it has to a greater extent been pushed 'behind the scenes' of public life – and rhetorical invocation of the supernatural in political discourse is now uncommon and embarrassing. On the other hand, it has been argued, notably by sociologists of religion like Greeley (1989, 2003) and Davie (2002), that on a global perspective it is secular Europe, not America, that is the exception. But whether or not that is the case, the apparent persistence of religion embodying a strong element of 'magic-mythical' thinking would appear to be at odds with Norbert Elias's sociological theory of knowledge and the sciences. This chapter will explore this persistence, and why in America a wider range of variation than in Europe endures in the social standards about what it is socially respectable to believe about the natural and social world, in what circumstances, and with what possible consequences.

Fantasy and the growth of knowledge

Elias does not say much about religion, and *The Civilizing Process* has often been criticized for omitting to discuss the civilizing influence that religion is very widely assumed to have had. That assumption, according to Goudsblom (2004), is rooted in the dominant intellectual tradition deriving from St Augustine, which singles out religious *belief* as a powerful force in the strong shift in socially induced individual self-control observed from the Renaissance onwards. In *The Protestant Ethic* (1930) – one of the most influential founding texts of modern sociology – Max Weber leaned heavily towards the Augustinian view. Elias, on the other hand, can be placed within what Goudsblom calls the Lucretian tradition. The first-century BC writer Lucretius, in *De rerum natura* (1951), anticipated the modern theory of evolution, and he attributed religious belief to people's ignorance of principles underlying life on earth. Elias recognized that religious *organization* may have played a part in exerting civilizing pressures; he treats princes of the church as no different from secular princes in the feudal power struggles out of which processes of state-formation arose (2000: 187). This idea has been developed by Mart Bax (1987), who argued that additional impetus was given to the European civilizing process by competition between religious and secular authorities. Unlike Weber, however, Elias gave little credence to the independent civilizing influence of religious *ideas*.[3]

What Elias did advance in many essays from the 1950s to the 1980s was a strong theory of the long-term development of knowledge and the sciences. Closely connected with the earlier theory of civilizing processes, it is not explicitly a theory of religion, still less of secularization, but it is concerned with the balance between 'involvement' and 'detachment', and between 'magic-mythical' and relatively more 'reality-congruent' thinking.[4]

Elias spoke of a balance between 'detachment' and 'involvement', rather than using more conventional dichotomies like 'rational' and 'irrational', 'objective' and 'subjective'. Most adult behaviour lies on a scale between total involvement and total detachment.

> One cannot say of a [person's] outlook in any absolute sense that it is detached or involved (or, if one prefers, 'rational' or 'irrational', 'objective' or 'subjective'). Only small babies, and among adults perhaps only insane people, become involved in whatever they experience with complete abandon to their feelings here and now; and again only insane people can remain totally unmoved by what goes on around them. (2007a: 68)

Besides, not only do 'irrational' and 'subjective' often have pejorative overtones, they also tend to imply 'psychological' characteristics of a particular individual, whereas the criteria by which Elias judges the balance between involvement and detachment cover both the 'psychological' and the 'social'. The balance of involvement and detachment varies between different human groups, from situation to situation within them, and from individual to individual within a situation. Nevertheless, '[t]he way in which individual members of a group experience whatever affects their senses, the meaning it has for them, depends on the standard forms of dealing with, and of thinking about, these phenomena gradually evolved in their society' (ibid.: 70). For example, in modern industrial societies people employ, as part of the knowledge they have inherited from the past and now take for granted, a very precise conceptual distinction between living and non-living things (ibid.: 120). The distinction is highly 'reality-congruent' – it consistently 'works' with a high degree of certainty. Individual reactions when experiencing the forces of nature – a thunderstorm, a forest fire, even an illness – may still vary from individual to individual and situation to situation, but in scientific societies the *concepts* which all individuals now use in thinking, speaking and acting represent a relatively high degree of detachment. That is true of concepts like 'hurricane', 'lightning', 'tree' and 'disease', as well as 'electricity', 'cause', 'time' and 'organism'. Today there is very little scope for hurricane, lightning and fire – and only a little more for illness – to be interpreted in terms of the intentions of supernatural living beings and their meaning for the particular humans affected. In other words, the range of individual variations in interpreting natural events is limited by the public standards of detachment embodied in modes of thinking and speaking about nature (ibid.). This is markedly less true of modes of thinking and speaking about things that happen in what we call 'society' as opposed to 'nature'.

Members of industrial societies have great difficulties in understanding that members of societies at earlier stages of development were often unable to distinguish what they themselves distinguish easily and as a matter of course. Their assumption of a clear distinction between living and non-living things, for instance, can be so easily confirmed by testing against reality that it is hard to imagine that anyone can ever have failed to make it. Yet in fact this distinction took a very long time to develop to its present form. At some stage in the past, human beings could not yet know that a hurricane or a raging sea which put their lives at risk was itself not alive. The very phrase 'raging sea', though now only a metaphor, helps the effort of imagination needed to put oneself in the place of people who were not aware that the storms which destroyed human life did so unintentionally, and were blind physical processes.

By the seventeenth century, when the colonization of North America began, the animate/inanimate distinction at least was fairly firm in the minds of English people. But they retained many other beliefs that from a modern standpoint seem absurd. Eggleston, in his pioneering study (1901) of the 'mental furniture' that early settlers took on board ship with them,[5] mentions the unclear distinction between astronomy and astrology, with horoscopes cast even by famous astronomers; comets being seen as portents; the belief in the spontaneous generation of worms, birds and fish from dead bodies, trees or the sea; the belief in an invisible world, including most famously the activities of witches and witchcraft. Noting the Salem witch trials of 1692, much studied by later historians, Eggleston observes that '[t]he phenomena known in later times as hysteria, and as mesmerism and hypnotism, were not yet recognized to be due to natural causes. The infinitely delicate shadings by which mental sanity passes without line of demarcation into madness could then not be imagined' (1901: 26–7). Similarly, people have not always been quite sure that a person could not transform him- or herself into an animal or a tree. To be certain that that was not possible was all the more difficult because these things did happen in dreams: people could easily see themselves or other people changing, or being changed, into trees or birds or animals. Such themes now persist for us mainly in the magic and myths of folklore and children's tales: if they happen in dreams, we know they are only dreams. But how could human beings know, from the very beginning, that many things which happen in dreams could not happen in reality? Elias points out that '[f]or small children everywhere, the difference between fantasy and reality is blurred. They learn the distinction between fantasy and reality, like other items of knowledge, in accordance with the standard reached in their society' (2007a: 121).

How distinctly the line is drawn between dreams and reality depends on public standards, which in industrial societies demand that people draw it very clearly and act accordingly. If they act out their dreams in a way not in line with the standard, their sanity may be questioned. Children have to learn this. But magical-mythical thinking, highly loaded with fantasy, is 'the primary mode of human experience' because it is part of the elementary makeup of human beings that 'their emotions, their affects and drives, are primarily attuned to other persons on whom they can fasten, rather than to lifeless things' (2007a: 128). This mode of experience does not simply cease to exist in industrial-scientific societies. As people grow up, it becomes a more or less submerged layer of the personality structure. Freud discovered it there and called it the 'unconscious'. The magical-mythical mode of experience remains alive in adults in modern societies, and is allowed relatively greater expression in some areas – cultural life, religion and politics for example – than in the domain of the natural sciences themselves. It is also seen in the popular appeal of science fiction, astrology and parapsychology.

If specific but differing balances between involvement and detachment are part of what is learned by every child in each particular society, the question is how the public standards available for learning are themselves formed and changed over time. By today's standards, what Eggleston called the 'mental outfit' of the early colonists displayed a high level of fantasy and a low level of reality-orientation. Rising standards of detachment of knowledge require a similar rise over many generations in the standards of self-control that have to be learned in the course of growing up, the same transformation of personality structure. Science, in fact, involves a species of detour behaviour, the detour via detachment. A necessary part of the detour is the conquest of the fears that inevitably spring from the dangers posed by hurricanes, by diseases, or by other human beings, abandoning supernatural explanations for all of them.[6] One of the results of a successful detour via detachment is greater human control of the forces – physical, biological or social – it is sought to understand.

Yet paradoxically, says Elias, the gradual increase in human beings' capacity for taking a more detached view of natural forces and gaining more control over them – a process which has also accelerated over the long term – has tended at least in the shorter term to *increase* the difficulties they have in extending their control over social relationships *and* over their own feelings in thinking about them. The reason for this paradox is that as humans have gradually come to understand natural forces more, fear them less and use them more effectively for human ends, this has gone hand in hand with specific changes in human relationships. More and more people have tended to become more and more interdependent with each other in longer chains and denser webs. The growth of the web of social interdependence tends to outstrip people's understanding of it. The same process which diminishes dangers and feelings of insecurity in the face of natural forces tends also to increase the dangers and feelings of insecurity in face of 'social forces' – the forces stemming from people's dependence on each other for the satisfaction of their needs and for their security. Elias puts the point vividly:

> It is as if first thousands, then millions, then more and more millions walked through this world with their hands and feet chained together by invisible ties. No one is in charge. No one stands outside. Some want to go this way, others that way. They fall upon each other and, vanquishing or defeated, still remain chained to each other. No one can regulate the movements of the whole unless a great part of them are able to understand, to see as it were from the outside, the whole patterns they form together. And they are not able to visualize themselves as part of these larger patterns because, being hemmed in and moved uncomprehendingly hither and thither in ways which none of them intended, they cannot help being preoccupied with the urgent, narrow and parochial problems which each of them has to face. . . . They are too deeply involved to look at themselves from without. Thus what is formed of nothing but human beings acts upon each of them, and *is experienced by many as an alien external force not unlike the forces of nature.* (2007a: 77; my italics)

In the natural sciences, the question characteristic of people's involvement, 'What does it mean for me or us?', has become more subordinated to questions like 'What is it?' or 'How are these events connected with each other?' The level of detachment represented by the latter questions has been buttressed and institutionalized as part of a scientific tradition transmitted by means of a highly specialized training, maintained by various forms of social control and socially induced emotional restraints. It has become embodied in the conceptual tools, the basic assumptions, the methods of speaking and thinking which scientists use. Scientific concepts and theories in the natural sciences embody the idea of a relatively autonomous, impersonal *order* in events. Scientific communities are relatively autonomous in their social *organization*, and exercise strong control over what it is acceptable for scientists to believe about the natural world.

As the stock of knowledge has grown, concepts of the more detached, scientific type have gradually spread to people at large. In industrial societies, most people use concepts and explanations of natural events based on the idea of a course of events independent of any specific group of human observers, without being aware of the long struggle that was necessary to develop these modes of thinking. Certainly, other more involved layers of experience persist alongside the more detached – as in the case of illness, where a scientific understanding of organisms may not quite drive out the question 'What have I done to deserve this?' In understanding social processes, the level of habitual detachment for most people remains much less than in the case of 'natural' processes. The institutionalized curbs on emotions and fantasy in the pursuit of understanding vary along a broad continuum. Many churches, especially in the past, sought to impose strict limits on acceptable belief through tight social discipline and elaborate doctrine. But, while the long-term trend may be towards higher social standards of detachment in some fields – most obviously the natural sciences and to the lesser extent the social sciences – in other fields it is arguable that spurts in the opposite direction are quite common.

American religion in long-term perspective

Organized religion and large-scale agriculture make their appearance in human history at the same time. The capacity for symbolic thought, permitting humans to speculate about the causes of natural and social events, is much older – it dates back at least to the emergence of *Homo sapiens sapiens* and probably much further. But specialized religious institutions, with organizational structures, specialized personnel – priests – and articulated bodies of doctrine, appeared only in connection with agriculture. 'Religious–agrarian regimes' tended to be supplanted by 'military–agrarian regimes', because the vulnerability of fields, crops and barns to marauding pillagers made defence (and exploitation) of farmers by specialist warriors more or less indispensable (Goudsblom, 1996a; 1996b). Yet priestly elites tended to endure, in alliance with the warrior rulers. The role and power of priests can be understood in relation to the kinds of danger that agriculturalists face. Natural dangers include droughts, floods, crop failures, infestations by weeds, insects and other parasites, soil exhaustion and erosion. These cannot always be prevented even today, let alone with the technology that was available in the past. But they can be exacerbated by human failings: negligence, ignorance, greed, lack of care, lack of discipline, lack of foresight. Priests seem to have played a part in deterring such failings. For millennia (Elias, 2007b: 42–5), they acted as timekeepers, using astronomic observations to determine the seasons for sowing and reaping. In many societies, religious ritual came to be employed as a means of promoting good practice and preventing bad through social control and discipline: people were made to fear the consequences, social and supernatural, of sowing crops at the wrong time, of bingeing on the new harvest and being hungrier later, of eating the seed corn.

Danger and superstition

The early European settlements in North America were no doubt very different from the early agrarian societies of millennia before, but they still faced many of the same dangers. Seventeenth-century people in both

Europe and North America lived with a pervasive sense of uncertainty, of having to cope with a capriciously dangerous world over which they could exert little control (Thomas, 1973: 3–24; Munchembled, 1985: 31–3, 119ff.). Drawing on diaries from the period, Carol Stearns shows that this extended even to the protection of children:

> [I]n the specific case of children, indeed, one is struck by how unprotected they were, with near-fatal accidents a commonplace in the diaries. The recording of these in part simply restated the view that one has no control over the world, but it indicated that the parents involved took little care to structure the environments of children in order to systematically protect them from danger. . . . [T]hey simply did not see the world as a controllable place and think in terms of controlling it. (1988: 56–7)

Stearns characterized the typical emotional response to misfortune in the early modern period as one of 'sadness' rather than anger, explaining it precisely by the lack of a sense of control. This enhanced the appeal to religious belief – explanations were routinely sought in 'the will of God' – but also, as Keith Thomas demonstrated, the appeal of superstition of all kinds and specifically the belief in witchcraft. Gradually, in the first half of the eighteenth century, the lack of a sense of control began to be replaced, especially among the middle and upper classes, by a sense that a greater degree of control was possible over at least some of the commoner dangers. It is tempting to relate this to intellectual developments, including the divorce between magic and science that gained momentum in the seventeenth century, and led into the Enlightenment of the eighteenth (Thomas, 1973: 767–800). The influence of ideas must not be dismissed entirely, and they do typically percolate very slowly downwards from intellectual elites to the wider society. But it could equally well be argued that Enlightenment ideas were a response to the world's becoming for some people somewhat less dangerous and more manipulable. (For instance, the threat of famine gradually diminished at this time because of improvements in transport and commerce.) Certainly the belief in witchcraft declined. Yet for many people, including farmers in the remoter parts of the expanding USA, life remained highly dangerous, capriciously so, and there are many accounts of the prevalence of superstition on the frontier in the nineteenth century. Herndon, in his *Life of Lincoln* first published in 1888, recalled that:

> Although gay, prosperous and light-hearted, these people were brimming over with superstition. . . . They believed in witches, pinned their faith to the curative power of wizards in dealing with sick animals, and shot the image of a witch with a silver ball to break the spell she was supposed to have over human beings. They followed with religious minuteness the directions of the

water-wizard with his magic divining rod, and the faith doctor who wrought miraculous cures by strange sounds and signals to some mysterious agency. The flight of a bird at the window, the breath of a horse on a child's head, the crossing by a dog of a hunter's path, all betokened evil luck in store for someone. The moon exercised greater influence on the actions of the people and the growth of vegetation than the sun and all the planetary system combined. Fence rails could only be cut in the light of the moon, and potatoes planted in the dark of the moon. Trees and plants which bore their fruit above ground could be planted when the moon shone full. Soap could only be made in the light of the moon, and it must only be stirred in one way and by one person. They had a horror of Friday, which with many exists to this day. Nothing was to be begun on that unlucky day, for if the rule were violated an endless train of disasters was sure to follow. (Herndon and Weik, 1983 [1888]: 55–6)

At first glance, the prevalence of superstition and magical beliefs may seem to be at odds with the traditional image of American settlers, especially with the rigid regulation of conduct and beliefs in early New England. As in the case of sexual behaviour, where the Puritan churches set high standards but recognized that practice fell short of precept, so the very rigidity of their codes of doctrine must be understood in relation to how widespread and relatively unbridled were popular supernatural beliefs. As in sex, so in beliefs: there remained to a great extent a volatility and impulsiveness still reminiscent of the Middle Ages. Learned and responsible men could still be carried away, as was Samuel Sewall, who came to look back with remorse on his role as judge in the Salem witch trials; he made a public confession of error and guilt in Old South Church in Boston just five years after the events. The rigid morality and doctrine of some of the early established churches – particularly in Massachusetts, which perhaps looms too large in popular perception – is only one side of the equation.

Established churches

Initially, established churches were a feature of several of the colonies. Virginia and other southern colonies began under the Anglican banner, and the Church of England received public subsidy, although it had little political power. In New York too, an attempt was made to impose Anglicanism as an established church, quite unsuccessfully. Maryland was founded by a Catholic, Lord Baltimore, partly as a refuge for English Catholics, although they were always outnumbered by Protestants. The Quaker colonies of Pennsylvania and Delaware always welcomed members of many sects. Only in Massachusetts was a serious attempt made to impose religious uniformity, to monopolize the means of orientation, in a theocratic state. From the beginning, that provoked conflict. In 1637, Anne Hutchinson was banished for her emphasis on the individual's intuition as a means of reaching God and salvation, rather than the observance of institutionalized beliefs and the precepts of ministers. Congregationalists, less enamoured of centralized religious authority, broke away to found Connecticut, and the liberal Roger Williams too fled Massachusetts to establish Rhode Island as a haven of religious tolerance. The Massachusetts theocracy effectively came to an end with the granting of a new royal charter in 1691, although religious elites remained powerful in New England for much longer. Eventually, the Bill of Rights was constitutionally to forbid the imposition of an established religion by the federal government: the First Amendment stipulated that 'Congress shall make no law respecting an establishment of religion, or prohibiting the free exercise thereof'.[7] As a result, in retrospect an established church appears distinctly un-American, although the last vestiges of establishment at state level persisted in Connecticut until 1818 and Massachusetts until 1833.

It has to be remembered that when the European settlement of North America began, the idea was not yet well established in Europe that a diversity of religious beliefs within one country was compatible with the maintenance of social order. After the initial religious wars that accompanied the Protestant Reformation, the Peace of Augsburg had in 1555 promulgated the principle of *cuius regio, eius religio*[8] – that the ruler of each state should choose the religion its people should all follow. But that was far from recognition of the possibility of tolerating a diversity of beliefs and practices among the subjects. Wars of religion were to devastate Europe again in the seventeenth century, and as late as 1685 Louis XIV's revocation of the Edict of Nantes resulted in the expulsion of the majority of the Huguenots, French Protestants, from Catholic France.[9] The degree to which European states enforced conformity varied. The Elizabethan Church Settlement, which re-established the Church of England, allowed considerable latitude by the standards of the time, but placed civil disabilities upon members of the Puritan sects and upon Catholics; indeed Catholic Emancipation – the restoration of their full civil rights – was not enacted in Britain until 1829. So the Maryland Toleration Act of 1649, which placed Protestants and Catholics on an equal footing (though it gave short shrift to Unitarians and non-Christians), was ahead of its time. More than a century later, Jefferson's Bill for Establishing Religious Freedom in Virginia, written in 1777 and enacted in 1786, was one of the achievements of which he was proudest.

It is of some long-term significance that not even in Massachusetts or Connecticut did clerical elites in the end secure a permanent place in the central monopoly of the power structure of American society. A comparison with Latin America is instructive. In the Spanish colonies, there was a classic symbiosis of priestly and warrior power. Darcy Ribeiro observes that the Catholic Church's association with the temporal power gave it everything the state could provide – an architectural heritage in its churches altogether more spectacular than those of North America is one sign of the use made of the state's taxing power – but in return the state acquired the church's 'co-operation in perpetuating colonial domination and maintaining the oligarchic order and in aristocratizing its upper hierarchy' (1971: 351). Ribeiro, like Elias (but in greater detail), paid more attention to the church's and the clergy's position in the power structure than to the 'psychological' effects of particular religious beliefs on which sociologists since Max Weber have tended to dwell.[10] In Latin America, the church's power gave rise to militant anti-clerical and secularist movements, whereas 'the clergy of Protestant America, excluded from the political power structure, could always safeguard itself better and exert a control that, though more informal, was more efficacious' (ibid.). This point connects well with Elias's argument that moderate, but sustained and consistent, social pressures are more effective in bringing about the internalization of changing social standards as taken-for-granted habitus or 'second nature'. Ribeiro contended that 'religion in Protestant America became actually more orthodox than Latin American Catholicism, generalizing as a more popular religiosity, less impregnated with syncretisms, *but also more intolerant*' (ibid.: 351–2; my italics). The last phrase is rather startling, unless one is thinking of the extreme right-wing Christians who have risen to prominence in the USA mainly since Ribeiro was writing in the 1960s. But Ribeiro's comparison does offer some insight into the persistence of religiosity in the USA, and why for a much larger proportion of Americans than Western Europeans it remains taken-for-granted 'second nature' to assent to religious belief and even belong to a religious organization.

Civil religion

One way in which taken-for-grantedness has taken root has been the institutionalization in the USA of what Robert Bellah (1967), following Rousseau, called a 'Civil Religion'. In spite of the constitutional prohibition of any religious establishment, the phrase 'In God we Trust' appears on American coins, children daily swear allegiance to 'one nation, under God', and reference has been made to 'God' in the inaugural addresses of every President.[11] Yet this God is not specifically Christian or Jewish, let alone Protestant or Catholic, and many of these invocations are phrased sufficiently abstractly, especially nowadays, not to exclude Islam. This generalized religion appears, from George Washington onwards, to be connected with the conviction that without belief in God, morality, public

or private, cannot be securely based – a proposition to which a large proportion of Americans assents today.[12] It is something separate from, but
drawing upon, conventional religion. As Bellah pointed out, the
Revolution has long been implicitly depicted as an American Exodus,
while the Civil War provided an American New Testament, with Lincoln
as the murdered God – an idea, as Frazer showed in *The Golden Bough*
(1958 [1890]), common in the mythology of the ancient world and central
to Christian belief. This civil religion can be dismissively stamped
'American Shinto' (Bellah, 1967: 12), but as a nationally sponsored syn-
cretism it appears to function in a way that legitimates more specific religious beliefs and their respective organizations, subtly casting a patriotic
cloak over them.[13]

Great awakenings

In ordinary religious observance among Americans, there would seem to
be several more or less long-term trends that are not altogether easy to
explain. One is a cyclical pattern of upsurges of religious fervour known
as 'Great Awakenings'. The First Great Awakening swept the colonies in
the 1730s and 1740s (Ahlstrom, 1972: 280–330); Jonathan Edwards,
minister at Northampton, Massachusetts, is generally seen as its intellectual leader, but the great English Methodist preacher George Whitefield
visited North America and preached from New England to the South.

The notion of being 'born again' in Christ, still prevalent in American
religion today, was prominent in the preaching of the First Great
Awakening. The opponents of the revival, particularly liberal pastors of
the established church in Massachusetts, criticized it for encouraging
emotional excess and religious delusions.

Two generations later, a further revival movement, known as the Second
Great Awakening (ibid.: 415–35), began once again in New England, but
swept westwards – Kentucky was an especially important centre – in the
early decades of the nineteenth century. It is associated with the 'camp
meetings' characteristic of religious enthusiasm as the frontier moved
west,[14] and was also linked with the growth of anti-slavery sentiment.
There is nothing very unusual about such upsurges, which occurred in
many pre-industrial agrarian societies.[15] Indeed, the First Great Awakening
was part of a broad international movement, linked directly to evangeli-
calism and the Methodist movement in England, and also having a broad
resemblance to the Pietism that was influential in German Lutheranism in
the seventeenth and eighteenth centuries (which emphasized personal faith
in protest against secularization in the church) and even to the Quietist
current in Roman Catholicism in the second half of the seventeenth century.
On the other hand, although the First and Second Great Awakenings

involved a highly emotional preoccupation with personal salvation, they did not veer towards encouraging the specifically magical experiences and visions that were common in Catholic Europe in the nineteenth century, when there were so many apparitions of the Virgin with consequent founding of Marian shrines as centres of pilgrimage and tourism.

The next widespread religious upsurge was very different in character. The Social Gospel movement (ibid.: 785–804), at its height from roughly the 1890s to the 1920s, unlike the First and Second Great Awakenings, was quintessentially a product of the new urban-industrial capitalist society rather than of the early Republic of small farmers.[16] It had affinities with the European Christian socialist movements in its criticism of the inequality and poverty produced by the unbridled market forces of American laissez-faire. It was the religious expression of the Progressive era, and had close intellectual links with social scientists such as the economist Richard T. Ely and the sociologist Albion Small, who stood in opposition to the dominant school led by William Graham Sumner, which, under the influence of Herbert Spencer, opposed all attempts to interfere with the survival of the fittest in the marketplace. Indeed, for Walter Rauschenbusch, one of the intellectual leaders of the Social Gospel movement, God's coming Kingdom on earth sounds quite Comtean (and also serves to recall Elias's theory of knowledge and the sciences): 'If the twentieth century could do for us in the control of social forces what the nineteenth did for us in the control of natural forces, our grandchildren would live in a society that would be justified in regarding our present social life as semi-barbarous' (1907: 422, quoted by Ahlstrom, 1972: 785).[17] Although as a religious movement it was in decline by the 1920s, the Social Gospel helped to prepare the way for the elements of an American welfare state enacted under Roosevelt.

The most recent upsurge in this cyclical pattern of religious enthusiasm began in the 1960s and still continues at the beginning of the twenty-first century.[18] This is the antithesis of the Social Gospel; dominated by evangelicals and Pentecostalists, its central religious concerns are with individual salvation, personal revelation and being 'born again', and thus it has much more in common with the First and Second Great Awakenings. Its individualism has allied it politically with a right-wing defence of laissez-faire and hostility to government – and to aspects of modern science. Its rise has been accompanied by the decline of old-style Protestantism. A columnist in the *New York Times* captured the trend in a family recollection:

My grandfather was fairly typical of his generation: A devout and active Presbyterian elder, he nonetheless believed firmly in evolution and regarded the Virgin Birth as a pious legend. Those kinds of mainline Christian are vanishing, replaced by evangelicals. Since 1960s, the number of Pentecostalists has increased fourfold, while the number of Episcopalians has dropped almost in half. (Kristof, 2003)

But that is not as new in American history as Kristof implies.

The replenishment of religious involvement

Popular revival movements, argued Bryan Wilson (1982: 152), were unwitting vehicles of increased secularization. From early Methodism to modern Pentecostalism, they drew people to church in larger numbers, stimulating but also disciplining religiosity, eradicating random superstitions, rationalizing understanding, undermining priestly authority and minimizing mystery. 'Eventually, they provide a new education of the emotions.' Wilson's view is consistent with one aspect of the rich historical data on American religious observance presented by Finke and Stark (2005). They show that the proportion of Americans who take part in organized religion has substantially *increased*. On the other hand, they show that this was accomplished by 'aggressive churches committed to vivid other-worldliness' (ibid.: 1) and high levels of emotional involvement. And, on a larger scale than in Europe, these revivalist movements have continued to the present day. That appears to contradict theories of secularization as well as my interpretation of Elias's theory about involvement and detachment.

Finke and Stark calculate that in 1776 only about 20 per cent of Americans took an active part in church affairs, whereas at the end of the twentieth century as many as 60 per cent did so. They do not claim that at Independence the other 80 per cent of Americans were necessarily irreligious, but their faith, if they had any, 'lacked public expression and organized influence' (ibid.: 26). And while the fervour of the First Great Awakening had subsided by then, Finke and Stark do not depict 1776 as a particularly low ebb in church participation. Our perception of religion in colonial America has been distorted by images of Puritans going to church (see p. 165 above); but – at least after the very earliest stages of settlement – Puritans were only ever a small minority in New England, and even in Puritan Massachusetts religious adherence never exceeded 22 per cent. By 1776, in New England as a whole only about one person in five had a religious affiliation. At Independence, Quakers amounted to only 5 per cent of the population of Pennsylvania, Catholics only 3 per cent in Maryland, and detailed calculations yield the overall figure of about 20 per cent religiously affiliated in all 13 colonies (ibid.: 25). So today's figure of almost two-thirds of Americans taking part in organized religion is a very striking fact.

More striking still is a general tendency for the emotional temperature of religion to increase over time. Or rather, there is a long history of denominations 'cooling down', of becoming rationalized or intellectualized, of

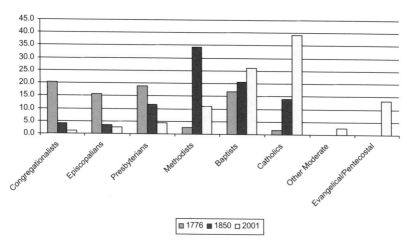

Figure 11.1: Adherents by Christian denomination, 1776, 1850 and 2001 (as per cent of total adherents)
Source: Finke and Stark (2005: 56) for 1776 and 1850; Kosmin et al. (2002).[19]

abandoning traditional belief in the literal truth of scripture, and of making fewer emotional demands on their adherents. But, as they did so, they lost 'market share': they ceased to prosper, and newer, more emotionally demanding, denominations grew in their place. The prototypical case was the decline of Congregationalism in Massachusetts. Partly in adverse reaction to the emotionalism of the First Great Awakening, many of the upper classes drifted away in the late eighteenth century towards Unitarianism. Similarly, a century later, many of the Quaker elite of Pennsylvania gravitated towards Episcopalianism: 'Although the "Protestant ethic" still spurred on the *parvenu*, Proper Philadelphia increasingly preferred the richness of the Anglican ritual' (Baltzell, 1958: 13). But trends among the elite did not make either the Unitarian or the Episcopal Church a market leader. Finke and Stark present quite precise calculations of the rise and fall of the principal denominations' shares of total adherents between 1776 and 1850, and I have made very roughly comparable calculations for 2001 (see figure 11.1).

As can be seen, among the Protestants, the Methodists gained massively in the first half of the nineteenth century; but towards its end, they in turn lost ground rapidly and it was the Baptists' turn to gain it. The Baptists have remained strong, perhaps because they are a diverse church, their congregations including both the relatively staid and the relatively emotionally highly charged (as well as the white and the black, and politically both left-wing and right-wing tendencies). During the twentieth century there had also grown up a substantial bloc of small evangelical and Pentecostalist churches, accounting for perhaps one in seven of people declaring a Christian denominational affiliation. Besides the various Christian denominations, there are of course substantial non-Christian minorities. The largest of these are the Jews, among whom there are also various theological tendencies, followed by growing numbers of Muslims, Buddhists and Hindus.[20]

Finke and Stark contend that the history of American religion has nearly always been written as an account of *intellectual* progress, of how religious ideas have undergone 'refinement', judged by the secular standards of parsimony, clarity, logical unity and graceful exposition. According to such accounts, 'religious ideas always become more refined (i.e. better) when they are shorn of mystery, miracle, and mysticism – when an active supernatural realm is replaced by abstractions concerning virtue' (2005: 7). That is to write the history of religion like the history of science, and indeed it brings back to mind Elias's stress on the significance of the 'detour via detachment' in the growth of scientific knowledge. Finke and Stark complain that 'one never encounters standards of theological progress or refinement based on how effectively a doctrine could stir the faithful or satisfy the heart'. Their major thesis is that 'religious organizations can thrive only to the extent that they can comfort souls and motivate sacrifice. . . . theological refinement is the kind of progress that results in organizational bankruptcy' (ibid.: 8).[21]

In fact, Finke and Stark's historical evidence seems to show that a sort of 'civilizing of religion' – including the curbing of the affects, and increasing constraints on the expression of fantasy – has been happening constantly, but the denominations in which it has been happening have declined in membership relative to others. The process has been equally constantly submerged by the rise of denominations that allowed their adherents to give vent more freely to the emotions and to emotionally satisfying fantasy.

Some explanations

What explanations can be offered for this continual replenishment of belief in 'an active supernatural realm' at the expense of 'abstractions concerning virtue'?

A 'utilitarian' explanation

First, is it possible that expressions of spiritual fervour are only a superficial sign of other more basic social benefits that are met by membership of a religious organization? Marvin Harris considered it more plausible that:

> [T]he deepest and most characteristic impulse of the Third Great Awakening is not the search for ultimate meaning but the search for solutions to America's unsolved economic and social problems. The human quest for ultimate meaning is a formidable force in history, but it rarely if ever exists apart from, above, beyond, or in opposition to the quest for solutions to practical problems. . . . At bottom, the Third Great Awakening is primarily a desperate response to the unsolved problems of malfunctioning consumerism, inflation, the upending of sex roles, break-up of the breadwinner family, alienation from work, oppressive government and corporate bureaucracies, feeling of isolation and loneliness, fear of crime, the bewilderment about the root causes of so many changes happening at once. (1987: 145, 165)[22]

Lest that still leave any room for a 'spiritual' interpretation, Harris spelled out that he saw the dominant motive force as utilitarian: executives prescribing encounter groups and sensitivity training 'to improve relationships among employees and to step up sales' (ibid.: 146). And, in his eyes, the born-again movement incorporates elements of a personal 'gospel of wealth', in which 'material success and physical well-being are signs of God's grace to the individual true believer' (ibid.: 157). That is not so very different from the historic mainstream of American Protestantism, except that Harris paid particular attention to the large fortunes accumulated as a sign of grace by leading tele-evangelists.

One problem with Harris's materialist interpretation is that the unsolved practical problems to which he refers are not unique – except perhaps in degree in certain localities – to the USA, so it does not easily explain why trends there are different from those in Europe. The same objection applies to the more popular and weaker version of the thesis, that the role of religion in the USA is less a matter of belief and more a matter of sociability. The argument is that for a population that is always on the move (see Jasper, 2000) and lacking rooted forms of social institution, religious organizations provide a socially sorted, open, available form of belonging, a kind of fraternity that assuages fears and anxieties. They provide networks, as well as moral reinforcement. Whatever people believe, and for whatever reason they believe it, there are rewards that accrue from congregating with believers.[23] Certainly, as Robert Putnam notes, 'Faith communities in which people worship together are arguably the single most important repository of social capital in America' (2000: 66). They support a wide range of social activities beyond mere worship; in some areas of the country, there are few other forms of social capital.[24] And in one historic instance, there is no doubt that religious organizations did help to solve one category of practical problems of everyday life – those arising from immigration, the scale of which, until very recent decades, distinguished the USA from most Western European countries.

As an extension to this utilitarian interpretation of American religiosity, it may be suggested that the rewards that accrue to believers include some that are typical of established–outsider relationships. Loud declarations of 'faith' are often accounts based on a 'minority of the best' – they are also proclamations of moral and social superiority. In particular, more powerful groups often use a conspicuous level of self-constraint as a mark of their social position. This is evident from the earliest years of settlement in New England. In other times and places in the course of American history, the discourse of some denominations has been linked to nativism and racism. On the other hand, other sects and denominations have served as vehicles for the emancipation of less powerful groups, helping them to eliminate a 'minority of the worst' from their we-feelings. Equally – as we shall note in a moment – religious groupings also frequently permit the relaxation of emotional self-constraints. Religious belief is protean in its social functions.

Immigration

Finke and Stark's data do not relate to a generation-to-generation process within a closed society of descendants of the people of colonial America. A very large part of America's population growth came from immigration, many of them from deeply religious peasant backgrounds. There is also some evidence that immigrants from fairly secular backgrounds – secularizing European Jews for instance – actually became *more* religious in America. The dangers and insecurities they faced in an alarming and unfamiliar society, together with the support that churches and synagogues provided in coping with them, would go a long way to explaining this. Immigration has obviously been a large factor in accounting for the size of the Catholic Church today – it is by far the largest single Christian denomination, even though all the numerous Protestant groups together still form an overall majority. The expansion of Catholicism in the USA was driven by the arrival first of Irish, then Italian, Polish and other European Catholic immigrants, and more recently Latin Americans. Nevertheless, as Finke and Stark emphasize, the Catholic Church could not take their adherence for granted, but had to compete with other churches, which it did among other things by developing a vast social infrastructure of schools and colleges.[25]

Some doubt remains, however, about whether an explanation of high rates of membership of religious organizations by the contribution it makes to solving practical problems of everyday life can equally explain the persistent drift towards the high-fervour forms of religion.

Fundamentalism

Especially notable is the strength in the USA of 'fundamentalism', a force that is particularly associated with the various evangelical and Pentecostalist churches that grew up in the course of the twentieth century, but is found in other churches (and other religions) too. The term 'fundamentalism' requires some explanation, particularly because at the beginning of the twenty-first century it is often preceded by the adjective 'Islamic'. Yet, as Karen Armstrong (2000: 141) has said, Islam was the last of the major world religions to develop a fundamentalist strain, from the 1960s and 1970s onwards. Before that came fundamentalist Judaism, fundamentalist Hinduism, fundamentalist Buddhism, fundamentalist Sikhism, 'and even fundamentalist Confucianism' (ibid.: 140). But first of all there was the fundamentalist Christianity that emerged in the USA early in the twentieth century.

Peter Berger (2006) has pointed out that contemporary America – but not just America – is in the grip of two apparently contradictory cultural currents: fundamentalism and relativism. Only apparently, because he sees them as closely interlinked, both being products of the same processes of 'modernization', and both precluding rational discussion. Relativism, in its various forms, is a reaction to social and cultural pluralization, while fundamentalisms in all faiths embody a rejection of modern society. As Armstrong argues:

> They reveal a deep disenchantment with the modern experiment [*sic*], which has not fulfilled all that it promised. They also express real fear. Every single fundamentalist movement that I have studied is convinced that the secular establishment is determined to wipe religion out. . . . Fundamentalists look back to a 'golden age' before the irruption of modernity for inspiration, but . . . all are intrinsically modern movements and could have appeared at no time other than our own. . . . Fundamentalists will often express their discontent with a modern development by overstressing those elements that militate against it. They are all – even in the United States – highly critical of democracy and secularism. Because the emancipation of women has been one of the hallmarks of modern culture, fundamentalists tend to emphasize the conventional, agrarian gender roles, putting women back into veils and into the home. The fundamentalist community can thus be seen as the shadow-side of modernity. (Armstrong, 2000: 141)

Fundamentalisms do not arise in immediate response to the onset of industrialization, urbanization and secularization, but only when these processes are quite far advanced. Armstrong contends that religious people typically try at first to reform their traditions and blend them with modern culture, but when that fails they resort to more extreme beliefs and methods. For that reason, 'with hindsight, we can see that it was only to be expected that fundamentalism should first make itself known in the United States, the showcase of modernity, and only appear in other parts of the world at a later date' (ibid.: 140–1). The rejection of modernity is made especially visible in the retention of late nineteenth-century costume by the Amish, notably in Pennsylvania, and some sects within the ultra-orthodox Jewish community, notably in New York. The celebrated Scopes trial in Tennessee in 1925 marked a stage in the rise of American Christian fundamentalism. That year, the state legislature had passed a law forbidding the teaching of any doctrine contradicting a literal reading of the biblical account of the Creation. A young schoolteacher was prosecuted for teaching the theory of evolution, and those responsible were so ridiculed in the press – as hillbillies and worse – that 'their theology became more reactionary and excessively literal, and they turned from the left to the extreme right of the political spectrum' (ibid.: 142). Over the coming decades, fundamentalist sentiments were reinforced by, among other things, the liberalization of sexuality from the 1960s onwards. By the end of the century, the political strength of fundamentalists was such that not even Vice-President Gore dared assent to the theory of evolution. (The Tennessee state law was repealed in 1967, but campaigns to enact similar legislation were launched in various states around the turn of the millennium.[26])

The 'supply side'

Yet fundamentalism, it might be argued, is more a part of the explanandum than the explanans for American religious trends: why has such an early rejection of modernity persisted and been renewed over so long a period? That question draws attention to the 'supply-side' theory of religious change advanced by Rodney Stark and his associates. Their argument is that too much attention has been paid to the 'demand side', to the preferences of religious consumers, with religious change being attributed to 'cultural realignments', 'crises of faith' or (as in the case of Armstrong's account of fundamentalism) 'flights from modernity' (Finke and Iannaccone, 1993). Yet survey research has failed to reveal significant shifts in underlying beliefs among the American population, or at any rate among the Christian majority of it (Greeley, 1989). Stark and his colleagues, in an argument directly derived from supply-side economic theory, set out to show that market forces govern the incentives and opportunities presented to religious producers. More specifically, they contend that, throughout American history, 'deregulation' in the religious marketplace – whether it be the disestablishment of state churches or the opening of the airwaves to evangelical preachers – has led to innovation and increased supply of religious products.

The 'supply-side' or 'rational choice' theory of religion poses many problems. It seems to rest upon a socio-biological assumption that all human beings have a constant, unchanging emotional 'need' for supernatural beliefs, that a market always exists in which 'producers' of more magical religious beliefs can sell their wares as older firms' more 'refined' products lose appeal. 'Secularization', write Finke and Stark (2005: 46), 'is a self-limiting process that leads not to irreligion, but to revival'. The founder of socio-biology, E. O. Wilson, has in fact written: 'Acceptance of the supernatural conveyed a great advantage throughout prehistory, when the brain was evolving' (1998: 262; see also Burkert, 1996).[27] Be that as it may, is it so essential today? All suppositions about an unchanging 'human nature' need to be treated with caution. Elias went so far as to speak paradoxically of humankind's 'natural changefulness as a social constant' (1978: 104–10). At a very general level, it is indeed possible to say that all human beings have a need for 'orientation' (De Swaan, 2001: 66–82); in contrast with other animals, even our nearest biological relatives the chimpanzees, very little of human behaviour is innately programmed. We humans have to *learn* a vast amount in order to live our lives together with others, and what has to be learned has varied widely between epochs and cultures. But to say that we have a basic need for orientation is very far from saying that we have a continuing need for orientation specifically in terms of an 'active supernatural realm'. There is some evidence that even in the USA a growing minority of people do not feel any such specific need. Between the two large-scale surveys of self-described religious identification in 1990 and 2001, the greatest increase in absolute as well as in percentage terms was among adults who did not subscribe to any. Their number had more than doubled from 14.3 million in 1990 to 29.4 million in 2001, representing a jump from 8 per cent of the total US population in 1990 to over 14 per cent in 2001 (Kosmin et al., 2002).[28]

Quest for excitement in religion

While there may be no universal need for specific belief in the supernatural, a good case can be made for the 'hotter' forms of religious participation meeting a need that has actually *increased* in contemporary 'advanced' societies. Elias and Dunning sought to show that people in contemporary 'advanced' societies have to be able to maintain a fairly even and stable control over their more spontaneous libidinal, affective and emotional impulses and over their fluctuating moods. Social survival and success depend on 'a reliable armour, not too strong and not too weak, of individual self-restraint' (1986: 41). This applies both to occupational roles and to many private relationships and activities. In these societies, there is relatively small scope for showing strong feelings, strong dislikes of people, let alone 'hot anger, wild hatred, or the urge to hit someone over the head'. 'People strongly agitated, in the grip of feelings they cannot control, are cases for hospital or prison. Conditions of high excitement are regarded as abnormal in a person, as a dangerous prelude to violence in a crowd' (ibid.). Opportunities for a more unreflected expression of excitement are, in many spheres of social life, severely limited (ibid.: 71). Yet containing strong feelings and maintaining an even control of drives throughout life are likely to lead to emotional staleness in most people (the extent varies between individuals). How is this problem to be handled socially?

In modern societies, there is an historically unparalleled variety of activities – concerts, opera, plays, films, dancing, paintings, card games, novels, detective stories, thrillers, sports of all kinds and, arguably, religion – that serve not simply to dissipate tensions generated in other spheres of life, but to provide opportunities for pleasurable excitement. The leisure sphere in modern societies, argue Elias and Dunning, provides an enclave within which *a controlled and enjoyable decontrolling of restraints on emotions is permitted* (ibid.: 65ff., 96). These activities generally allow the emotions to flow more freely in a specially constructed setting in some ways reminiscent of non-leisure reality. Sports are an especially clear illustration of this: they always consist of a controlled struggle in an imaginary setting (ibid.: 50–1), but it is striking that some forms of religion, especially the evangelical–Pentecostalist and fundamentalist types, also involve an emotionally satisfying mimetic struggle against the forces of darkness. Sometimes, it would appear, the degree of control over the decontrolling of emotional controls is not very effective, so religious mimetic struggle spills over into the political realm. (A comparison of super-patriotic Christian fundamentalists in America with super-patriotic football hooligans in Britain might prove illuminating.)

If excitement followed by catharsis is a common need enhanced by life in modern societies, why is it that a larger proportion of Americans than of Europeans seek this kind of mimetic release of the emotions in religious pastimes, and apparently have done so for a long time? The constraints of the marketplace, as Haskell (1985; see also pp. 110–13 above) suggests, may have made themselves felt in the growing commercial Republic at a exceptionally early stage, and the main emotional upsurges of religious feeling began before the full range of sports and cultural activities was available to most Americans. There nevertheless remains a broad question of why today Americans are more likely than Europeans to take their principal means of orientation from religious beliefs.

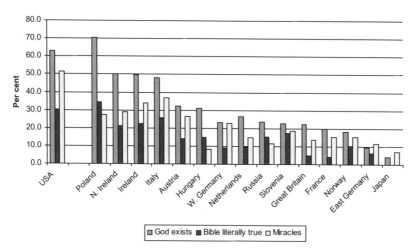

Figure 11.2: Religious beliefs in USA, selected European countries and Japan
Source: International Social Survey Programme (1998): <www.issp.org>.

Odd one out – Europe or the USA?

Comparisons between the USA and Western Europe are more than usually relevant in this case, because there is a debate about whether America or Europe is the exceptional case in the world today.[29] For decades it has been generally assumed among social scientists that secularization was one of the characteristic part-processes of 'modernization'. The assumption can be found in most of the classical sociologists – Marx, Durkheim, Tönnies and, most quintessentially, in Max Weber's account of rationalization and the 'disenchantment of the world'. But most of the classical sociologists were European, and drew their conclusions mainly from observing European society. They argued that 'individualism threatened the communal basis of religious belief and behaviour, while rationality removed many of the purposes of religion and rendered many of its beliefs implausible' (Bruce, 1996: 230). Why, then, should that not apply to the USA, so often characterized by its individualism?

Church membership and attendance has certainly been in steep decline in most countries of Europe for decades, even if the decline tended to set in later in Catholic regions than in Protestant. Many of those who do not attend a church may continue to have some general religious beliefs, and Grace Davie has often used the phrase 'believing without belonging' (1990, 1994). Even so, key aspects of belief also seem noticeably lower in most European countries than in the USA. Figure 11.2 displays findings from the 1991 survey of religious behaviour and beliefs in the International Social

Survey Programme (ISSP). In the ISSP survey, 62.8 per cent of Americans responded positively to the statement, 'I know that God exists and I have no doubts about it'; although this is much lower than the 95 per cent reported from the Gallup polls as believing in God (the wording of the ISSP question, excluding every scintilla of doubt, probably set the bar higher), it is still far higher than all but a few – mainly Catholic – countries in Europe. The same is true of belief in the literal truth of the Bible, miracles and (not shown in figure 11.2) heaven, hell and the devil.

Sociologists of religion have advanced diametrically opposite interpretations of these contrasts. Some have argued that religious pluralism weakens faith, because where multiple religious groups compete, each discredits the other. That was the prevalent view before the Stark group advanced their 'rational choice' or 'supply-side' thesis. Certainly it seems to have made some difference, for example, that in France a strong anti-clerical and secularist alternative has existed since the Revolution. And more recently, large non-Christian minorities have arrived in most Western European countries. In America, the largest such minority for more than a century has been the Jews, but, as already remarked, a sort of Judaeo-Christian synthesis has become embodied in American 'civil religion'. The more recent growth of Islamic, Hindu, Buddhist, Sikh and other non-Christian minorities could be connected with the apparently steep increase in the non-believing minority during the 1990s, but it is far too early for that to be more than speculation.[30]

In contrast, Stark and his associates contend that religious pluralism, and competition for market share between religious producers, promote religious participation and belief overall. They claim that 'religious economies can never be successfully monopolized, even when backed by the state' and that monopoly producers 'tend to be lazy' (Finke and Stark, 2005: 11). They point out that even in medieval Europe, where the Catholic Church enjoyed a monopoly, heresy was rife. (I am not sure that at the time of the Albigensian Crusade, when it deployed the most brutal means to enforce orthodoxy, the church could be described as lazy, even if the crusade was driven by the territorial ambitions of northern French noblemen.) As for today, 'close inspection of the religious situation in societies where "everyone" is a Roman Catholic reveals levels of religious participation that are astonishingly low compared with those in America' (ibid.: 10).

They make an exception for the cases of Ireland and Poland, where 'the church has also served as the primary vehicle for political resistance to external domination'. But they grossly exaggerate the power of legally established churches in recent times. The Church of England, for example, has had minimal monopoly power since at least the eighteenth century, and its establishment did little to impede the expansion of

Methodism, Nonconformism and Catholicism then and in the nineteenth century. Much the same could be said about the Scandinavian state churches. Religious monopolies may also form without a legal basis in establishment – the Catholic Church was never legally established in Ireland, for example, though it did for a time enjoy a verbal 'most favoured nation' status in the Republic's constitution. As Inglis (1998) has demonstrated, the Catholic Church established a hugely effective 'moral monopoly' in the Republic of Ireland. The bedrock of the moral monopoly was the church's ownership and control of most schools and hospitals and much other social infrastructure, and the foundation for that had been laid through its alliance with the *British* state until shortly before the country gained independence. Weekly mass attendance persisted at extremely high rates – over 90 per cent – until near the end of the twentieth century, and heterodoxy was not a significant problem, since the church actively encouraged magical beliefs.

The argument about the effect of religious monopolies can perhaps be turned on its head. Is it possible that American civil religion has served as a functional equivalent to an established national church? Certainly Stark and his colleagues are right to point to the very low level of monopolization and the vigorous competition at the micro-level of specific theological doctrines and styles of worship in America. But at the more macroscopic level of fundamental beliefs in the supernatural, how much competition is there in the USA? If people are forced from childhood to swear daily allegiance to 'one nation under God', some measure of cognitive dissonance as well as courage will be involved in announcing one's belief that there is no God and no supernatural world.

Conclusion

Ultimately, whether Western Europe or America is seen as the odd one out in the process of secularization depends on the comparators. On the face of it, it would seem obvious to compare the USA with the European countries and Japan, because those are the advanced industrial-scientific states that in other respects most resemble it. The case for America being 'normal' and Europe being exceptional rests on comparing it with nations of the global 'South' – or what used to be called the Third World, and before that the 'underdeveloped' world. For instance, global survey data (Pew Global Attitudes Project, 2003: 115–16) show that the proportion of Americans (58 per cent) in whose view it is necessary to believe in God in order to be moral – in effect a statement that moral behaviour depends upon external constraint, the fear of punishment, rather than self-constraint – is closer to that found in developing countries than in the rest of the industrialized world.

In the light of the connection Elias draws between fears, dangers and the balance between emotional involvement and detachment, it is worth asking whether the USA is in any respect a more fearful and dangerous place than Western Europe. In certain ways, the *real* level of danger is higher in America. Although the risks are geographically and socially unequally distributed, the probability of being murdered, encountering someone carrying a gun or being unable to afford necessary medicine or surgery are examples of this higher level of danger. There is also a matter of the *perceived* level of danger, which may be greater or less than the statistically computed factual measures of danger. The terrorist raids on New York and Washington on 11 September 2001 killed a relatively small number of people compared with massacres and civil wars in recent years elsewhere in the world, but they undoubtedly, and with good cause, raised the level of perceived danger and of fear among Americans in general.

But setting aside a recent world-historical event like '9/11', it has been argued that there has grown up in America in recent decades a 'culture of fear' (Glassner, 1999), in the most literal sense of fear being cultivated. Glassner examines the fears ranging from violent crime and school massacres through paedophiles to epidemic disease and road rage – all the objects of moral panics among the public – and finds that in most cases the threat presented is greatly exaggerated. People feel the fear on the basis of media reports rather than their own direct experience. Glassner locates the source of these fears in the media, in businesses and among politicians who stand to gain by first raising and then exploiting popular fears. Glassner argues that this culture of fear is really an oblique expression of concern about problems such as poverty, poor schools, gun ownership and inadequate health insurance that are widely recognized but which no decisive action has been taken to solve (1999: 209). That also points to a connection between fears of this type and a sense of the low possibility of control over natural and social forces, including low confidence in other people's (and possibly one's own) capacity for self-control. Elias mentioned how advances in technological control could result in increased levels of fear by outstripping the potential control over social forces. The religiously charged political debates over bio-medical research, genetic engineering, prolonging the life of the brain-dead, fertility treatment and abortion are relevant instances of science becoming entangled with 'culture wars'.

There remains the possibility that the relatively high level of emotional release and fantasy permitted in substantial parts of the American religious marketplace is something as innocuous as an informalization process (see pp. 75–80 above) marked by increasing varieties. Finke and

Stark, after all, attribute the buoyancy of the market to religious deregulation. But processes of informalization, according to both Elias and Wouters, characteristically involve a *highly controlled* decontrolling of emotional controls, the decontrolling being dependent upon the development of actually *more* demanding public standards of habitual self-control. Whether that applies in the case of American religiosity is a topic for further research.

One reasonably certain conclusion can, however, be drawn from the discussion that has unfolded in this chapter. Trends in religious affect, belief and behaviour cannot be understood by looking at religion as if it were a self-contained institutional and discursive field of its own. If, the role of civil religion notwithstanding, there is a low degree of monopolization of the means of orientation in the field of religion, that is only part of a broader picture of relatively weak authoritative model-setting centres in American society as a whole.

12

America and Humanity as a Whole

> How strange these people are
> How strange I am
> How strange we are
>   Norbert Elias (1987: 59)

Writing in the 1960s, the historian David Potter noted the 'curious fate' of the United States, to exert immense influence in the modern world 'without itself quite understanding the nature of this influence':

> In the twentieth century the United States developed what was perhaps the first mass society, but the American cult of equality and individualism prevented Americans from analysing their mass society in realistic terms. Often they treated it as if it were simply an infinite aggregation of Main Streets in Zenith, Ohio. (1968: 136)

Major trends, both bad and good, had often first become evident in America. Potter mentioned that in its earliest years the United States had achieved the first democratic political revolution;[1] that later it had witnessed episodes of extreme industrial conflict; that it had led the world in technological changes, with profound social consequences; and that it had in more recent years experienced a sweeping transformation in sexual behaviour. Yet none of these had been fully incorporated into the way Americans understood themselves. American society – white society – at the time of Independence was already so relatively egalitarian that the revolution seemed conservative in comparison with the French and other subsequent revolutions. Industrial conflict in the nineteenth and twentieth centuries was not interpreted in Marxist terms. And changes in sexuality had 'not been incorporated into the system of values by which

[America] explains itself'. Overall, while the USA 'had often been a step ahead in the process of social change, it has often been a step behind in its awareness of the meaning of new developments' (ibid.: 135–6). Potter attributed these misperceptions to the lingering effects of Americans' preconceptions about the frontier, the agrarian basis of 'democracy', a 'classless' society and, above all, 'individualism'. These had all helped to make developments seem to Americans to be distinctively American when they were actually widespread across the world.

To achieve a balanced view of what is distinctively American and what is not necessitates some comparative perception. I would contend that Elias's theory of civilizing processes, which has provided the guiding thread running through this book and the main framework for comparing traits of American and Western European society, has proved its usefulness.

As chapters 3–5 showed, the broad trend of the development of manners and habitus in the USA was very similar to that which Elias observed between the late Middle Ages and the nineteenth century in Western Europe, and later studies (notably by Cas Wouters) suggest that in the twentieth century the pattern was one of further convergence. Having in the first place inherited most of its social conventions from its European parent society, America has in some respects been ahead of Europe, notably (as Tocqueville saw in the 1830s) in the avoidance of overt expressions of social superiority and inferiority. That is to say, the USA tended to lead Europe in the avoidance of both excessive deference and most forms of 'superiorism' – a word coined by Wouters to embrace the *expression* of feelings of superiority on all grounds, from wealth and social status to sex and ethnicity. On both sides of the Atlantic, changes in social standards were driven by similar, though not identical, processes. In America, it is true, there was no two-front stratum of courtiers of the kind studied by Elias in *The Court Society*, although there were quasi-aristocratic formations in certain regions and periods. From an early stage, markets rather than courts were the crucial institution leaving their stamp on Americans' habitus, setting standards and enforcing conformity. Yet, because America has experienced several centuries of barely interrupted rapid economic and demographic growth, what Elias called 'pressure from below' has continually made itself felt in the struggle to achieve and retain 'respectability'. Through a growing social constraint to self-constraint, the same advance in the thresholds of shame and repugnance is evident in American as in Europe. One example in which America may have been in advance of Europe by the late nineteenth century is in standards of cleanliness as a badge of social respectability. The advancing threshold of repugnance is also associated with the hiding of troublesome practices behind the scenes of social – and mental – life: dirt, nakedness, cruelty, suffering, violence. America is clearly very much 'civilized' in this respect.

In broad terms, as was demonstrated in chapter 6, the long-term trends in the incidence of violence in the USA are similar to those in Western Europe and other 'European countries overseas' like Australia, New Zealand and Canada. What is distinctive about the USA is not the *trend* but the absolute *rates* of certain kinds of violence, which are much higher per capita than in comparable countries. From the standpoint of the theory of civilizing processes, it is most interesting that the difference appears to lie in the category of affective or impulsive homicides rather than in relation to instrumental violence, in the course of robbery for example. This rather suggests that, in those parts of American society that chiefly account for these higher rates, the 'muting of drives' (Elias, 2000: 397–414) has been less effective than in equivalent parts of Europe. Yet that too can be explained from within Elias's theory: it appears to derive from the relative weakness of the state monopoly of the means of violence, either now or in the past, especially in the South and West, and in particular to be related to relatively high levels of danger and consequent fears that inhibit the social constraint towards self-constraint.

Although the *internal* pacification of American society was rather taken for granted by some of the Founding Fathers (notably Jefferson) as something already achieved, inherited from its European antecedents, and firmly incorporated into American habitus, the European process of the 'courtization of warriors' (Elias, 2000: 387–97) does have its counterparts in American history: the taming of the Southern planters, the process of westward expansion. They have seemed to cast a shadow into present-day America, perhaps because of their relative recency.

Yet, again from within Elias's thinking, the point can be made that recency has little to do with it, because however slowly a civilizing process may advance, decivilizing processes can set in very rapidly when conducive circumstances arise: to quote Elias's remark again, if danger became as incalculable as it once was, 'corresponding fears would soon burst the limits set to them today' and 'the armour of civilized conduct would crumble rapidly' (2000: 532). In Europe, the traumatic episode of the destabilization of German society after the First World War and its consequences in the Second World War and the Holocaust have been much analysed; and decivilizing processes were seen even more recently in the break-up of Yugoslavia (Zwaan, 2001). In America, the connection between rising danger and rising fears has been seen in the aftermath of the attacks on New York and Washington in 2001, known as '9/11'.

An important contribution to understanding these processes, and a significant extension to Elias's ideas, is Thomas Scheff's (1994) concept of 'shame–rage spirals' (or 'shame–rage feeling traps'). Fear is not the only element in the emotional response to threats and rising danger; humiliation plays a great part too. According to Scheff, in situations ranging in scale from the face-to-face to the international, anger is a characteristic response to shame, but then anger triggers further feelings of shame, and so on in an upwards spiral. Scheff has applied his theory to the origins of both world wars (ibid.: 75–124), and it appears to fit the sequence of events after 9/11 too. The American government was led to resort to the routine use of torture, to abrogate the Geneva conventions and the law of habeas corpus, and under the cloak of being 'at war' to embark on a programme of domestic surveillance and an expansion of the powers of central government that is greatly at odds with what is generally perceived to be American tradition.

One of Elias's major theses is that people's habitus typically bears the marks of their country's history and government, of the state under which they live. The processes of state-formation that have unfolded in America since the beginnings of European settlement were, as shown in chapters 7–9, not so radically different from those that took place in Western Europe. The USA was not exclusively an emanation of the human spirit or an expression of civilized 'values' from the American Enlightenment. It was as much the product of wars and violence as were the states of Europe. And, at least as much as in Europe, that side of the national story is to some extent hidden behind the scenes of collective memory. In North America, too, there took place an elimination contest, a struggle for supremacy that was initially driven exogenously by rivalries among European powers, but soon came to be driven more by an inexorable contest for territory that was largely endogenous to the American continent.

The long-term experience that has left its mark on Americans' habitus is of the steady tilting of balances of power in their favour – starting with the power ratio between the white settlers and the indigenous population, and continuing up to its domination of many other countries of the world at the beginning of the twenty-first century. Its power advantage came into play even when it gained territory not by military conquest but by apparently peaceful means, including diplomacy and purchase. This long-term tilting of power ratios in the United States' favour is also associated with changes in another balance. The planned and intentional elements in its state-formation processes gradually gained ground at the expense of the unplanned and unintended: as its power advantage increased, the USA needed less to react to events determined by others, and could more actively shape the world to its advantage. Overall, however, large elements of a compelling process beyond anyone's control remain: the USA still seeks to extend its control over certain parts of the world from fear that, if it does not, someone else will do so to its disadvantage. More will be said about the growth of America's external empire in a moment.

Thus far, many parts of Elias's theory of civilizing processes appear to fit quite well the American case. However, at several points in the book (particularly in chapters 5 and 10), difficulties have arisen in connection with Elias's idea that lengthening chains of interdependence are associated with functional democratization (relatively more equal power ratios between links in the chains), which in turn are associated with a widening of the circle of mutual identification between people. At least in the long term, the latter part of the proposition is probably valid, even though in the short term the immediate result is often the intensification of conflict in 'integration struggles'. The first part of the proposition looks more questionable: longer chains of interdependence seem often to lead to growing inequalities and power imbalances, and to a narrowing of the circle of human sympathy. In the rest of this chapter, I shall therefore adapt some of the overall themes that Elias raised in the concluding section of *The Civilizing Process*² to problems that have arisen in this study of American society: the trend towards diminishing contrasts and increasing varieties; the problem of American 'individualism'; market fundamentalism and diminishing foresight; functional de-democratization within America and between America and the rest of the world; and the American empire.

'American social character': diminishing contrasts, increasing varieties

From Crèvecœur and Tocqueville to the present day, both Americans and non-Americans have attempted to capture the 'essence' of American social character. Not all of the most disparaging views of American character have been expressed by foreigners. The patrician diplomat George Kennan, a twentieth-century Midwestern descendant of the old New England *Bildungsbürgertum*, described the typical Californian (and by implication Americans in general) in these terms: 'childlike in many respects: fun-loving, quick to laughter and enthusiasm, unanalytical, unintellectual, outwardly expansive, preoccupied with physical beauty and prowess, given to sudden and unthinking seizures of aggressiveness, driven constantly to protect his status in the group by eager conformism – yet not unhappy' (1972: 81). That amusing caricature is worth quoting if only because Kennan contrived to make his Californians reminiscent in certain respects of the emotionally volatile temperament of medieval Europeans as described by Elias, Huizinga and others.

More rigorous attempts by social scientists to capture 'national character' have run into numerous difficulties. Theorists in the middle of the twentieth century expended enormous intellectual energy in drawing conceptual distinctions between the 'cultural', 'social' and 'personality' traits that groups of people have in common. In the end, though, when it comes to measuring cultural 'values', social habitus or modal personality, researchers generally seem to be looking at the same thing from marginally different points of view. Kluckhohn and Murray (1948: 35) made a useful point when they remarked that every person is in certain respects (a) like all other people, (b) like some other people and (c) like no other person. Studies of groups of people, up to and including whole nations, are concerned with (b). At that level, Goudsblom (2002) has suggested, the key element in 'national character' is how in a country members of different social classes deal with each other. By that criterion, somewhat contradictory inferences could be drawn from Americans' everyday courtesy on the one hand, and from mass incarceration on the other.

The problem with attempting to pontificate about the common characteristics of Americans in general is the sheer diversity to be found in so vast a country. In attempting to compare Americans in general with the peoples of other countries, one needs to bear in mind both (metaphorically) the mean and standard deviation. Diversity is a matter of perspective. Some commentators have always been impressed by the relative homogeneity of American society. Lord Bryce, for instance, wrote that within Britain, France, Germany, Italy or Spain there were 'more varieties between individuals' than among Americans from any part of the USA (1891: II, 691). Many forces tending still further to reduce diversity gained in strength during the twentieth century: 'instant nationwide communications, constant mobility, a homogeneous popular culture, and the standardization inherent in mass production and a technological culture have steadily reduced the margins of idiosyncratic behaviour in the United States' (Luedtke, 1992: 7). (But not only in the USA: also in most other developed countries.)

Conformity was a theme common to several prominent commentators in the latter half of the twentieth century. In *The Lonely Crowd* (1961), David Riesman and his collaborators spoke of a transition in the typical mode of the steering of behaviour from 'inner-directedness' to 'other-directedness' (see pp. 106–7 above). 'Inner-directed' people had been predominant in the nineteenth century; their behaviour had been steered by social norms and values acquired from their parents, and in adulthood had been marked by conformity to the extent that it was compatible with the values internalized and with earning other people's esteem. 'Other-directed' people, in contrast, had come to be steered mainly by the peer-group of their own generation, were motivated by a wish to be liked, and responded flexibly to changing group tastes and fashions. There had been a shift from cultural heroes of industry to heroes of consumption. Similarly, in *The Organization Man* (1956), William H. Whyte depicted the decline of the ethic of work, thrift and deferred gratification in favour of consumption and conformity in large-scale organizations. And David Potter, in *People of Plenty* (1954), picked out abundance as the decisive influence, through child-rearing onwards, on American character. A few decades later, other-directed Americans resurfaced in the writings of Christopher Lasch, notably *The Culture of Narcissism* (1979), as narcissistic self-gratifiers dependent on others for recognition and approval. Lasch, reflecting on the 'me generation' of the 1960s and 1970s, took a notably more negative view than his precursors in the 1950s, seeing in the later kind of conformism a deeper selfishness and manipulativeness representing a continuation of a long-term trend of egoistic individualism under capitalism.

On the other hand, many processes promoted diversity. Immigration in particular has constantly replenished the sources of diversity in American society through most of its history. Yet even the massive wave of immigration in the second half of the nineteenth century and the first decade of the twentieth century was not sufficient to challenge the predominantly white, Northern European and Protestant character of the country: around 1900, about three-quarters of American citizens still fitted into that category. In the middle years of the twentieth century, the 'Yankee ethos' was still sufficiently strong that scholars such as Riesman could write about a general American social character that still strongly bore its marks. And Louis Hartz could still depict the USA as a European 'fragment society', much as Herbert Baxter Adams and the Johns Hopkins school's 'germ theory' had in the 1880s. Yet over recent decades the scale of changes in American society has been so great that Alan Wolfe (1991: 3–4) for one has contended not just that the Yankee ethos is no longer dominant, but that in important ways the USA is no longer a 'European' country. If that is the case, it is something that other commentators find hard to accept: Samuel P. Huntington (2004) advocated a return to not merely 'European' but 'Anglo-Protestant' as the core of American identity.

One leitmotif of this book is that the USA never really had a single dominant model-setting 'good society' of the kind that was found in several Western European countries. Instead it had several competing social formations, differing in geographical location as well as social character. This did not mean that social emulation played no part in American social history, but that in America, earlier and more clearly than in Europe, an overall trend is evident towards what Elias called 'diminishing contrasts, increasing varieties' (2000: 382–7). The complexity of competition between elites and aspirant elites increased over time; in Dahl's phrase, there was a trend (at least in the broad middle ranges of power) 'from cumulative to dispersed inequalities' (1961: 85–6). As successive outsider groups challenged older established groups, they themselves became established and resisted for a time the challenge of the next waves of rising outsiders. In such a situation, standards spread both downwards and upwards to form new varieties of civilized conduct. 'The contrasts in conduct between the upper and lower groups are reduced . . . ; the varieties or nuances of civilized conduct are increased' (Elias, 2000: 386). That people at every level of society, including the highest social ranks, are expected to *work* for their living is one instance of an important aspect of this process becoming firmly established sooner in America than in Europe.

In his study of the integration of American culture in the eighteenth and nineteenth centuries, Peter Dobkin Hall (1982: 3) captured both facets of this process. Mass culture, he said, was paradoxical. On the one hand it involved the equalization and standardization of opportunities and styles of life, and in a modern mass culture people were presented with a nearly incalculable range of choices. On the other hand, that went along with the existence of elites who defined and limited the range of choices by gauging and shaping public desires and expectations. The importance of celebrities in mass culture is one facet of this. Something more analogous to a competitive market than to the feudal remnant of a well-defined status hierarchy has shaped the cultural traits of Americans. Yet, as emphasized in chapter 5, markets are structures of power in which, generally, not everyone is equal. The individualistic image of everyone having a free and unconstrained choice of goods, information and opinions needs some qualification. There are always many interdependent people – usually unequal in their mutual dependence – so that the choices made by some people always to a greater or lesser extent limit and constrain the choices available to others. The power of the great corporate elites, including those who control the mass media, appears to be growing rather than shrinking. Furthermore, in the late 1930s in his discussion of 'diminishing contrasts, increasing varieties', Elias considered the West as a kind of world upper class whose standards were spreading to, as well as being influenced by, the then colonial countries of the world. At the beginning of the twenty-first century, the power of the USA is such that it is not unreasonable to consider it as fulfilling the functions of a sort of upper class even in the West, as well as throughout the world.

The problem of the American *homo clausus*: the we–I balance

America, said Alexis de Tocqueville in 1840, was one country in the world where the precepts of Descartes were least studied and most followed. In their common assumptions Americans sought 'to evade the bondage of system and habit, of family maxims, class opinions, and, in some degree, of national prejudices; to accept tradition only as a means of information, and . . . to seek the reason of things for oneself, and in oneself alone' (1961 [1835–40]: II, 1–2). In short, 'each American appeals to the individual exercise of his own understanding alone'. Tocqueville employed the concept of 'individualism' for the purpose of characterizing the Americans. Since then, it has acquired many nuances of meaning (Lukes, 1973; Curry and Goodheart, 1991), but this statement of Tocqueville's elegantly captures an American proneness to what Elias calls the *homo clausus* conception of human beings – a mode of self-experience as a 'closed person', as a single isolated individual separate from other individuals. But that is only one side of the coin, for Tocqueville (1961: II, 268) also noted that Americans tended to be exceptionally sensitive to criticism of their country by outsiders. That appears to be as true early in the twenty-first century as it was in the 1830s, and it is symptomatic of what Elias, again, would call their strong 'we-feelings'. How can these superficially contrary observations be reconciled? Through the application, I would suggest, of yet another of Elias's concepts, the 'we–I balance' (1991: 155–237).

The term 'individual', just like 'civilization', has acquired a whole complex of evaluative connotations. Today, Elias points out, 'the primary function of the term "individual" is to express the idea that every human being in the world is or should be an autonomous entity, and at the same time that each human being is in certain respects different from all others' (ibid.: 156). These evaluations indeed appear to have arisen as part of a civilizing process; and if America has for so long been characterized by its dominant 'individualism', that is not because it is unique but because this may be one more instance of a trait where America came to be somewhat in advance of Europe. Its roots, however, antedate the European settlement of America.

In its most intellectualized form, the *homo clausus* conception is central to the Western tradition of philosophical epistemology. It is a conception of the person as the 'subject' of knowledge: a single, adult, thinking mind inside a sealed container, from which each one looks out and struggles to fish for knowledge of the 'objects' (including other minds) outside in the 'external world'. This can be found as far back as Plato's image of the prisoners in a cave, watching the shadows cast upon the wall by the fire behind them. It came to the fore in early modern Europe in Descartes' proposition *cogito ergo sum*, and then runs like a thread through Berkeley and Kant right up to twentieth-century phenomenology and existentialism (Elias, 1991: 196–201). Elias contended that this Cartesian philosophical tradition was merely an academic manifestation of a much more fundamental and widespread change in the way that more and more people were coming to experience themselves. It was a process of individualization associated with the intensifying social constraint

towards self-constraint, starting among elites – as has been typical of civilizing processes up to now – but gradually spreading to all ranks of
society. 'Individualization' can only be realistically conceptualized as a
tilting of the we–I balance, for, as Elias argues, there can be no 'I-identity'
without a 'we-identity'; 'I' makes sense only if we can also say 'we', 'you',
'they'. The point is even evident in people's names: in almost every society
there are both forenames, distinctive and possibly unique to a particular
person, and surnames that indicate to which family or tribe a person
belongs (ibid.: 184). The philosophers gave expression to a 'We-less I'
(ibid.: 201) that is impossible; what people actually experience are shifts
in the we–I balance: 'Only the weighting of the I–We balance, the pattern
of the I–we relation are variable' (ibid.: 184). The emergence of the self-
disciplined, 'individualistic' Protestant capitalists described by Max
Weber was just one part-process within the more general social process.

The notion of a we–I balance helps to make sense of a number of familiar observations, such as the problems of 'particularism' and 'corruption'
in less developed societies.[3] At earlier stages of social development, the
balance leaned heavily to the 'we' pole. Individuals were far more tightly
bound for life to the groups into which they were born – to their kinship
group, their tribe, or their local community – for the very good reason
that these were their 'survival groups', the groups to which they could
turn for help and protection in time of need. People felt obligations to
their kith and kin that to our eyes may appear a denial of self. And when
those loyalties survive into the 'modern' administration of a new state, we
call it 'corruption'.

The processes of state-formation, Elias suggests, have a peculiar effect
on the prevailing we–I balance. States represent a more complex and comprehensive form of survival unit than, for example, tribes; but for its citizens a state has a dual function that may seem self-contradictory:

> On the one hand it irons out the differences between people. In the state
> registers and offices, the individual is largely divested of his or her distinc-
> tive personality. The individual is a name with a number, a taxpayer or . . .
> a person seeking help and protection, which the state authorities can grant
> or refuse. But although the state apparatus in this way embeds the individ-
> ual in a network of rules which is by and large the same for all citizens, the
> modern state does not relate to people as sisters or uncles, as members of a
> family group or one of the other pre-state forms of integration, but to
> people as individuals. . . . [T]he process of state-formation makes its own
> contribution to a new advance of mass individualization. (Ibid.: 180–1)

Yet the extent and pattern of this individualization vary according to the
structure of the state, and 'particularly the distribution of power
between government and governed, state apparatus and citizens'. Under

dictatorships, a state's external control heavily outweighs the self-control of individuals, and personal initiative may be punished rather than rewarded; people become attuned to external control, and may in the short term become disorientated if it is removed (ibid.: 181). It follows that there can rarely be a quick fix, in which an overthrown dictatorship is immediately replaced by a smoothly functioning democracy.[4]

The notion of the we–I balance also puts into perspective certain features of American society. There, in accordance with a much more reciprocal control between rulers and ruled, individual initiative is greatly valued. Yet to see ever-greater 'individualism' as a symptom of some inevitable law of historical 'progress' is wrong; that minority of Americans who still consider that they have the right and duty to protect their own property and family, unfettered by the forces of the state, can be seen not as the leading edge of progress but as a throwback to an earlier stage of state-formation. At the same time, it is also clear why – much more widely spread than that minority view – there is also a strong sense of 'patriotism' or American nationalism; in historical perspective, it appears probable that humans have generally felt the greatest emotional identification, had the most emotionally charged we-images, in relation to whatever social entity serves for the time being as their survival unit. For the last century or two, in the more 'advanced' societies, that has in general been a nation-state. The emotional focus of we-identities can narrow when danger levels rise – as in civil wars (Mennell, 1994), or if one's country is invaded – as well as widen. But as the source of the principal dangers facing humanity as a whole shifts to the planetary level, nation-states are probably becoming too small to function as effective survival units.

Finally, even if 'individualism' as a philosophical idea (not the word itself) can be found in John Locke, whose writings are known to have influenced the framing of the American polity, it is clear that it has not been an eternal and unchanging component of everyday American habitus. The character of this practical individualism has undergone change. In the days of the predominantly agrarian republic, Americans may have been individualistic by comparison with European villagers, but not by today's standards. Crèvecœur, speaking about the relatively isolated farmer of the late eighteenth century, writes:

> Thus this man devoid of society learns more than ever to centre every idea within that of his own welfare. To him, all that appears good, just, equitable has a necessary relation to himself and his family. He has been so long alone that he almost forgot the rest of mankind, except it is [sic] when he carries his crops on the snow to some distant market. (1981 [1782]: 260)

But this is almost certainly misleading. Although well into the nineteenth century American farm people 'were attached to few strings pulled from long distances by faceless bureaucrats', they were 'enmeshed in a web of family and community relationships in which subordination to the wishes of the group, rather than spirited individualism, was the essential rule' (Collier, 1991: 22).[5] As Wilkinson (1984: 71) notes, in human groups small and large, individuals' impulses towards tough assertiveness always stimulate controlling behaviour on the part of other members of the group. Richard Hofstadter (1969: 141–6) contended, furthermore, that in the course of American history the pendulum has repeatedly swung between creative individualism and group solidarity, the one and then the other alternating in dominance.

In short, while the ideal of self-reliance was strong, Tocqueville was right to observe that conditions of social equality were conducive to conformity, because, in Potter's words, 'it places the stigma of arrogance upon any man who ventures to set his personal judgement against the judgement of a majority of his equals' (1963: 145). That has acted as a check on excessive emphasis on the rights of individuals, which, as Potter observed, 'essentially implies a component of privatism which would sacrifice the interests of the group to the interests of a limited number of its members; and this implication is not acceptable in the long run to a democratic society' (ibid.: 151). The snag is that the check is dependent on conditions of relative equality, of relatively evenly balanced power ratios within a society. Can it operate as effectively in a society in which, as observed in chapter 10, inequality is increasing? Does social, economic and political inequality slacken the reins on the pursuit of private self-interest, enabling some people simply to ignore the wider consequences of their actions?

Market fundamentalism and diminishing foresight

A key component of a civilizing process, according to Elias, is the spreading social pressure on people habitually to exercise foresight. Corresponding to the integration of more and more people into an ever more widespread worldwide network of interdependence is 'the necessity for an attunement of human conduct over wider areas and over longer chains of action than ever before', with commensurate standards of self-constraint (2000: 379). In order to play their part at their own node in a nexus of interdependences, individual people have acquired the social skills to anticipate all sorts of dangers, from breaches of social codes that cause embarrassment, through the dangers of economic risk, all the way to dangers to life and limb. Here, Elias seems to be on firm ground. Every organization in the modern world appears to be enslaved to a 'strategic plan', complete with 'mission statements' and 'vision statements' which seek to picture the organization and its members in the future perfect tense, as (it is hoped) they will have become at some point in the future.[6]

The effective exercise of foresight involves trying to anticipate the unanticipated, foresee the unforeseen – to deal with the side effects or unintended consequences of intended actions.

In the modern world, however, the key concept is not the sociologists' idea of *unintended consequences*, but rather the economists' notion of *externalities*. The two are closely related, but it is externalities that give the keener critical edge, because (although economists would not put it in this way) the concept focuses attention on the distribution of power chances in a social figuration. Externalities are side effects, in the sense that they arise from activities that cause costs or benefits to people other than the person or group who initiates those activities. They give rise to a discrepancy between social and private net costs. Externalities may or may not be foreseen. If foreseen, they may or may not be considered desirable by the decision-maker. The critical point is that externalities can, by definition, be ignored by those whose activities cause them. That is to say, plans and strategies may have side effects that impose costs on other people or a wider community – indeed the world in general – but they are not costs that have to be met by those who make the plans and carry them out.

A decision to ignore external costs (using the term in a broad, not narrowly economic, sense) that are not hidden, and of which those responsible for causing them are fully aware, soon raises questions of morality. Tom Lehrer captured the problem in his song about the famous rocket scientist:

> Once the rockets are up,
> who cares where they come down?
> That's not my department,
> says Werner von Braun

Here our concern is less with moralizing than with explaining, and if the 'not my department' syndrome appears to be prevalent in a world supposedly subject to increasing foresight, it needs to be explained. Part of an explanation is that it has to a considerable extent been legitimated by economic theorists. The roots of the idea that the pursuit of self-interest will inevitably lead to the greatest happiness of the greatest number can be traced back to the classical economists. Adam Smith, Jeremy Bentham and David Ricardo, however, usually expressed themselves with more caution than do today's advocates of unregulated capitalism; they characteristically spoke, for instance, of *enlightened* self-interest – meaning that it was balanced by a regard for others' interests and needs. In the absence of such a moderating influence, and if it were believed that the 'laws' of supply and demand automatically transmuted each individual's pursuit of narrow self-interest into the common good, then as Haskell (1985: 549; see p. 111 above) pointed out, no one need be concerned with the 'public' interest and the very possibility of moral obligation would be put in doubt. Or, as Tocqueville put it in *L'Ancien Régime*, 'people are far too much disposed to become self-seekers, practising a narrow individualism and caring nothing for the public good' (1955 [1856]: xiii). Today, what the Nobel prize-winning economist Joseph Stiglitz (2002) calls *market fundamentalism* tends to absolve individuals, organizations and even governments from wider ethical considerations regarding the consequences of their actions. Like Werner von Braun, they need not concern themselves with where the rockets come down, because their faith is that free and untrammelled ('undistorted') markets will always guarantee that the rockets land on target. 'Faith' is the apposite word here, for in some circles of American politics, market fundamentalism and religious fundamentalism have become symbiotic. Adam Smith's 'hidden hand' of the market merges with the hand of God: the market, like God, will provide. 'Market failure' becomes an exceptional case, something requiring specialist study.

What determines whether, in practice, recognized externalities can be ignored? (Or, more exactly: why can externalities, even though recognized, still remain externalities?) To reiterate a point stressed in chapter 5, markets are, among other things, structures of power. A faith in their always benevolent functioning would be a little easier to sustain if America (and the world at large) really were, in Potter's words, 'an infinite aggregation of Main Streets in Zenith, Ohio'. An isolated small-town community comprising only small traders might be able to use its moral suasion to impel people to take account of the externalities that their activities created for the community.

That kind of local corrective measure, redolent of town meetings and consensus among equal enfranchised citizens, is less likely in the modern economy dominated by vast corporations. A classic study, *The Un-Politics of Air Pollution* by Matthew Crenson (1971), provides just one illustration of how a problem may not even find its way onto a city's political agenda when the culprit is US Steel and the major employer in the town. (And that was in America itself, not in some poor but oil-rich overseas country.) Regulation then becomes possible only at higher levels of integration. That might be the state rather than federal level; but even states, like towns, may be frightened that they will drive away business and employment to their competitors. National governments may be prepared to legislate for taxation measures that enshrine, for instance, the 'polluter pays' principle. In the USA, that would raise questions about whether the federal government had that constitutional power. In other countries, even national governments may find themselves confronting corporations more powerful than themselves, and face the same fear of trade and jobs moving to other, less scrupulous, countries.

As Stiglitz (2002) shows, the self-regulating market is, and always was, a myth. Stiglitz's challenge to the neo-liberal orthodoxy of the last quarter of the twentieth century is less surprising than it seems, because he is reviving what economists used to know perfectly well: that markets do not, and never did, cope very effectively either with externalities or with uncertainty and with the long term. For all the rhetoric about missions and visions and strategic plans, modern corporations are often myopic: market pressures often ensure that the need to maximize 'shareholder value' in the short term obliterates longer-term perspectives. Markets do not work all on their own; there *is* no hidden hand. Adam Smith himself was well aware of the framework of social and political institutions necessary for markets to function well. In modern economies, the economic footprint of government – taxation, transfer payments, employment, contracts – is such that there is no conceivable way in which its functions can be 'neutral'. A decision by a government *not* to intervene in a market – in order to regulate it, to enforce charging for externalities, or to ensure social justice – amounts just as much to an intervention as a decision *to* intervene.

Karl Polanyi's classic study of the industrialization phase of world development, *The Great Transformation* (1944), puts contemporary problems in historical perspective. Its major thesis is that economies are always *embedded* in a society, and that it is impossible to 'disembed' them from broader social structures and pretend that they function quite separately as self-regulating machines. His discussion of the world's governments' adherence to the Gold Standard in the late nineteenth and early twentieth centuries is especially relevant to the early twenty-first. What they saw as a self-regulating mechanism was, in effect, a very rigorous form of constraint imposed by governments and central bankers on each other and on themselves. The resulting economic straitjacket caused wild fluctuations in the trade cycle and widespread suffering on the part of the poorest strata in industrial societies. Moreover, contended Polanyi, it was also one of the forces driving the acquisition of colonial empires by those industrial countries: it made it in their interest to establish long-term control over sources of raw materials and over overseas markets for their manufactured products.

Polanyi's book has attracted renewed attention in recent years because today's revived faith in free-market doctrines has similarly brought wealth for some at the cost of greater insecurity for large numbers of the less well off in the USA and other old industrial countries. Their implementation worldwide by the World Bank and the International Monetary Fund –

largely under American domination, and especially since the collapse of the Soviet bloc – has resulted in extreme instability in ordinary people's standards of living in many other countries. The most spectacular example was the collapse of the Russian economy after forced marketization, which has been followed by an extended period of massive export of capital by a kleptocracy of 'oligarchs', directly causing poverty and insecurity for many other people. IMF policies have counterproductively undermined social cohesion elsewhere, notably in Chile, Argentina and Indonesia, while in Africa enforced privatization with ineffective governments has been a recipe for massive corruption and short-sighted asset-stripping.

Perhaps the most spectacular illustration of Polanyi's thesis of embeddedness was the priority given by the American vice-regal government to the forced marketization of the Iraqi economy, with the goal of benefiting American corporations and securing control of the oil reserves. In the short term, none of the intended economic objectives could be gained, given the collapse of the basic security necessary for everyday life to proceed. (We shall not know the long-term outcome for many years after the publication of this book.) Curiously, the belief in disembedded markets as self-regulating machines comes to resemble a kind of anti-socialist Marxism: a belief that if the economy (the base) is designed in a certain way, all the social and cultural qualities of a Western democracy (the superstructure) will arise automatically.

These macroeconomic processes are largely driven by a micro-political economy in which the short-term interests of major corporations are normally given priority over any conception of a longer-term public interest. One reason for this is the increasing dependence of individual politicians and political parties on donations from business to finance their political campaigns. This is a major source of corruption in many countries, but it is especially open and acknowledged in the USA. The problem runs deeper than that, however. In Britain, which has more closely imitated American models than have most other countries, recent decades have witnessed what David Marquand calls a *Kulturkampf* against the culture of public service and citizenship. He complained that deregulation, privatization of public utilities, open disbelief in the motivation of civil servants and professionals who saw themselves as working for the public good, and mimicking of the private corporate sector narrowed the public domain and blurred the distinction between it and the market domain (2004: 2). In America, Talcott Parsons used to say that no society could afford to have economic rationality as its highest value system, precisely because it corroded any sense of the public interest; and many other commentators (such as Frank, 2000) have since echoed that thought. Perhaps the sense of the public interest was always weaker in the USA than in Europe, and one effect is that American influence in the world appears to be exerted towards giving narrowly economic considerations priority over broader questions of the viability and cohesiveness of society more widely.

To nothing is this more relevant than the great problem of environmental change and global warming. Here, the denial of the problem of externalities is especially clear: the world's oil companies do not stand to gain, in the short term, from the effective restriction of carbon dioxide emissions. The USA, with 5 per cent of the world's population but producing 25 per cent of its emissions, plays the part on the world stage of the individual or company who denies any responsibility for the external costs it imposes on the rest of the world. On 29 March 2001, President George W. Bush stated this principle quite explicitly: 'In terms of the CO_2 issue, I will explain as clearly as I can today and every other chance I get that I will not do anything that harms our economy. Because first things first are the people of America. That [sic] is my priority' (quoted in the *Guardian*, 19 August 2005).

Global warming is only one instance – albeit the greatest – of a problem that can be solved, if at all, only by collective action at the international level.[7] But, given the USA's current power position in the world, such collective action in the wider 'public' interest is inconceivable without the active participation and enthusiasm of the Americans.

It is not as if Americans, any more than people in other countries, would assent to the principle that the private interest should always or generally take precedence over the public interest. Here the static polarity between the 'private' and the 'public', like all such static conceptualizations (Elias, 1978: 111ff.), is unhelpful. The problem is how the 'public' is defined, whether the definition is wider or narrower and, above all, who has the right to define what is the public and the public interest. Too often, the activities of one person – chopping down a little bit of a rain forest, for instance – seem harmless enough; the harm arises when many people simultaneously do the same thing. Moreover, the benefits or profits accruing to an individual or business are quite tangible and immediate, whereas the external costs falling on a wider entity are more diffuse and uncertain, and arise only over a longer time horizon. Perhaps even more than in other countries, the American political system, where all members of the House of Representatives and many other public officials have to seek re-election every two years (and where the pork barrel plays an acknowledged part), is not conducive to farsighted legislation in the long-term general interest. Above all, however, what is deemed to constitute the general interest is fundamentally shaped by the central power ratios within a nation-state and between it and other states of the world.

Functional de-democratization

Two trends present a particular challenge to the way many Americans see themselves and their country. Internally, the central economic and political power balances have tended to become more unequal. That does not make the USA different from many other countries, but it does run counter to a belief common among Americans that their country is more 'democratic' and egalitarian than others. The second trend is much more distinctively American: it is the long-term national experience of the power ratios between the Americans and their neighbours swinging steadily in their favour over a very long period. As argued in chapters 7 and 8, this process began in relation to the Native Americans, and continued through the growth of hemispheric hegemony to the present status of the USA as (for the moment) the world's sole superpower.

As noted several times before, Norbert Elias generally perceived functional democratization as a dominant trend in increasingly complex and more closely integrated societies. The twentieth century witnessed an astonishing sequence of emancipation struggles: of workers, of colonial people, of ethnic groups, of women, of homosexuals, of students and even of children. In each case, the power balance between these outsider groups and their established counterparts changed, not to equality certainly, but towards a somewhat less uneven balance. These trends were real and important; they played a key part in the process of 'informalization', and from some standpoints may appear the dominant feature of the last century. In the counterpoint of history, however, they can be interwoven with contrary trends. Elias paid less attention to the possibility of what may be called *functional de-democratization* and its effects. Yet in his writings and those of subsequent researchers who have followed his lead, there are important clues as to the sociogenesis and consequences of functional de-democratization.

When some people have a large power advantage, the experience affects in quite specific ways how they perceive themselves and others. This can be seen at every level from the microcosm – the partners in a marriage, for instance – right up to the macrocosm of international relations. A study of a Dutch refuge for battered women and of their violent partners is revealing. These were marital relationships with a very unequal power balance, and the authors (Van Stolk and Wouters, 1987) found that the women took much more notice of their men than the men did of the women, and the women were much more attuned to their men's wishes and needs than the men were to theirs. When the women were asked to give a character sketch of their partner, they could do so with considerable precision, nuance and insight, while the men could not describe their wife's except in terms of clichés applicable to women in general. These men's self-esteem depended mainly on what other *men* thought of them, in other words on their ranking within the established group. The result was that the women were forced to identify more with their men than vice versa. It appears to be a general characteristic of established–outsider relations that the outsiders 'understand' the established better than the established do the outsiders. This seems to have been true of some aspects at least of relations between masters and slaves in the old South. Similarly with colonized people and their colonizers (Elias, 2000: 432). And as a British-born person now resident in Ireland, it is obvious to me that Irish people in general have a very detailed and knowledgeable understanding of their more populous and powerful neighbouring island, of British affairs and British people; in contrast, British people tend to know very little of Irish politics and to think about 'John Bull's other island' in terms of thoroughly outdated stereotypes.

Much the same, I would argue, goes for the grandest-scale established–outsider relation of all, between the US superpower and the rest of the world. Billions of educated people outside the USA know an immense amount about America, its constitution, its politics, its manners and culture; all these are extremely visible to the rest of the world. But it is as if they were looking through a one-way mirror.[8] America's huge power advantage seems to function something like a black hole in reverse: a mass of survey evidence suggests that Americans do not see out at all clearly, and tend to think about the 'outside world' if at all in stereotypical and indeed Manichean terms. (As always, there are of course large numbers of Americans of whom this is not true: we are speaking of general tendencies and differences in averages between Americans and, in particular, Europeans.) Like Elias's 'Villagers' (see p. 19 above), and like established groups in general, they tend to think and talk about themselves in terms of a national narrative based on the 'minority of the best'. That is sometimes coupled with an account of the rest of the world derived from a 'minority of the worst'. Gore Vidal, a master of irony, alleged that there was always 'a horrendous foreign enemy at hand to blow us up in the night out of hatred of our Goodness and rosy plumpness' (2004: 6). Amusing as that is, it captures something that cannot be wholly ignored. As noted right at the beginning of chapter 1, in American (and to a lesser extent Western) rhetoric at the beginning of the twenty-first century there has been a whiff of the nineteenth-century polarity of 'civilization' versus 'barbarism'.[9]

The other side of the coin in Elias's model of established–outsiders relationships is that the outsiders typically to some extent take the more powerful party's image of themselves into their own we-image. Van Stolk and Wouters's battered women were highly ambivalent: in part, the woman's conscience still took the husband's side, and *his* view remained embedded in her personality; that was why they were 'torn two ways', and typically returned at least once to their husbands. In the same way, people in the rest of the world tend in part to take the American world-view into their own we-image, and this is connected with the widespread adoption of American styles and traits. But that does not mean that their resentments disappear. On the contrary: their ambivalence may be increased. By analogy, many bourgeois people in *ancien régime* France followed aristocratic models as best they could in manners, speech and fashion, but that did not prevent them simultaneously resenting aristocratic privileges. Nor did it prevent the French Revolution.

What has been said about functional de-democratization in an international context also applies to increasing disparities in wealth and power within the USA. As observed in chapter 6, in about the last third of the twentieth century there appears to have taken place a realignment of perceived class interests. Many members of the 'protected strata', including large numbers who might be described as 'respectable working class', now identify themselves with an established group and no longer seem easily able to identify with the American poor who form a corresponding outsider group. Indeed, the poor tend to become hidden behind the scenes (or behind the one-way mirror), and, when they irrupt into visibility, may be perceived as 'bad people'.

There is a very strong tendency in American intellectual life to seek explanations in American 'values', 'ideas' and 'cultural traditions'. At several points in this book it has been argued that such explanations are rarely adequate in themselves: one should always look for the sociogenesis and psychogenesis of the values and traditions in changing social structures (particularly balances of power and control), and then at the ways in which values and traditions have become embodied in social structures and practices.

The tendency to think in terms of 'good' people and 'bad' people is no exception. James Morone, in his book *Hellfire Nation* (2003), gives many examples of moral fervour in American history. It has motivated emancipation movements – the abolition of slavery, the enfranchisement of women, civil rights – but also witch-hunting (literal in colonial days, metaphorical in the McCarthy era), slavery and Prohibition (which depended to a great extent on the stigmatizing of bibulous ethnic groups (Mennell, 1969)). Morone argues that the legacy of Puritanism has always conflicted with the checks-and-balances Enlightenment liberalism of the Constitution, which was in effect designed to work irrespective of whether individual people were 'good' or 'bad'. The moralizing tradition, in contrast, Morone points out, has always operated to make it easy to define some people as 'bad' and outside the privileges of liberal democracy, as can be seen in racism, in nativism, in what Hofstadter (1967) called 'the para-noid style in American politics', all the way through to the culture wars over sexuality and abortion and to the treatment of prisoners at Abu Ghraib and Guantanamo Bay in the course of the 'war on terror'.

No doubt Morone is correct in pointing to the recurrence of such episodes ever since early colonial times. What is more questionable is whether religious ideas alone can account for them. Why do some groups have the power to pin the badge of inferiority on others? Each of these episodes needs to be viewed in the context of the relevant power differ-entials of the time. And the moral fervour that has fired various emanci-pation movements can be seen to have achieved its leverage because, at the times in question, relevant power ratios within the nexus of interde-pendence were becoming relatively more equally balanced.

The American empire

Is the United States now an all-embracing world state? The question sounds preposterous unless it is posed specifically in terms of Max Weber's definition of a state as an organization which successfully upholds a claim to binding rule-making over a territory, by virtue of com-manding a monopoly of the legitimate use of violence (1978 [1922]: I, 54). The USA came very close to claiming such a monopoly in its National Security Strategy of 2002. How did it come to be in a position to be able to assert such a claim? As described especially in chapters 7 and 8, the processes of state-formation in America differ in interesting but minor ways from the Western European experience, but were broadly similar. The principle that 'He didn't want all the land; he just wanted the land next to his' (Elias, 2000: 312; see pp. 15, 181 above) applied extensively in both continents. In later centuries, of course, it was not a matter solely of land, which had been the pre-eminent power resource in the European Middle Ages, but also control over natural resources, markets and trade routes, and latterly perhaps over technical knowledge – although that is problematic to monopolize. By the beginning of the twenty-first century, the outcome is something that has been extensively discussed under the rubric of 'the American Empire' (Johnson, 2001, 2004; Bobbitt, 2002; Chomsky, 2003; Mann, 2003; Bacevitch, 2004; Todd, 2004).

Many Americans are uncomfortable with the idea that their country is an imperial power. Its tradition, they say, is anti-imperialist. Yet again, the idea of eternal and unchanging American 'values' blocks perception. Yes, the USA did oppose other imperial powers: in its own War of Independence, in the Monroe Doctrine (see pp. 190–1), and in urging decolonization on the British and French after the Second World War. In the nineteenth and twentieth centuries, it served American interests to be against other people's empires. That did not prevent America acquiring its own 'first empire' through the war with Spain at the end of the nineteenth century, nor something subtler towards the end of the twentieth. Contrasts are often drawn between America's position in the world today and the British Empire in its heyday (O'Brien and Clesse, 2002; Porter, 2006). America does not rule through governors wearing cocked hats, nor usually indulge in constitution-drafting and 'nation-building' (the occupations of Germany and Japan may be seen as exceptions). It does not, as a rule, aim to occupy countries for long periods, nor to create a class of colonial civil servants who may become deeply immersed in and knowledgeable about the cultures in which they serve (the cost–benefit balance of the British having done so is debated). American domination is normally achieved by more indirect means; but the difference should not be exaggerated, for the British also ruled many parts of their empire indirectly through puppet regimes.

Were the USA able in the course of the twenty-first century to achieve the final internal pacification of the world, the goal implied in the 2002 National Security Strategy, that ought to be an immense blessing to humanity as a whole. To live in peace, security and safety is a privilege that large parts of the world's population do not enjoy. The consequences would be immense, and they would be expected to precipitate a civilizing spurt: to quote Elias once more: '[I]f . . . people are forced to live in peace with each other, the moulding of the affects and the standards of emotion management are very gradually changed as well' (2000: 169; see p. 12, above). If the USA came to serve in effect as a world government – as Mandelbaum (2006) shows that it does already in some respects – there would be enormous external benefits for the rest of the world. The governments of the other countries of the world could well regard these benefits as worth the price of their lands undergoing a kind of mediatization – a term used to describe how in the nineteenth century the rulers of many of the small hitherto independent German statelets became subordinated to one or other of the larger states, while retaining their titles and some powers and privileges.

But the benefits would remain externalities, because there is no reason to suppose that the US would be so acting with the primary purpose of benefiting others. Governments of the USA, like those of other countries throughout history, act primarily in what they perceive to be the national interest; part of the definition of what constitutes a 'sovereign' country is that it has some degree of freedom to pursue its own interests. To oppose the pursuit of 'interests' to 'altruism' is another example of a false static polarity. What is labelled altruism may sometimes involve the calculation of interests, but over a longer time horizon. For instance, the Marshall Plan for the rebuilding of Europe after the Second World War was undoubtedly one of the most benevolent acts in the history of American foreign policy, but its motivation was to some extent qualified by the recognition that an economically crippled and politically vulnerable Europe was not in the longer-term interests of the USA. Very little in the record of US foreign policy since then suggests that it is guided by the promotion of political democracy for its own sake; sometimes democratic regimes have been assisted when it has been in the political and economic interest of the USA; at least as often, US power has been deployed on the side of dictatorships when that has seemed in the national interest (see Blum, 1995, for details of many US military and CIA interventions since the Second World War). Close reading of American government rhetoric about promoting 'freedom' reveals that what is meant by that is primarily free markets and access to them by American businesses.

Yet whatever the motivation, the external benefits of US global domination have been very considerable. Especially during the Cold War, in bipolar competition with the Soviet empire, it provided a highly stable world order. According to Godfried van Benthem van den Bergh (1992), when the two superpowers held each other in check, the principle of Mutually Assured Destruction (MAD) served as a functional equivalent to a world monopoly of violence. Even though there was a pervasive fear of nuclear war, the Western world enjoyed a high level of peace and security. Wars of the conventional type were fought mainly in the Third World by proxies for the two superpowers.[10]

The collapse of the Soviet empire in the early 1990s, whatever benefits it may have brought, had the effect of disturbing this bipolar balance of mutual restraint. What effects should have been anticipated from this? Elias's idea of the balance between external constraints and self-constraints in the steering of behaviour appears highly relevant to the question. Normally, great caution is needed in drawing analogies between the psychology of individual people and the processes that guide the actions of collectivities such as nations. Nevertheless, in this case it seems safe to conceptualize both as being steered by the balance between, on the one hand, internalized or socially institutionalized standards of conduct and, on the other, the external constraints exerted by other people or other collectivities. In both cases, a sudden diminution of external constraint may be expected to give rise to an increased probability of impulsive or opportunistic behaviour. Crudely, both individual people and collectivities will tend to probe the limits of what they can get away with, although the strength of internalized or institutionalized standards may prevent anything dramatic happening immediately. In the case of the Soviet collapse, there was very soon a certain amount of intellectual triumphalism

(Fukuyama, 1992), but only gradually did more practical evidence of the probing of the limits of power become evident.

Only a few commentators (such as Nye, 2003) perceived that the 'unipolar' world that succeeded the bipolar one was, in practice, a more *multi*polar world, which paradoxically meant that the central ruler had less rather than more scope to act unilaterally. Once again, Elias's historical investigations may shed light on a modern problem. Blomert (2003) drew on Elias's *The Court Society* to propose an intriguing analogy between France at the zenith of the 'absolutist' *ancien régime*, and the position of the USA in the world at the beginning of the twenty-first century. By the reign of Louis XIV, the earlier territorial princes had been transformed fairly thoroughly from knights to courtiers, losing their military autonomy. By analogy, after the Second World War the plans to create a military force under United Nations control, envisaged under the UN charter, were vitiated by the immediate onset of hostility between the USA and Russia, and the USA began to create a military system for the Western world against the threat of communism. The European powers lost their military autonomy and were transformed into functionaries within the new American-dominated alliance, NATO. But, argued Blomert, neither French kings nor American presidents were absolutely free to do just what they wanted: they were bound by rules and protocols. In such hierarchical networks, there are fetters of legitimacy and authority. Elias spoke of the 'binding' or 'enchainment' of the king (2006a: 127–57). Despite the apparently thorough subordination of the courtly aristocracy, even Louis XIV did not have *absolute* power. A highly effective ruler, he showed great sensitivity to the management of a finely balanced system, and as the 'first nobleman' was bound by rules of conduct and protocol that were accepted by the princes and courtiers as the basis of their cooperation. Any figuration of this sort needs more than just obedience; it needs intelligent cooperation. Had the king broken these rules, he would have lost authority and weakened his position.

By analogy, it does seem clear that, in the aftermath of the Soviet collapse and particularly after the attacks on America in 2001, the United States showed a growing insensitivity to the attitudes and interests of other countries. In particular, Blomert argued that the claim to have the right, contrary to international law, to launch pre-emptive wars had the potential to destabilize the whole structure of collective security because, if its head 'does not feel obliged to obey the rules by which the whole system of loyalties and soft constraints works, how can anyone feel secure?' Or, in other words, the net advantage of accepting the limitations imposed by American leadership in return for the benefits of security provided by the USA as an externality could come to be outweighed by the costs.

Acceptance of the constraints of international law is one area in which America and Europe have diverged. The lesser powers have come greatly to value the corpus of international law that has grown especially since the Second World War; it serves their collective interests. Like any law, it is not always observed to the letter, but in Europe the commitment to international law is stronger; the rule of law has replaced war as the ultimate arm of policy; the national sovereignty of a state vis-à-vis its citizens has been subordinated to the European Court of Human Rights[11] (and, as part of that, capital punishment has been abolished throughout the EU); there is a stronger commitment than in the USA to development aid and to global ecology; and the EU but not the USA has committed itself (and its soldiers) to the jurisdiction of the new International Criminal Court. These developments may be interpreted as a further phase in the European civilizing process. Kagan (2003: 3) expressed the same idea in his celebrated statement that 'Americans are from Mars and Europeans are from Venus', and he went on to say that 'they agree on little and understand one another less and less'.[12] At least two authors – Rifkin (2004) and Haseler (2004) – have suggested that Europe will in the coming century pose a major challenge to the USA, Rifkin arguing that a European Dream focused on sustainable development, quality of life, a social market and multilateralism will supplant the American Dream. As I write, that seems hard to believe, for the EU is itself for the moment internally divided between advocates of the two dreams; such internal conflicts are very much characteristic of outsider groups.

Whether these discords in the international arena are short-term aberrations or longer-term trends remains to be seen. If they are indeed the product of functional de-democratization in the international order, they may perhaps be expected to go into reverse, for it is widely considered that the USA has already, in the early twenty-first century, passed the peak of its world dominance. Its military adventures appear to have served to demonstrate the limits of its might; and indeed the self-imposed burden of very nearly half of all the world's military expenditure may threaten to do to the USA itself what it claims to have done to the Soviet Union: cause economic collapse through military spending that cannot be afforded. The USA of course has no monopoly over the means of taxation across the globe, although its domination of the world's financial system does ensure large flows of capital into the American economy. Yet it is hard to see how America, with less than 5 per cent of the world's population, can in the long term continue to consume as much as one-third of Gross World Product, with the rapid growth of new economic giants like China, India and Brazil. Indeed, American military expenditure is already largely financed through the willingness of China, in particular, to continue investing the product of its trade surpluses in US government stocks. As for what is now called ideological or 'soft power', including the global appeal of American culture and consumer products, we have already noted that that is not incompatible with persisting resentment among the very outsider groups to whom they appeal. For these reasons among others, Michael Mann (2003) has spoken of an 'incoherent empire'.

If indeed the zenith of American dominance in the world has already passed, at least two scenarios are possible. The first is gloomy. A multi-polar world order would (as Elias's game models (1978: 71–103; see above, p. 182) demonstrate) very likely be far more unstable and less sus-ceptible to planning and control by any single player. It would also develop in ways that – even less than in the past – represented the outcome of the plans and intentions of no single player: in Elias's words (1991: 64):

> From plans arising, yet unplanned
> By purpose moved, yet purposeless.

For Americans, this could be a traumatic time. The whole history of their country has been an almost unbroken glorious ascent through unparal-leled national achievement. As Elias remarked, there are connections 'between a people's long-term fortunes and their social habitus at any sub-sequent time'. In America's case, at what he tentatively refers to as the 'we-layer' of their personalities, there is a deep well of national pride. The experience of national decline in other countries has been painful: 'there are often complex symptoms of disturbance at work which are scarcely less in strength and capacity to cause suffering than the individual neu-roses' (1996: 19). 'Britain in the recent past', remarked Elias (ibid.: 4), 'is a moving example of the difficulties a great power of the first rank has had in adjusting to its sinking to being a second- or third-class power.' The United States is a very long way from becoming a second- or third-class power, but it may have to experience reverses and humiliations to which it has not been accustomed. The shame–rage spiral triggered by the events of 11 September 2001 suggests the kind of danger that may arise for Americans and for humankind in general.

A more cheerful scenario – which could happen even if the relative power of the USA did not begin to decline – might eventuate from an American government coming to recognize that unilateral world domi-nation by the USA was unsustainable for much the same reason that American anti-imperialists like Mark Twain and Carl Schurz argued at the beginning of the twentieth century. That was an adaptation of the slogan of Independence: 'No taxation without representation'; in other words, in the era of America's first empire, they said that the USA could not in the long term dominate the people of its colonies – the Philippines (Go, 2003), Hawaii or Cuba – without giving them representation. They would have to be either given independence or made citizens and given the vote.[13] Today's American dominion is much more extensive. (Europeans sometimes joke that the American presidency is far too important to be left to Americans, so they should have the vote too.) In these circumstances, American governments might gradually decide that, after all, the prudential course might be to make use of the structures of the United Nations. At the moment that seems unlikely.[14] Yet in the light of history, it can safely be predicted that – unless there is a prior catastrophic collapse of the world's ecosystems or an annihilating nuclear war that reduces humankind to a much lower level of social organization – new levels of integration will in the long term take shape to deal with the problems that are arising from new forms of global interdependence.

Internationalism is not in fact so foreign to American traditions as it may now seem. The problem is that there is no single American tradition in this field: opposite tendencies have coexisted in a tension-balance with each other, sometimes one facet and sometimes another gaining ascendancy. In this case, Walter Russell Mead (2001: xvii) has identified no fewer than four such traditions: the Jeffersonian principle that America avoid all 'entangling alliances', and not only refuse to rule over other nations, but refrain from meddling in their affairs altogether; the Hamiltonian tradition of maintaining an international system and preserving a balance of power, acknowledging equals in the world rather than seeking hegemonic domination; the Jacksonian tradition, which defined America's interests narrowly and avoided intervention unless there was a very direct and immediate threat to them; and the Wilsonian tradition, which attempted to spread American-style democracy across the globe, through international organizations. Arguably, since 2001, American policy has breached all four traditions. The important point, however, is that all four were formed in and had relevance to a world characterized by a much lower level of interdependence among humanity as a whole. Again, discussions of American traditions and culture are too often couched statically in terms of ideas and 'values' inherited from the past that then function as independent variables steering national behaviour.

Conclusion: path-dependency in America and the world

In this book, I have attempted to take a very long-term view of the processes of development through which America has reached its present position in the world. There is always a danger of writing through the prism of concerns of the moment; the human sciences – including history and sociology – continue to struggle to achieve an adequate balance between involvement and detachment. That they do not always succeed is one reason why history often needs to be written anew in every generation (Elias, 2006a: 3–38). Even if a writer strives hard to prevent the intrusion of heteronomous evaluations, readers will inevitably read the text in the light of contemporary social and political problems. So in conclusion I shall emphasize a single point.

It is that there is some danger both to America itself and to the world at large in the belief that there exists a largely unchanging and internally consistent set of distinctive American cultural and ideological orientations that continue to work as a kind of magnetic compass in global development. For a start, as noted in many parts of this book, the interestingly distinctive features of America have to be seen against the background of broad similarities with other countries, notably those of Western Europe; Americans have often been tempted to exaggerate the extent to which their country is different. Nor are American 'values' internally consistent; they are marked by tension-balances between opposing elements. Most of all, however, it is erroneous to see them as a fixed set of free-floating ideas that shape history. Starr has expressed clearly how the influence of 'values' is better viewed in a more institutional and historical way:

> Once values are applied and entrenched in stable institutional structures (as they were, for example, through the Constitution), the institutions channel development along particular paths and 'carry' the values to some extent independently of public belief. Value orientations are not irrelevant. In any conflict, the opposing sides are likely to try to mobilise widely shared values in support of their position, but the outcome may depend on institutional structures and the resources and strategies each side employs as well as the resonance of its appeal in public sentiment. Values are always at the mercy of politics; their influence is not direct but mediated by the forces at work in a given historical time. (2004: 405*n*)

Thus the Constitution reflects the interplay of values and politics in the USA as it was in the late eighteenth century, when in an inspired way it resolved many (not all: never forget slavery) of what were the problems of that time. The checks and balances for which Madison, in particular, so brilliantly saw the need continue to have a practical impact both within the USA and in the world at large, but they *now* pose a serious obstacle to solving world problems such as global warming. Madison's patron Jefferson himself believed that the Constitution would need to be rewritten every generation to meet new problems. Checks and balances are certainly still needed, but perhaps a different set of them.

American 'values' and political arrangements have on the whole worked very well for America. But there is no good reason to suppose that they provide a universal recipe that will prove equally successful wherever it is baked by whatever cook. They are, rather, an instance of 'path-dependency' (Puffert, 2005), more like the 4ft 8½ ins standard railway gauge, the QWERTY keyboard, or the Windows computer operating system than the most perfect solution imaginable for all time. They solved problems at particular times, and then became so entrenched that they came to seem inevitable. Not to recognize this poses a double danger. For America itself, it enhances the risk of collective self-satisfaction and reduces the self-reflexive capacity for finding new solutions to new problems. For the rest of the world, the danger is that US models will be imported even where the nexus of forces that made them work in one era and one place is so different as to ensure their failure in another.

By any measure, the USA has been an immensely successful nation-state, and not for its own benefit alone. At the beginning of European settlement, thinking of the potential of the supposed wilderness, John Locke (1960 [1690]: Second Treatise, Sec. 49) remarked: 'Thus in the beginning, all the World was America.' Since then, America's vast achievements – in technology, science, government and culture – have helped to transform the world, mostly for the better. At times it seems that in the end, too, all the world will be America. Yet in humanity as a whole there are many people who view that prospect with trepidation.

At the end of *The Civilizing Process*, writing in 1939, a black moment in world history, Norbert Elias quoted Holbach: '*[L]a civilisation . . . n'est pas encore terminée.*' Elias was temperamentally an optimist, and at the end of his life could still predict that in later centuries the age through which he had lived would probably be seen as that of the 'late barbarians' (1991: 146–7). Is it merely a difference in personal temperament that makes me more pessimistic in 2007 than Elias was in 1939? Perhaps. Let us hope that Charles Dickens was wrong when he wrote: 'I do believe that the heaviest blow ever dealt at liberty's head will be dealt by this nation in the ultimate failure of its example to the earth.'[15]

Notes

Prologue: Civilizing Processes

1 Japan also retains the death penalty.
2 To my mind, Harriet Martineau (1837: III, 5–6) made the point better than Hartz: 'While the republics of North America are new, the ideas of the people are old. While these republics were colonies, they contained an old people, living under old institutions, in a new country. Now they are a mixed people, infant as a nation, with a constant accession of minds from old countries, living in a new country, under institutions newly combined out of old elements. It is a case so singular, that the old world may well have patience for some time, to see what will arise.'
3 Charles Tilly (1995) complained that analysts of large-scale processes frequently invoke invariant models that feature self-contained and self-motivating social units. More specifically in relation to American history, Ian Tyrell (1991a) has pleaded the necessity of a 'transnational history'. See also the response by McGerr (1991), and Tyrell's rejoinder (1991b).
4 The allusion here is to Robert H. Lowie's famous remark: 'To that planless hodgepodge, that thing of shreds and patches called civilization, its historian can no longer yield superstitious reverence. He will realize better than others the obstacles to infusing design into the amorphous product; but in thought at least he will not grovel before it in fatalistic acquiescence but dream of a rational scheme to supplant the chaotic jumble' (1920: 520).
5 A fuller summary and discussion of Elias's writings can be found in Mennell (1998); see also the selections of Elias's writings in Mennell and Goudsblom (1998) and Goudsblom and Mennell (1998).
6 All references to *The Civilizing Process* in this book are to the revised edition and translation published in 2000. A further revision, entitled *On the Process of Civilization*, is to be published by University College Dublin Press in due course as volume 3 of the Collected Works of Norbert Elias in English.

7 The word appears to have been coined by Mirabeau the elder in 1756 (Mazlish, 2004: 19). Elias drew upon Lucien Febvre's classic 1930 essay, '*Civilisation*: evolution of a word and a group of ideas' (Febvre, 1973: 12–26).

8 The word was fairly widely current in social science between the wars, and seems to have first been used in French by Marcel Mauss, but it became more familiar to social scientists much later through the work of Pierre Bourdieu.

9 There were always some foods, such as chicken legs, that could be handled – at least if the host or hostess agreed. In the late twentieth century it was often noted that, with the increasing diversity of takeaway food, the prohibition on eating with the fingers seemed to have been relaxed. The question of reversals of the trend of civilizing processes, of which this is a rather trivial example, will be discussed later in the book.

10 On the connection between the emergence of a warrior class and the rise of large-scale agriculture, see Goudsblom (1996b: 49–62).

11 Not everywhere and always, of course, but the treatment meted out to the inhabitants of Srebrenica by the Serbian army in July 1995 did at least shock the world at large.

12 It is an oversimplification to see the 'curbing of affects' as a question merely of *more* self-constraint or self-control. How later Europeans differ from their medieval forebears is, according to Elias, more precisely formulated as involving *more automatic, more even* and *more all-round* operation of self-constraints. By 'more automatic' is meant that the controls over emotional expression become more reliable or calculable, involving less conscious reflection. By 'more even', Elias meant that individuals' oscillations of mood become less extreme – people are less volatile. 'More all-round' refers to a decline in the differences between the various spheres of life, such as contrasts between what is allowed in public and in private, between conduct in relation to one category of people as against another, or between 'normal' behaviour and that permissible on special occasions like a carnival which are seen as exceptions to the rules. See Mennell (1998: 241–6).

13 See the 'Excursus on some differences in the paths of development of England, France and Germany' (Elias, 2000: 261–7).

14 The idea of the monopolization of power resources, of course, goes back well before Elias – to Marx, and especially to Weber, who wrote: 'the more powerful . . . entrench their privileges by monopolizing economic, social, and political advantages. This became particularly acute when competition for scarce resources increased . . .' (1978 [1922]: II, 341–2). Elias plays down the voluntaristic element, showing how competitors are enmeshed in a compelling process. He stresses the centrality of land as a power resource in medieval Europe, while recognizing that many other sources of power can be subject to monopolization processes. See for instance Stone (2002) on ethnic group formation or Inglis (1998) on the monopolization of 'moral' power by the Catholic church in Ireland.

15 'Courtization', however deplorable a word, was Elias's preferred translation of *Verhöflichung*.

16 See Elias in *Quest for Excitement* (Elias and Dunning, 1986: 26–40); he contends that the principal differences were that the Tories were on the whole

lesser landowners, more sympathetic to royal power and Catholicism, and more hostile to the Dissenters than were the great Whig grandees.

17 Quotations from *Democracy in America* are from the original English translation by Henry Reeve, sometimes with minor modifications. Several modern translations have been published, but none seems to me to equal the elegance and charm of Reeve's.

18 Elias's writings on the sciences are scattered among many journal articles, but some of the most important are collected in his *Involvement and Detachment* (2007a [Collected Works, vol. 8]). The other essays on this subject will be included in volume 14 of Elias's Collected Works.

Chapter 1 'American Civilization'

1 National Day of Prayer and Remembrance for the Victims of the Terrorist Attacks on September 11, 2001. By the President of the United States of America. A Proclamation, 13 September 2001: <www.whitehouse.gov/news/releases/2001/09>.

2 The Italian Prime Minister of the time, Silvio Berlusconi, broke ranks with other Western leaders when in an apparent allusion to Samuel Huntington's popular book (1999) he spoke of 'the clash of civilizations', asserting the superiority of Western Christian 'civilization' over Islam. He said: 'The attacks on New York and Washington are attacks not only on the United States but on our civilization, of which we are proud bearers, conscious of the supremacy of our civilization, of its discoveries and inventions, which have brought us democratic institutions, respect for the human, civil, religious and political rights of our citizens, openness to diversity and tolerance of everything.' He called on Europe to recognize 'its common Christian roots', and remarked that respect for human rights 'certainly does not exist in the Islamic countries' (*Guardian*, 27 September 2001).

3 For comparative studies of the French, Scottish and American Enlightenments, see Gay (1997 [1968]) and Himmelfarb (2004); on the American Enlightenment specifically, see the collection of papers from the *Journal of the History of Ideas* edited by Shuffelton (1993).

4 Barbara Ehrenreich (2004) noted the ironic accuracy with which these words describe the USA's use of large numbers of mercenaries ('contractors') in its occupation of Iraq following its invasion of that country in 2003.

5 The Beards, eminent among the Progressive historians of the first half of the twentieth century (see Hofstadter, 1969), made plain in this wartime work their own identification with the values of the Enlightenment. This contrasts with the orthodoxy among social theorists in the latter part of the century, who, under the influence of the Frankfurt School and especially of *Dialectic of Enlightenment* by Horkheimer and Adorno (1972), have tended to stress the darker side of the Enlightenment faith in reason, progress and human perfectibility. The rationalization of killing in the Nazi genocides certainly implies the need for caution and scepticism. Yet the pendulum of opinion surely swung too far from the optimism of the Beards' generation. That rationalization has a darker side does not warrant the rejection of all applications of

reason to the improvement of the human lot. The Beards' book, it should be noted, contains the earliest extensive discussion in America of Elias's *Über den Prozess der Zivilisation* (see Beard and Beard, 1942: 58–9, 64ff.).

6 These data are drawn from a search of the 1907 edition of *The Writings of Thomas Jefferson* in 19 volumes by Albert Ellery Bergh, which is available on CD-ROM. For a more recent scholarly edition, see *The Papers of Thomas Jefferson*, edited by Julian P. Boyde et al. and published by Princeton University Press from 1950 onwards.

7 *The Adams-Jefferson Letters: The Complete Correspondence between Thomas Jefferson and Abigail and John Adams*, ed. Lester J. Cappon (1959). All subsequent references to the correspondence between Jefferson and John Adams are to this edition.

8 'Enthusiasm' is used here in its then current pejorative sense, denoting disapproval of a breach of the prevailing (upper-class) standard of emotion management.

9 This principle applies even to the mother and her baby; it is at first a very unequal power ratio – though as long as the baby is loved and valued it is not entirely without power chances of its own – but the ratio characteristically tilts over the course of their lifetimes, first becoming relatively more equal and then eventually often nearing the reverse of its original balance. See Elias (1978: 78).

10 It has often been noted that Jefferson dropped the reference to property rights that were so central to Locke, and he appears to have done so on his own initiative when drafting the Declaration of Independence (Ellis, 1997: 65–6).

11 That this point still has to be made in contemporary political polemics is shown by Hillary Rodham Clinton's book *It Takes a Village* (1996).

12 Crèvecœur refers to the king because he was writing before the outcome of the War of Independence was settled. His sympathies were Tory, and as a result he was briefly imprisoned in New York before taking refuge in his native France.

13 For a review of the debates in those days about 'functionalism' and 'social systems', and about 'consensus' and 'conflict', see Mennell (1974: 116–40).

14 This passing reference to debtor and creditor interests is intended to allude to, but not re-open, the intricate debates which for many years followed the publication of Charles Beard's *An Economic Interpretation of the Constitution* (1913).

15 Even very recently, a purportedly serious work of scholarship could represent the Federalists as having attempted a 'counter-revolution' in a 'retreat from liberty' – see Tise (1998).

Chapter 2 'Fellow Americans' and Outsiders

1 Writing the history of westward expansion at the end of the nineteenth century, another soon-to-be President Theodore Roosevelt (1995 [1889–99]) demonstrated a similar deep ambivalence towards the Indians, often writing about them in what would today be considered rankly racist terms: 'The most ultimately righteous of all wars is a war with savages, though it is apt also to

be the most terrible and inhuman. The rude, fierce settler who drives the savage from the land lays all civilized mankind under a debt to him' (quoted by Zimmerman, 2002: 219). Yet he also often posed the paradox of 'how a people could claim to be civilized if it behaved as barbarously as its barbarous foes' – a paradox as relevant to the USA's military adventures at the beginning of the twenty-first century as it was then.

2 It has lately been fashionable in the humanities and social sciences to refer to 'the "other"' in the singular; I follow Elias in bearing in mind that there are always many 'others', and that it is very generally misleading to speak of human beings in the singular.

3 The Beards' quotation from the second volume of *Democracy in America*, Book II, chapter II, differs slightly from the Reeve translation used elsewhere in this book.

4 I am grateful to Johan Goudsblom (personal communication) for this reflection.

5 When making broad statements about dominant opinion in America, and especially about the behaviour of US governments, it has to be constantly borne in mind that there are always American critics too. One small example is a comment by Molly Ivins in the *Charleston Gazette*, 28 January 2002, on the denial of prisoner of war status to the men captured by US forces in Afghanistan after the events of 11 September 2001: 'Now we've won the war . . . So we take the prisoners we've captured off to our base at Guantanamo Bay and suddenly announce that they are not prisoners of war after all because this isn't really a war we've been fighting . . . This is why a lot of people hate us. For the sheer bloody arrogance of having it both ways all the time. For thinking that we are above the rules, that we can laugh at treaties, that we can do whatever we want.'

Chapter 3 American Manners Under Scrutiny

1 For an iconoclastic critique of Tocqueville, especially his methods of research and his tendency to overgeneralize, see Wills (2004).

2 In a similarly understated way, Elias's *The Civilizing Process* is also a three-way comparative study of France, Germany and England.

3 I am hinting here that the explanation for English aristocratic manners being somewhat less rococo than the French by the late eighteenth century may be similar to that which I offered for the French developing a more elaborate *haute cuisine* than the English, whose cookery maintained greater continuities from medieval styles (see Mennell, 1996a: 102–33). For a thorough study of codes of conduct in early modern England, see Bryson (1998).

4 These estimates were originally made by Samuel Goodrich, in *Recollections of a Lifetime* (1856), but were accepted by Hellmut Lehmann-Haupt et al. (1951: 124, 195). See Kasson (1990: 47), and also Starr (2004: 113–50).

5 Again, there is a parallel between manners and cookery: a process of Americanization of cookery books took place at roughly the same time (see Mennell, 1996a: 341–4).

6 See Degler (1974: 1479) and Seidman (1991: 6) for good discussions of the caution with which the evidence of advice literature must be handled. In both cases their concern is mainly with advice concerning sexuality, but their

remarks are of more general application (and, again, the parallel with cookery books is striking – see Mennell, 1996a: 65–9).

7 The German anthropologist Hans-Peter Duerr (1988) has attempted to show, contrary to Elias, that there is no pattern of development in feelings about nakedness, and that all societies more or less equally have rules of avoidance concerning it. For a counter-critique of Duerr, see Mennell and Goudsblom (1997).

8 Standards still vary considerably among the countries of Europe. Today, it is common in Germany, the Netherlands and Scandinavia for both sexes – strangers as well as friends – to sit naked together in a public sauna, something unthinkable in Britain, Ireland and (I would guess) all the Mediterranean countries, let alone America. I suspect, however, that the tolerance, where it exists, is the product of a twentieth-century reversal of the trend in some countries and not in others.

9 According to the resident historian at the Mammoth Hot Springs Hotel, Yellowstone Park, in the summer of 2003, visitors to the hotel had been expected to share a bed with a stranger (of the same sex) as late as 1900.

10 There has in consequence been some discussion among historians about whether Lincoln had homosexual tendencies (see Tripp, 2005, and the summary of the controversy by Philip Nobile in History News Network, <http://.hnn.us/articles>, 10 January 2005). Whether he did or not, his sharing his bed is not in itself valid evidence either way; and inferring sexual proclivities from a social practice common at the time is a classic instance of the dangers of an ahistorical conception of psychology, against which Elias strongly warned.

11 For studies of other 'civilizing offensives', see Mennell (1998: 121).

12 This point is elaborated with further historical evidence on leprosy, syphilis, the plague and cholera by Goudsblom (1986a).

13 The term is mine, not Elias's, though I use it as shorthand in summarizing one aspect of his argument; see Mennell (1998: 47).

14 More recent scholarship has suggested that Elias somewhat exaggerated the extent of the impoverishment of the *noblesse d'épée*, though not its general subordination to the monarchy; see Roche (1998: 658–9).

15 D. H. Lawrence, in his *Studies in Classic American Literature* (1924: 8) wrote: 'America has never been easy, and is not easy today. Americans have always been at a certain tension. Their liberty is a thing of sheer will, sheer tension: a liberty of THOU SHALT NOT.' But he went on: 'And it has been so from the first', and that is more questionable. Larkin (1988: 199) dates the feeling (more in the North than the South and West) that sex itself is a problem to the 1830s – roughly the same time as E. P. Thompson speaks of an 'all-embracing "Thou Shalt Not"' in England. He notes changing patterns of courtship, involving greater control, and the decline of bundling (institutionalized forms of heavy petting among young people) in rural areas. Religion was not the only factor, however. Bundling declined in America, as in many parts of Europe, with high geographical mobility: men just arrived in a community and soon to depart could not so easily be trusted to abide by the rules of bundling.

16 Collier's book – entitled *The Rise of Selfishness in America* – was mainly concerned with what he saw as a subsequent reversal of this trend.

17 On the social significance of the use of the pronouns, see Brown and Gilman (1960).

18 For a fuller account of the origins of the debate among Dutch sociologists about informalization and the theory of civilizing processes, and a bibliography of the main contributions to it up to 1988, see Mennell (1998: 241–6). I shall not develop the discussion of informalizing trends over the last century in as much detail as I otherwise would do here because Wouters's two books (2004; 2007) present the fruit of three decades of research, comparing trends in four countries: the USA, Britain, Germany and The Netherlands. Wouters's research proceeds from the same perspective as mine, and readers are referred to his work.

19 He did not at that stage use the word 'informalization', nor did he fully incorporate the process into his theory of civilizing processes. That came much later, in a chapter of *The Germans* (1996: 23–43), after informalization had been extensively discussed among his associates, particularly by Cas Wouters.

20 Wouters (2004: 141–2) has suggested that the apparently greater popularity of oral sex in America than in Europe stems from this code.

Chapter 4 American Aristocracies

1 Of course it is easy to overgeneralize both about categories of people and about periods. Voltaire (1980 [1734]: 52) noted that in England the younger sons of peers could go into trade with no disgrace, although he regretted that this trait was beginning to disappear. 'This custom', he wrote, 'seems monstrous to Germans who are mad about their quarterings; they cannot understand that the son of a Peer of England may only be a rich and influential bourgeois, whereas in Germany everybody is a Prince. . . . In France anyone is a Marquis who wants to be . . . and loftily despise[s] a business man.'

2 Eaton draws upon Daniel R. Hundley's *Social Relations in Our Southern States* (1860), a pioneering sociological study, albeit pro-slavery. The 1860 US Census used a more generous definition, counting as a 'planter' anyone who owned 20 slaves or more; this yielded as many as 46,000 planters, which is still a small proportion of the total population; see Bowman (1980: 781).

3 Bowman contrasts the persistence of the 'private law state' with the growth in Britain since about the seventeenth century of first civil, then political and finally social rights of 'citizenship' applicable equally to all (on which see Marshall, 1950).

4 The fullest account of duelling and the code of honour in America is by Stevens (1940).

5 It is indeed a little reminiscent of the distinction drawn by the old 'culture and personality' school of anthropology between 'shame cultures' and 'guilt cultures'; see, for instance, Benedict (1946: 156–9).

6 Steward argues, furthermore, that although duelling largely died out at the end of Reconstruction, the idea of people killing each other over matters of reputation has persisted (see pp. 125–6 below).

7 I am grateful to Tom Garvin for pointing this out to me.

8 The novelty of a *working* upper class emerging in seventeenth- and eighteenth-century France, consisting of the *noblesse de robe* and other professionals along with the financiers and commercial elite, is not always appreciated. See Elias (2006a). Elias (1996) also discusses the vicissitudes of the equivalent *berufsbürgerlich* groups in Germany.

9 See epigraph to chapter 3 above.

10 Of course, there are complex trends and counter-trends, and some members of the northern educated elite might be said to have sympathy with military and imperial values; see, for example, Zimmerman's study (2002) of Theodore Roosevelt and his circle – Alfred T. Mahon, Henry Cabot Lodge, John Hay and Elihu Root – five Americans 'who made their country a world power'.

11 And some, like Joshua Lawrence Chamberlain of Bowdoin College, who were quintessentially members of the northern *Bildungsbürgertum*.

12 This too is a trait more readily associated with Europe. The German nobility's obsession with their 'quarterings' – being able to claim unsullied descent from 16 aristocratic great-great-grandparents – is notorious. Weber remarked that 'in Germany the appropriate avenue to social honour led from the purchase of a feudal estate to the foundation of an entailed estate, and the acquisition of titular nobility, which in turn facilitated the reception of the *grandchildren* in aristocratic "society"' (1946: 309). The aristocratic rule later appeared in coarser form in the Nazi definition of what constituted 'Aryan' purity (Elias, 1996: 15).

13 For a discussion of the taken-for-granted assumptions underlying sociologists' use of the metaphors of 'high' and 'low', see Goudsblom (1986b).

14 See Weber's famous discussion of 'class, status and party' as dimensions of the distribution of power and patterns of stratification (1978: i, 926–40).

Chapter 5 The Market Society

1 Indeed Riesman's conception of the 'other-directed' person was substantially indebted to Erich Fromm's (1947: 67–82) discussion of the 'marketing orientation' (Riesman et al., 1961 [1950]: 22*n*).

2 This had important political and economic consequences in the 1830s. Andrew Jackson's bad experience with local bankers earlier in his life fed into his hostility as President to the Second Bank of the United States, his destruction of which led to a prolonged economic slump. Americans of Jackson's persuasion may be said to have drawn the wrong conclusions from unreliable banks: bigger and better credit institutions were what they needed. See pp. 227–33 below.

3 Thus, at least in the later essay on 'The Protestant Sects and the Spirit of Capitalism', Weber's argument does not fundamentally rest on the supposed social psychological effects of various theological beliefs. In this instance, the argument is more Lucretian than Augustinian (see Goudsblom, 2004, and p. 268 below for my use of these terms) – it does not depend on the supposed 'civilizing' effects of religious beliefs. In spite of Weber's famous denial of his

intention 'to substitute for a one-sided materialistic an equally one-sided spir-itualistic causal interpretation of culture and of history' (1930: 183), on close reading the more famous essay *The Protestant Ethic and the Spirit of Capitalism* does tip over into idealism.

4 Carol Z. Stearns (1988: 58) implies that the 'tearfulness' of women in this period was associated with them being less subject to the constraints of the market in emotion management. Today, with so many women in the work-place, this difference will have disappeared. Stearns's argument is at odds in an interesting way with Elias's discussion of the constraints upon upper-class women in medieval courts, whom he saw as being subjected to more intense civilizing pressures earlier than men (2000: 249).

5 'Tout n'est pas contractuel dans le contrat' (Durkheim, 1893: 189).

6 Haskell writes, 'to *the* remote consequences', but remoteness in this context is a matter of degree.

7 The 'explosion' of contract law, coupled with a relatively non-interventionist state and corresponding reliance on market mechanisms, also goes a long way to explaining the peculiar prominence of lawyers in American society.

8 In his discussion of the 'forced division of labour', Durkheim (1984: 318–20) spoke of the necessity for equality of power between parties to a contract. That is utterly unrealistic. But the idea persists, especially among protagonists of the free market, that – because there is nearly always a 'market-clearing price' at which a deal can be struck – any contract represents an agreement between parties of equal power.

9 I refer to these economic models as 'ideal-types' to draw attention to their logical similarity to the ideal-types that sociologists associate especially with the work of Max Weber. Following Otto Hintze, Norbert Elias (2000: 533, *n*22) expressed a distrust of ideal-type conceptualizations, preferring 'real types' – investigating specific examples of social formations rather than build-ing models whose features were rarely if ever met with all together in the real world. Most 'figurational' sociologists have shared this distrust; but the success and influence of the classic economic models of competition mean that in this case reference to them is unavoidable.

10 In the first years of the new century, scandals have engulfed Andersen, Worldcom, Enron, Xerox, Fanny Mae and many smaller corporations.

11 See p. 17 above.

Chapter 6 Violence and Aggressiveness

1 In his pioneering study, Gurr concluded that while there had, since the nine-teenth century, been an underlying downward trend in the USA, as there was in Europe, it was partly obscured by a massive upsurge of violent crime in the first three decades of the twentieth century. The upsurge appeared to be attrib-utable to a sharp increase in homicides among black Americans (1981: 324). Eckberg (1995), however, has shown that the upsurge was a statistical arte-fact: there had been serious underreporting of homicides at the beginning of the century. Using econometric techniques, he was able to estimate corrections that are incorporated in figure 6.2.

2 Killing the lover might be condoned even when killing the wife was not. Wives in general were not permitted to kill even their husbands' lovers, although in one early sign of women's emancipation, Georgia in 1925 extended to wives the right to kill in cases of adultery.

3 States in which adultery had been made a criminal act repealed these laws under the impact of its coming to be regarded only as a 'misdemeanour'.

4 Indeed Gurr made passing reference to Elias. In his response to Gurr's findings, Lawrence Stone (1985) counterposed the *violence au vol* thesis as a 'social' explanation to the 'cultural' explanation derived from Elias. The opposition is a false one, since Elias seeks to provide a social explanation of cultural changes. I pointed this out at the time in personal correspondence with Stone, who accepted that – largely because he had not read the second volume of *The Civilizing Process* (which was published in English only in 1982, *after* Gurr's essay) – he had overlooked the broader context of Elias's work.

5 Spierenburg (1996: 70–1) conceptualizes the distinction slightly differently. He proposes two related but distinct axes: 'impulsive violence' versus 'planned' or 'rational' violence, and 'ritual' or 'expressive' versus instrumental violence. The main difference from my own usage is that he employs the terms 'ritual' or 'expressive' violence to denote acts that are guided by cultural codes – notably honour codes of the type that persisted especially in the American South – and are designed to degrade the victim. In his own research on early modern Amsterdam, he stresses the significance of stabbing a victim in the buttock.

6 This is the essence of Bauman's (1989) argument about modernity and the Holocaust, though it is not at odds with Elias's own studies of Germany and the Holocaust (1996).

7 Charles Tilly (1979: 78) notes that in France, too, 'urbanization damped collective violence in the short run'. Tilly's concern, however, is with *collective* violence – the resort to violent means by groups of people protesting at their communal, industrial or political grievances. He explains the initial downturn by noting that new urban residents are not yet organized in associations, trade unions or political movements, and that 'modern' collective violence is marked by a degree of organization and foresight that mirrors the more effective policing and administration emphasized by Lane.

8 See the note in *The Civilizing Process* (2000: 531–2n), together with later writings such as 'The Breakdown of Civilization' (1996: 299–402).

9 Wacquant's allusion is to an essay of my own (Mennell, 1990a), in which I sought to distinguish such cases from, among other things, informalization processes.

10 In certain respects only, because it can be argued that increased identification with the suffering of the poor worldwide went paradoxically hand in hand with a revival of the distinction of the deserving and undeserving poor within state-societies.

11 'White flight' is partly a misnomer, because members of the 'black bourgeoisie' took part in it too.

12 O'Donnell (2004) has criticized Garland's 'culture of control' thesis, pointing

out that the southern states and California contribute disproportionately to the overall national increase in incarceration. A comparison of the five states with the highest prison population per capita (all in the South) and the five with the lowest (in New England and the northern Midwest, which have rates more like those of England and Wales) shows that, while the rates have risen in all of them, the gap between the high and low groups has actually widened. In other words, it would be rash to assert that the shift towards a culture of control, or the retreat from penal welfarism, have taken place equally across the USA as a whole.

13 Canada's homicide rate has been consistently lower than the USA's for many decades. Daly and Wilson (1988: 282) track the two countries' rates for the period 1921–85.

14 The 'Turner thesis' is discussed more fully in chapter 8 below.

15 Spierenburg (2004) emphasizes that in Europe there was also, further down the social scale, a long tradition of the popular duel with knives.

16 Israel resembles Switzerland in this respect, yet has a homicide rate more closely resembling those in the EU.

17 It is possible that undeclared illegal possession of guns may be higher in cities than in rural areas.

18 Gun ownership also has some academic defenders; see, for example, Olson and Kopel (1999).

19 The entire controversy is documented in the archives of the History News Network (<http://hnn.us>). In my opinion, the errors were comparatively trivial; Bellesiles corrected them in a revised edition of *Arming America* (2003). It is the corrected edition that is listed in the bibliography.

20 This should not be taken in too literal a sense: David Garland points out that democracy in a developed, non-corrupt sense, came to the South very late, after the 1960s (personal communication); but it is certainly clear that the Southern whites had not become accustomed to being disarmed.

21 Thus, using the term in this loose sense, Marika Sherwood (1999) traced what she called racial 'lynchings' in Britain from 1919 to the 1990s; but, in the stricter sense of the killing of a specific person accused of a specific offence, one would have to go back much further in the history of Great Britain – Ireland is a separate issue – to find a classic US-style communal 'necktie party' lynching.

22 John Melish, a Glasgow textile manufacturer who travelled in the South in the first decade of the nineteenth century, witnessed the scene after two slaves had been lynched (Nevins, 1948: 48); he appears to have taken the hanging of one in his stride, but to have been deeply shocked by the other's burning alive.

23 National Association for the Advancement of Colored People (1919), based on newspaper reports and the NAACP's own investigations.

24 Zimring's reference to the number of native Americans lynched points to the intriguing possibility that, for this melancholy purpose at least, they were classified as 'white' in the official statistics charted in figure 6.7 above.

25 Zimring (2003: 110) points out that, unlike in the South, the legacy of this early vigilantism on the Pacific coast has left few marks today, because 'much

of the population . . . has attenuated links with the region's history and historical identity'.

26 Richard Evans (1996), in his monumental study of capital punishment in Germany, discusses Spierenburg's work at length. The bulk of Evans's evidence favours Spierenburg's interpretation, although in his conclusions Evans draws back from fully endorsing Elias's theory.

27 Public executions continued longer elsewhere in the USA, the last one taking place in 1936 (Banner, 2002).

28 Homicide is generally a matter for state jurisdictions. In a few cases, such as terrorism or assassination of a President, it falls under federal law, but the execution of Timothy McVeigh in 2001 for the 1995 Oklahoma City bombing was the first federal execution for many years.

29 Still the best formulation of this necessary balance is, I think, to be found in William Kornhauser's *The Politics of Mass Society* (1959).

30 Another discussion of American character by a member of the 'culture and personality' school of anthropologists is by the British writer Geoffrey Gorer (1948).

Chapter 7 And Wilderness is Paradise Enow: From Settlements to Independence

1 See for instance Lipset (1963), Greenfeld (1992: 397–484). Such has been the strength of American social scientists' focus on the collective subjectivity of 'nation-building' that the very term 'state-formation' is a rare usage for them. When it is used, as in Charles Tilly's work, it tends to be applied to Europe rather than to the USA itself. The ambiguity of the word 'state' in the US context undoubtedly contributes to the avoidance of the *term* 'state-formation', but perhaps also to a neglect of the factual process to which the term refers.

2 Miller could then still describe his book *Errand into the Wilderness* as a study of 'the movement of European culture into the vacant wilderness'.

3 But see Loewen (1995: 93–7) for a frank reassessment of this story.

4 See also Kupperman (2000); Oberg (1999); Sokolow (2003); Merritt (2003).

5 For a model of purely ecological interdependence between two human groups, see Elias's discussion of a 'Primal Contest' – a 'game without rules' (1978: 76–80).

6 This point was emphasized especially by Herbert E. Bolton, a student of Frederick Jackson Turner's who specialized in the history of the Hispanic borderlands of the southwest. Bolton's work (1921) is the point of departure for the critique of the 'new western history' by Adelman and Aron (1999).

7 For just such an exercise, of considerable interest, see J. C. D. Clark (1997).

8 A compelling process is one which, though propelled by the interweaving actions of many interdependent people pursuing their particular goals, as a whole takes an unplanned course and gains a momentum which constrains and compels the activities of the people caught up in it. See Elias (1978: ch. 6, 'The Problem of "Inevitability"') and Dunning (1977).

9 There has been vigorous debate about this. Some of the principal contributions in favour of Iroquois influence are Grinde (1977); Johansen (1982;

1998); Grinde and Johansen (1991). A contrary view, denying that the Iroquois played any role in shaping American democracy, can be found in Elisabeth Tooker (1988). Advocates of Iroquois influence make strong cases for, among other things, Franklin having been impressed by their non-coercive form of government as early as his participation in the Albany Congress of 1754, and that in his *Defence of the Constitutions of the Government of the United States of America* John Adams can be seen to have 'believed that Indian governments provided an excellent example of the separation of the three branches of government' (Grinde and Johansen, 1991: xvii–xxv).

10 The significance of this point seems first to have been emphasized by the Mississippi Congressman Lucius Q. C. Lamar during the Reconstruction era; see Turner (1947: 24).

Chapter 8 But Westward, Look, the Land is Bright: From Frontier to Empire

1 It is not helpful to think in terms of a polar dichotomy (as Popper [1957] famously did) between history as following 'inevitable' laws and history as an unstructured sequence of more or less 'accidental' events; see Mennell (1996b); Dunning (1977). The question of whether a sequence of social development can ever be said to be 'inevitable' has tended to become entangled with the philosophers' metaphysical antithesis of 'determinism' and individual 'free will'. The muddle is then further compounded when 'free will' is linked to 'freedom' in the sense of political and social liberty, and 'determinism' to lack of liberty. This link is false. As Elias points out, 'it is usually forgotten that there are always simultaneously many mutually dependent individuals, whose interdependence to a greater or lesser extent limits each one's scope for action' (1978: 167). That simple sentence pithily cuts across centuries of metaphysical debate. More subtle and reality-orientated modes of thinking are necessary to come to grips with the issue of prediction and 'inevitability' in sequences of social development. Elias proposes that we think of such development as a continuum of changes, or figurational flow. Within the flow, we can identify a sequence of figurations, which we can label A, B, C, D; these are not static, discontinuous *stages* of development, but points inserted in a flow – various figurations of people, each figuration flowing from the previous one as the development takes its course from A to D. The kernel of Elias's argument is then as follows:

> Retrospective study will often clearly show not only that the figuration is a *necessary* precondition for D, and likewise B for C and A for B, but also why this is so. Yet, looking into the future, from whatever point in the figurational flow, we are usually able to establish only that the figuration at B is *one possible* transformation of A, and similarly C of B and D of C. In other words, in studying the flow of figurations there are two possible perspectives on the connection between one figuration chosen from the continuing flow and another, later figuration. From the viewpoint of the earlier figuration, the later is – in most if not all cases – only one of several possibilities for change. From the viewpoint of the later figuration, the

earlier one is usually a necessary condition for the formation of the later. (1978: 160)

> There is, then, an asymmetry in the two time-perspectives. The reason is that figurations vary greatly in their pliability, plasticity, potential for change (or, conversely, in their rigidity). Retrospective investigation will usually show that the possible outcomes have to be thought of in terms of probabilities; moreover, as a particular figuration changes, and a scatter of possible outcomes narrows down to a single one, *another range of possible outcomes, once more with differing probabilities*, hoves into view in the next phase of development.

2 The Mexican War thus established the boundaries of the conterminous USA as it exists today, with minor exceptions such as the Gadsden Purchase (a further sliver of Mexican territory) in 1853.

3 Saying attributed to Mexican President Porfirio Díaz (1830–1915).

4 The exact wording of Roosevelt's message to Congress in December 1904 was: 'Chronic wrongdoing, or an impotence which results in a general loosening of the ties of civilized society, may in America [i.e., the American hemisphere], as elsewhere, ultimately require intervention by some civilized nation, and in the western hemisphere the adherence of the United States to the Monroe Doctrine may force the United States, however reluctantly, in flagrant cases of such wrongdoing or impotence, to the exercise of an international police power' (Zimmerman, 2002: 440–1).

5 Ray Allen Billington (1977: 51–73) charts the circulation of books and the desire to maintain eastern culture, mainly among the more settled farming communities.

6 For further detail on the costs of setting up a farm even on cheap land in the West in the mid-nineteenth century, see Billington (1967: 10).

7 Two excellent compendia of contributions to the earlier phase's debate about 'the frontier thesis' are those edited by Taylor (1956) and by Hofstadter and Lipset (1968). The contents of the two partly overlap, but the latter includes some contributions from the late 1950s and 1960s. A balanced survey of the controversy can be found in Hofstadter, *The Progressive Historians* (1969: 118–64). A selection of papers marking the revival of the debate in 'the new Western history' is Cronon et al., 1992.

8 Hofstadter's exact words were 'the vast *empty* interior of the continent', which demonstrates that even so recently it was possible for a major American historian to ignore the existence of prior inhabitants.

9 Elias commented: 'Nothing is more fruitless, when dealing with long-term social processes, than to attempt to locate an absolute beginning' (2006a: 249).

10 Cuban sovereignty was severely curtailed by the incorporation of the 'Platt Amendment' into its constitution; see Zimmerman (2002: 376–86).

11 See Bergh (1992). For an account of the friendly disagreement between Bergh and Elias (who in his later years was preoccupied with the danger of nuclear war), see Mennell (1990b).

Chapter 9 Integration Struggles

1 The great campaign for civil rights in the South in the 1950s and 1960s is one instance of an 'integration struggle', but I use the term in a broader sense.

2 See *Statistical Abstract of the United States* 2002, table 28, p. 30.

3 See White and White (1962) and Smith (1966: 183–212, 258–83).

4 The Lynds captured this process very well in their classic study of one small Midwestern town (1937).

5 Note, however, Higham's (1968: 92–3) discussion of the distinction between 'immigrant' and 'settler': '[T]he term immigrant presupposed the existence of a receiving society to which the alien could attach himself. The immigrant . . . is not a colonist or settler, who creates a new society and lays down the terms of admission for others. He is rather the bearer of a foreign culture.' This is to state the difference in excessively polar terms. The difference between settlers and immigrants is one of power ratios; as discussed in chapter 7, European settlers rapidly gained the power advantage in their dealings with Indian societies, while even at the peak of immigration to the USA at the turn of the nineteenth to twentieth century that was never remotely true of immigrant groups in relation to the receiving society. The significance of differing power ratios is best captured in William McNeill's (1984) schema of forms of migration: conquest – infiltration – forced immigration (including indented labour as well as slavery) – forced emigration (expulsion). In effect, this forms a spectrum which, like many spectrums, is actually a circle: conquest may entail expulsion.

6 In the 1850 and 1860 censuses, no information was recorded about slaves' place of birth.

7 In Europe as much as the United States, the period 1870–1914 was a fecund one for the invention of traditions. Examples range from Mother's Day, which began in the USA in 1904, to the Tour de France and the FA Cup Final; see Terence Ranger's essay 'Mass-producing traditions: Europe, 1870–1914', in Hobsbawm and Ranger, eds (1983).

8 Of *groups*, that is true; but, as Godfrey Hodgson (2004: xx) has pointed out, it is less well known that over almost a century and a half, roughly one-third of individual immigrants went home again.

9 Legally, this was permitted by the Hart–Celler amendments, which took effect in 1968, to the 1952 Immigration and Nationality Act. Needless to say, the official statistics cited in this chapter do not take account of illegal immigrants, who add substantially to the figures for recent decades.

10 Hispanic migrants are slower than most others to undergo naturalization.

11 British police forces outside London today are answerable to regional police authorities, but decentralization is considerably tempered by the existence of a central supervisory agency, HM Inspectorate of Police, and by fairly frequent 'advice' to chief constables by the Home Secretary (the member of the government who would, in many other countries, be called 'Minister of the Interior'). Britain differs from both the USA and most European countries in that (setting aside minor exceptions like the British Transport Police and the Ministry of Defence Police whose writ runs nationally), there is effectively only *one* police force in any city or region.

12 Great Britain, not United Kingdom: the Royal Irish Constabulary, and after partition the Royal Ulster Constabulary, were always armed.

13 Lane's studies of the effects of policing and effective urban administration in nineteenth-century Boston (1967) and Philadelphia (1979) are referred to on p. 127 above.

14 But only its *origins*; its proximate cause was the Reagan administration's sponsorship of financial deregulation which gave the savings and loan banks the incentive to sell as many mortgages to the public as possible, while knowing that the state would ultimately rescue the banks from debts arising from consumers' bankruptcies. See Calavita et al., 1997.

15 President Woodrow Wilson (1913–21) was born in Virginia, but spent his adult life in New Jersey; in any case, he owed his election to the accident of the Republican vote being split between William Howard Taft and Theodore Roosevelt.

16 The traditional view was that sympathy for the rebel cause was widespread among the British elite, although not among the working classes. The detailed research of Campbell (2003), however, yields a more complicated picture.

17 Ransom (2005) lays out an intriguing counterfactual scenario of a Confederate victory.

18 See Key's classic *Southern Politics* (1949) – no less a classic just because the system it described was soon to vanish.

19 Andreski (1968 [1954]: 33) defines the MPR as 'the proportion of militarily utilised individuals in the population'. Lenski (1966: 49), taking over Andreski's concept, defines it more precisely as 'the proportion of *adult male* population utilised in military operations'; however, not only is that more difficult to calculate, but with the increasing numbers of women in the military it has recently also become a less necessary restriction. Data presented here are based on total population, male and female, children and adults.

20 In placing the beginnings of professionalization of the officer class in the early nineteenth century, Skelton differs from Samuel P. Huntington who, in *The Soldier and the State* (1957), argued that the process only dated from after the Civil War, when most of the army was posted on the western frontier in isolation from the rest of society.

21 I have omitted detailed data; the huge fluctuations between peacetime and war make them difficult to display visually. The French historical statistics are in any case surprisingly incomplete.

22 They fell back somewhat in the 1990s, between the fall of communism and the attacks on New York and Washington in 2001, but military theorists now argue that the link between personnel and firepower is no longer so great, because advanced technology has transformed both weapons and the means of surveillance over potential enemies.

23 See the review of this concept in Roland (2000).

Chapter 10 The Curse of the American Dream

1 This aspect of Sombart's argument rested on a rather crude version of the frontier thesis; he stressed the role of the Homestead Act in providing a safety

valve for the achievement of prosperity by those willing to settle on farms in the West. Over the ensuing century, an enormous literature arose on the question of the weakness of socialism in the USA; Lipset and Marks (2000) provide a comprehensive review, as well as essaying up-to-date answers of their own.

2 For comparative data on income distribution and poverty in all OECD countries in the second half of the 1990s, see Förster and d'Ercole (2005), and also Wright (1996) and Marshall (1997).

3 I am indebted to Helmut Kuzmics for this thought.

4 Even to use the expression 'welfare state' can be a source of transatlantic misunderstanding. Broadly speaking, for most people in Europe it has positive connotations – although that may be changing – whereas for a large bloc of opinion in the USA it is a pejorative term.

5 'Rational choice' theorists in sociology attempt to apply concepts and models derived from economics; for a debate about the merits of this approach, see Coleman and Fararo (1992), and notably the paper by Scheff (pp. 101–19) connecting this debate to the work of Elias.

6 A small proportion of the uninsured will be those who are so rich that they have no need to pay the premiums, but most are relatively poor, who rely on receiving free emergency care at hospitals – the cost of which then puts up premiums for the insured (*Economist*, 2006b: 26).

7 In passing, it is interesting that Newburyport, MA, the object of Thernstrom's study, was also the 'Yankee City' studied in the 1930s by W. Lloyd Warner (1960), who pioneered the sociological study of small details of lifestyle by which strata distinguish themselves.

8 Whether what Thernstrom found in nineteenth-century Massachusetts or Runciman in Britain in the 1960s still holds true in an America where more distant inequalities are constantly brought into everyone's home by television remains to be seen. Any such effect of media coverage is probably offset by the realignment, on the part of broad sections of the American population, of their perception of their actuarial interests (see p. 133 above).

9 'Reality-congruence' may jar, but it is a technical term from Elias's theory of knowledge.

10 I am indebted to Nico Wilterdink for this formulation.

Chapter 11   Involvement, Detachment and American Religiosity

1 The Gallup Organization periodically surveys American adults about their beliefs in evolution and creation, and its findings were remarkably stable throughout the 1980s and 1990s. In the 1997 survey, only 10 per cent assented to the proposition that 'Man has developed over millions of years from less advanced forms of life. God has no part in this process.' A further 39 per cent believed in God-boosted evolution ('intelligent design') – they accepted that Man had developed from less advanced forms of life, but that the process, including the creation of human beings, was guided by God. As many as 44 per cent believed that God had created Man much in his present form, at one time within the last 10,000 years. Among a sample of scientists, in contrast, the corresponding figures were 55, 40 and 5 per cent respectively.

International Social Survey Programme data from 1993 also showed the USA to be the least informed among 21 countries about evolution; see Ontario Consultants (2004), Bishop (1999). Slightly different wording in a 2005 survey yielded the finding that 42 per cent of Americans at large believed that life on earth had existed in its present form since the beginning of time; although 48 per cent believed that life had evolved over time, that figure broke down into 26 per cent who believed evolution took place through natural selection and 18 per cent who believed it was guided by a supreme being (Pew Research Center, 2005; balances made up of 'Don't Knows'). The same survey found that 64 per cent of respondents were favourable towards creationism being taught in schools alongside evolution, and 38 per cent wished it to replace evolution.

2 On the other hand, mass pressures towards conformity are once again evident in the large proportion of Americans who assent to religious belief.

3 A notable and fascinating example of the Augustinian approach in the study of American religion is Baltzell's *Puritan Boston and Quaker Philadelphia* (1979), in which he attributes to 'two Protestant Ethics' a decisive difference in 'class authority and leadership' and ultimately economic growth in the two cities. For all the interest of the cultural differences between two elites, however, the causal inference is weak.

4 A few of the most important of Elias's essays on the sociology of knowledge and the sciences can be found in *Involvement and Detachment* (2007a; Elias Collected Works, vol. 8). The rest, originally published in contributions to many different journals and books, will be published in 2008 as volume 14 of the Elias Collected Works. For an overall account of Elias's writings in this area, see Mennell (1998: 158–99).

5 At the very outset of his book, Eggleston wrote: 'What are loosely spoken of as national characteristics are probably a result not so much of heredity as of controlling traditions. Seminal ideas received in childhood, standards of feeling and thinking and living handed down from one overlapping generation to another, make the man English or French or German in the rudimentary outfit of his mind. A gradual change in fundamental notions produces the difference between the character of the nation at an early epoch and that of the same people in a later stage' (1901: 1) – a formulation that would have been congenial to Elias several decades later.

6 To show how all these processes are connected, Elias (2007a: 105–78) draws on a famous American short story, Edgar Allan Poe's 'A Descent into the Maelström' (1845).

7 Among the anti-Federalists during the debate on the Constitution were many who were shocked by its secular character; they argued that religion was a crucial support of government, and Richard Henry Lee wrote to Madison that 'the experience of times shows a religion to be the guardian of morals' (quoted by Kramnick (1987: 59). Debate has continued until the present day about how far the Founders intended a strictly secular state, or whether their secularism was narrowly confined to the prohibition of religious establishment. A strong case can be made for the more broadly secularist interpretation: see Jacoby (2005) for a brief summary.

8   Talcott Parsons (1971: 51, 54–6, 58, 88, 128) laid great emphasis on this political compromise, seeing it as a major cultural breakthrough.

9   One of Elias's earliest essays, published in 1935 when he was himself in Paris as a refugee from Hitler's Germany, was 'The Expulsion of the Huguenots from France' (2006c: 97–104).

10 Ribeiro does not dismiss ideological differences out of hand. He notes the influence of the encouragement to read the Bible in the case of the Protestants, in contrast with 'the conservatism, expressed in the insistence on attitudes of resignation to ignorance, backwardness and poverty, in the traditional Catholic ideology' (1971: 350). But he nevertheless attributes the famous 'Protestant work ethic' more to differences in the prevalent mode of labour recruitment: the predominance of the wage-earner class and a resulting view of dignity of labour in the one case, and serfdom and slavery in the other.

11 Max Weber commented (1946: 303n): 'The opening by prayer of not only every session of the US Supreme Court but also of every Party Convention has been an annoying ceremonial for quite some time.'

12 In a national survey conducted by the Pew Research Centre in March 2002, 47 per cent of respondents assented to the view that a belief in God was necessary in order to be a moral person, but slightly more (50 per cent) deemed it unnecessary. The vagaries of opinion surveys are exposed, however, by 84 per cent of respondents also expressing the view that a person can be a good American if he or she does not have religious faith, while just 13 per cent disagreed. One commentator calculated that this implied that nearly half of Americans believed that it was possible to be a good citizen without being moral.

13 And it has served as a thurible from which the odour of sanctity is spread around American foreign policy. Bellah's famous essay was written at the time of the Vietnam War, just as this book has taken shape during the war in Iraq, and he noted that the civil religion 'has often been used and is being used today as a cloak for petty interests and ugly passions' (1967: 16, 18–19). Catherine Albanese (1992) contended that the civil religion had gone into decline from the 1960s, but it has arguably reasserted itself in the early years of the twenty-first century.

14 See Fanny Trollope's account of a Methodist camp-meeting and its emotional excesses (1997 [1832]: 126–32).

15 That is not to imply that such upsurges represent totally spontaneous movements of the spirit; both the First and Second Great Awakenings were highly organized and planned campaigns (Finke and Stark, 2005: 55ff.).

16 The economist Robert W. Fogel (2000) counts this as a Third Great Awakening, but Christian fundamentalism (see below), which began to emerge in the USA at about the same time, is much closer in character to the first two than is Social Gospel.

17 It is highly improbable that Elias had read Rauschenbusch, but this does bring to mind Elias's much-quoted comment that later generations might well see the late twentieth century as an age of 'the late barbarians' (1991: 146–7).

18 Fogel has labelled this 'the Fourth Great Awakening', though its roots lie further back, early in the twentieth century. He sees each of them as the result of technological advances outstripping ethical norms, a hypothesis distantly

recalling what in the present book are referred to as integration struggles. Running through all four, he argues, is an unbroken egalitarian impulse. Most reviewers, however, have been unconvinced by Fogel's argument, and there is not space here to discuss his ideas at length.

19 The third column in each denomination, that for 2001, is a rough-and-ready calculation which is probably only approximately comparable with the Finke and Stark data. From the American Religious Identification Survey of 2001 (Kosmin et al., 2002) I excluded the respondents who described themselves as 'Christian', 'Protestant' without further specification of a denomination, or as 'Non-denominational'; the resulting total was then used as the enumerator in calculating percentages. The remaining respondents were tabulated into the five denominations mentioned by Finke and Stark, plus two new composite groupings that I labelled 'Other Moderate' (containing for example the Orthodox, Quakers, Unitarians and – debatably – the Salvation Army) and 'Evangelical/Pentecostalist', into which I divided (perhaps impressionistically) the numerous remaining sects.

20 Figures for self-described non-Christian religious identification in the American Religious Identification Survey 2001 (Kosmin et al., 2002) are:

	Number	% US pop.
Jewish	2,831,000	1.30
Muslim	1,104,000	0.50
Buddhist	1,082,000	0.50
Hindu	766,000	0.40
Other	1,306,000	0.67
No Religion	29,481,000	14.20
Refused	11,246,000	.5.40

Note that in this table percentages are calculated in relation to the *total* population of the USA, not, as in figure 11.1, in relation to the total of those describing themselves as having a denominational affiliation.

21 While Finke and Stark are no doubt right in detecting a judgement about what is 'better' in traditional accounts of religious progress, they are making a value judgement of their own about what *they* consider 'better': they clearly imply that it is a good thing to 'stir the faithful or satisfy the heart'. In contrast, it should be noted that Elias's theory of knowledge and the sciences is not a theory of 'progress', in the sense of things becoming 'better' in any moral sense, but rather about an unplanned direction of development that may have both 'good' and 'bad' effects.

22 Harris's thesis has something in common with Wilson's view that 'what goes on in the major churches of Britain is very much more "religious" than what occurs in American churches; in America secularizing processes appear to have occurred *within* the church' (1982: 152).

23 I owe this pithy formulation to David Garland (personal communication).

24 Putnam has described (in personal conversation) an area of California where a massive 'church campus' is virtually the monopoly supplier of social capital,

in industrial quantities, organizing everything from recreation to counselling and crèches.

25 The counter-intuitive fact that a majority of Irish-Americans is Protestant (Greeley, 1979) can be cited in evidence for the effectiveness of inter-denominational competition. It is likely that, especially in small towns and along the advancing frontier where a full portfolio of denominations was not available, many Catholic families were recruited into Protestant churches that were present and welcoming. Greeley's surprising finding may also owe something to the fact that much Irish immigration before the mid-nineteenth century was of Ulster Protestant origin (several of the early Presidents were of 'Scotch-Irish' stock), so they had several generations' start in breeding descendants.

26 Susan Jacoby (2005) provides a very good brief historical account of evolutionism versus creationism controversies since the Scopes trial of 1925.

27 See Hunt (1999) for a critical discussion of these socio-biological writers.

28 Over the same period there was also a substantial increase in the number of adults who refused to reply to the question about their religious preference, from about four million or 2 per cent in 1990 to more than eleven million or over 5 per cent in 2001. This may, however, include many religious people – for example Muslims – who wish not to disclose their affiliation.

29 The debate gains a certain piquancy from many proponents of secularization not being believers, while most of their opponents among sociologists of religion appear themselves to be religious. See Davie (2002) for an excellent survey and bibliography of the extensive literature. Besides Europe and America, Davie includes chapters on Latin America, Africa and parts of the Far East, which I cannot discuss here. Overall, the evidence does point to a more decisive secularization in Western Europe than anywhere else, but not so much to an 'exceptionalism' as to the highly differentiated trajectories of religious development across the globe. It appears to me, however, that some of the explanations (drawn largely from *outside* the normal sociology of religion) that I advance here to explain the persistence and renewal of religiosity in the USA also apply to some extent in the other continents.

30 An equally speculative thought is that there could be an unbelieving backlash to the political campaigns of fundamentalist pressure groups; one thinks of the T-shirt slogan 'So many right-wing Christians, so few lions'.

Chapter 12 America and Humanity as a Whole

1 Whether it was in fact the first such revolution is debatable. A good case can be made for the Dutch Republic as an early example of a state in which the nobility lost its leading position and became subordinated to the merchant patricians, and in which control of the monopolies of violence and taxation was dispersed. See Vree (1999: 189–93).

2 The sub-headings in Elias's concluding 'synopsis' (2000: 363–447) were: spread of the pressure for foresight and self-constraint; diminishing contrasts, increasing varieties; the courtization of warriors; the muting of drives: psychologization and rationalization; shame and repugnance; increasing constraints on the upper class: increasing pressure from below; and a final section

in which Elias discussed his theory against the background of the international politics of the late 1930s.

3 Terms like 'less developed' are often criticized for seeming to belittle the societies so described. Elias took exactly the opposite viewpoint. 'It would be denigrating them not to speak of them in this way, so closing one's mind to the structure of the change these groups are undergoing as societies and as individuals in the transition from one stage of development to another' (1991: 180). Elias's view runs completely counter to the orthodoxy that has prevailed for several decades among anthropologists.

4 To labour the point, that was forgotten when the USA invaded Iraq.

5 In his study of political ideas in the era of Independence, based on sources such as newspapers and sermons rather than explicit political statements, Shain concluded that the life of the mass of Americans was not governed by abstract ideas, whether of liberal individualism or republicanism. Rather, 'The vast majority of Americans lived voluntarily in morally demanding agricultural communities shaped by reformed-Protestant social and moral norms. These communities were defined by overlapping circles of family- and community-assisted self-regulation and even self-denial, rather than by individual autonomy . . .' (1994: xvi).

6 This sounds like a *cri de coeur*, and is. My own experience in universities suggests to me that the American management orthodoxy of 'missions' and 'visions' actually serves to promote relatively unrealistic planning, oblivious to manifold unintended consequences.

7 Another example is the conservation of the world's fish stocks (the Grand Banks off the shore of the USA and Canada have already been fished out of cod).

8 For the analogy of a one-way mirror, I am indebted to Goudsblom (1986c). A similar insight is encapsulated in Chakrabarty's concept of 'asymmetric ignorance' (2000: 28).

9 In a book that otherwise tends rather to glorify the role of the American military in the world today, Kaplan (2005) nevertheless stresses that the soldiers – 'Imperial grunts', he calls them – feel a loyalty only to the USA, and have a very limited knowledge of or sympathy for the local cultures in which they are intervening. A similar criticism was made by a senior British army officer (Ailwyn-Foster, 2005), writing in the US Army's *Military Review*.

10 Among the general public, the fear of nuclear war has declined, although politicians appear to regard the risk as higher today, when nuclear weapons have proliferated to several other countries, including India, Pakistan, Israel, North Korea and, imminently, Iran. At first glance, a multipolar balance of power would seem less stable than a bipolar one. Bergh, however, considers that the MAD principle still holds: the cost of suffering a retaliatory nuclear strike is so great that the governments that have now acquired them will be as reluctant to use them as the USA and USSR were (personal communication).

11 The Court of Human Rights is an arm of the 46-member Council of Europe, an older entity than the European Union with its current 25 member states.

12 There is a public debate in the USA about the extent and validity of international law. One view that is openly stated and influential is that international

law should be ignored whenever it is an obstacle to the exercise of American power, and should be used only when it serves to promote American interests (as, on the whole, it does in relation to trade, where the rules were broadly designed by and for American interests). Besides international law itself, a trend is evident in many countries for their courts to cite cases and use precedents from other jurisdictions; this trend is less clear in the USA. At least one Justice of the US Supreme Court (Scalia) has argued that international law has no relevance to the Court's task of expounding the US Constitution, although according to Cleveland (2005: 124) the 'historical record established that our constitutional tradition is significantly more receptive to international norms than is understood in the current scholarly and judicial debate'.

13 This is a very practical question today. Stiglitz (2006: 120–2, 211n) gives the example of the USA's insistence for narrowly commercial reasons of trade-related aspects of intellectual property rights (TRIPs) in the Uruguay round of world trade negotiations which, through preventing the production of cheaper generic drugs in poor countries, probably condemned hundreds of thousands of people to death (especially from AIDS). In contrast, for all the imperfections of the American political system and the inequality of American society, notions of 'fairness' do usually play some residual part in determining domestic policy, for fear of the electoral consequences of not doing so.

14 Fukuyama (2006), drawing lessons from the catastrophically unilateral invasion of Iraq, urges a return to more multilateral methods, but still scorns the UN; the more or less equal representation of all countries under the Charter makes the UN recalcitrant to monopoly management.

15 Charles Dickens, letter to John Forster, 24 February 1842; in Forster (n.d.), p. 151.

References

Abrams, Philip (1982) *Historical Sociology*. Shepton Mallet: Open Books.

Adams, Henry (1999 [1919]) *The Education of Henry Adams*. Oxford: Oxford University Press.

Adams, Herbert Baxter (1882) *The German Origin of New England Towns*. Baltimore, MD: Johns Hopkins University Press.

Adelman, Jeremy and Stephen Aron (1999) 'From Borderlands to Borders: Empires, Nation-States, and the Peoples in Between in North American History', *American Historical Review*, 104 (3): 814–41.

Ahlstrom, Sydney E. (1972) *A Religious History of the American People*. New Haven, CT: Yale University Press.

Ailwyn-Foster, Nigel (2005) 'Changing the Army for Counterinsurgency Operations', *Military Review* (November–December): 2–15.

Alba, Richard D. (1990) *Ethnic Identity: The Transformation of White America*. New Haven, CT: Yale University Press.

Albanese, Catherine (1992) *America: Religions and Religion*. Belmont, CA: Wadsworth.

Alderson, Arthur S. and François Nielsen (2002) 'Globalization and the Great U-turn: Income Inequality Trends in 16 OECD Countries', *American Journal of Sociology*, 107 (5): 1244–99.

Alesina, Alberto, Edward L. Glaeser and Bruce Sacerdote (2001) 'Why Doesn't the United States Have a European-style Welfare State?' Cambridge, MA: Harvard Institute of Economic Research, Discussion Paper 1933.

Allestree, Richard (1658) *The Whole Duty of Man*. London.

Andreski, Stanislav (1968 [1954]) *Military Organization and Society*. London: Routledge.

Anon. (1859) *The Habits of Good Society*. London: J. Hogg.

Aptheker, Herbert (1961) *The American Civil War*. New York: International Publishers.

Armstrong, Karen (2000) *Islam: A Short History*. London: Phoenix.

Atkinson, A. B. and Thomas Piketty (2007) *Top Incomes Over the Twentieth Century: A Contrast Between English-speaking and European Countries*. Oxford: Oxford University Press.

Bacevich, Andrew J. (2002) *American Empire: The Realities and Consequences of US Diplomacy*. Cambridge, MA: Harvard University Press.

Bailey, Beth L. (1988) *From Front Porch to Back Seat: Courtship in Twentieth-Century America*. Baltimore, MD: Johns Hopkins University Press.

Bailyn, Bernard, Robert Dallek, David Brion Davis, David Herbert Donald, John L. Thomas and Gordon S. Wood (1992) *The Great Republic: A History of the American People*. Lexington, MA: D. C. Heath.

Baltzell, E. Digby (1953) '*Who's Who in America* and *The Social Register*: Elite and Upper Class Indexes in Metropolitan America', in Reinhard Bendix and Seymour Martin Lipset, eds, *Class, Status and Power*. New York: Free Press.

Baltzell, E. Digby (1958) *Philadelphia Gentlemen*. Glencoe, IL: Free Press.

Baltzell, E. Digby (1979) *Puritan Boston and Quaker Philadelphia: Two Protestant Ethics and the Spirit of Class Authority and Leadership*. New York: Free Press.

Banner, Stuart (2002) *The Death Penalty: An American History*. Cambridge, MA: Harvard University Press.

Barclay, Gordon and Cynthia Tavares (2002) 'International Comparisons of Criminal Justice Statistics 2000'. <www.homeoffice.gov.uk/rds/>, accessed 12 July 2002.

Bauman, Zygmunt (1989) *Modernity and the Holocaust*. Cambridge: Polity Press.

Bax, Mart (1987) 'Religious Regimes and State Formation: Towards a Research Perspective', *Anthropological Quarterly*, 60 (1): 1–13.

Beard, Charles A. (1913) *An Economic Interpretation of the Constitution*. New York: Macmillan.

Beard, Charles A. and Mary A. Beard (1940) *The Making of American Civilization*. New York: Macmillan.

Beard, Charles A. and Mary A. Beard (1942) *The American Spirit: A Study of the Idea of Civilization in the United States*. New York: Macmillan.

Bederman, Gail (1995) *Manliness and Civilization: A Cultural History of Gender and Race in the United States, 1880–1917*. Chicago: University of Chicago Press.

Beeghley, Leonard (2003) *Homicide: A Sociological Explanation*. Lanham, MD: Rowman & Littlefield.

Bellah, Robert N. (1967) 'Civil Religion in America', *Daedalus*, 96 (1): 1–21.

Bellah, Robert N., Richard Madsen, William M. Sullivan, Anne Swidler and Steven M. Tipton (1985) *Habits of the Heart: Individualism and Commitment in American Life*. Berkeley, CA: University of California Press.

Bellesiles, Michael A. (2003) *Arming America: The Origins of a National Gun Culture*. Brooklyn, NY: Soft Skull Press.

Benedict, Ruth (1946) *The Chrysanthemum and the Sword*. Boston: Houghton Mifflin.

Berger, Peter (2006) 'Between Relativism and Fundamentalism', *The American Interest*, 2 (1): 9–17.

Bergh, Godfried van Benthem van den (1992) *The Nuclear Revolution and the End of the Cold War: Forced Restraint*. London: Macmillan.

Billington, Ray Allen (1967) *Westward Expansion: A History of the American Frontier*. New York: Macmillan.

Billington, Ray Allen (1969) 'Frontiers', pp. 75–90 in C. Vann Woodward, ed., *The Comparative Approach to American History*. Oxford: Oxford University Press.

Billington, Ray Allen (1977) *America's Frontier Culture: Three Essays*. College Station, TX: Texas A&M University Press.

Bishop, George (1999) 'What Americans Really Believe: And Why Faith Isn't as Universal as They Think', *Free Inquiry*, 19 (3): 38–42.

Blake, William (1958 [1793]) 'America: A Prophecy', in Jacob Bronowski, ed., *William Blake: A Selection of Poems and Letters*. Harmondsworth: Penguin.

Blakely, Edward J. and Mary Gall Snyder (1998) *Fortress America: Gated Communities in the United States*. Washington, DC: Brookings Institute.

Blanden, Jo, Paul Gregg and Stephen Machin (2005) 'Intergenerational Mobility in Europe and North America'. A Report supported by the Sutton Trust. London: Centre for Economic Performance, London School of Economics.

Block, Richard (1998). 'Firearms in Canada and Eight Other Western Countries: Selected Findings of the 1996 International Crime (Victim) Survey'. Ottawa: Canadian Firearms Centre, Department of Justice, Canada.

Blok, Anton (1974) *The Mafia of a Sicilian Village, 1860–1960*. Oxford: Basil Blackwell.

Blomert, Reinhard (2003) 'The Disobedient King-President', *Figurations: Newsletter of the Norbert Elias Foundation*, 19.

Blum, William (1995) *Killing Hope: US Military and CIA Interventions since World War II*. Monroe, ME: Common Courage Press.

Blumer, Herbert (1930) 'Science Without Concepts', pp. 153–70 in Blumer, *Symbolic Interactionism: Perspective and Method*. Englewood Cliffs, NJ: Prentice-Hall, 1969.

Bobbitt, Philip (2002) *The Shield of Achilles: War, Peace and the Course of History*. London: Allen Lane The Penguin Press.

Bolton, Herbert E. (1921) *The Spanish Borderlands*. New Haven, CT: Yale University Press.

Boorstin, Daniel and William H. Goetzmann (1972) *American Civilization*. London: Thames & Hudson.

Borjas, George J. (2000) *Heaven's Door: Immigration Policy and American Economy*. Princeton, NJ: Princeton University Press.

Bourdieu, Pierre (1996) *The State Nobility*. Cambridge: Polity.

Bowman, Shearer Davis (1980) 'Antebellum Planters and *Vormärz* Junkers in Comparative Perspective', *American Historical Review*, 85 (4): 779–808.

Bowman, Shearer Davis (1993) *Masters and Lords: Mid-Nineteenth Century United States Planters and Prussian Junkers*. New York: Oxford University Press.

Brathwayt, Richard (1630) *The English Gentleman*. London: Robert Bostock.

Brinkgreve, Christien (1982) 'On Modern Relationships: The Commandments of the New Freedom', *Netherlands Journal of Sociology*, 18 (1): 47–56.

Broad, David B. (1996) 'The Social Register: Directory of America's Upper Class', *Sociological Spectrum*, 16 (2): 173–81.

Brown, Richard D. (1989) *Knowledge is Power: The Diffusion of Information in Early America, 1700–1865*. New York: Oxford University Press.

Brown, Richard Maxwell (1975) *Strain of Violence: Historical Studies of American Violence and Vigilantism*. New York: Oxford University Press.

Brown, Richard Maxwell (1991) *No Duty to Retreat: Violence and Values in American History and Society*. New York: Oxford University Press.

Brown, Roger (1965) *Social Psychology*. New York: Free Press.

Brown, Roger and A. Gilman (1960) 'The Pronouns of Power and Solidarity', in T. A. Sebeok, ed., *Style in Language*. Cambridge, MA: MIT Press.

Bruce, Steve (1996) *Religion in the Modern World: From Cathedrals to Cults*. Oxford: Oxford University Press.

Brundage, W. Fitzhugh (1993) *Lynching in the New South: Georgia and Virginia, 1880–1930*. Urbana, IL: University of Illinois Press.

Bryce, James (1891) *The American Commonwealth*, 2 vols. London: Macmillan.

Bryson, Anna (1998) *From Courtesy to Civility: Changing Codes of Conduct in Early Modern England*. Oxford: Clarendon Press.

Bryson, Bill (1994) *Made in America*. London: Secker & Warburg.

Burkert, Walter (1996) *Creation of the Sacred: Tracks of Biology in Early Religions*. Cambridge, MA: Harvard University Press.

Bushman, Richard L. (1993) *The Refinement of America: Persons, Houses, Cities*. New York: Knopf.

Calavita, Kitty, Henry N. Pontell and Robert H. Tillman (1997) *Big Money Crime: Fraud and Politics in the Savings and Loans Crisis*. Berkeley, CA: University of California Press.

Campbell, Duncan Andrew (2003) *English Public Opinion and the American Civil War*. Woodbridge: Royal Historical Society/Boydell.

Cancian, Francesca (1987) *Love in America: Gender and Self-Development*. Cambridge: Cambridge University Press.

Casa, Giovanni della (1994 [1558]) *Galateo*. Toronto: Centre for Reformation and Renaissance Studies.

Castiglione, Baldesar (1967 [1528]) *The Book of the Courtier*, trans. George Bull. Harmondsworth: Penguin.

Ceaser, James W. (1997) *Reconstructing America: The Symbol of America in Modern Thought*. New Haven, CT: Yale University Press.

Chakrabarty, Dipesh (2000) *Provincializing Europe: Postcolonial Thought and Historical Difference*. Princeton, NJ: Princeton University Press.

Chesnut, Mary Boykin (1961 [1905]) *A Diary from Dixie*. Gloucester, MA: Peter Smith.

Chesterfield, Philip Dormer Stanhope, 4th Earl of (1774) *Letters to his Son*. London.

Chinoy, Ely (1955) *Automobile Workers and the American Dream*. Garden City, NY: Doubleday.

Chomsky, Noam (2003) *Hegemony or Survival: America's Quest for Global Dominance*. New York: Henry Holt.

Clark, David (2005) 'West Wing Wanabees: Wake Up and Smell the Coffee', *Guardian*, 18 January 2005.

Clark, J. C. D. (1997) 'British America: What If There Had Been No American Revolution', pp. 125–74 in Niall Ferguson, ed., *Virtual History: Alternatives and Counterfactuals*. London: Picador.

Cleveland, Sarah H. (2005) 'Our International Constitution', *Yale Journal of International Law*, 31 (1): 1–125.

Clinton, Hillary Rodham (1996) *It Takes a Village*. New York: Simon & Schuster.

Coleman, James S. and Thomas J. Fararo, eds (1992) *Rational Choice Theory: Advocacy and Critique*. London: Sage.

Collier, James Lincoln (1991) *The Rise of Selfishness in America*. Oxford: Oxford University Press.

Condorcet, Marie-Jean-Nicolas de Caritat, marquis de (1955 [1795]) *Sketch for a Historical Picture of the Progress of the Human Mind*. London: Weidenfeld & Nicolson.

Corbin, Alain (1986) *The Foul and the Fragrant: Odour and the French Social Imagination*. Cambridge, MA: Harvard University Press.

Courtin, Antoine de (1672) *Nouveau traité de civilité qui se pratique en France, parmi les honnestes gens*. Amsterdam: J. Le Jeune.

Crenson, Matthew (1971) *The Un-Politics of Air Pollution*. Baltimore, MD: Johns Hopkins University Press.

Crèvecœur, J. Hector St John de (1981 [1782]) *Letters from an American Farmer and Sketches of Eighteenth-Century America*. New York: Penguin.

Cronon, William, George Miles and Jay Gitlin (1992) *Under an Open Sky: Rethinking America's Western Past*. New York: W. W. Norton.

Curry, Richard O. and Lawrence B. Goodheart (1991) *American Chameleon: Individualism in Trans-National Context*. Kent, OH: Kent State University Press.

Curti, Merle Eugene (1953) *A History of American Civilization*. New York: Harper.

Dahl, Robert A. (1961) *Who Governs?* New Haven, CT: Yale University Press.

Daly, Martin and Margo Wilson (1988) *Homicide*. New York: Aldine de Gruyter.

Darnton, Robert (1984) *The Great Cat Massacre and Other Episodes in French Cultural History*. London: Allen Lane.

Davidoff, Leonore (1973) *The Best Circles: Society, Etiquette and the Season*. London: Croom Helm.

Davie, Grace (1990) 'Believing Without Belonging: Is This the Future of Religion in Britain?', *Social Compass*, 37 (4): 456–69.

Davie, Grace (1994) *Religion in Britain Since 1945: Believing Without Belonging*. Oxford: Blackwell.

Davie, Grace (2002) *Europe: The Exceptional Case: Parameters of Faith in the Modern World*. London: Darton, Longman & Todd.

Degler, Carl N. (1974) 'What Ought To Be and What Was: Women's Sexuality in the Nineteenth Century', *American Historical Review*, 79 (5): 1467–90.

Dickens, Charles (1957 [1842]) *American Notes*. Oxford: Oxford University Press.

Doob, Christopher (1988) *The Open Covenant: Social Change in Contemporary Society*. New York: Praeger.

Douglass, Frederick (1995 [1845]) *Narrative of the Life of Frederick Douglass*. New York: Dover.

Drucker, Peter (1969) *The Age of Discontinuity*. New York: Harper & Row.

Duerr, Hans-Peter (1988) *Nacktheit und Scham: Der Mythos vom Zivilisationsprozeße*. Frankfurt/Main: Suhrkamp.

Dunning, Eric (1977) 'In Defence of Developmental Sociology: A Critique of Popper's *Poverty of Historicism* with Special Reference to the Theory of Auguste Comte', *Amsterdams Sociologisch Tijdschrift*, 4 (3): 327–49.

Dunning, Eric (1999) *Sport Matters: Sociological Studies of Sport, Violence and Civilization*. London: Routledge.

Dunning, Eric and Kenneth Sheard (1979) *Barbarians, Gentlemen and Players*. Oxford: Martin Robertson.

Dunning, Eric, Patrick Murphy and John Williams (1988) *The Roots of Football Hooliganism: An Historical and Sociological Study*. London: Routledge & Kegan Paul.

Durkheim, Emile (1893) *De la division du travail social*. Paris: Alcan.

Durkheim, Emile (1984) *The Division of Labour in Society*, trans. W. D. Halls. London: Macmillan.

Eaton, Clement (1968) *The Waning of the Old South Civilization, 1860–1880s*. Athens, GA: University of Georgia Press.

Eckberg, Douglas Lee (1995) 'Estimates of Early Twentieth-Century US Homicide Rates: An Econometric Forecasting Approach', *Demography*, 32 (1): 1–16.

Economist (2004) 'Ever Higher Society, Ever Harder to Ascend', *The Economist* (29 December).

Economist (2006a) 'America's Headache: How to Start to Fix the World's Costliest Health-Care System', *The Economist* (28 January), p. 12.

Economist (2006b) 'Special Report: America's Health-Care Crisis', *The Economist* (28 January), pp. 26–8.

Eggleston, Edward (1901) *The Transit of Civilization from England to America in the Seventeenth Century*. New York: D. Appleton.

Ehrenreich, Barbara (2004) 'Their George and Ours', *New York Times*, 4 July.

Eisenhower, Dwight D. (1961) 'Farewell Address to the Nation', 17 January, pp. 1035–40 in *Public Papers of the Presidents of the United States*. Washington, DC: United States General Printing Office, 1960–.

Eisner, Manuel (2001) 'Modernization, Self-Control and Lethal Violence: The Long-Term Dynamics of European Homicide Rates in Theoretical Perspective', *British Journal of Criminology*, 41 (4): 618–38.

Eisner, Manuel (2003) 'Long-term Historical Trends in Violent Crime', *Crime and Justice: A Review of Research*, 30: 83–142.

Eisner, Manuel (2005) 'Modernity Strikes Back? The Latest Increase in Interpersonal Violence (1960–1990) in a Historical Perspective'. Paper presented at the Fourth Workshop on Interpersonal Violence, Rotterdam, April 2005.

Elias, Norbert (1950) 'Studies in the Genesis of the Naval Profession', *British Journal of Sociology*, 1 (4): 291–309.

Elias, Norbert (1974) 'Foreword: Towards a Theory of Communities', in Colin Bell and Howard Newby, eds, *The Sociology of Community: A Selection of Readings*. London: Frank Cass.

Elias, Norbert (1978) *What Is Sociology?* New York: Columbia University Press.

Elias, Norbert (1987) *Los der Menschen: Gedichte/Nachdichtungen*. Frankfurt: Suhrkamp.

Elias, Norbert (1991) *The Society of Individuals*. Oxford: Blackwell.

Elias, Norbert (1994) 'Introduction: A Theoretical Essay on Established and Outsiders', pp. xi–lii in *The Established and the Outsiders: A Sociological Enquiry into Community Problems*. London: Sage.

Elias, Norbert (1996) *The Germans: Power Struggles and the Development of Habitus in the Nineteenth and Twentieth Centuries*. Cambridge: Polity.

Elias, Norbert (2000 [1939]) *The Civilizing Process: Sociogenetic and Psychogenetic Investigations*, trans. Edmund Jephcott, ed. Eric Dunning, Johan Goudsblom and Stephen Mennell. Oxford: Blackwell.

Elias, Norbert (2006a) *The Court Society*, trans. Edmund Jephcott, ed. Stephen Mennell. Dublin: University College Dublin Press.

Elias, Norbert (2006b) 'The Kitsch Style and the Age of Kitsch', pp. 85–96 in *Early Writings*, ed. Richard Kilminster. Dublin: University College Dublin Press.

Elias, Norbert (2006c) 'The Expulsion of the Huguenots from France', in *Early Writings*, ed. Richard Kilminster. Dublin: University College Dublin Press.

Elias, Norbert (2007a) *Involvement and Detachment*, trans. Edmund Jephcott, ed. Stephen Mennell. Dublin: University College Dublin Press.

Elias, Norbert (2007b) *An Essay on Time*. Dublin: University College Dublin Press.

Elias, Norbert and Eric Dunning (1986) *Quest for Excitement: Sport and Leisure in the Civilizing Process*. Oxford: Blackwell.

Elias, Norbert and John L. Scotson (1994 [1965]) *The Established and the Outsiders: A Sociological Enquiry into Community Problems*. London: Frank Cass.

Elkins, Stanley (1959) *Slavery: A Problem in American Institutional Life*. New York: Grosset & Dunlop.

Elkins, Stanley and Eric McKittrick (1954) 'A Meaning for Turner's Frontier: Democracy in the Old Northwest', *Political Science Quarterly*, 69 (3): 323–99.

Ellis, Joseph J. (1997) *American Sphinx: The Character of Thomas Jefferson*. New York: A. A. Knopf.

Emsley, Clive (2004) 'Control and Legitimacy: The Police in Comparative Perspective in Europe Since 1800', pp. 193–209 in Clive Emsley, Eric A Johnson and Pieter Spierenburg, eds, *Social Control in Europe*. Colombus, OH: Ohio State University Press.

Erasmus, Desiderius of Rotterdam (1530) *De civilitate morum puerilium*. Köln: J. Gymnicus.

Erikson, Robert and John H. Goldthorpe (1992) *The Constant Flux: A Study of Class Mobility in Industrial Societies*. Oxford: Clarendon Press.

Espy, M. Watt and Juan Ortiz Smylka (1994) 'Executions in the US, 1608–1897: The Espy File'. <www.icpsr.umich.edu/NACJD>.

Evans, Richard J. (1996) *Rituals of Retribution: Capital Punishment in Germany, 1600–1987*. Oxford: Oxford University Press.

Febvre, Lucien (1973) '*Civilisation*: Evolution of a Word and a Group of Ideas', pp. 219–57 in Peter Burke, ed., *A New Kind of History: From the Writings of Febvre*. London: Routledge & Kegan Paul.

Fenton, William N. (1998) *The Great Law and the Longhouse: A Political History of the Iroquois Confederacy*. Norman, OK: University of Oklahoma Press.

Finke, Roger and Laurence R. Iannaccone (1993) 'Supply-Side Explanations for Religious Change', *Annals of the American Academy of Political and Social Science*, 527: 27–39.

Finke, Roger and Rodney Stark (2005) *The Churching of America, 1776–2005: Winners and Losers in our Religious Economy*. New Brunswick, NJ: Rutgers University Press.

Fitzhugh, George (1854) *Sociology for the South, or The Failure of Free Society*. Richmond, VA: A. Morris.

Flandrin, Jean-Louis (1979) *Families in Former Times: Kinship, Household and Sexuality*. Cambridge: Cambridge University Press.

Fogel, Robert W. (2000) *The Fourth Great Awakening and the Future of Egalitarianism*. Chicago: University of Chicago Press.

Foner, Eric (1988) *Reconstruction: America's Unfinished Revolution, 1863–77*. New York: Harper & Row.

Forster, John (n.d. [orig. 1872]) *The Life of Charles Dickens*. 1-vol. edn, London: Chapman & Hall.

Förster, Michael and Marco Mira d'Ercole (2005) 'Income Distribution and Poverty in OECD Countries in the Second Half of the 1990s'. Paris: Organization for Economic Co-operation and Development. OECD Social, Employment and Migration Working Papers 22.

Foucault, Michel (1977) *Discipline and Punishment*. London: Allen Lane.

Frank, Robert H. and Philip J. Cook (1996) *The Winner-Take-All Society*. New York: Penguin.

Frank, Thomas (2000) *One Market Under God*. Garden City, NY: Doubleday.

Franklin, Adrian (1999) *Animals and Modern Cultures: A Sociology of Human–Animal Relations in Modernity*. London: Sage.

Franklin, Benjamin (1905–7) *The Writings of Benjamin Franklin*, 10 vols., ed. A. E. Henry. New York: Macmillan.

Frazer, Sir James (1958 [1890]) *The Golden Bough*. New York: Macmillan.

Fromm, Erich (1947) *Man for Himself: An Enquiry into the Psychology of Ethics*. New York: Fawcett Premier.

Fukuyama, Francis (1992) *The End of History and the Last Man*. London: Hamish Hamilton.

Fukuyama, Francis (2006) *After the Neocons: America at the Crossroads*. London: Profile.

Fulbright, J. W. (1966) *The Arrogance of Power*. New York: Random House.

Garland, David (1985) *Punishment and Welfare*. Aldershot: Gower.

Garland, David (1990) *Punishment and Modern Society: A Study in Social Theory*. Oxford: Clarendon Press.

Garland, David (2001) *The Culture of Control: Crime and Social Order in Contemporary Society*. Oxford: Oxford University Press.

Garland, David (2004) 'A Peculiar Institution? Capital Punishment and the American Civilizing Process'. Moffett Lecture on Ethics, Princeton University, 9 December.

Garland, David (2005a) 'Capital Punishment and American Culture', *Punishment and Society*, 7 (4): 347–76.

Garland, David (2005b) 'Penal Excess and Surplus Meaning: Public Torture Lynchings in Twentieth-Century America'. (Unpublished paper.)

Gay, Peter (1997 [1968]) 'The Enlightenment', pp. 34–46 in C. Vann Woodward, ed., *The Comparative Approach to American History*, new edn. New York: Basic Books.

Gerhard, Dietrich (1959) 'The Frontier in Comparative View', *Comparative Studies in Society and History*, 1 (2): 205–29.

Glassner, Barry (1999) *The Culture of Fear: The Assault on Optimism in America*. New York: Basic Books.

Glazer, Nathan (1998) 'The American Welfare State: Exceptional No Longer?', pp. 7–19 in Henry Cavanna, ed., *Challenges to the Welfare State: Internal and External Dynamics for Change*. Cheltenham: Edward Elgar.

Glazer, Nathan (2005) 'Why Americans Don't Care About Income Inequality', *Irish Journal of Sociology*, 14 (1): 5–12.

Gleichmann, Peter R. (1979) 'Zur zivilisationssoziologischen Begriffsbildung', in J. Diederich et al., eds, *Sozialer Wandel in Westeuropa*. Berlin: Universitätsbibliothek der Technischen Universität Berlin.

Gleichmann, Peter R. (1980) 'Einige soziale Wandlungen des Schlafers', *Zeitschrift für Soziologie*, 9 (3): 236–50.

Go, Julian (2003) 'Introduction: Global Perspectives on the US Colonial State in the Philippines', pp. 1–42 in Julian Go and Anne L. Foster, eds, *The American Colonial State in the Philippines*. Durham, NC: Duke University Press.

Go, Julian and Anne L. Foster, eds (2003) *The American Colonial State in the Philippines*. Durham, NC: Duke University Press.

Goodhart, David (2004) 'Too Diverse?', *Prospect*, 95, February.

Goodrich, Samuel (1856) *Recollections of a Lifetime*. New York: Miller, Orton & Mulligan.

Goodwin, Jason (2003) *Greenback: The Almighty Dollar and the Invention of America*. London: Hamish Hamilton.

Gordon, John Steele (1998) *Hamilton's Blessing: The Extraordinary Life and Times of our National Debt*. New York: Penguin.

Gorer, Geoffrey (1948) *The Americans*. London: Cresset Press.

Goudsblom, Johan (1977) *Sociology in the Balance*. Oxford: Blackwell.

Goudsblom, Johan (1980) *Nihilism and Culture*. Oxford: Blackwell.

Goudsblom, Johan (1986a) 'Public Health and the Civilizing Process', *The Millbank Quarterly*, 64 (2): 161–88.

Goudsblom, Johan (1986b) 'On High and Low in Society and in Sociology: A Semantic Approach to Social Stratification', *Sociologisch Tijdschrift*, 13 (1): 3–17.

Goudsblom, Johan (1986c) 'Dutch Sociology in the 1950s: A View from Behind the One-Way Mirror', pp. 112–20 in R. Kroes and Martin van Rossum, eds, *Anti-Americanism in Europe*. Amsterdam: Free University Press.

Goudsblom, Johan (1989) 'Stijlen en beschaving', *De Gids*, 152: 720–2.

Goudsblom, Johan (1992) *Fire and Civilization*. London: Allen Lane The Penguin Press.

Goudsblom, Johan (1996a) 'Ecological Regimes and the Rise of Organized Religion', pp. 31–47 in Johan Goudsblom, Eric Jones and Stephen Mennell, *The Course of Human History: Economic Growth, Social Process, and Civilization*. Armonk, NY: M. E. Sharpe.

Goudsblom, Johan (1996b) 'The Formation of Military-Agrarian Regimes', pp. 49–62 in Johan Goudsblom, Eric Jones and Stephen Mennell, *The Course of Human History: Economic Growth, Social Process, and Civilization*. Armonk, NY: M. E. Sharpe.

Goudsblom, Johan (1996c) 'Rational and Other Choices: Comments on the Rational Choice Model', *Netherlands Journal of the Social Sciences*, 32 (1): 16–25.

Goudsblom, Johan (2001) *Stof waar honger uit ontstond: over evolutie en sociale processen*. Amsterdam: Meulenhoff.

Goudsblom, Johan (2002) 'Terug naar Nederland', *De Gids*, 165: 989–1002.

Goudsblom, Johan (2004) 'Christian Religion and the European Civilizing Process: The Views of Norbert Elias and Max Weber compared in the Context of the Augustian and Lucretian Traditions', pp. 265–80 in Steven Loyal and Stephen Quilley, eds, *The Sociology of Norbert Elias*. Cambridge: Cambridge University Press.

Goudsblom, Johan and Stephen Mennell, eds (1998) *The Norbert Elias Reader: A Biographical Selection*. Oxford: Blackwell.

Graham, Hugh Davis and Ted Robert Gurr, eds (1979) *Violence in America: Historical and Comparative Perspectives*, 2nd edn. Beverly Hills, CA: Sage.

Grant, Ulysses S. (1994 [1885]) *Personal Memoirs of U. S. Grant*. New York: Smithmark.

Greeley, Andrew M. (1979) 'Ethnic Variations in Religious Commitment', pp. 113–34 in Robert Wuthnow, ed., *The Religious Dimension: New Directions in Quantitative Research*. New York: Academic Press.

Greeley, Andrew M. (1989) *Religious Change in America*. Cambridge, MA: Harvard University Press.

Greeley, Andrew M. (2003) *Religion in Europe at the End of the Second Millennium: A Sociological Profile*. New Brunswick, NJ: Transaction.

Greenfeld, Liah (1992) *Nationalism: Five Roads to Modernity*. Cambridge, MA: Harvard University Press.

Grinde, Donald Jr (1977) *The Iroquois and the Founding of the American Nation*. San Francisco: Indian Historian Press.

Grinde, Donald Jr and Bruce E. Johansen (1991) *Exemplar of Liberty: Native America and the Evolution of Democracy*. Los Angeles: American Indian Studies Center.

Gurr, Ted Robert (1981) 'Historical Trends in Violent Crime', *Crime and Justice: An Annual Review of Research*, 3: 295–353.

Hacker, Jacob S. (2002) *The Divided Welfare State*. Cambridge: Cambridge University Press.

Hacker, Louis M. (1933) 'Review of Turner, *The Significance of Sections in American History*', pp. 43–6 in George Rogers Taylor, ed., *The Turner Thesis concerning the Role of the Frontier in American History*. Boston: D. C. Heath.

Hall, Peter Dobkin (1982) *The Organization of American Culture, 1700–1900: Private Institutions, Elites and the Origins of American Nationality*. New York: New York University Press.

Harrington, Michael (1962) *The Other America: Poverty in the United States*. New York: Macmillan.

Harris, Marvin (1987) *Why Nothing Works: The Anthropology of Daily Life*. New York: Simon & Schuster.

Hartz, Louis (1964) *The Founding of New Societies: Studies in the History of the United States, Latin America, South Africa, Canada and Australia*. New York: Harcourt, Brace & World.

Haseler, Stephen (2004) *Super-State: The New Europe and its Challenge to America*. London: I. B. Tauris.

Haskell, Thomas R. (1985) 'Capitalism and the Origins of Humanitarian Sensibility', *American Historical Review*, 90 (2–3): 339–61, 547–66.

Hayes, Carlton J. H. (1946) 'The American Frontier – Frontier of What?', *American Historical Review*, 51 (2): 199–216.

Headland, Thomas N., Kenneth L. Pike and Marvin Harris (1990) *Emics and Etics: The Insider/Outsider Debate*. Newbury Park, CA: Sage.

Hemphill, C. Dallett (1996) 'Middle Class Rising in Revolutionary America: The Evidence from Manners', *Journal of Social History*, 30 (2): 318–44.

Hemphill, C. Dallett (1999) *Bowing to Necessity*. New York: Oxford University Press.

Herndon, William H. and Jesse W. Weik (1983 [1888]) *Herndon's Life of Lincoln*. New York: Da Capo.

Higham, John (1968) 'Immigration', pp. 91–106 in C. Vann Woodward, ed., *The Comparative Approach to American History*. New York: Oxford University Press.

Himmelfarb, Gertrude (2004) *The Roads to Modernity: The British, French and American Enlightenments*. New York: A. A. Knopf.

Hobbes, Thomas (1904 [1651]) *Leviathan*. Cambridge: Cambridge University Press.

Hobsbawm, E. J. and T. O. Ranger, eds (1983) *The Invention of Tradition*. Cambridge: Cambridge University Press.

Hodgson, Godfrey (2004) *More Equal than Others: America from Nixon to the New Century*. Princeton, NJ: Princeton University Press.

Hofstadter, Richard (1967) *The Paranoid Style in American Politics and Other Essays*. New York: Vintage Books.

Hofstadter, Richard (1969) *The Progressive Historians: Turner, Beard, Parrington*. London: Jonathan Cape.

Hofstadter, Richard and Seymour Martin Lipset, eds (1968) *Turner and the Sociology of the Frontier*. New York: Basic Books.

Horkheimer, Max and Theodor W. Adorno (1972) *Dialectic of Enlightenment*. New York: Herder & Herder.

Howe, Daniel Walker (1997) *Making the American Self: Jonathan Edwards to Abraham Lincoln*. Cambridge, MA: Harvard University Press.

Hoy, Suellen M. (1995) *Chasing Dirt: The American Pursuit of Cleanliness*. New York: Oxford University Press.

Huizinga, Johan (1972a) *America: A Dutch Historian's Vision, from Afar and Near*. New York: Harper & Row.

Huizinga, Johan (1972b [1924]) *The Waning of the Middle Ages*. Harmondsworth: Penguin.

Hundley, Daniel R. (1860) *Social Relations in Our Southern States*. New York: H. B. Price.

Hunt, Morton (1999) 'The Biological Roots of Religion: Is Faith in Our Genes?', *Free Inquiry*, 19 (3): 30–3.

Huntington, Samuel P. (1957) *The Soldier and the State: The Theory and Politics of Civil–Military Relations*. New York: Vintage Books.

Huntington, Samuel P. (1999) *The Clash of Civilizations*. New York: Simon & Schuster.

Huntington, Samuel P. (2004) *Who Are We? The Challenges to America's National Identity*. New York: Simon & Schuster.

Inglis, Tom (1998) *Moral Monopoly: The Rise and Fall of the Catholic Church in Modern Ireland*. Dublin: University College Dublin Press Press.

Inouye, Senator Daniel K. (1992) 'Preface', in Oren Lyons et al., eds, *Exiled in the Land of the Free: Democracy, Indian Nations, and the United States Constitution*. Santa Fe, NM: Clear Light Publishers.

Jacoby, Susan (2005) 'Caught between Church and State', *New York Times*, 19 January.

Janowitz, Morris (1960) *The Professional Soldier: A Social and Political Portrait*. Glencoe, IL: Free Press.

Jasper, James M. (2000) *Restless Nation: Starting Over in America*. Chicago: University of Chicago Press.

Jeffers, H. Paul (2000) *An Honest President: The Life and Presidencies of Grover Cleveland*. New York: HarperCollins.

Jefferson, Thomas (1907) *The Writings of Thomas Jefferson*, 19 vols., ed. Albert Ellery Bergh. Washington, DC: Thomas Jefferson Memorial Association.

Jefferson, Thomas (1950) *The Papers of Thomas Jefferson*, ed. Julian P. Boyd et al. Princeton, NJ: Princeton University Press.

Jefferson, Thomas, John Adams, and Abigail Adams (1959) *The Adams–Jefferson Letters: The Complete Correspondence between Thomas Jefferson and Abigail and John Adams*. Chapel Hill, NC: University of North Carolina Press.

Jennings, Francis (2000) *The Creation of America: Through Revolution to Empire*. Cambridge: Cambridge University Press.

Jensen, Merrill (1997) 'The Colonial Phase', pp. 18–33 in C. Vann Woodward, ed., *The Comparative Approach to American History*. New York: Oxford University Press.

Johansen, Bruce E. (1982) *Forgotten Founders: Benjamin Franklin, the Iroquois, and the Rationale for the American Revolution*. Ipswich, MA: Gambit.

Johansen, Bruce E. (1998) *Debating Democracy*. Santa Fe, NM: Clear Light Publishers.

Johnson, Chalmers (2001) *Blowback: The Costs and Consequences of American Empire*. Boston: Little Brown.

Johnson, Chalmers (2004) *The Sorrows of Empire: Militarism, Secrecy, and the End of the Republic*. London: Verso.

Johnson, Eric A. (1995) *Urbanization and Crime: Germany 1871–1914*. Cambridge: Cambridge University Press.

Johnson, Eric A. and Eric H. Monkkonen, eds (1996) *The Civilization of Crime.* Urbana, IL: University of Illinois Press.

Johnston, David Cay (2005) 'Richest Are Leaving Even the Rich Far Behind', *New York Times*, 5 June.

Kagan, Robert (2003) *Of Paradise and Power.* London: Atlantic Books.

Kammen, Michael (1972) *People of Paradox: An Enquiry Concerning the Origins of American Civilization.* New York: Knopf.

Kaplan, Robert D. (2005) *Imperial Grunts: The American Military on the Ground.* New York: Random House.

Kasson, John F. (1987) 'Rituals of Dining: Table Manners in Victorian America', pp. 114–41 in Kathryn Grover, ed., *Dining in America, 1850–1900.* Amherst, MA: University of Massachusetts Press.

Kasson, John F. (1990) *Rudeness and Civility: Manners in Nineteenth-Century Urban America.* New York: Hill & Wang.

Keegan, John (1976) *The Face of Battle: A Study of Agincourt, Waterloo and the Somme.* London: Jonathan Cape.

Kennan, George F. (1972) *Memoirs 1950–1963.* London: Hutchinson.

Key, V. O. Jr. (1949) *Southern Politics in State and Nation.* New York: Alfred A. Knopf.

Kilminster, Richard (1987) 'Introduction to Elias', *Theory, Culture and Society*, 4 (2–3): 213–22.

Kingston, Paul W. (2000) *The Classless Society.* Stanford, CA: Stanford University Press.

Kluckhohn, Clyde and Henry A. Murray, eds (1948) *Personality in Nature, Society and Culture.* New York: A. A. Knopf.

Kornhauser, William A. (1959) *The Politics of Mass Society.* New York: Free Press.

Kosmin, Barry A., Egon Mayer and Ariela Keyser (2002) 'American Religious Identification Survey 2001'. New York: City University of New York, Graduate Centre.

Kramnick, Isaac (1987) 'Editor's Introduction', pp. 11–82 in Madison, Hamilton and Jay, *The Federalist Papers.* London: Penguin.

Krech III, Shepard (1999) *The Ecological Indian: Myth and History.* New York: W. W. Norton.

Kristof, Nicholas D. 2003. 'Believe It, Or Not', *New York Times*, 15 August.

Krug, Eugene G., Linda L. Dahlberg, James A. Mercy, Anthony B. Zwi and Rafael Lozano (2002) *World Report on Violence and Health.* Geneva: World Health Organization.

Krugman, Paul (2005) 'Cleaning Up the Health Care Mess', *New York Times*, 26 December.

Kupperman, Karen O. (1980) *Settling with the Indians: The Meeting of English and Indian Cultures in America, 1580–1640.* London: J. M. Dent.

Kupperman, Karen O. (2000) *Indians and English: Facing Off in Early America.* Ithaca, NY: Cornell University Press.

La Salle, Jean-Baptiste de (1729/1774) *Les Règles de la bienséance et de la civilité chrétienne* (Rouen/Reims; 1st edn 1695).

Lane, Roger (1967) *Policing the City: Boston, 1822–1885.* Cambridge, MA: Harvard University Press.

Lane, Roger (1979) *Violent Death in the City: Suicide, Accident and Murder in Nineteenth-Century Philadelphia.* Cambridge, MA: Harvard University Press.

Lane, Roger (1997) *Murder in America: A History.* Columbus, OH: Ohio State University Press.

Larkin, Jack (1988) *The Reshaping of Everyday Life, 1790–1840.* New York: Harper & Row.

Lasch, Christopher (1979) *The Culture of Narcissism: American Life in an Age of Diminishing Expectations.* New York: W. W. Norton.

Lawrence, D. H. (1924) *Studies in Classic American Literature.* London: Heinemann.

Lehmann-Haupt, Hellmut, in collaboration with Lawrence C. Wroth and Rollo G. Silver (1951) *The Book in America.* New York: R. R. Bowker.

Lenski, Gerhard (1966) *Power and Privilege: A Theory of Social Stratification.* New York: McGraw-Hill.

Lerner, Max (1957) *America as a Civilization: Life and Thought in the United States Today.* New York: Simon & Schuster.

Light, Donald (2006) 'Making Competition Fair for Health Insurance in Ireland', pp. 61–74 in Desmond McCluskey, ed., *Health Policy and Practice in Ireland.* Dublin: University College Dublin Press.

Limerick, Patricia Nelson (1987) *The Legacy of Conquest: The Unbroken Past of the American West.* New York: W. W. Norton.

Limerick, Patricia Nelson (1995) 'Turnerians All: The Dream of a Helpful History in an Intelligible World', *American Historical Review*, 100 (3): 697–716.

Lincoln, W. Bruce (1994) *The Conquest of a Continent: Siberia and the Russians.* New York: Random House.

Lipset, Seymour Martin (1963) *The First New Nation: The United States in Comparative and Historical Perspective.* London: Heinemann.

Lipset, Seymour Martin and Gary Marks (2000) *It Didn't Happen Here: Why Socialism Failed in the United States.* New York: W. W. Norton.

Locke, John (1960 [1690]) *Two Treatises of Government.* New York: Mentor.

Lockwood, David (1966) 'Sources of Variation in Working-Class Images of Society', *Sociological Review*, 14: 249–67.

Loewen, James W. (1995) *Lies My Teacher Told Me: Everything Your American History Textbook Got Wrong.* New York: New Press.

Lowie, Robert H. (1920) *Primitive Society.* New York: Boni & Liveright.

Lucretius (1951) *On the Nature of the Universe.* Harmondsworth: Penguin.

Luedtke, Luther S. (1992) *Making America: The Society & Culture of the United States.* Chapel Hill, NC: University of North Carolina Press.

Lukes, Steven (1973) *Individualism*. Oxford: Blackwell.

Lukes, Steven (1974) *Power: A Radical View*. Basingstoke: Macmillan.

Lynd, Robert S. and Helen Merrill Lynd (1937) *Middletown in Transition*. New York: Harcourt Brace.

McClymer, John F. (1982) 'The Americanization Movement and the Education of the Foreign-Born Adult, 1914–25', in Bernard J. Weiss, ed., *American Education and the European Immigrant, 1840–1940*. Urbana, IL: University of Illinois Press.

McDowell, David (1995) 'Firearms and Self-Defence', *Annals of the American Academy of Political and Social Sciences*, 539 (May): 130–40.

McGerr, Michael (1991) 'The Price of the "New Transnational History"', *American Historical Review*, 96 (4): 1056–67.

McNaught, Kenneth (1969) *The Pelican History of Canada*. Harmondsworth: Penguin.

McNeill, William H. (1983) *The Great Frontier: Freedom and Hierarchy in Modern Times*. Princeton, NJ: Princeton University Press.

McNeill, William H. (1984) 'Human Migration in Historical Perspective', *Population and Development Review*, 10 (1): 1–18.

McPherson, James M. (1990) *Abraham Lincoln and the Second American Revolution*. New York: Oxford University Press.

Madison, James, Alexander Hamilton, and John Jay (1987 [1788]) *The Federalist Papers*. London: Penguin.

Mandelbaum, Michael (2006) *The Case for Goliath: How America acts as the World's Government in the Twenty-First Century*. New York: Public Affairs.

Mann, Michael (2003) *Incoherent Empire*. London: Verso.

Mannheim, Karl (1953) 'Conservative Thought', pp. 74–164 in *Essays on Sociology and Social Psychology*. London: Routledge & Kegan Paul.

Marquand, David (2004) *Decline of the Public*. Cambridge: Polity.

Marshall, Gordon (1997) *Repositioning Class: Social Inequality in Industrial Societies*. London: Sage.

Marshall, T. H. (1950) *Citizenship and Social Class and Other Essays*. Cambridge: Cambridge University Press.

Martin, Judith (1996) *Miss Manners Rescues Civilization: From Sexual Harassment, Frivolous Lawsuits, Dissing, and Other Lapses in Civility*. New York: Crown.

Martineau, Harriet (1837) *Society in America*, 3 vols. London: Saunders & Otley.

Mastenbroek, Willem F. G. (1999) 'Negotiation as Emotion Management', *Theory, Culture and Society*, 16 (4): 49–73.

Masur, Louis P. (1989) *Rites of Execution: Capital Punishment and the Transformation of American Culture, 1776–1865*. Oxford: Oxford University Press.

Mauk, D. and J. Oakland (1995) *American Civilization: An Introduction*. New York: Routledge.

Mazlish, Bruce (2004) *Civilization and its Contents*. Stanford: Stanford University Press.

Mead, Margaret (1942) *And Keep Your Powder Dry: An Anthropologist Looks at America*. New York: Morrow.

Mead, Walter Russell (2001) *Special Providence: American Foreign Policy and How it Changed the World*. New York: Century Foundation.

Mennell, Stephen (1969) 'Prohibition: A Sociological View', *Journal of American Studies*, 3 (2): 159–75.

Mennell, Stephen (1974) *Sociological Theory: Uses and Unities*. London: Thomas Nelson.

Mennell, Stephen (1990a) 'Decivilizing Processes: Theoretical Significance and Some Lines for Research', *International Sociology*, 5 (2): 205–23.

Mennell, Stephen (1990b) 'The Globalization of Human Society as a Very Long-term Social Process: Elias's Theory', *Theory, Culture and Society*, 7 (3): 359–71.

Mennell, Stephen (1994) 'The Formation of We-Images: A Process Theory', pp. 175–97 in Craig Calhoun, ed., *Social Theory and the Politics of Identity*. Oxford: Blackwell.

Mennell, Stephen (1996a) *All Manners of Food: Eating and Taste in England and France from the Middle Ages to the Present*, rev. edn. Champaign, IL: University of Illinois Press.

Mennell, Stephen (1996b) 'Introduction: Bringing the Very Long-Term Back In', pp. 3–13 in Johan Goudsblom, Eric Jones and Stephen Mennell, *The Course of Human History: Economic Growth, Social Process, and Civilization*. Armonk, NY: M. E. Sharpe.

Mennell, Stephen (1998) *Norbert Elias: An Introduction*, rev. edn. Dublin: University College Dublin Press. [First published as *Norbert Elias: Civilization and the Human Self-Image*. Oxford: Blackwell, 1989.]

Mennell, Stephen and Johan Goudsblom (1997) 'Civilizing Processes – Myth or Reality? A Comment on Duerr's Critique of Elias', *Comparative Studies in Society and History*, 39 (4): 729–33.

Mennell, Stephen and Johan Goudsblom, eds (1998) *Norbert Elias on Civilization, Power and Knowledge*. Chicago: University of Chicago Press.

Merritt, Jane T. (2003) *At the Crossroads: Indians and Empires on a Mid-Atlantic Frontier, 1700–1763*. Chapel Hill, NC: University of North Carolina Press.

Merton, Robert K. (1968) *Social Theory and Social Structure*. New York: Free Press.

Messner, Steven F., Robert D. Baller and Matthew P. Zevenbergen (2005) 'The Legacy of Lynching and Southern Homicide', *American Sociological Review*, 70 (4): 633–55.

Meyrowitz, Joshua (1985) *No Sense of Place*. Oxford: Oxford University Press.

Mikesell, Marvin (1960) 'Comparative Studies in Frontier History', *Annals of the Association of American Geographers*, 50 (1): 62–74.

Miller, Perry (1956) *Errand into the Wilderness*. Cambridge, MA: Belknap Press.

Mills, C. Wright (1956) *The Power Elite*. New York: Oxford University Press.

Mills, C. Wright (1959) *The Sociological Imagination*. New York: Oxford University Press.

Monkkonen, Eric H. (1981) *Police in Urban America, 1860–1920*. Cambridge: Cambridge University Press.

Monti, Daniel (1999) *The American City: A Social and Cultural History*. Malden, MA: Blackwell.

Moody, Eleazer (1715) *The School of Good Manners*. Boston.

Moore, Barrington, Jr. (1998) *Moral Aspects of Economic Growth, and Other Essays*. Ithaca, NY: Cornell University Press.

Morgan, Edmund S. (1975) *American Slavery, American Freedom: The Ordeal of Colonial Virginia*. New York: W. W. Norton.

Morgan, Edmund S. (2002) *Benjamin Franklin*. New Haven, CT: Yale University Press.

Morone, James (2003) *Hellfire Nation: The Politics of Sin in American History*. New Haven, CT: Yale University Press.

Mumford, Lewis (1957 [1926]) *The Golden Day: A Study in American Literature and Culture*. New York: Dover.

Munchembled, Robert (1985) *Popular Culture and Elite Culture in France, 1400–1750*. Baton Rouge, LA: Louisiana State University Press.

National Association for the Advancement of Colored People (1919) *Thirty Years of Lynching in the United States, 1889–1918*. New York: Arno Press.

Nevins, Allan, ed. (1948) *America Through British Eyes*. New York: Oxford University Press.

Nevins, Allan and Henry Steele Commager (1992) *A Pocket History of the United States*. New York: Simon & Schuster.

Newton, Tim (2003) 'Credit and Civilization', *British Journal of Sociology*, 54 (3): 347–71.

Noble, Charles (1997) *Welfare As We Know It: A Political History of the American Welfare State*. New York: Oxford University Press.

Nye, Joseph S. Jr. (2003) *The Paradox of American Power: Why the World's Only Superpower Can't Go It Alone*. New York: Oxford University Press.

Oberg, Michael L. (1999) *Dominion and Civility: English Imperialism, Native America, and the First American Frontiers, 1585–1685*. Ithaca, NY: Cornell University Press.

O'Brien, Patrick (1988) *The Economic Effects of the American Civil War*. Basingstoke: Macmillan.

O'Brien, Patrick and Armand Clesse (2002) *Two Hegemonies: Britain 1846–1914 and the United States 1941–2001*. Aldershot: Ashgate.

O'Donnell, Ian (2004) 'Interpreting Penal Change: A Research Note', *Criminal Justice*, 4 (2): 199–206.

Ogle, Maureen (1996) *All the Modern Conveniences: American Household Plumbing, 1840–1890*. Baltimore, MD: Johns Hopkins University Press.

Olson, Joseph E. and David B. Kopel (1999) 'All the Way down the Slippery Slope: Gun Prohibition in England and Some Lessons for Civil Liberties in America', *Hamline Law Review*, 22 (2): 399–465.

Ontario Consultants on Religious Toleration (2004) 'Public Beliefs about Evolution and Creation'. <http://www.religioustolerance.org/ev_publi.htm>, accessed 31 May.

Packard, Vance (1957) *The Hidden Persuaders*. New York: David McKay.

Parsons, Talcott (1971) *The System of Modern Societies*. Englewood Cliffs, NJ: Prentice-Hall.

Peacham, Henry (1622) *The Compleat Gentleman*. London.

Pearce, Roy Harvey (1988) *Savagism and Civilization: A Study of the Indian and the American Mind*. Berkeley, CA: University of California Press.

Perrow, Charles (2002) *Organizing America: Wealth, Power, and the Origins of Corporate Capitalism*. Princeton, NJ: Princeton University Press.

Persons, Stow (1973) *The Decline of American Gentility*. New York: Columbia University Press.

Perucci, Robert and Earl Wysong (2002) *The New Class Society: Goodbye American Dream*. Lanham, MD: Rowman & Littlefield.

Pessen, Edward (1980) 'Wealth in American before 1865', in W. D. Rubinstein, ed., *Wealth and the Wealthy in the Modern World*. London: Croom Helm.

Pettit, Becky and Bruce Western (2004) 'Mass Imprisonment and the Life Course: Race and Class Inequality in US Incarceration', *American Sociological Review*, 69 (2): 151–69.

Pew Global Attitudes Project (2003) *Views of a Changing World*. Washington, DC: Pew Research Center for the People and the Press.

Pew Research Center for the People and the Press (2002) 'Americans Struggle with Religion's Role at Home and Abroad'. Washington, DC: Pew Research Center for the People and the Press/Pew Forum on Religion and Public Life.

Pew Research Center for the People and the Press (2005) 'Public Divided on Origins of Life: Religion a Strength and Weakness for Both Parties'. Washington, DC: Pew Research Center, 30 August.

Pfeffer, Jeffrey and Robert I. Sutton (2006) *Hard Facts, Dangerous Half-Truths and Total Nonsense*. Cambridge, MA: Harvard Business School Press.

Phillips, Kevin (2002) *Wealth and Democracy: A Political History of the American Rich*. New York: Broadway Books.

Pierson, George W. (1942) 'The Frontier and American Institutions: A Criticism of the Turner Theory', *New England Quarterly*, 15: 224–55.

Piketty, Thomas (2003) 'Income Inequality in France, 1901–1998', *Journal of Political Economy*, 111 (5): 1004–42.

Piketty, Thomas and Emmanuel Saez (2003) 'Income Inequality in the United States, 1913–1998', *Quarterly Journal of Economics*, 118 (1): 1–38.

Poe, Edgar Allan (1967 [1845]) 'A Descent into the Maelström', pp. 225–46 in *Selected Writings*. Harmondsworth: Penguin.

Polanyi, Karl (1944) *The Great Transformation: The Political and Economic Origins of Our Time*. Boston: Beacon Press.

Popper, Karl R. (1957) *The Poverty of Historicism*. London: Routledge & Kegan Paul.

Porter, Bernard (2006) *Empire and Superempire: Britain, America and the World*. New Haven, CT: Yale University Press.

Potter, David M. (1954) *People of Plenty: Economic Abundance and the American Character*. Chicago: University of Chicago Press.

Potter, David M. (1963) 'American Individualism in the Twentieth Century', *Texas Quarterly*, 6 (2): 140–51.

Potter, David M. (1968) 'Civil War', pp. 135–45 in C. Vann Woodward, ed., *The Comparative Approach to American History*. New York: Oxford University Press.

Pratt, John (2002) *Punishment and Civilization: Penal Tolerance and Intolerance in Modern Society*. London: Sage.

Puffert, Douglas (2005) 'Path Dependence'. <http://www.eh.net/encyclopedia>, accessed 16 June.

Putnam, Robert (2000) *Bowling Alone: The Collapse and Revival of American Community*. New York: Simon & Schuster.

Quilley, Stephen and Steven Loyal (2005) 'Eliasian Theory as a "Central Theory" for the Human Sciences', *Current Sociology*, 53 (5): 809–30.

Ransom, Roger L. (2005) *The Confederate States of America: What Might Have Been*. New York: W.W. Norton.

Rauschenbusch, Walter (1907) *Christianity and the Social Crisis*. New York: Macmillan.

Remini, Robert V. (2001) *Andrew Jackson and his Indian Wars*. New York: Viking Penguin.

Remini, Robert V. (2002) *John Quincy Adams*. New York: Henry Holt.

Ribeiro, Darcy (1971) *The Americas and Civilization*. London: George Allen & Unwin.

Ridley, Hugh (1983) *Images of Imperial Rule*. London: Croom Helm.

Riesman, David, with Nathan Glazer and Reuel Denney (1961 [1950]) *The Lonely Crowd: A Study of the Changing American Character*. New Haven, CT: Yale University Press.

Rifkin, Jeremy (2004) *The European Dream: How Europe's Vision of the Future is Quietly Eclipsing the American Dream*. Cambridge: Polity.

Roche, Daniel (1998) *France in the Enlightenment*. Cambridge, MA: Harvard University Press.

Roland, Alex (2000) *The Military-Industrial Complex*. Washington, DC: American Historical Association.

Roosevelt, Theodore (1923–6) *The Works of Theodore Roosevelt*, ed. Hermann Hagedorn, 24 vols. New York: Charles Scribner's Sons.

Roosevelt, Theodore (1995 [1889–99]) *The Winning of the West*, 4 vols. Lincoln: Nebraska University Press.

Rose, Arnold M. (1967) *The Power Structure: Political Process in American Society*. New York: Oxford University Press.

Rothschild, Emma (2000) *Economic Sentiments: Adam Smith, Condorcet and the Enlightenment*. Cambridge, MA: Harvard University Press.

Rotundo, E. Anthony (1993) *American Manhood: Transformations in Masculinity from the Revolution to the Modern Era*. New York: Basic Books.

Runciman, W. G. (1966) *Relative Deprivation and Social Justice*. London: Routledge & Kegan Paul.

Said, Edward W. (1978) *Orientalism*. New York: Random House.

Scheff, Thomas J. (1992) 'Rationality and Emotion: Homage to Norbert Elias', pp. 101–19 in James S. Coleman and Thomas J. Fararo, eds, *Rational Choice Theory: Advocacy and Critique*. London: Sage.

Scheff, Thomas J. (1994) *Bloody Revenge: Emotions, Nationalism and War*. Boulder, CO: Westview Press.

Schlesinger, Arthur M. Jr. (1992) *The Disuniting of America: Reflections on a Multicultural Society*. New York: W.W. Norton.

Schlesinger, Arthur M. Jr. (1993) *The Almanac of American History*. New York: Barnes & Noble.

Schlesinger, Arthur M. Jr. (2006) 'History and National Stupidity', *New York Review of Books*, 27 April.

Schlesinger, Arthur M. Sr (1922) *New Viewpoints in American History*. New York: Macmillan.

Schlesinger, Arthur M. Sr (1947) *Learning How to Behave: A Historical Study of American Etiquette Books*. New York: Macmillan.

Seidman, Steven (1991) *Romantic Longings: Love in America, 1830–1980*. New York: Routledge.

Sennett, Richard (1998) *The Corrosion of Character*. New York: W. W. Norton.

Shackelford, George Green (1995) *Thomas Jefferson's Travels in Europe, 1784–1789*. Baltimore, MD: Johns Hopkins University Press.

Shain, Barry Alan (1994) *The Myth of American Individualism: The Protestant Origins of American Political Thought*. Princeton, NJ: Princeton University Press.

Sherwood, Marika (1999) 'Lynching in Britain', *History Today* (March).

Shorter, Edward (1976) *The Making of the Modern Family*. London: Collins.

Shuffelton, Frank (1993) *The American Enlightenment*. Rochester, NY: University of Rochester Press.

Skelton, W. B. (1992) *An American Profession of Arms: The Army Officer Corps, 1784–1861*. Lawrence, KS: University Press of Kansas.

Skocpol, Theda (1992) *Protecting Soldiers and Mothers: The Political Origins of Social Policy in the United States*. Cambridge, MA: Belknap Press.

Skowronek, Stephen (1982) *Building a New American State: The Expansion of National Administrative Capacities, 1877–1920*. Cambridge: Cambridge University Press.

Slotkin, Richard (1973) *Regeneration through Violence: The Mythology of the American Frontier, 1600–1860*. New York: Atheneum.

Slotkin, Richard (1985) *The Fatal Environment: The Myth of the Frontier in the Age of Industrialization*. New York: Atheneum.

Slotkin, Richard (1992) *Gunfighter Nation: The Myth of the Frontier in Twentieth-Century America*. New York: Atheneum.

Smith, Page (1966) *As a City Upon a Hill*. New York: Alfred A. Knopf.

Sokolow, Jayme A. (2003) *The Great Encounter: Native Peoples and European Settlers in the Americas, 1492–1800*. Armonk, NY: M. E. Sharpe.

Sombart, Werner (1969 [1913]) *Luxury and Capitalism*. Ann Arbor, MN: University of Michigan Press.

Sombart, Werner (1976 [1906]) *Why Is There No Socialism in the United States?* London: Macmillan.

Sontag, Susan (2001) 'The Talk of the Town', *The New Yorker*, 24 September.

Spierenburg, Pieter (1984) *The Spectacle of Suffering: Executions and the Evolution of Repression*. Cambridge: Cambridge University Press.

Spierenburg, Pieter (1996) 'Long-Term Trends in Homicide: Theoretical Reflections and Dutch Evidence, Fifteenth to Twentieth Centuries', pp. 63–105 in Eric A. Johnson and Erik H. Monkkonen, eds, *The Civilization of Crime: Violence in Town and Country since the Middle Ages*. Urbana, IL: University of Illinois Press.

Spierenburg, Pieter (2004) *Written in Blood: Fatal Attraction in Enlightenment Amsterdam*. Columbus, OH: Ohio State University Press.

Spierenburg, Pieter (2006) 'Democracy Came Too Early: A Tentative Explanation for the Problem of American Homicide', *American Historical Review*, 111 (1): 104–14.

Stannard, David E. (1992) *American Holocaust: Columbus and the Conquest of the New World*. New York: Oxford University Press.

Starr, Paul (1982) *The Social Transformation of American Medicine*. New York: Basic Books.

Starr, Paul (2004) *The Creation of the Media: Political Origins of Modern Communications*. New York: Basic Books.

Stearns, Carol Z. (1988) '"Lord Help Me Walk Humbly": Anger and Sadness in England and America, 1570–1750', pp. 39–68 in Carol Z. Stearns and Peter N. Stearns, eds, *Emotion and Social Change: Toward a New Psychohistory*. New York: Holmes & Meier.

Stearns, Carol Z. and Peter N. Stearns (1986) *Anger: The Struggle for Emotional Control in America's History*. Chicago: University of Chicago Press.

Stearns, Peter N. (1989) *Jealousy: The Evolution of an Emotion in American History*. New York: New York University Press.

Stearns, Peter N. (1994) *American Cool: Constructing a Twentieth-Century Emotional Style*. New York: New York University Press.

Steiker, Carol (2002) 'Capital Punishment and American Exceptionalism', 81 *Oregon Law Review* 97.

Stevens, William Oliver (1940) *Pistols at Ten Paces: The Story of the Code of Honour in America*. Boston: Houghton Mifflin.

Steward, Dick (2002) *Duels and the Roots of Violence in Missouri*. Columbia, MO: University of Missouri Press.

Stiglitz, Joseph (2002) *Globalization and its Discontents*. London: Allen Lane.

Stiglitz, Joseph (2006) *Making Globalization Work*. London: Allen Lane.

Stokvis, Ruud (1999) *Concurrentie en beschaving: ondernemingen en het commercieël beschavingsproces*. Amsterdam: Boom.

Stolk, Abraham van and Cas Wouters (1987) 'Power Changes and Self-Respect: A Comparison of Two Cases of Established–Outsiders Relations', *Theory, Culture and Society*, 4 (2–3): 477–88.

Stone, John (2002) 'Max Weber on Race, Ethnicity, and Nationalism', pp. 28–42 in John Stone and Rutledge Dennis, eds, *Race and Ethnicity*. Malden, MA: Blackwell.

Stone, John and Stephen Mennell (1980) 'Introduction', pp. 1–46 in John Stone and Stephen Mennell, eds, *Alexis de Tocqueville on Democracy, Revolution and Society*. Chicago: University of Chicago Press.

Stone, Lawrence (1985) 'Interpersonal Violence in English Society, 1300–1980', *Past & Present*, 101: 3–24.

Swaan, Abram de (1988) *In Care of the State: Health Care, Education and Welfare in Europe and the USA in the Modern Era*. Cambridge: Polity.

Swaan, Abram de (2001) *Human Societies: An Introduction*. Cambridge: Polity.

Taylor, George Rogers, ed. (1956) *The Turner Thesis Concerning the Role of the Frontier in American History*. Boston: D. C. Heath.

Tester, Keith (1991) *Animals and Society: The Humanity of Human Rights*. London: Routledge.

Thernstrom, Stephan (1964) *Poverty and Progress: Social Mobility in a Nineteenth-Century City*. New York: Columbia University Press.

Thomas, Keith (1973) *Religion and the Decline of Magic*. Harmondsworth: Penguin.

Thomas, Keith (1983) *Man and the Natural World*. London: Allen Lane.

Thompson, E. P. (1963) *The Making of the English Working Class*. Harmondsworth: Penguin.

Thucydides (1972) *History of the Peloponnesian Wars*. Harmondsworth: Penguin.

Tilly, Charles (1979) 'Collective Violence in European Perspective', pp. 83–118 in Hugh Davis Graham and Ted Robert Gurr, eds, *Violence in America: Historical and Comparative Perspectives*, 2nd edn. Beverly Hills, CA: Sage.

Tilly, Charles (1990) *Coercion, Capital and European States, AD 990–1990*. Oxford: Blackwell.

Tilly, Charles (1995) 'To Explain Political Processes', *American Journal of Sociology*, 100 (6): 1594–1610.

Tise, Larry E. (1998) *The American Counter-Revolution: A Retreat from Liberty, 1783–1800*. Mechanicsburg, PA: Stackpole Books.

Tittle, Charles R. (1995) *Control Balance: Toward a General Theory of Deviance*. Boulder, CO: Westview Press.

Tocqueville, Alexis de (1955 [1856]) *The Old Régime and the French Revolution*. Garden City, NY: Doubleday.

Tocqueville, Alexis de (1961 [1835–40]) *Democracy in America*, trans. Henry Reeve, 2 vols. New York: Schocken.

Tocqueville, Alexis de (1971 [1893]) *Recollections*. Garden City, NY: Doubleday.

Todd, Emmanuel (2004) *After the Empire: The Breakdown of the American Order*. New York: Columbia University Press.

Tonry, Michael (2004) *Thinking about Crime: Sense and Sensibility in American Penal Culture*. New York: Oxford University Press.

Tooker, Elisabeth (1988) 'The United States Constitution and the Iroquois League', *Ethnohistory*, 35 (Fall): 305–6.

Tripp, C. A. (2005) *The Intimate World of Abraham Lincoln*. New York: Free Press.

Trollope, Anthony (1968 [1862]) *North America*. London: Penguin.

Trollope, Fanny (1997 [1832]) *Domestic Manners of the Americans*. London: Penguin.

Turner, Frederick Jackson (1932) *The Significance of Sections in American History*. New York: Henry Holt.

Turner, Frederick Jackson (1947 [1920]) *The Frontier in American History*. New York: Holt, Rinehart & Winston.

Tyrell, Ian (1991a) 'American Exceptionalism in the Age of Transnational History', *American Historical Review*, 96 (4): 1031–55.

Tyrell, Ian (1991b) 'Rejoinder to McGerr', *American Historical Review*, 96 (4): 1068–72.

Ubelaker, Douglas H. (1988) 'North American Indian Population Size, AD 1500–1985', *American Journal of Physical Anthropology*, 77: 289–94.

US Census Bureau (various dates) *Statistical Abstract of the United States*. <http://www.census.gov/compendia/statab/>.

US Department of Commerce and Bureau of the Census (1975) *Historical Statistics of the United States: Colonial Times to 1970*. Washington, DC: US Government Printing Office.

US Department of Defense (2002) 'Selected Manpower Statistics, Fiscal Year 2001'. Washington, DC: US Department of Defense.

United States Government (2002) 'The National Security Strategy of the United States of America'. Washington, DC: US Government Printing Office.

Uviller, H. Richard and William G. Merkel (2002) *The Militia and the Right to Bear Arms: or, How the Second Amendment Fell Silent*. Durham, NC: Duke University Press.

Veblen, Thorstein (1899) *The Theory of the Leisure Class*. New York: Macmillan.

Vidal, Gore (2002) *The Last Empire*. London: Abacus.

Vidal, Gore (2004) *Imperial America: Reflections on the United States of Amnesia*. London: Clairview.

Vidich, A. J. and Joseph Bensman (1968) *Small Town in Mass Society: Class, Power and Religion in a Rural Community*. Princeton, NJ: Princeton University Press.

Voltaire, François-Marie Arouet (1980 [1733]) *Letters on England*. Harmondsworth: Penguin.

Vree, Wilbert van (1999) *Meetings, Manners and Civilization: The Development of Modern Meeting Behaviour*. London: Leicester University Press.

Wacquant, Loïc (2004) 'Decivilizing and Demonizing: The Remaking of the Black American Ghetto', pp. 95–121 in Steven Loyal and Stephen Quilley, eds, *The Sociology of Norbert Elias*. Cambridge: Cambridge University Press.

Wade, Richard C. (1968) 'Urbanization', pp. 187–205 in C. Vann Woodward, ed., *The Comparative Approach to American History*. New York: Oxford University Press.

Wakeford, John (1969) *The Cloistered Elite*. London: Macmillan.

Wallace, Anthony F. C. (1999) *Jefferson and the Indians: The Tragic Fate of the First Americans*. Cambridge, MA: Belknap Press.

Wallerstein, Immanuel (1974) *The Modern World-System*, vol. I. New York: Academic Press.

Walling, Karl-Friedrich (2000) *Republican Empire: Alexander Hamilton on War and Free Government*. Lawrence, KS: University Press of Kansas.

Warner, W. Lloyd, Marchia Meeker and Kenneth Eells (1960) *Social Class in America: A Manual of Procedure for the Evaluation of Status*. New York: Harper.

Washington, George (1890) *Rules of Civility*. London: Chatto & Windus.

Webb, Walter Prescott (1952) *The Great Frontier*. Boston: Houghton Mifflin.

Weber, Eugen (1977) *Peasants into Frenchmen*. London: Chatto & Windus.

Weber, Max (1930 [1904–5]) *The Protestant Ethic and the Spirit of Capitalism*. London: George Allen & Unwin.

Weber, Max (1946) 'The Protestant Sects and the Spirit of Capitalism', pp. 302–22 in H. H. Gerth and C. Wright Mills, eds, *From Max Weber: Essays in Sociology*. New York: Oxford University Press.

Weber, Max (1978 [1922]) *Economy and Society*, ed. Guenther Roth and Claus Wittich, 2 vols. Berkeley, CA: University of California Press.

Wharton, Edith (1982 [1920]) *The Age of Innocence*. London: Virago.

Wharton, Edith (1990 [1905]) *The House of Mirth*. London: Virago.

Wharton, Francis (1907) *The Law of Homicide*. Rochester, NY: Lawyers Cooperative Publishing Co.

White, Morton and Lucia White (1962) *The Intellectual Versus the City: from Thomas Jefferson to Frank Lloyd Wright*. Cambridge, MA: Harvard University Press.

Whitman, James Q. (2003) *Harsh Justice: Criminal Punishment and the Widening Divide Between America and Europe*. New York: Oxford University Press.

Whyte, William H. (1956) *The Organization Man*. New York: Simon & Schuster.

Wilkinson, Rupert (1984) *American Tough: The Tough-Guy and American Character*. Westport, CT: Greenwood Press.

Williams, Basil (1960) *The Whig Supremacy, 1714–1760*. Oxford: Clarendon Press.

Williams, Raymond (1958) *Culture and Society, 1780–1950*. London: Chatto & Windus.

Wills, Garry (2004) 'Did Tocqueville "Get" America?', *New York Review of Books*, 51 (7), 29 April.

Wilson, Bryan (1982) *Religion in Sociological Perspective*. Oxford: Oxford University Press.

Wilson, E. O. (1998) *Consilience*. New York: A. A. Knopf.

Wilson, Woodrow (1918) *History of the American People*. New York: Harper.

Wilterdink, Nico (2000) 'The Internationalization of Capital and Trends in Income Inequality in Western Societies', pp. 187–200 in Don Kalb et al., eds, *The Ends of Globalization*. Lanham, MD: Rowman & Littlefield.

Winthrop, John (1994 [1630]) 'A Modell of Christian Charity', pp. 108–12 in Giles Gunn, ed., *Early American Writing*. New York: Penguin.

Wister, Owen (1998 [1902]) *The Virginian*. Oxford: Oxford University Press.

Wolfe, Alan (1991) *America at Century's End*. Berkeley, CA: University of California Press.

Wolfe, Tom (1988) *The Bonfire of the Vanities*. London: Jonathan Cape.

Wolff, Edward N. (2002) *Top Heavy: The Increasing Inequality of Wealth in America and What Can Be Done About It*. New York: New Press.

Woodward, C. Vann (1974) *The Strange Career of Jim Crow*. New York: Oxford University Press.

Wouters, Cas (1977) 'Informalization and the Civilizing Process', pp. 437–53 in Peter R. Gleichmann, Johan Goudsblom and Hermann Korte, eds, *Human Figurations: Essays for/Aufsätze für Nobert Elias*. Amsterdam: Stichting Amsterdams Sociologisch Tijdschrift.

Wouters, Cas (1987) 'Developments in Behavioural Codes Between the Sexes: Formalization of Informalization in the Netherlands 1930–85', *Theory, Culture and Society*, 4 (2–3): 405–20.

Wouters, Cas (1998a) 'Balancing Sex and Love Since the 1960s Sexual Revolution', *Theory, Culture and Society*, 15 (3–4): 187–214.

Wouters, Cas (1998b) 'Changes in the "Lust Balance" of Sex and Love Since the Sexual Revolution: The Example of The Netherlands', pp. 228–49 in Gillian Bendelow and Simon J. Williams, eds, *Emotions in Social Life: Critical Themes and Contemporary Issues*. London: Routledge.

Wouters, Cas (1998c) 'Etiquette Books and Emotion Management in the Twentieth Century: American Habitus in International Comparison', pp. 283–304 in Peter N. Stearns and Jan Lewis, eds, *An Emotional History of the United States*. New York: New York University Press.

Wouters, Cas (2002) 'The Quest for New Rituals in Dying and Mourning: Changes in the We–I Balance', *Body & Society*, 8 (1): 1–27.

Wouters, Cas (2004) *Sex and Manners: Female Emancipation in the West, 1890–2000*. London: Sage.

Wouters, Cas (2007) *Informalization: Manners and Emotions Since 1890*. London: Sage.

Wright, Benjamin F. Jr. (1930) 'American Democracy and the Frontier', *Yale Review*, 20: 349–65.

Wright, Benjamin F. Jr. (1934) 'Political Institutions and the Frontier', pp. 15–38 in Dixon Ryan Fox, ed., *Sources of Culture in the Middle West*. New York: D. Appleton–Century.

Wright, Erik Olin (1996) *Class Counts: Comparative Studies in Class Analysis*. New York: Cambridge University Press.

Wright, Louis B. (1940) *First Gentlemen of Virginia*. San Marino, CA: Huntington Library.

Wright, Ronald (2001) 'Living on Haunted Land', *Times Literary Supplement*, 9 February.

Wrong, Dennis H. (1961) 'The Oversocialized Conception of Man in Modern Sociology', *American Sociological Review*, 26 (2): 183–93.

Wyatt-Brown, Bertram (1982) *Southern Honor: Ethics and Behavior in the Old South*. New York: Oxford University Press.

Zimmerman, Warren (2002) *First Great Triumph: How Five Great Americans Made Their Country a World Power*. New York: Farrar, Straus & Giroux.

Zimring, Franklin E. (2003) *The Contradictions of American Capital Punishment*. Oxford: Oxford University Press.

Zimring, Franklin E. and G. Hawkins (1997) *Crime is Not the Problem: Lethal Violence in America*. New York: Oxford University Press.

Zwaan, Ton (2001) *Civilisering en decivilisering: Studies over staatsvorming en geweld, nationalisme en vervolging*. Amsterdam: Boom.

Index

9/11 (attacks on New York and Washington, 11 Sept. 2001) 21, 23–5, 47, 225, 261, 292, 296–7

absolutism, absolutist monarchies
  in continental Europe 10, 69, 170, 176, 317
  effects on courtiers 107
  tendencies towards in England 16, 171–2
Abu Ghraib prison 314
Adams, Charles Francis 95, 236
Adams, Henry 75, 94–5, 97, 100
Adams, Herbert Baxter 2, 194, 300
Adams, John
  on banking 232
  constitutional views 33–6, 181
  correspondence with Jefferson 27–8, 36–8, 81
  courtly traits of 84
  as Enlightenment intellectual, 25, 81
  knowledge of Native Americans 41, 161, 335*n*
  opposition to slavery 43
Adams, John Quincy 180, 185, 188, 190, 196
Adams–Onís Treaty (1819) 185–6
Adams, Samuel 35
Adorno, Theodor W. 325*n*
affects
  curbing of 18, 82, 86, 282, 324*n*

  moulding of 12, 158, 315, 110
  restraint of as mark of upper class 92
  see also emotions
African Americans
  'black bourgeoisie' 332*n*
  early population estimates 164
  early stigmatization of 24, 26, 40–1, 43–4
  incidence of poverty among 264
  rates of imprisonment 130
  social exclusion in North 92
  social exclusion in South 93, 147, 237–8
aggressiveness 11–13, 15, 126–7
  civilizing of 125–7
  and gun culture 140
  role in competition for territory 15, 166–7
  as supposed characteristic of Americans 155–6, 298
  survival value of 201–2
  whether innate in humankind 11–13
Ahlstrom, Sydney E. 278, 279
Ailwyn-Foster, Nigel 344*n*
Alba, Richard D. 222
Alderson, Arthur S. 254
Alesina, Alberto 264
allegiance, pledge of 221, 277, 291
Allestree, Richard 55
altruism 315–16

American Dream 73, 105, 249–50, 254, 263–5, 318
American Federation of Labour 239, 258
American Medical Association 239
American Revolution 25–6, 85, 176–9, 294
Amherst, General Jeffrey 175
Amish, Old Order 286
Andreski, Stanislav 242, 338*n*
Anne, queen of England (1702–14) 171
anti-Americanism 48–9
anticipatory socialization 74, 82–3
anti-trust legislation 112–13, 119, 239
Argentina 219, 221, 319
aristocracy
    European 70–1, 89, 98, 317
    Northern patricians 101–3, 119
    of office 103–4; *see also noblesse de robe*; *Junker* class
    pseudo- or artificial 36–8, 81
    of southern planters 85–8, 92–3
    see also plutocracy
armies
    British 170, 175, 176, 240–1, 244
    officers 52, 188, 242–3
    standing 148, 176, 228, 240–2, 245, 246
    in support of civil power 237–8, 244–5
    Union 69, 72, 97, 235–6, 257
    US, size of 88, 97, 148, 243
    see also under wars
Armstrong, Karen 285–6
Articles of Confederation 34, 177–8, 241
assassinations, political 133–4
Atkinson, A. B. 251
Augsburg, Peace of 276
Augustine, Saint 268
Australia 3, 53, 134, 164, 221, 296
autarky
    of early colonies in N. America 159–60, 168, 198
    political and economic linked 14, 169, 228

Bacon's rebellion (1676) 168
Bailey, Beth 75
balance of power: *see* power ratios
Baltzell, E. Digby 98, 102, 103, 281, 340*n*
Bancroft, George 95
banks
    Bank of the United States (1st) 231
    Bank of the United States (2nd) 232–3
    central 231
    commercial 229
    'national' 229
Baptists 281
barbarism, contrasted with 'civilization' 24–28, 32
    in 18th and 19th centuries 26–8, 32, 327*n*
    after 9/11 24, 312
    in frontier thesis 197, 201
barter 169, 228–9
Baudelaire, Charles 49
Baudrillard, Jean 49
Bauman, Zygmunt 332*n*
Bax, Mart 268
Beard, Charles and Mary 26, 43, 45–6, 325–6*n*
'behind the scenes of social life'
    poverty 253, 313
    religion 267, 297
    repugnant or embarrassing activities 8–9, 64, 295
    violence 13, 37, 201, 246–7
Bellah, Robert N. viii, 78, 341*n*
Bellesiles, Michael 143, 144, 333*n*
Benedict, Ruth 329*n*
Bensman, Joseph 217
Bentham, Jeremy 306
Berger, Peter 285
Bergh, Godfried van Benthem van den 316, 336*n*, 344*n*
Berkeley, George 302
Berlusconi, Silvio 324*n*
Billington, Ray Alan 196, 201, 336*n*
Bismarck, Otto von 257
blacks: *see* African Americans
Blackstone, Sir William 112
Blaine, James C. 187

Blair, Tony 23, 258
Blake, William 48
Blanden, Jo 263
Blok, Anton 147
Blomert, Reinhard 317
Bolton, Herbert E. 334*n*
Boston 90, 94–5, 102, 127, 168, 338*n*
Bourdieu, Pierre 20, 103, 226, 267
bourgeoisie 7, 10–11, 16, 94–100, 236, 332*n*
Bowman, Shearer Davis 87–8, 329*n*
Braddock, General Edward 175
Brathwayt, Richard 55
Brinkgreve, Christien 77–8
Britain
    banks in 108, 230–1
    civil service 226, 309
    colonies in North America 159–62, 167–76
    constitution 36, 170, 171, 176
    diplomatic relations with USA 184–91, 236
    empire 173, 212, 315
    inequality in 251, 253
    police 224–5, 337*n*
    social conventions in 71–3, 75–6, 82
    social classes in 57, 82–3, 94, 128–9, 263, 264
    and USA, changing balance of power between 55–6, 58, 244, 319
    welfare state 257–8
    see also under England, armies, wars, 'good society'
Brown, Richard D. 83, 94, 234
Brown, Richard M. 127, 133, 137, 138–9, 144, 146–7, 207–8
Brown, Roger 250–1, 329*n*
Bruce, Steve 289
Bryce, James, Lord 72, 299
Bryson, Bill 228–9
Buddhists 282
bureaucracy 16
    patrimonial 171
    see also civil service
Burke, Edmund 29
Burr, Aaron 90

Bush, George W. 23, 24, 47, 211–12, 310
Bushman, Richard L. 55, 85
Byrd William II 234

Calvinism 46, 113
Canada 134, 173–5, 186–7, 196–7, 219, 333*n*
Cancian, Francesca 78
Canning, George 190
capital punishment: see under punishment
capitalism 87–8, 107–8, 117–19
Carnegie, Andrew 97, 262
carpetbaggers 237
Casa, Giovanni della 53, 54
Castiglione, Baldesar 7, 53, 54
catharsis 288
Catholicism
    in America 275, 280–1, 284, 343*n*
    in Europe 276, 278, 279, 289–91
    hostility towards 147, 220
    in Latin America 277, 341*n*
Caxton, William 7, 8
Ceaser, James 49
Central Intelligence Agency (CIA) 316
Chamberlain, Joshua Lawrence 330*n*
charisma
    group 67
    of office 103–4, 226
Charlemagne 169
Charles I, king of England and Scotland (1625–49) 171, 172
Charles II, king of England and Scotland (1660–85) 169
Cherokee 42, 192–3, 244
Chesnut, Mary 86–7, 88–9
Chesterfield, Philip Stanhope, Lord 55
Chinoy, Ely 250
Chomsky, Noam 210
Christian Right 218, 277, 343*n*
churches
    established 275–7, 290–1
    membership of 108–9, 280–85, 289–90

cities, growth of 33, 215–16
citizenship, rights of 210, 223, 237,
    329n
civility 1, 16, 26, 115
civilization
    emic and etic meanings 25
    as term of Western self-
        approbation 5–6, 23–5, 40
    as used by Jefferson 27
civilizing offensives, campaigns
    66–7, 328n
civilizing processes
    in America 21–2, 156
    in Europe 6–13, 50, 52, 109,
        152–3, 268, 318
    hygiene as explanation of 67–9
    and markets 110–12
    possible reversals 76, 324n
    no zero point 7, 67
    theory of 1, 4–18, 60, 91–3, 120,
        296–8
    and violence 124, 126–7, 128–9,
        141
    see also decivilizing process
civil service
    British 226
    French 226
    USA 225–7
Civil War, American (1861–5) 86,
    88, 233–6
    consequences 97
    disease in 69
    end at Appomattox 236
    legacy on western frontier 207–8
    veterans 257
Civil War, English 171, 240
Clark, David 22
Clark, J. C. D. 334n
Clausewitz, Karl M. von 187
cleanliness, personal 65–6
clergy: see priests
Cleveland, Grover 191, 210, 245
Cleveland, Sarah H. 345n
Clinton, Hillary Rodham 326n
Clive, Robert 173
Cold War 210–11
Collier, James L. 73–4, 94, 99, 305
colonial governments 168–72
colonialism 26

colonization–repulsion mechanism
    11, 70
Commager, Henry Steele 202
compelling forces 133, 172, 212,
    334n
Comte, Auguste 87, 279
concept avoidance 20
Condorcet, Marie-Jean Nicolas de
    Caritat, marquis de 27, 33
Confederate States of America
    235–6
conformism, conformity 106, 113,
    118, 121, 300, 340n
Congregationalism 281
Congress, Continental 30, 32, 34,
    230
Congress, United States 152, 221,
    225, 235, 237, 243, 245
conservative thought 87
Constitution of United States 33,
    34–6, 147–9, 233
    Bill of Rights 148
    checks and balances 313, 321
    drafting of 178
    Iroquois influence on 176, 334–5n
    Second Amendment 147–9
    and slavery 233–4
    Third Amendment 148
constraints
    external 6, 17–18, 34, 37, 77, 91
    internal or self- 6, 17–18, 29, 34,
        77, 89, 91
    mutually expected self-restraint
        78–9
    relaxation of 284
consumption, conspicuous 75, 81,
    93, 100
contracts 111, 112; see also law,
    contract
Cooke, Jay 230
cookery 57, 327–8n
corporations, American scandals
    114–15, 331n
corruption 226, 303
Courbin, Alain 65
courtiers 10–11, 69–70, 87, 107
Courtin, Antoine de 7–8, 54, 55
courtization 16, 39, 109–10, 296,
    324n

courts
  royal and aristocratic 6–7, 10–11,
    54–5, 70, 83–4, 103
  of colonial governors 84–5
  court society 16, 18, 86, 92, 98,
    109–10
cowboys 199–200
creationism 266, 286, 339–40n
creditworthiness 108–9, 110
Crenson, Matthew 307
Crèvecœur, J. Hector St John de 22,
    32, 34, 304
criminology 12, 124, 126
cruelty 11–12, 126, 141, 296
Crusades 209, 290
Cuba 210, 319
culture 5–6, 26
  mass 301
culture wars 79–80, 153, 154, 218,
    292

Dahl, Robert A. 100–2, 300
danger, levels of
  in agrarian societies 200, 271–4
  on frontier 198–9, 201–2
  in modern societies 12, 32, 128–9
  in relation to fears 198, 260, 292,
    296–7
Darnton, Robert 141
Darwinism: see evolution, theory
    of
dating, codes governing 79
Davidoff, Leonore 75, 82, 98
Davie, Grace 267–90, 343n
Davis, Jefferson 88
decivilizing processes 22, 198–9,
    260, 296
Declaration of Independence 26,
    30–1, 236n
de-democratization, functional
    311–14, 318
deference 56, 58, 69–70, 72, 83,
    295
defunctionalization 93, 100
democratization, functional 17, 76,
    115, 120, 128–9, 182, 298, 311
  and American Dream 250
Descartes, René 301–2
detour behaviour 271

detour via detachment 199, 271,
    282
Díaz, Porfirio 336n
Dickens, Charles 59, 62, 322
disease 41, 69, 160, 328n
division of labour 16
Douglass, Frederick 92
drives, muting of: see affects,
    curbing of
Drucker, Peter 260–1
duelling 89–92, 96, 103, 139, 329n
Duerr, Hans-Peter 328n
Duncan Smith, Iain 23
Dunning, Eric 126, 128–9, 287–8
Durkheim, Emile 35, 111, 289, 331n

Eaton, Clement 85, 92–3, 329n
Edwards, Jonathan 278
egalitarianism, American 70–3,
    120–1, 204, 249–51, 311
Eggleston, Edward 2–3, 56, 270,
    271, 340n
Ehrenreich, Barbara 325n
Eisenhower, Dwight D. 245–7
Eisenhower, Milton 134
Eisner, Manuel 124, 126, 129
Elias, Norbert
  author's meeting with viii
  The Civilizing Process ix–x, 4,
    6–9, 323n
  on communities 216–18
  on constraints of market 109
  The Court Society ix, 10, 74, 87,
    109–10, 137–8, 295, 317
  The Germans 89–90, 329n
  reception of works ix–x
  on religion 268–9
  see also 'behind the scenes of
    social life'; civilizing processes;
    colonization–repulsion
    mechanism; compelling forces;
    constraints; courtization;
    established–outsiders relations;
    game models; homo clausus;
    magic-mythical thinking;
    monopoly mechanism; reality-
    congruence; repugnance; royal
    mechanism; we–I balance; we-
    feelings; we-images

elimination contest
  in Europe 15, 181
  in North America 166–8, 172–9
Elizabeth I, queen of England
  (1558–1603) 171
Elkins, Stanley 44, 204
Ellis, Joseph J. 31–5
Ely, Richard T. 279
Emancipation Proclamation 236
emancipation struggles 20
embarrassment: *see* shame
emic and etic perspectives 50; *see
  also under* civilization
emotions
  decontrolling of controls 79,
    282–4, 288, 293
  and fantasy 270–2, 282
  'hard' style 89, 94, 97
  management of 12, 18, 29, 74–9,
    118, 155–6, 159
  and religion 278–82, 288, 293
  in violence 126–7, 129
Empire, American
  first acquisition of 209–10
  post-Second World War 314–20
Emsley, Clive 224
England
  manners 6, 52, 55, 59, 83–5
  Parliament 16
  religion in 266, 275–6, 289–91,
    342*n*
  Restoration (1660) 16
  Tudor and Stuart periods 16
  violence in 124, 127, 130,
    138–40
  see also under Britain
Enlightenment 25–6, 33, 37, 297,
  325*n*
Episcopalianism 281
Erasmus, Desiderius 7, 8, 53, 61,
  64, 68
Erikson, Robert 263
established–outsiders relations
  18–20, 41, 55, 58, 66–7, 74
  in relation to immigration 218
  in South 93
European Court of Human Rights
  318, 344*n*
European Union 152, 318

Europeans as 'others' 44
Evans, Richard 334*n*
evolution, theory of 46, 266–7,
  339*n*
exceptionalism, American x, 22, 38,
  150, 213
excitement
  quest for in religion 287–8
  at spectacle of punishment 12
executions 12
externalities 116, 256, 306–7

famine, Irish potato 87
Faubus, Governor Orville 245
fear: *see under* danger, level of
Febvre, Lucien 324*n*
Federal Bureau of Investigation 225
Federal Reserve Board 233
Federalist Papers 34–5, 148, 241,
  246
Federalist party 33, 35, 230
feudal society 10, 14, 87, 125
figurational sociology 20
Finke, Roger 280–2, 286–7, 290
Fitzhugh, George 87
Florida 175, 185
Fogel, Robert W. 341–2*n*
Foner, Eric 235–6, 237, 238, 239
foresight 17–18, 29, 113–14, 305–8
fork, use of 58–60
Foucault, Michel 110, 149
Fourier, Charles 87, 88
fragment societies 3, 296, 300
France
  anti-Americanism in 49
  civil service 103
  colonies in North America 164,
    167, 173, 175, 183–4
  compared with USA 51–2, 65,
    140–1, 143, 169, 172, 239
  concept of *civilisation* in 5
  inequality in 251, 255
  Jefferson in 27, 35
  manners in 52, 54, 59
  military power 244
  religion in 289
  state formation in 14–16, 181
  see also absolutism; absolutist
    monarchy; court society

Franklin, Benjamin 25, 30, 34, 37, 40, *55*, 172
  cited by Weber 249
  European experience 8
Frazer, Sir James 278
Frederick the Great, king of Prussia 173
French colonists in America 40
French Revolution 28, 33, 52, 143, 170, 294
Freud, Sigmund 271
friendly societies 256–7
Fromm, Erich 330*n*
frontier
  closing of 33, 208–9
  Turner's thesis 3, 32, 53, 141, 193–9, 203–9, 336*n*
Fukuyama, Francis 317, 345*n*
Fulbright, Senator J. W. 48
fundamentalism
  market 305–7
  religious 266, 285–6, 288
fur trade 163, 177, 199, 201–2

Galbraith, J. K. 230
game models (Elias) 182, 319, 334*n*
Garland, David 126, 131, 132–3, 145, 150–3, 333*n*
gated communities 132
Gay, Peter 25, 325*n*
Geneva conventions 297
genocide 11, 162, 296, 324*n*, 332*n*
gentry
  American colonial 82–5, 94
  British 82–3
George I, king of Great Britain and Ireland (1714–27) 172
George III, king of Great Britain and Ireland (1760–1820) 26
Germany 14
  comparison with USA 102–3
  Kaiserreich (1870–1918) 89–90, 239, 247
  religion 289
  reunification (19th cent.) 96–7
  social mobility 263
  welfare state 257
  see also Prussia

'germ theory' (of American institutions) 2–3, 194, 300
Gerry, Elbridge 35
Gettysburg, battle of 236
Gilded Age 74–5, 100, 113, 262–3
Glassner, Barry 292
Glazer, Nathan 261, 264
global warming 310
Glorious Revolution (1688–9) 3, 169, 171
Gold Standard 308
Goldthorpe, John H. 263
Goodhart, David 264
'good society'
  American 81, 300
  European 81–2
  London 74–5, 82, 95
Gordon, John Steele 230–1
Gore, Al 266, 286
Gorer, Geoffrey 334*n*
Goudsblom, Johan 26–7, 78, 113, 214, 265, 328*n*, 330*n*
  on fire 160
  on national character 299
  on priests and warriors 39, 200, 206, 273, 324*n*
  on religion 268, 330*n*
  see also pacification, paradox of
Gould, Jay 97
governors, colonial 83–4
  see also under courts
Grant, Ulysses S. 9, 188–9, 233–4, 238
  views on duelling 90
Great Awakenings 278–80, 283, 341*n*
Great Britain, formed from union of England and Scotland (1707) 171
  see also under Britain; England
Great Crash (1929) 251
Great Depression 258
Greeley, Andrew M. 267, 286–7, 343*n*
Greenfeld, Liah 334*n*
Greenstock, Sir Jeremy 23
Guantánamo Bay 314, 327*n*

guns
    in American culture 122, 136,
        139–42, 155
    control of 39, 142, 149, 217
    gunfight, Western, 139, 207
    use and ownership 1, 140–3, 145,
        148–9, 292
Gurr, Ted Robert 125, 128, 131,
    332n
Gustavus II Adolphus, king of
    Sweden (1611–32) 240

habitus
    American 29, 52, 75, 84, 104,
        139, 142–3
    effects on of markets and
        organizations 115, 117
    formation and change 6, 11, 18,
        73, 127, 277, 319
    meaning of term ix, 5–6, 299
    Northern 96, 142, 238
    Southern 88–9, 142, 238
    in small communities 216–17
    and state formation 194, 319
    see also aggressiveness
Hacker, Jacob 254
Hall, Peter Dobkin 216, 225, 301
Hamilton, Alexander 25, 33, 34–6,
    230
    death 90
    financial expertise 230–1
    Inspector-General of the Army
        242
    on navies 241
Harrington, Michael 252–3
Harris, Marvin 283, 342n
Hartz, Louis 3, 300, 323n
Haseler, Stephen 318
Haskell, Thomas 110–13, 288,
    307
Hawaii, 210, 319
Hawkins, Gordon 135
Hayes, Rutherford B. 238
Headland, Thomas N. 25
health care 259–62
health insurance 260, 261
Hegel, G. W. F. 49
Heidegger, Martin 49
Hemphill, C. Dallett, 55, 56, 57

Henry, Patrick 35
Heraclitus 21
Herndon, William 64, 274–5
hidden hand 32, 112, 307–8
Higham, John 219, 221, 337n
Himmelfarb, Gertrude 325n
Hindus 282, 285, 290, 342n
Hintze, Otto 321n
Hobbes, Thomas 31
Hobsbawm, Eric 337n
Hodgson, Godfrey 337n
Hofstadter, Richard 204, 208, 305,
    314
Holbach, Paul-Henri Thiry, baron
    d' 322
Hollywood 104, 160, 200, 207
Holmes, Justice Oliver Wendell 139
Holocaust: see genocide
Homestead Act 235, 338–9n
homicide, justifiable 138–40
homicide rates 123–6
    international comparisons of
        134–5
    romantic triangle 125–6, 127
homo clausus 301–2
honour
    contrasted with dignity 91–2
    social code of 90–2, 247, 329n
Horkheimer, Max 325n
Howe, Daniel Walker 37, 95
Hoy, Suellen M. 61, 66
Hugo, Victor 48–9
Huizinga, Johan xi, 12, 298
human nature 28, 36
Hundley, Daniel R. 329n
Huntington, Samuel P. 300, 325n,
    338n
Hutchinson, Anne 276
Huxley, T. H. 266
hyphenated Americans 222

ideal type v. real type 331n
identification, mutual 17, 120–1,
    126, 132
    and American Dream 250, 263–5
    between settlers and Native
        Americans 162–3
immigration 33, 101, 218–23, 337n
    and religion 284

Indians, American: *see* Native
    Americans
individualism 45–8, 115, 116, 295,
    302–5
    'rugged' 197, 213
industrialization 33, 93, 251, 285
inequality 250–4, 305
inevitability, historical 128, 172,
    182–3, 334*n*, 335–6*n*
informalization 75–80, 126
    as challenge to theory of civilizing
        processes 76–7, 329*n*
Inglis, Tom 291, 324*n*
Inouye, Daniel 193
interdependence, webs or chains of
    17, 112, 126, 271–2, 298
International Criminal Court 318
International Monetary Fund (IMF)
    308–9
International Social Survey
    Programme (ISSP) 289–90,
    340*n*
involvement–detachment (Elias)
    269–73, 280
Iraq, war in 24, 122, 344*n*, 345*n*
Ireland 291, 312, 324*n*
Iroquois 175–7, 191, 334*n*
    system of government 175–6
Islam 24, 325*n*
    see also Muslims
Israel 24, 333*n*
Italy 6, 12, 14, 299
Ivins, Molly 327*n*

Jackson, Andrew 33, 42, 52, 66,
    185, 188, 196
    creation of 'spoils system' 225
    hostility to banks 232–3
Jackson, Thomas J., Stonewall 88
James, C. L. R. 65
James I, king of England and
    Scotland (1603–25) 172
James II, king of England and
    Scotland (1685–8) 9, 171
Janowitz, Morris 246
Japan 134, 210, 251–5, 289, 323*n*
Jay, John 25, 84
Jeffers, H. Paul 191, 245
Jefferson, Thomas x, 25–39

belief in mild government 28–33,
    155, 223
correspondence with John Adams
    27–8, 36–8, 81
debts 86
experience in Europe 84
hostility to banks 232
hostility to cities 138, 216
knowledge of Native Americans
    41–2, 161
Louisiana Purchase 183–5
owned manners book 55
on religious freedom 276
slave owner 43, 81
on westward expansion 180
on rewriting Constitution 321
Jennings, Francis 177
Jews 282, 286, 290
Jim Crow laws 146, 147, 238
Joffe, Josef 24
Johnson, Andrew 237
Johnson, Lyndon B. 137, 258
    Great Society 253
Johnson, Samuel 263–4
Jünger, Ernst 49
Junker class, Prussian 87–8

Kagan, Robert 318
Kant, Immanuel 302
Kaplan, Robert D. 344*n*
Kasson, John F. 55, 61, 96
Keegan, John 240
Kennan, George F. 298
Key, V. O. Jr 85–6, 338*n*
Kilminster, Richard x
kitsch 107
kleptocracy 309
Kluckhohn, Clyde 299
knife, use of, differences between
    Europe and America 59–60
Know-Nothings (American Party)
    220
Knox, Henry 42
Kornhauser, William A. 334*n*
Kosmin, Barry A. 281
Kramnick, Isaac 34, 35, 178,
    181
Kristof, Nicholas D. 279–80
Krugman, Paul 260

Ku Klux Klan 238, 244
Kupperman, Karen 162–3

Lader, Philip 23
Lane, Roger 91–2, 127–9, 139,
    141–3, 146, 338n
Larkin, Jack 58, 61, 63–4, 66, 67–8,
    71, 228–9
La Salle, Jean-Baptiste de, Saint 54,
    63
Lasch, Christopher 22, 78, 300
Latin America
    Amerindians in 44, 162
    immigrants from, to USA 222,
        284
    religion in 276–7, 343n
    Spanish colonies in 3, 161, 190
    slavery in 86
    US interventions in 190–1
law
    contract 331n; see also contracts
    international 318, 344–5n
Lawrence, D. H. 328n
lawyers 83
League of Nations 210
Lee, Joe (J. J.) 24
Lehrer, Tom 306
Leibniz, Gottfried W. 161–2
Light, Donald 261
Limerick, Patricia Nelson 203–6,
    208
Lincoln, Abraham 64, 234, 237
Lipset, Seymour Martin viii, 165,
    259, 334n, 339n
literacy 37, 57
Livingston, Robert 184
Locke, John 16, 31, 35, 161–2, 304,
    322, 326n
Lockwood, David 249–50
Lodge, Henry Cabot 102, 187,
    330n
Loewen, James W. 160, 334n
Louis XIV, king of France
    (1643–1715) 10, 16, 69–70,
    100, 170–1, 317
Louisiana Purchase (1803) 180,
    183–5
L'Ouverture, Toussaint 184
Lowie, Robert H. 323n

Loyal, Steven x
Lucretius 268, 330n
Luedtke, Luther S. 299
lust balance 78
Lyell, Sir Charles 70, 90
lynching 144–6, 151, 238

McCarthy era 313
McDowell, David 141
MacIver, Robert 26
Mackay, Alexander 62, 65
McKittrick, Eric 2
McNeill, William H. 337n
McPherson, James M. 234–5
Madison, James 25, 32, 34–5, 185,
    232
magic-mythical thinking (Elias)
    268–71
Maistre, Joseph de 45, 49
Mandelbaum, Michael 315
manifest destiny 180–2
Mann, Michael 319
manners
    changes in Renaissance 6–9
    medieval 6–9
    table 7–8, 54, 58–60
    under democracy 17, 120–1
manners books
    American 53–6, 74, 98
    European 6–9
Mannheim, Karl 87
markets
    in civilizing processes 21, 105,
        121, 126, 156–7, 295
    constraints of 107–15, 125, 288
    free 31–2, 87–8, 279, 307–9, 316
    labour 132–3
    social 318
    as structures of power 112–15,
        121, 301, 307
Marks, Gary 259, 339n
Marquand, David 309
Marryat, Captain Frederick 71
Marshall Plan 316
Marshall, T. H. 329n
Martin, Judith 76
Martineau, Harriet 66, 90, 95–6,
    99, 251, 323n
Marx, Karl 107, 247, 289, 324n

Massachusetts Bay Company 169
Mastenbroek, Willem F. G. 118
Maurice of Nassau, prince
    (1567–1625) 240
Mauss, Marcel 324*n*
May, Karl 138
Mazlish, Bruce 324*n*
Mead, Margaret 155
Mead, Walter Russell 320
Medicare, Medicaid 258, 259
Mennell, Stephen 132, 171, 220,
    313, 332*n*
mercantilism 229
mercenaries (soldiers) 26
merchants 52, 82–4, 100, 112, 176,
    231
Merkel, William G. 147–8
Merton, Robert K. 82–3, 220, 257
Messner, Steven F. 145
Methodism 278, 281
Mexico 180, 188–9, 191, 242,
    243
Middle Ages, European
    manners and habitus 6–8, 10–14,
        57–64, 76, 98, 275, 295, 298
    migration in 196
    religion 290
    state formation 14–16, 159, 166,
        169, 189, 206
    violence in 124, 149, 166
military expenditure 211
military participation ratio (MPR)
    242, 243–4, 338*n*
military-industrial complex 245–7
militias 147–8, 245
Miller, Perry 334*n*
Mills, C. Wright ix, 101, 245–6
minority of the best, of the worst
    19, 93, 284, 312
Mirabeau, Victor de Riqueti,
    marquis de (1715–89) 324*n*
mobility
    geographical 283
    social 262–3
model-setting elites
    America as, for world 121
    in Germany 103, 239
    plurality of in America 22, 52,
        81–2, 153, 293, 300

money 16, 228–9
    paper 229, 232–3
Monkkonen, Eric 224
monopolies
    market structures 113–14, 120,
        261
    of means of orientation 267, 275,
        276, 290–1, 293
    model-setting groups 81, 83, 104
    public and private 16, 170–1
monopoly mechanism 15–16, 179,
    211–12
Monroe Doctrine 190–1, 211, 314
Monroe, James 32, 42, 184, 190
Monti, Daniel 215
Moody, Eleazer 54–5
Moore, Barrington Jr 107–8
Moore, Michael 144
Morone, James 313–14
Motley, John Lothrop 97
muckrakers 75
Muirhead, James 72
Mumford, Lewis 197
Munchembled, Robert 274
murder: *see* homicide
Murray, Henry A. 299
Muslims 282, 343*n*; *see also* Islam
Mutually Assured Destruction
    (MAD) 211, 316, 344*n*

nakedness 8–9, 54, 62–3, 77, 296,
    328*n*
Nantes, revocation of Edict of 276
Napoleon I, emperor of France
    (1804–14) 184
national character 136, 298–9,
    340*n*
national debt (US) 230–1
National Guard 148, 243, 245
National Rifle Association 142, 147
nationalism, American 213, 250,
    263–4, 304
nation-building contrasted with
    state-formation 158
Native Americans 26, 40–3
    contrast with Australian
        aborigines 16–1
    dignity under torture 88
    Plains Indians 244

Native Americans (*cont.*)
  population estimates 163–5
  pre-Columbian condition 41
  relations with early European
    settlers 160–5
  treaties with 191, 197
  we-image 43
nativism, American 66, 219–20,
  314
NATO 317
natural functions 8–9, 54
  and cleanliness 64–7
Navy
  Royal (British) 241
  US 209–10
New Deal 253
negotiation, civilizing of 118
Netherlands 52, 78, 124, 140
  Dutch colonies in America 167–8
  Dutch Republic 343*n*
Nevins, Allan 58, 202
New Deal 227, 258
New Haven, CT 100–2
Nielsen, François 254
Nietzsche, Friedrich 46
noblesse d'épée 87, 328*n*
noblesse de robe 103, 330*n*
nose-blowing 8–9, 54, 60–2
nouveaux riches 81, 97–101
Nullification Crisis 233

O'Donnell, Ian 333*n*
organizations
  international 115
  large-scale 115–20
O'Sullivan, John L. 180

pacification
  internal 15–16, 30, 39, 158–9,
    255, 296
  paradox of 214
Packard, Vance 117–18
Panama Canal 209
Paris, Treaty of (1783) 175, 185,
  241
Parliament 16, 171–2, 176, 240,
  253
Parsons, Talcott viii, 33–4, 309,
  341*n*

parties, political 16, 171, 249–50,
  350
path-dependency 320–2
patriotism: *see* nationalism
Peacham, Henry 55, 56
Pearce, Roy Harvey 41
Pennsylvania 'Dutch' 40, 164, 218
Pentecostalism 279–80, 282
Perrow, Charles 115–17, 119
Persons, Stow 83, 85, 94
Perucci, Robert 252
Pettit, Becky 130
Philippines 43, 210, 319
Pierson, George W. 204
Pietism 278
Piketty, Thomas 251
Plato 302
plutocracy 11, 81, 97–8, 239, 263
Plymouth Plantation 41, 160, 165
Poe, Edgar Allan 340*n*
Polanyi, Karl 107, 308–9
police
  British 224, 337*n*
  development of in USA 224–5
  Royal Irish Constabulary 196,
    338*n*
  Royal North-West Mounted
    Police 196
Polk, President James 186, 188, 190
Poor Law, Elizabethan 256, 258,
  261
Potter, David 72, 204, 294–5, 300,
  305, 307
poverty in USA 252–3
Powell, Colin 23
power ratios, meaning of term 21
Pratt, John 131
'pressure from below' 10, 83,
  99–100, 295
priests 7, 39, 83, 273, 277
prisons 155
  incarcerated population (USA)
    122, 130–1, 133, 259
  see also Abu Ghraib prison;
    Guantánamo Bay
privacy 9, 63, 66
private law state 88
process sociology: *see* figurational
  sociology

processes, relatively unplanned
  social 29, 181, 183–90, 247,
  253, 297, 319
progress 25, 26–8, 194, 206, 342n
Progressive movement 257
Prohibition 220, 313
protected/unprotected strata 129,
  132, 260, 313
Protestant ethic 249, 268
Protestantism
  in America, 220–1, 275, 277,
    279, 283–4, 300
  in Europe 276, 289
  see also under Weber, Max
Prussia 10, 87–90, 103, 173, 187,
  224, 243
  see also under wars
psychogenesis 37, 50, 313
publishing in America 55
Puffert, Douglas 321–2
punishment
  capital 1, 122–3, 149–54, 334n
  state monopoly of 13–14
Puritans 14, 165, 280
Putnam, Robert 283, 342–3n

Quakers 275, 280, 281, 340n
Quietism 278
Quilley, Stephen x

railways 235, 236, 238
Ranger, Terence 337n
rational choice theory 255, 287,
  290, 339n
rationality 18, 29, 86, 289, 311
rationalization 17–18, 29, 110,
  325–6n
Rauschenbusch, Walter 279, 341n
Reagan, Ronald 258
reality-congruence (Elias) 268–9,
  339n
Reconstruction 93, 145, 237–8
reformalization 79
relative deprivation 128
relativism 285
religion
  'civil' (Bellah) 277–8, 290, 291,
    293, 341n
  civilizing effect of 266

definition of 267
organized 273
and science 266–7
Renaissance 6–10, 63, 67, 268
repugnance, threshold of 64–5,
  68–9, 126, 295
Restoration (England, 1660) 240
Ribeiro, Darcy 86, 161, 277, 341n
Ricardo, David 306
Riesman, David viii, 22, 106–7,
  117, 118, 330n
Rifkin, Jeremy 318
Robber Barons 113
Roman Empire 14
romanticism, romanticization 93,
  137–8
Roosevelt, Franklin D. 227, 253,
  279
Roosevelt, Theodore
  and military, imperial values 187,
    330n
  and Native Americans 326n
  as President 239, 243
  Roosevelt Corollary 191, 211,
    336n
  social circle 102
  and the West 41, 47, 136, 177,
    323n
Root, Elihu 243, 330n
Rose, Arnold M. 246
Rousseau, Jean-Jacques 35
royal mechanism (Elias) 16
Runciman, W. G. 262, 339n

Said, Edward 5
Sanitary Commission, US 69
Sartre, Jean-Paul 49
'savagery', discursively contrasted
  with 'civilization' 24, 27, 41–3,
  199, 206, 326–7n
scalawags 237
Scalia, Antonin 345n
Scheff, Thomas J. 296
Schlesinger, Arthur M. Jr 23, 222–3
Schlesinger, Arthur M. Sr 53, 55,
  56, 74, 84–5, 97–8
Schurz, Carl 210, 319
sciences, natural 271–2, 292
Scopes trial (1925) 286, 343n

sect, membership of 108–9, 284, 342n
secularization 268, 280, 284, 285, 287, 289–91, 343n
self-aggrandisement 58, 70–1
Sennett, Richard 118
shame
  feelings of 9
  –rage spirals 296–7, 319
  threshold of 6, 68–9
Shay's Rebellion 34, 148, 241
Sherman, William Tecumseh 242
Siberia, Russian expansion into 196
Simmel, Georg 10, 21
Skelton, W. B. 241–2
Skowronek, Stephen 239, 243, 244
slavery 43–4, 85–6, 87–8
  abolitionists 43
  emancipation of 93, 234, 236, 313
  in Northern states 234
sleeping arrangements 6, 54, 63–4
Slotkin, Richard 136–7, 141
Small, Albion W. 279
Smith, Adam 21, 31–2, 112, 306, 307, 308
Smith, Page 218
Social Gospel movement 279
Social Register 102–3
socialism 87–8
society
  civil 115
  permissive 76, 79–80
  post-industrial 129
  see also 'good society'
sociogenesis 37, 50, 311, 313
softening of manners
  Jefferson 28
  Tocqueville 96, 120–2
Sombart, Werner x, 249, 338–9n
Sontag, Susan 24–5
South (Southern states of USA) 85–94
  ante-bellum dominance of federal officers 235
  levels of violence 125, 154–5
  one-party politics 238
sovereignty 190–1, 213, 315, 318
Soviet Union 114, 211, 317, 318
  nomenklatura 103

Spain
  empire 164, 169, 185–6
  in European great power politics 173, 184, 187, 190
  relations with USA 184
  territories in North America 167, 175, 183, 186, 190
  see also absolutism, absolutist monarchies; Florida; Latin America; wars
spectatorship, pleasures of xi, 126, 149
Spencer, Herbert 247, 279
Spierenburg, Pieter 123, 125, 127, 143–4, 149–50, 202–3, 332n, 333n
  on capital punishment 149–50, 334n
  hypothesis that 'democracy came too early' 143–4, 151–2, 203
  on types of violence 125, 127, 333n, 333n
spitting 8–9, 54, 61–2
spoils system 225–6, 238
sports 77, 126, 141, 288
Stalin, Josef 210
Standish, Miles 165
Stannard, David E. 161–2
Stark, Rodney 280–2, 286–7, 290
Starr, Paul 260, 321
state: see private law state; and under Weber, Max
state-formation 12–17
  Europe and N. America compared 159–60, 297
  in USA 158, 214
Stearns, Carol Z. 155, 331n
Stearns, Peter N. 75, 77, 125–6, 155
Steward, Dick 91
Stiglitz, Joseph 307, 308, 345n
Stokvis, Ruud 119
Stolk, Abraham van 311–13
Stone, John 324n
Stone, Lawrence 332n
stratification, social, in USA 250–4
Stuyvesant, Pieter 167
Sumner, William Graham 46, 279
superiorism 295
superstition 273–5, 280

Supreme Court 148, 152–3, 192–3,
    245, 345*n*
survival unit 159, 303
Swaan, Abram de 132, 255–7
    on collectivizing process 256–7,
    261–2
Swedish colonies in America 167
Switzerland 333*n*

table manners: *see under* manners
Tannhäuser 7
taxation
    in state formation 13–14, 227–8,
        230–1
    in USA 84, 133, 176–7, 197,
        251–3, 264, 307–8
    see also violence, monopolization
        of means of
technology, advance of 67–8, 260
Texas, annexation of 188
Thatcher, Margaret 258
Thernstrom, Stephan 262, 339*n*
Thomas, Keith 141, 274
Thompson, E. P. 73, 328*n*
Thucydides 211
Tilly, Charles 168, 323*n*, 332*n*,
    334*n*
Tittle, Charles R. 12
tobacco, chewing 61–2
Tocqueville, Alexis de 17, 22, 51–2,
    81
    on American manners and social
        character 17, 22, 51–2, 70–2,
        81, 96, 298
    comparisons of USA and Europe
        51, 295, 295
    on ease of social encounters 92,
        96, 251
    on individualism 45, 301–2, 307
    on invidious status distinctions 72
    on prisons and punishment
        122–3, 150, 155
    on tyranny of the majority,
        conformism 153, 106–7, 267,
        305
    on unintended consequences
        238
    on voluntary associations 204
    see also softening of manners

Tönnies, Ferdinand 35, 216, 289
Tonry, Michael 130
torture 297
trade unions 220, 229–30, 249, 253
'trickle up' and 'trickle down' 71
Trollope, Anthony 62, 71–2, 88
Trollope, Fanny 62, 70, 341*n*
Truman, Harry S. 210–11
Turner, Frederick Jackson 3, 136,
    267
    and Norbert Elias compared
        198–9
    image of self-reliant frontiersman
        217
    see also under frontier
Twain, Mark 104, 210, 319
two-front stratum 10, 69–70, 83
    post-bellum South 93
tyranny of the majority
    (Tocqueville) 106, 267
Tyrrell, Ian 323*n*

undressing: *see* nakedness
unintended consequences 116,
    181–3, 233, 253, 260, 306,
    344*n*
Unitarianism 281
United Kingdom: *see under* Britain;
    England
United Nations 212, 317, 320, 345*n*
universities 95
urbanization 128, 215–18, 285
Uviller, H. Richard 147–8

values, American 21, 131, 294–5,
    330–2
Van Buren, Martin 188
Veblen, Thorstein 11, 97
Vicksburg, siege of 236
Victorian period 73–5
Vidal, Gore 210–11, 312
Vidich, A. J. 217
vigilantes 137, 146–7, 224, 333*n*
violence 11–13, 296
    impulsive 127
    instrumental 127
    monopolization of means of 39,
        88, 143–4, 158, 267, 324*n*
    upturn in 1960s 127–9

Virginia Declaration of Rights 30–1
Voigt, Kurt 23
Voltaire, François-Marie Arouet 92,
  329n

Wacquant, Loïc 129, 130, 332n
Wade, Richard 102, 215
Wagner, Richard 137–8
Wallerstein, Immanuel 87
Warner, W. Lloyd 339n
warrior class 10, 11, 13, 16
warrior code, in Germany 46–7, 88,
  89–90
warriors
  taming of 39, 87, 147
wars
  of 1812 186, 232, 242
  Anglo-Dutch 167
  First World War 15, 210
  Franco-Prussian (1870) 15,
    239
  French and Indian 172–3
  of Independence 41, 48, 185–6,
    179, 191–2, 210, 314
  King Philip's (1675–6) 168
  Mexican (1846–8) 188–9, 242–3,
    336n
  Peloponnesian 211
  Prussian-Austrian (1866) 239
  Second World War 16, 210
  Seven Years War 173, 174, 176
  Spanish-American (1898) 210,
    243
  Vietnam 245, 341n
  see also Civil War
Washington, George 33, 36, 54,
  174, 241–2
wealth, growing inequalities of 116,
  120
Weber, Max
  on bureaucracy 171
  definition of state 13, 158, 212,
    314
  on disenchantment 289
  on markets 107–9, 112–14, 119
  on monopolization of power
    resources 324n
  observations on visit to USA 72,
    98, 108–9, 341n

Protestant ethic 249, 268, 277,
  303
  on rationality 18
we-feelings 40, 121, 284
we–I balance 74, 301–4
we-images 19–20, 21, 40, 48
welfare state, US 254–62, 279, 339n
West Point, US Military Academy
  88, 242
Western, Bruce 130
Wharton, Edith 98–9
'white flight' 132, 135, 332n
Whitefield, George 278
Whitney, Eli 43
Whyte, William H. 118, 299–300
Wilkinson, Rupert 97, 305
Williams, Raymond 26–7
Williams, Roger 276
Wilson, Bryan 267, 280, 342n
Wilson, Edward O. 287
Wilson, Woodrow 47, 233, 338n
Wilterdink, Nico 253–4
Winthrop, John x, 44
Winthrop, John the Younger 54
Wister, Owen 139
witches
  belief in 274–5
  hunting 313
  Salem trials (1692) 270, 275
Wolfe, Alan 300
Wolfe, General James 175
Wolfe, Tom 253
Wood, Gordon S. 169
Woodward, C. Vann 146
workhouses 256
World Bank 308–9
Wouters, Cas 70, 75–6, 78–9, 295,
  311–13, 328n
Wright, Louis B. 55, 56
Wright, Ronald 49
Wrong, Dennis 34
Wyatt-Brown, Bertram 90–1
Wysong, Earl 252

Young, Hugo 47–8

Zimmerman, Warren 102, 187
Zimring, Franklin E. 135, 145–6,
  150, 151, 224, 333n